A SPECIAL GIFT

PRESENTED TO:

_____

FROM:

_____

DATE:

_____

Keep yourselves in the love of God,
looking . . . unto eternal life.
                    —Jude 21

COLORS OF GRACE

The Women's Devotional Series

Among Friends

The Listening Heart

A Gift of Love

A Moment of Peace

Close to Home

From the Heart

This Quiet Place

In God's Garden

Fabric of Faith

Alone With God

Bouquets of Hope

Colors of Grace

To order, call **1-800-765-6955.**
Visit us at **www.reviewandherald.com**
for more information on other Review and Herald® products.

COLORS OF GRACE

A Daily Devotional for Women by Women

ARDIS DICK STENBAKKEN, EDITOR

REVIEW AND HERALD® PUBLISHING ASSOCIATION
HAGERSTOWN, MD 21740

The author assumes full responsibility for the accuracy of all facts and quotations as cited in this book.

This book was
Edited by Jeannette R. Johnson
Copyedited by Delma Miller and James Cavil
Cover design by FreshCut Designs
Cover photo by Getty Images/Taxi
Electronic makeup by Shirley M. Bolivar
Typeset: Minion 11/13.5

PRINTED IN U.S.A.

07 06 05 04 03   5 4 3 2 1

R&H Cataloging Service
Stenbakken, Ardis Dick, 1939-   ed.
        Colors of grace, edited by Ardis Dick Stenbakken.

        1. Devotional calendars—SDA.   2. Devotional calendars—women.
3. Women—religious life.   4. Devotional literature—SDA.   I. Title.

242.643

ISBN 0-8280-1761-1

A New Year's Promise

Though your sins be as scarlet, they shall be as white as snow. Isa.1:18.

I AWOKE THIS MORNING TO a fresh blanket of snow that had silently, stealthily covered the landscape during the night. The ground of yesterday had been patchy with grass, roots, and decaying leaves protruding through scattered patches of ice and snow from the winter's previous storms. Human footprints and animal tracks had crisscrossed the paths and lawn areas, revealing the brown earth beneath. It had not been a pretty picture.

But this morning revealed a total, incredible transformation. As I looked out the picture window at the tiny snowflakes that were still falling, I mused on these tiny crystals whose light-reflecting surfaces made the whole landscape bright. Each tiny, six-sided flake sparkled its reminder to me that it was unique, no two of them exactly alike, each flake doing its part to create a beautiful picture.

Am I, in my uniqueness, doing my part to reflect God's love in my neighborhood? Am I a viable part of the larger picture God wants to show to this earth?

The Night Artist had outlined each branch and twig of the naked trees with a beautiful lining of white, making their gaunt frames picturesque on the snowy landscape. One little snowflake didn't make an impression on the muddy ground, but hundreds and thousands together created an impressive scene. Together they had covered the barren places of yesterday.

New Year's Day. I needed this message from God that He was lovingly covering my mistakes of yesterday—the ugly places, the roots of bitterness, the decaying leaf words, the footprints of feet going their own way. He was covering them one snowflake, one blessing at a time. He was giving me a new slate, a new day, a new year in which to emulate the lovely character and person of His Son, my Savior, Jesus Christ. He was giving me another chance to reflect His love in my family and in my neighborhood.

His promise is sure. "Though your sins be as scarlet, they shall be as white as snow" (Isa. 1:18).

Thank You, Lord, for this message of incredible love today.

JOAN MINCHIN NEALL

On Land and in the Air

But let him ask in faith, nothing wavering. For he that wavereth is like a wave of the sea driven with the wind and tossed. James 1:6.

DURING THE EARLY YEARS of our marriage, my husband, children, and I would travel to visit our parents, who lived in the Carolinas. We would always pray before leaving and before coming back, asking God in faith to take charge of the wheel and give us traveling mercies.

As we traveled we encountered many accidents, some minor and some of a more serious nature, but God always sent His angel to watch over us. We'd always leave early in the morning, waking Cynthia and her brother, Alexander, so they could appreciate things of nature God had made. Cynthia liked to stay awake, watching whatever came in sight, whereas her brother liked to sleep as we traveled.

Since those days I've thought about my Christian life and often asked myself, "Am I—are we—sleeping spiritually? Or are we awake—working, obeying Jesus, doing what He would have us do?"

As the years passed and the children grew up, the distance and my husband's physical condition meant we had to resort to taking the airplane. Praying before traveling and asking Jesus to be the pilot and copilot is still part of our travel preparation.

One Sunday there was snow on the ground. But I had to get home. I boarded the plane about 20 minutes before takeoff. I decided not to let any negative thought enter my mind. Then the pilot announced we were ready for takeoff, but we would have a bumpy ride. How glad I was I had prayed for traveling mercies! Sure enough, about 10 minutes into our flight the plane suddenly seemed to drop, then tilted sideways. This continued off and on for some time. Just as the pilot had warned, it was a bumpy ride.

Having prayed with faith in God, I reached my destination. In life we sometimes have bumpy roads and flights. But God will help us travel, no matter how bumpy the roads or skies are. Jesus will always be there.

ANNIE B. BEST

A Glorious Gift

It is God's gift that all should eat and drink and take pleasure in all their toil. Eccl. 3:13, NRSV.

THIS MORNING, AFTER DOING my exercises, I sat on my bed with my ice pack wrapped around my wrist. My cat, Chester, showed up and curled up on my lap. He's become a real lap kitty since I've been home recuperating, and he often claims those 12 minutes with the ice pack as his own. As I petted him with my good hand, I thought what a blessing it was to have time to pet my cat until he decides he's had enough. I decided not to get up today until Chester did, and he sat there purring happily for an extra 15 minutes. Chester hasn't always been such a cuddler, and I have to wonder if my having time to sit with him has made him want to sit with me more.

My therapy sessions and the exercises have helped me get much of the use of my hand back since my cast came off nearly a month ago, but I'm not there yet. Sometimes not being able to do the things I love really gets to me. But a couple weeks ago I realized that in the midst of it all I have been given a glorious gift.

After surgery I had to stop doing almost everything I'd been able to do prior to surgery. I couldn't bathe or get dressed by myself, and I had to get my hair done at "Hair by Gary." On the other hand (no pun intended), not being able to wash dishes or clean the cat's litter box has been a nice break. However, not being able to write in my journal or play my guitars was heartbreaking. Then one day it hit me: all the activities I'd had to put on hold—I didn't have to start them all up again. Maybe there were some things I could just let go. Or as Todd, one of my wonderful occupational therapists, put it, "You discovered you don't have to have three million things going at once to survive."

In all honesty, I wouldn't have chosen this particular path to get myself to slow down, sit still, and take inventory, but I'm thankful that God has used it to help me do that. It hasn't always been a lot of fun, and it continues to be a lot of work, but I now know better what my true passions are. I'm thankful to have been relieved of my one-thing-after-another mode of operation, and my prayer is that when I'm able to do it all again—I won't.

TOYA MARIE KOCH

My Father's Joy

In my Father's house are many mansions: if it were not so, I would have told you. I go to prepare a place for you. John 14:2.

THERE'S A FAMILY OF five from the Philippines visiting us in Maryland. These friends had dreamed about this trip, planned, and saved to make it possible. Finally, they are here. The father is a frequent traveler because of the nature of his job, but every time he visited new places, he always wished that one day he could bring his family with him.

I have enjoyed so much watching the joy the children are having, even in simple things such as seeing squirrels. Each morning Kimberly goes out on the lawn to watch or feed the squirrels. This simple thing that we take for granted brings joy to this little one.

I notice that after each tour or trip the family takes, or after they have done or experienced something new, the father says, "See children, this is what I told you. Isn't it beautiful?" I see the joy in the father's face as he watches his children enjoying the new experience.

While we were visiting with the parents one evening the father told me how happy he was that his family was able to make this trip. He said there were times during his travels when tears rolled down his cheeks as he thought of his children when he saw beautiful places and things.

"But this trip is different," he said, "because I have my children and wife with me, and I am so happy." His face was full of smiles as he said this.

This made me think of our heavenly Father. I think of the mansions and all the beauty He has prepared for us. I can imagine us leaping for joy when we first see heaven, as we take a ride on a lion's back, as we feed the birds from our hand, as we drink from the stream, as we pick some fruit in the garden, or just stand there, in the midst of the garden, absorbing all the beauty. But most of all, I imagine the great joy in the Lord's face as He watches us enjoy the beauty of the things He has prepared for us.

Yes, I know joy will overflow when we get to heaven; but, more important, I will love to see the joy in my Father's face when we all get there—His children with Him at last.

JEMIMA D. ORILLOSA

Does Prayer Really Make a Difference?

Praying always with all prayer and supplication in the Spirit, and watching thereunto with all perseverance and supplication for all saints. Eph. 6:18.

MY HUSBAND AND I do not send Christmas greetings anymore. Several years ago we began the practice of saving all the greetings we receive and putting them in a special box. After New Year's we choose two greetings each morning, reminisce about the folks they are from, and have special prayer for them. Then I write a letter to each person or family. I tell each of them about the other and ask them to pray for each other and for us on the day they receive the letter. The joy we have received from doing this is overwhelming, and the responses we receive have caused us to know what power there is in prayer.

We've learned that people were having surgery on the day we drew their greetings, or someone in the family was in an accident the same day. The saddest was the time a friend lost her son the very morning that we were praying for her, and God gave her peace and strength.

This year we received a letter that absolutely gave us chills to think how much our prayers were needed at the very time we were praying. A portion of the letter said, "We always appreciate your time of prayer for us. Besides surviving the earthquake just after we received your letter, let me tell you another miracle that happened as you prayed for us. Darrel and a group of businessmen get together every weekday morning at a local restaurant (as they have for the past 29 years). The numbers have dwindled over the years, and fortunately that morning some of the group were in Arizona on winter vacation. A Ford Bronco came right through the restaurant wall, slamming away the end of the table, missing Darrel by only one chair. The heat vent and light fixture crashed onto the middle of the table; Sheetrock and dust rained down. Everyone was shaken, but miraculously no one was hurt. We praise God for the safety of Darrel and his friends and for that of the elderly couple in the car, whose brakes had failed them."

I'm not saying it was only our special prayers on their special day that protected everyone that morning, but I do know there is great power in prayer, and it is truly awesome to know what God can do for us and our friends when we ask Him. ANNA MAY RADKE WATERS

Secret Heart

I praise you because I am fearfully and wonderfully made. . . . My frame was not hidden from you when I was made in the secret place. Ps. 139:14, 15, NIV.

FOR YEARS MY GRANDMA'S old bureau held a special charm for me. Everything she owned resided in that bureau, except for her clothes. Whenever we went to visit her, she would lower the lid of the bureau and rest it carefully on the pullout supports. Behind the lid were lots of tiny drawers, cupboards, and little shelves. Out of one of these my grandma would always take a special treat. Maybe it would be a bar of chocolate, a balloon, a pretty card someone had sent her, a tiny toy, or a coin. And the old bureau continued to hold surprises when I visited her with my own children. They soon learned that it was a treasure chest for them, as well.

Then one day my grandma moved, and she had a new bureau. She knew how much the old piece of furniture had meant to me, so my dad brought the bureau down to my home. It wasn't a particularly beautiful bureau. The drawers had woodworm, years of wear had darkened the wood, and some of the little handles were broken, but it was still something to treasure. We would treat the woodworm and mend the broken parts.

It was only when I began to clean the old wood that I noticed something—the tiny door in the middle of the shelves was inlaid with wood. There was a tiny border around the edge of the door and a delicate heart design right in the middle. The rest of the wood was oak, solid and functional, but this tiny door was a labor of love, something beautiful, hidden away in the heart of the old desk.

I wondered who had made the little door, and why. Had the bureau once been a gift of love? Did the carpenter always add a special touch to their furniture like this? Had an old door been replaced with this pretty one for some reason? I'll never know.

But I do know that every person is a treasure. They may look old or worn or broken or dirty and diseased, just like the bureau. But everyone has a special something hidden away, just waiting to be discovered by someone who cares.

There's a secret heart waiting to be discovered in each person you meet today.

KAREN HOLFORD

A Precious Message

"For I know the thoughts that I think toward you," says the Lord, "thoughts of peace and not of evil, to give you a future and a hope." Jer. 29:11, NKJV.

A GROUP OF FRIENDS AND relatives joined me for lunch recently. During a lull in the conversation my sister Rose spoke up. "The Lord has done something extraspecial for me this week," she began. She immediately had our undivided attention.

"To give you a little background," she went on, "I have a friend who's been having a real battle with discouragement and depression, and I've been trying to support her as best I can. When she began talking of suicide, I managed to get her to promise me she would call me before she did anything drastic."

Some time later she did call Rose, and they spent the day together. Talking and praying together seemed to help, but as Rose was leaving, her friend again was much troubled. She confessed that she felt hopeless, a person without a future. That's when Rose remembered the text in Jeremiah 29:11, in which the Lord promises to give us a future and a hope. They looked it up in the Bible and read it together. Her friend said she'd never heard this passage before. Much encouraged, she claimed it as God's special message for her.

"This week I remembered that her birthday would be the next Saturday," related Rose. "Since I knew my supply of birthday cards was limited, I decided I'd need to run into town to get a really nice card for her. Then I thought I'd just look through my old cards, just in case. Sorting through the cards, I could see I had nothing suitable. Then, there—stuck in the middle of a bunch of thank-you notes—was a beautiful birthday card. I knew I had never seen it before. Not only was it a lovely card but printed beautifully on the front was the text, Jeremiah 29:11! Needless to say," Rose added, "the card provided a wonderful blessing for both of us. I'm so thankful the Lord gave us this precious experience."

Thank You, Father, for Your love shining through Your Word, for Rose and her friend, and for all of us. Praise Your name. MARILYN KING

The Invitation

The Spirit and the bride say, "Come," And let everyone who hears say, "Come." And let everyone who is thirsty come. Let anyone who wishes take the water of life as a gift. Rev. 22:17, NRSV.

DOESN'T EVERYONE LIKE TO be invited to a birthday party, a graduation celebration, a wedding, an anniversary, or other special occasion? Personally, I may not want to go to every event to which I'm invited, but I always feel honored whenever I get an invitation to a wedding. I think weddings are some of the most beautiful and joyous gatherings. Some other happy occasions are inaugural celebrations of different kinds.

Two weeks before the forty-third president of the United States was inaugurated, my older daughter, Lynda, received an invitation to attend the president's inauguration. When she told me about the invitation, I was very excited. Who would spurn such an invitation? When I asked her if she was going, she said she wasn't. She has a 4-month-old baby, and she didn't have enough money to donate to the political party inviting her. All the time I had thought it was free, as long as one was invited. After all, she had an invitation to the inaugural ball. She said that she needed to give a donation of at least $5,000.

Reading the Word, I pondered seriously on God's invitation: "The Spirit and the bride say, 'Come.' And let everyone who hears say, 'Come.' And let everyone who is thirsty come. Let anyone who wishes take the water of life as a gift."

The Lord's invitation is offered freely to all—to everyone, no matter what her station in life. She doesn't need to pay a contribution of $5,000. True, a ticket is necessary to enter the banquet hall, but that entry ticket has already been paid for by our Lord and Savior, Jesus Christ. We have only to wear the robe of righteousness He offers to each. Wearing Christ's righteousness will give us abundant entry to the city where the inauguration of the reign of the King of kings and the Lord of lords will be celebrated. Oh, what a grand celebration that will be!

Dear Lord, thank You for paying the way for me to be in the grandest inauguration ever—of Your reign when You shall claim Your own. Amen.

OFELIA A. PANGAN

My Pictorial Guest Book

And he had a Book of Remembrance drawn up in which he recorded the names of those who feared him and love to think about him. Mal. 3:16, TLB.

THE THREE-RING GUEST BOOK on my coffee table is a conversation piece. My ever-ready camera sits beside it. An entire page is devoted to each person or group who visits; I place a snapshot next to their message. I discovered the idea when I visited my sister, who had borrowed it from her daughter-in-law.

A picture, they say, is worth a thousand words, and so it seems. Every page is a colorful reminder of a friend, family member, or loved one. Scrawled, printed, or written carefully are inscriptions that characterize each individual. Some are brief, and the picture fills the rest of the page. Other messages consume the entire space, and the picture or pictures are relegated to the opposite page. Each is unique in its own interesting style, even as that person is unique to me and holds a special place in my heart.

As friends peruse my guest book, fond memories are frequently recalled. Often, a guest will recognize a mutual friend in the book, and a bridge to renewed communication is established between them.

Early one morning an especially warm feeling pervaded my heart as I thought about that pictorial guest book. And then it came to me: How like my little book is the book of remembrance God keeps in His celestial realm. Each page is colorful with pictures of His children, and their loving deeds are accurately inscribed. How it must warm His great heart of love!

Some day soon I want to visit heaven's vast library and leaf through God's book of remembrance, where noble endeavors by residents of heaven are inscribed. Each person is His unique creation. Each one bears His special signature.

Sadly, some of my carefully planned deeds may never be entered there because I failed to touch the life of someone God placed within my reach. So each day, as I glance at that guest book lying on my table, I purpose to create a page in God's book that my guardian angel may read with joy as he reflects on some loving Christlike achievement I've tried to perform with His help. I pray there will be no blank pages. LORRAINE HUDGINS-HIRSCH

The Rainbow

I do set my rainbow in the cloud, and it shall be a token of a covenant between me and the earth. Gen. 9:13.

HAVE YOU EVER FELT abandoned by God? Have you ever wondered, deep in your heart, if this time He moved—not you? Have you ever questioned, as did Job, why the wicked prosper? Have you ever asked God, Why me?

It's usually when I'm lying quietly in my bed reviewing the events of the day and anticipating events to come, just as I'm drifting into quiet rest, that the questions come. In my quiet moments, when life for me is still, I wrestle with the questions about my God.

My days as a social worker are filled with extending myself to others, with the giving of myself—the phone calls, family meetings, home visits, counseling. And let's not forget the paperwork. Even on my way home from work I feel the hustle and bustle, the reality of living in crowded isolation in the concrete jungles of success.

As I roll up the car windows to stay warm, the noise once so loud and distracting is hushed. The conversations on the streets and in the cars next to me are stilled. In my car all is quiet, and in that moment I strain to hear God. But there is nothing—and I need something, Someone. The social worker, the giver, is now the needy one. I begin to feel utterly alone in the hush. Why is God so silent when I'm hurting and in need of healing? Why is He so still when I need His strength and power? Why does it seem He is not a relevant God?

Then something catches my eye, and my attention is quickly drawn to the sky. Directly in front of me, in the middle of a perfectly sunny day, I see a rainbow encased in a cloud. It is truly incredible to see! I begin to smile, then laugh. God is no longer silent. He is no longer motionless. He is relevant. He is my healer, my power, and my attentive God. He revealed Himself to me in the symbol of a rainbow-encased cloud, God's covenant, His token of love, His promise to be Terrie Ruff's God. His token bridges the gap between heaven and earth. I thank God for the gift of a rainbow that day, but, more important, I'm thankful for the Giver of the rainbow.

TERRIE RUFF

God in a Community Center?

Religion . . . is this: to look after orphans and widows in their distress. James 1:27, NIV.

THE CLIENT'S FACE WAS glowing. Her smile was captivating, her energy infectious.

As a community service volunteer, most of my clients greet me politely, but seldom enthusiastically. No, they display different emotions. They might be morose, sullen, angry, discouraged. Some are plagued by inertia, low self-esteem, and depression. Their negativism is understandable. It is spawned by their experiences—layoffs, discrimination, illnesses, divorce, abuse. They struggle with lack of job skills, inadequate income, and even inclement weather.

But today one thirtysomething client was happy. I had seen her first just last month, a victim of job cutbacks. Now, with spirits soaring, she told me she had secured employment in a coastal town some 50 miles away. Until her first paycheck, though, she needed food. And could she have a few items of clothing suitable for the new job? Of course she could!

While I prepared food and clothing vouchers she asked, "Does your organization have a church in the city where I'll be working?"

"We do," I responded, "and we also have a hospital there."

She blinked. "A hospital? I'll go there to volunteer. I've done some social work. A church, too. I need your church."

God, she explained, had never seemed important to her, although she was involved in service-oriented work. "I just left God out," she said. Rather pensively she continued, "You know I came here a month ago. I was discouraged and depressed. I left feeling encouraged by the genuine love and compassion shown me here. It must be God's love and concern that prevails."

I handed her the vouchers and assured her of the joy she would experience discovering the God of love. Unexpectedly, she embraced me warmly.

Where does one find God? Anywhere, really, for God and love are inseparable, and God is omnipresent. But a community center? Why not? Isn't that what James, who saw Jesus' compassion firsthand, meant when he spoke of widows and orphans?

"For God so loved . . . that he gave . . . everlasting life."

LOIS E. JOHANNES

19

Unfailing Love

How precious is your unfailing love, O God! All humanity finds shelter in the shadow of your wings. Ps. 36:7, NLT.

I WAS ALMOST TO THE entrance to my place of employment one morning when the car in front of me suddenly slowed to a crawl. I did likewise and soon saw that a goose was wandering aimlessly in the street. As I carefully inched my way toward the area where she was standing, I noticed a small mound on the pavement. *Oh no,* I thought, *a baby goose.* I felt sick at heart as I imagined how confused or distraught this mother goose was.

I parked my car in the lot and started walking toward the building. Then I noticed something on the sidewalk near the employee entrance. As I approached the walkway I realized that another large goose was walking around, ever so slowly. Now and then it would pause, then begin walking again. As I got nearer I saw a small heap of baby geese, sleeping rather soundly, right there on the pavement. How cute they looked, and they had not a care in the world despite the fact that they were in a very peculiar spot with no grass or dirt or pond anywhere. As they were only a foot or so from the street, I worried for their safety. *Lord, please protect these geese and help their parents to lead them to safety,* I prayed as I opened the door to the building and stepped inside.

As I prepared for my day's work I reflected on the love these parent geese had for their babies—staying close by, trying to offer shelter, protection, and safety. Sadly, in one case it wasn't enough. Hopefully, it would be in the other.

And I thought of how God provides shelter, comfort, and protection for me. He loves me so much that He is always by my side, faithfully guiding me in the path that I should go, forever leading me to my eternal home. Even when I try to choose my own way or run into the dangerous pathways of life, He is there. What unfailing love!

Thank You, Father, that under Your wings of love and mercy I find shelter and safety.

IRIS L. STOVALL

The Simplicity of Trust

In quietness and confidence shall be your strength. Isa. 30:15, NKJV.

A S I PACKED THE LAST of my things into the car, I took one more look at the house full of memories that I was leaving, never to return. There had been a few happy times there, but mostly the heartaches stood out in my mind. Marital abuse takes many forms, and mine had been invisible to the untrained eye. Only God knew all the details. But I was leaving all that behind. I would have to trust God for my future.

Learning to trust fully in God's care did not come early to my strong-willed heart. I had the habit of going ahead on my own without stopping to pray or ask for guidance. But when I had to face a major change in my life, it was devastating to me because I had not formed the practice of first asking God for direction. Now I felt totally helpless.

Fear gripped my heart as I struck out on my own to rebuild a shattered life, the result of a bitter divorce. Friends tried to console me, and I did jot down the verses they repeated to me. Plunging headlong onto the trail of escape, I thought I could run away from my fears and worries, only to discover that they followed me. Reaching my secluded hidden valley, I settled down to nurse my fearful self-pity.

Then I felt a loving presence surround me every time I cried to God for help. Someone was praying for me a lot! Isaiah 30:15 was one of those verses friends had given me, and reading it again, I finally relinquished my will in utter despair. Praying my own supplicant prayer, I began to find the quietness and to gain the confidence I needed.

Another verse I clung to was 2 Timothy 1:7: "For God has not given us a spirit of fear, but of power and of love and of a sound mind" (NKJV). I certainly needed that power to overcome my fears. By taking hold of God's power and trusting in Him, I was able, step by step, to carry on in rebuilding my life.

Dear Lord, I want to thank You for helping me long ago when I was so alone and afraid. And for all the help You have given me since then as I've learned to trust You more, I bless Your holy name. BESSIE SIEMENS LOBSIEN

God Gave a Malta

The islanders [of Malta] showed us unusual kindness. . . . They honored us in many ways. Acts 28:2-10, NIV.

I T HAD BEEN THE most stressful nine months of my professional career. One after another, national, state, and regulatory surveys had descended on each of my three facilities. Pushed beyond my limit and drained, it was difficult to get out of bed in the morning or tackle each new day with anything remotely resembling enthusiasm. Would my vim and vigor ever return?

The phone rang, and I heard a familiar voice. "Come to Malta for the weekend."

"Malta?"

"Yes, Malta," she chuckled. "I'll be your 'Publius,' welcome you to my home, and entertain you hospitably for three days. Please come. You need it!"

Malta. My mind went to Paul's account of the wonderful three months he'd spent on Malta after the shipwreck on the journey to Rome. I went. It was a wonderful experience, and I learned firsthand about a Malta.

In our healing and recovery process God sometimes gives us a Malta—placing individuals in our path who can help us, or putting us in a place where we can receive needed rest, nurturing, and affirmation. Each of us has something from which to recover, some woundedness to heal. We need to be patient and respect the process in ourselves and in others.

Has anyone ever said, "Why don't you snap out of it?" "When are you going to get your ducks in a row?" "A few nights of sleep should put you back on your feet." Not very helpful, were they? Those would-be do-gooders obviously have little if any concept of the recovery process or understand that healing takes time.

Now a Malta, on the other hand, is a gift! How I cherish mine. I offer it to others, too. A Malta provides opportunity to reflect on the progress we've made. We can use the vital respite time to get outfitted for the next phase of our journey. And with Paul we can rest assured that we will land in safety.

Has God given you a Malta? Did you recognize it? take advantage of it? give thanks for it? Have you shared that gift with someone else?

ARLENE TAYLOR

The Art Lesson

Whether therefore ye eat, or drink, or whatsoever ye do, do all to the glory of God. 1 Cor. 10:31.

HANGING ABOVE MY DESK is a beautiful painting of a snow scene that was given to me by my sister, Betty. She has a unique flair for doing landscapes, birds, and other wildlife, but I especially enjoy this winter view of our farmlands. The snow appears almost three-dimensional in its depth. The lengthening shadows of a lone, bare tree and the white-capped old barn stand just beyond a stump fence near the rim of the frozen meadow.

This talent started with our mother but lay dormant until her last child was in school. With 16 children, there was no time. It was but a few years later that some of her daughters and most of her sons began to show a real artistic talent.

One day I decided it was time for me to try my hand at painting. So I approached my mother and said, "Can you show me how to paint a picture?"

She got out an easel, some brushes, and a few cans of paint and proceeded to give me an art lesson. I watched as she demonstrated the methods of mixing paint, blending, and shading. It all sounded so exciting and looked so easy. But it didn't take long into the session before I knew this wasn't for me. Right then I was convinced I would never be a painter like other members of my family. So my very first art lesson also became my last.

Eventually, I began composing some music along with some poetry, and for a few years I thought perhaps I'd found my niche in life. But the remnants of the poems and the 48 songs I wrote remain buried in the bookcase, waiting to be rediscovered.

Talent is a gift. According to the dictionary it's "a particular aptitude for some special work or activity." Some talent may come naturally, like art did to the Weaver family. It was evident even with no formal instruction. Other would-be artists choose proper training and become professionals in their field. We may not all be able to paint a picture, and we certainly can't all be poets, nor can everyone write a song, but we all have abilities in some area.

Perhaps it isn't so important where my ability lies. Maybe what really counts is what I do with what I have. "Do all to the glory of God."

CLAREEN COLCLESSER

Trucks and Other Traffic

When you pass through the waters, I will be with you; and when you pass through the rivers, they will not sweep over you. When you walk through the fire, you will not be burned; the flames will not set you ablaze. Isa. 43:2, NIV.

WE LIVED FOR A short time on one of the busiest roads in Brisbane, where the traffic never stopped. There were countless traffic light intersections. One such intersection was near our home. Because of the continuous traffic, I always drove into our driveway as quickly as possible—I didn't want to cause a nose-to-tail accident by slowness on my part.

One afternoon I was a little annoyed to see a small parked utility truck partially blocking our driveway so that I had to swerve out and around it to get in. After I'd put my car away, the driver was still sitting in his truck, engine running. I realized something wasn't right.

"How long has that truck been there?" I asked my mother-in-law, who was staying with us at the time.

"About 20 minutes," she said.

As I walked out to the footpath, the driver slowly turned and looked at me with overbright eyes. What was I to do? My husband was still at work, so I ran next door to my neighbor, Bill. When he opened the cab door, he noticed that the driver had a Medic Alert wristband on.

We called an ambulance for "our" truck driver, who was by then in a diabetic coma, and they rushed him to the hospital. The police came to park and lock the truck on a vacant block of land nearby until the owner's immediate family could take possession of it.

The driver's wife phoned later that evening to say thank you and to report that her husband was going to be fine. He'd been driving home from work and had thought he could make it home OK, even though he wasn't feeling well.

I thought how similar my life is to that. Satan snares me so many times when I think I'm doing OK. I pray there will be those along the way willing to help and that I'll make it all the way safely home to heaven.

LEONIE DONALD

Simply Dust and Ashes

If any of you is lacking in wisdom, ask God, who gives to all generously and ungrudgingly, and it will be given you. James 1:5, NRSV.

A FEW MONTHS AGO I was assigned by the head of my college to pay out more than 60,000 Gambian dalasi to some regional directors for appropriation. The first bundle of notes that I counted was D4,000, so I assumed that all the remaining bundles were also D4,000 each. I was so confident and sure of myself that I even told the officers not to waste time recounting what I gave them. So they both signed off and left. Then I realized that I didn't have enough to pay the last four. I consulted my boss.

"Count the notes properly, Mabel," she said, "because I brought the exact amount from the bank."

After a careful check I noticed it was only the top bundle of notes that was D4,000— all the others were D5,000. I had given them away as D4,000. Then I realized that even though I thought I knew all, I am nothing "but dust and ashes" (Gen. 18:27), so I could make mistakes.

Sometimes I forget that wisdom and knowledge are from God, as today's text says, so that I always need to ask God for wisdom before I start my assignments. The devil makes us feel so confident that we at times forget all about God and act unwisely and get into big trouble. But Psalm 46:1 says that "God is our refuge and strength, an ever-present help in trouble" (NIV).

I left the office, running after the two people whom I'd overpaid. But where would they be? They should be on their way up-country miles away. Looking around hopelessly, I bowed my head in shame and prayed. A soft voice told me to look up. About a hundred yards away I saw the two men. I called them back to the office, the necessary correction was done, and I got the lost money back.

One of the men then testified that they had been struggling for some time to start their motorbike but hadn't been able to do so until I called them. They thought God kept them there for a purpose.

Yes! Isn't God awesome?

MABEL KWEI

The Right Stuff

Do your best to win full approval in God's sight, as a worker who is not ashamed. 2 Tim. 2:15, TEV.

A S A FAVOR TO A friend I agreed to talk to an aspiring writer. I teach a writing class, and I enjoy encouraging new talent. Most of my students are willing and eager to learn their craft.

Five minutes into our conversation, though, I knew that this woman didn't have the right stuff for the job. When I asked her why she wanted to be a writer, she told me it was because she was so gifted. Since she was so talented, she felt it was her duty to share her talent with the world. Over the course of our conversation she informed me several more times how gifted she was. I mentioned different books and magazines about writing, but she had never heard of any of them.

"What do you like to read—what type of books do you look for in the library?" I asked her.

Then she told me she didn't enjoy reading and didn't have a library card. Anyway, she informed me, she didn't want to read what other people wrote because she didn't want them to influence her writing. Take a writing class? Never. It might spoil her natural talent.

I am confident that I have the characteristics needed to be a writer. I am always reading and learning more. I can be objective with my writing and ruthless in cutting out words that don't work. But talking to the would-be writer got me to thinking. Do I have the right stuff to be a Christian?

Am I willing to admit my ignorance of portions of the Bible and eager to study to learn more? Am I willing to worship God not just once a week in church but every day of my life? Am I willing to stand up for my beliefs in the face of ridicule? Can I forgive people when they wrong me, and turn the other cheek? Am I generous with my time? Do I truly love others?

When I ask these questions, I find myself lacking in several areas. I do, however, possess an abiding love for Jesus Christ, and that is a good start. Someday I hope to have all the right stuff for the job of being a Christian.

GINA LEE

Stranded

For He Himself has said, "I will never leave you nor forsake you."
Heb. 13:5, NKJV.

WHEN I STARTED MY car I knew something was wrong with the engine. Since I had completed an eight-hour day at work, I hoped my automobile would make it home, where my husband could help me decide how to handle the problem.

It looked as if I was going to make it when, with only 10 miles to go, my engine started to sputter and skip before coming to a complete stop. I couldn't coax it to life again.

I called my husband, telling him where I was. He said, "Don't worry. I have a chain in my vehicle, and I should have no problem towing you home."

When he arrived, he secured my car to his heavy-duty automobile, and we started down the highway, with me remaining in my car to help with steering and any braking that might be needed. About three miles down the road the chain came loose, leaving me stranded in the slow lane, watching my husband's vehicle disappearing in the distance. I guess I should have tooted my horn, but I was so amused by the situation that I just sat there laughing.

He returned in a few minutes, and we both had a good laugh. "I wondered why it was so easy to pull your car," he said, "until I looked in my rearview mirror."

Many years passed by before I thought again about that amusing day. My husband had died after a five-and-a-half-year battle with colon cancer, and the weight of being alone dawned on me. Once again I had been left in life's slow lane, this time permanently disconnected from my companion of 42 years. Then I remembered that day when I had watched the disappearing automobile, and my thoughts turned to God's promise never to leave me nor forsake me—not accidentally; not on purpose.

God is there for us in all our sorrows, trials, and disappointments. We are safe in His care, and we can rely on Him to be there always. Sometimes we can't sense His presence, but if we allow Him to stretch our faith heavenward He is there, His everlasting arms surrounding us.

Thank You, dear Lord, for staying connected with us today and through all our tomorrows. Amen.

MILDRED C. WILLIAMS

The Old Volkswagen Van

For God so loved the world, that he gave his only begotten Son, that whosoever believeth in him should not perish, but have everlasting life. John 3:16.

IN MY WORK AS educational adviser in a school, many times I go a little beyond my professional activities and become involved in the personal life of the students when this assistance is requested.

Once the mother of a seventh grader came to my office, asking me to help convince her son to stay in school. We were in the middle of the school year and, to his mother's despair, her son had decided to give up on everything. We set up an appointment to visit him the next day.

As arranged, this mother came to pick me up. When I saw the old VW van, I could tell that this woman had financial problems, but I only realized how bad the situation was when we drove away. The steering wheel was loose, and the gears were hard to shift. The seats had broken springs and no seat belts. Bad brakes rounded out the package. At each curve in the road (and there were many), I tried to hold on to the seat; but since I was seated in the middle, I didn't have anything to brace against.

Just before we reached our destination the woman said, "Mrs. Oliveira, Anderson is going to be surprised to see that you liked him enough to face a trip in this old Volkswagen van just to visit him."

When she said that I remembered Someone who faced a much worse situation for you and me. When Jesus came to this earth, He came willing to face whatever was necessary to save humanity. But people didn't recognize His sacrifice. Prior to His death in Gethsemane the weight of responsibility was so great and the anguish so intense that He perspired blood. He could have given up, but He didn't, because of His love for you and me. He knew that the eternal life of all fallen humanity depended upon Him. Jesus prayed three times, and on these three occasions He entrusted His will to that of the Father.

Dear Jesus, thank You for not being overcome by fear, anguish, and discouragement. Help me not to become discouraged before difficulties and to face them with good humor and trust.   INGRID RIBEIRO WOLFF DE OLIVEIRA

Lost and Found

Rejoice, because your names are written in heaven. Luke 10:20.

I HAVE LOST A NUMBER of things in my lifetime. Some losses can be shrugged off, while others cause a state of panic. My misplaced umbrella and gloves were easily replaced, so I didn't lose any sleep over them. But when I lost an airline ticket, my heart raced and I felt ashamed. Fortunately, I was able to get a duplicate ticket for $25. God heard how grateful I was for not having to pay the full price.

The most regrettable losses are those of sentimental value that can't be replaced. Although such items may have no dollar value, it's the meaning or memory evoked by them that makes them invaluable.

"Do you recognize this?" the school janitor asked one day, holding out a small black book.

"I sure do!" I exclaimed, snatching up my 50-year-old autograph book, which had been missing for 36 years.

After many questions, the mystery was solved. When moving from one school to another, I had sorted the books. There were the books I would be taking with me, books I'd give to a teacher friend, and books that would remain at the school. The autograph book was mistakenly put in the box for my friend, whom I never got to see again.

When the janitor attended her brother-in-law's funeral in the hometown of my teacher friend, she decided this was a good opportunity to return my book. It is full of treasured verses, written by special people in my life. There were the artistic pages by Andy, Bambi, and Gladys; my dad's wise counsel copied from Philippians 4:8; my grandmother's Icelandic script that I couldn't read; and many valued messages from other family and friends.

This gives me a glimpse of how God feels about our names being written in the book of life. Each of us is invaluable to Him; He doesn't want any of us to be lost. Let's guard each day so that the record on our page will bring joy to the heavenly hosts. A friend wrote this prayer in my book, which is my prayer for each of us:

"When life on earth is ended, and this path no more you trod,
    May your name in gold be written, in the autograph of God."

EDITH FITCH

Lord, Help Me Be a Blessing

Thanks be to God for his indescribable gift! 2 Cor. 9:15, NIV.
He gives power to the tired and worn out, and strength to the weak.
Isa. 40:29, TLB.

I AWOKE ONE MORNING, grateful that God had spared my life to see another day. During my devotion time I prayed that God would help me be His instrument to speak a word of encouragement to someone. Today I wanted to try to make a difference in someone's life.

I was walking across campus when I glimpsed a young man sitting under a large tree, looking alone and sad. I felt impressed to greet him, so I walked over and said, "How are you doing today? I'm sure you're eager to get home to see your folks and get some good home cooking." He responded that he had just finished taking midterm exams and was tired. When I asked him where his home was he said that his parents had moved while he was in school, and he hadn't seen his new house, but he guessed it was all right. His countenance took on a smile as we continued to chat. He seemed happy that I took the time to greet him. I wished him safe travel, and he responded with a cheery "Thank you, ma'am."

Later on, a young man visited my office and asked me to purchase items he was selling to raise money for tuition. I inquired how he was doing in school. He said that it was not so good; he worked long hours to help pay his tuition, and when it was time to study he was usually tired. He mentioned that his mother worked very hard, and he was trying to do his part. As we chatted I encouraged him to try to spend a little more time with his studies so that his grades would improve and wished him God's blessings. Before leaving, he said, "My mother would be happy to know that you took the time to talk to me. I appreciate your encouragement. Thank you very much."

That incident took a few minutes, but it sparked a friendship. This young student frequently visits or calls to see how I'm doing and to let me know how things are with him.

As I reflect on my day, one of my favorite songs comes to mind: "If I can help somebody as I pass along, then my living shall not be in vain." May that be our prayer each day.

SHIRLEY C. IHEANACHO

Wiped Out!

The Lord will be your confidence and will keep your foot from being snared.
Prov. 3:26, NIV.

I KNOW THERE IS MORE in the checking account than that," I told my husband. He replied that the credit union said we were overdrawn. I didn't see how that could be; I was always very careful to watch how much I wrote checks for, and since I did it on the computer, I knew the calculations were done correctly. My mathematical mistakes were overridden by the computer, which made doing bank reconciliations much easier. And I also knew that we had a $9,000 overdraft for protection. So how could it all be gone?

I immediately called the credit union. The person who answered tried to tell me that we had written checks for more than we had in our account. I told him that was not possible. He looked at our account carefully and then said, "There is a check for $35,000, written to your water account." I told him the check I wrote was for $35, not $35,000. He finally admitted that the bank had made the error, and in so doing had wiped out our overdraft and put us in heavy debt. That was on a Friday, and the credit union could do nothing about it until the following Monday. He assured me that all of my other checks would be honored and that no charges would be assessed. I was also assured that our credit would not be affected.

"Thank You, Lord." I breathed a sigh of relief. We had always had good credit, and this seemed like a terrible thing to happen.

On Monday it was all straightened out, and we were solvent again. As I thought about the situation I wondered if I was always as careful to have good credit with the Lord. Do I guard my Christian reputation as carefully as I do my monetary reputation? It's true that my Christian reputation won't earn me eternal life—that only comes as the gift of Christ, who died for me. But as a Christian I'm admonished to avoid the appearance of evil. Everything I do and say affects those around me, even those who don't know me. Am I reflecting Christ's love in all I do and say?

Please help me, Lord, to reflect Your character. This is my prayer for myself, and for those who are reading this today.   LORAINE F. SWEETLAND

Covered With His Hands

*For thou hast been a shelter for me, and a strong tower from the enemy.
Ps. 61:3.*

I LOVE TO TRAVEL, AND of all the modes of travel available to us, flying
is my favorite. I have seen many an eyebrow raise when I have said that,
but it's true. I love to fly.

In 1996, when I was called to work for the Caribbean Union
Conference as women's and children's ministries director, my feelings were
very different. I knew my job would entail much flying to various islands in
airplanes of different shapes and sizes. I heard my fellow directors tell of
their adventures in the air, and I shuddered at each tale recounted.

The first few trips were fine, but then came the hurricane season, which
meant lots of rain and winds, even on good days. One particular trip, however, changed my view of flying. I was flying from St. Lucia to Guadeloupe
in a 12-seat airplane. The sky was dark and ominous-looking, and the rain
was coming down. It was just a regular thunderstorm, but that airplane was
going up and down and sideways, and my stomach was doing the same.

I remember my eyes were tightly shut when I thought, *If I am going to
die, I want to see what's happening.* I opened my eyes just as the airplane
took a sudden drop and noticed that I could see nothing out the window
but clouds. Suddenly I realized how beautiful that was. God began to speak
to me at that moment and reminded me that I was safe in His arms and
therefore had no need to see beyond the clouds. I consequently had nothing
to fear.

Just as I could see nothing beyond that window, so at times in my own
life I cannot tell what the next moment will bring. I want to know; I want
to see and feel secure. But Jesus reminds me that once I know He is holding
me safe in His arms, I have nothing to fear.

And so flying for me is an experience I look forward to. I long to be in
the clouds where I can see nothing beyond the window, for then I remember my God is holding me safe, and I have nothing to fear.

Father, keep me safe in Your arms today and always. I love You.

HEATHER-DAWN SMALL

Time to Listen

I will instruct thee and teach thee in the way which thou shalt go: I will guide thee with mine eye. Ps. 32:8.

A RMED WITH A DAILY devotional guide in one hand and the lesson guide and Bible in the other, I headed to the study to have my devotional reading. I hurried through one thing after the other, whisked a prayer heavenward, and started out the door.

Then I heard an audible voice: "And what did God say to you this morning?"

"Excuse me? Had God wanted to say something?"

I didn't know what God said because I hadn't stopped to listen to what He had to say. My devotion had consisted of reading and praying, and then I was done. There had been no time to listen.

Communicating with God has to be more than a duty. It is developing a relationship with a friend. What is the sense in holding a conversation if you're the only person talking? Any meaningful relationship must have dialogue. It doesn't feel very good when we stop to talk to a friend or an acquaintance and they ignore us completely. Somehow this was what I was doing to God each day.

One author says, "Prayer is the opening of the heart to God as to a friend" (*Steps to Christ,* p. 93). Through sincere prayer we are brought into connection with the mind of the Infinite. He speaks to us, but we will not hear His voice until we stop to listen.

Today, pause a little longer and listen to what He is saying. Your Partner and Friend is waiting to say something important to you, but you must be willing to listen. If the morning is not a good time to spend with Him, choose another time of the day that is more convenient.

What did He say to you this time? Did you hear? He says, "I am with you always." Even when you anticipate a terrible day, when you are driving in traffic, when the babies are crying, and you haven't even started your to-do list, He is with you.

I know that you feel better already, knowing that there is no situation that you'll face today that He isn't facing with you. Aren't you happy that you stopped to listen?

GLORIA GREGORY

A Child's Heart

And he said: "I tell you the truth, unless you change and become like little children, you will never enter the kingdom of heaven." Matt. 18:3, NIV.

ONCE AGAIN THE CHILDREN were all piled into the school bus and heading for the local skating rink. This hour of fun and exercise was a weekly highlight for the kids of the small church-operated school where I taught. Few of the teachers skated, so we mostly huddled around, supervising and shivering.

One particular day stands out vividly in my memory. It was early spring, and the gang had just arrived at the rink. Warm air outside contrasted markedly with the cold inside. There was the usual bedlam of yelling, struggling into skates, and racing for the ice. Older kids helped younger, and teachers helped all. Finally I rested on the slatted wooden bench as one or two stragglers fought with an ornery mitten before tottering off toward the rink.

Just then the main door opened, and our pastor walked in. He was a tall man with a ready smile, and his skates were slung loosely over his broad shoulder. He offered a cheery hello as he sank down to the bench across from me and began to untangle his laces.

As if out of nowhere, a mob of kids materialized around him. They were jumping, shouting, and pulling on his arms in their excitement. To have the pastor skating with them was going to be a great treat. They all seemed to be vying for his attention. I watched the scenario—detached yet amused. It was good to see them so happy and eager.

Suddenly I became aware of a presence by my side. I turned to see one of my girls, a very precious and sensitive child. She sat quietly for a moment while the raucous action continued, then gently tugged at my sleeve. Her eyes were clouded with concern.

"I didn't want you to feel left out," she explained. Her thoughtful words caught me quite off guard. Soon her arms encircled me in a deliberate hug that said that I too was special.

Is it really any wonder that Jesus said we must become like little children in order to enter heaven?

Dear Lord, How far am I from heaven today? Please give me the heart of a child as I long for Your kingdom.   DAWNA BEAUSOLEIL

Express Yourself

A little child will lead them. Isa. 11:6, NIV.

"MS. ELAINE, I LOVE YOU," blurted out one of the children. Another said, "Hey, Ms. Elaine!" A third asked, "Can I be your helper, Ms. Elaine?" These are some of the things children at the day care where I've worked for the past eight years say to me on any given morning to brighten up my day. That's why a child is presented as a gift from God.

When things get stressful at work and I want to just quit, one of my "children" is there to pick me up. It seems as if they know when I am not at my best. Children have that sensitivity toward the feelings of others. We adults have this ability also, but rarely use it.

If I am in a joyful mood, my babies are more lovable and cuddly. We have a fun day together, unless their personal needs haven't been met. But don't let me come in angry, upset, or even just tired. The babies feel my emotions and cry, scream, or even yell.

Our heavenly Father also has a sensitivity toward our feelings. "For we do not have a high priest who is unable to sympathize with our own weaknesses" (Heb. 4:15, NIV).

Several days ago I was having one of those rough days and was about to call it quits. The next morning I was still undecided. When I drove into the parking lot I looked out of my window toward the main entrance. I saw and heard two of my former students jumping out of their truck and running toward me, smiling. In their hands they each carried a beautiful white carnation. Their mom told me they had picked them out of their yard for me! Then she said their nana was going to pick them up that day after lunch, so they decided to give the carnations to Nana instead because they thought she would be sad. They asked if I could put the flowers in some water. This would give me a chance to enjoy them before Nana came.

"For all who exalt themselves will be humbled, and those who humble themselves will be exalted" (Luke 14:11, NIV).

Thank You, Lord, for Your "gift" and for allowing me to be a part of their lives.   ELAINE J. JOHNSON

All He Did Was Part the Sea

He hath said, I will never leave thee, nor forsake thee. So that we may boldly say, The Lord is my helper, and I will not fear what man shall do unto me. Heb. 13:5, 6.

GOD IS SUCH AN awesome God! Just look at what He did for the Israelites. He brought down the mightiest king in the world, leaving a powerful nation in ruin just to free a tribe of slaves. When they were cornered between impassable mountains and the Red Sea, He parted the sea and turned it into a dry highway for them to escape. Heavy-duty miracles! He even gave them private rivers in the desert, catered every meal from Heaven's own bakery, and camped right there with them in a pillar of fire and cloud. They could see signs of His presence whenever they looked, but they still lost faith every time things got a little rough. Petty little problems, and they whined, complained, and threatened.

For 40 years they never once turned to God when a problem came up. They turned up the attitude instead. I think, *They surely were dim-witted back in Bible times. That's why I'm glad I'm a modern Christian who knows all about the manna, streams in the desert, and the parting of the Red Sea. I'm not a faithless, whining Israelite. I'm not, am I?*

What about the time someone gossiped about me to the conference president. It was untrue, but I panicked because the president might believe the lies. God couldn't defend me. All He'd ever done was part the Red Sea!

Then there was the time my toddler wandered off. I was tearing my hair out and never thought about praying until someone else reminded me. After all, why turn to God for help with a lost son when all He ever did was guide Israel through trackless desert?

What about the time a powerful man tried to get me fired because of my religion? I stewed all night and didn't remember to pray until 2:00 a.m. After all, what could God do against the might of a community leader? All He did was bring Pharaoh to his knees.

God works the miracles that keep the world alive and turning every day. He also finds time to listen to every prayer and keep an eye on every sparrow in the world. Why am I worrying? Why don't I pray more? My God parted the Red Sea, and my God is listening to me.   JULIA VERNON

The Lost Key

Ask, and it shall be given you; seek, and ye shall find. Matt. 7:7.

IT WAS 8:00 P.M.; I'd just gotten home from work. As I prepared to open the door, I realized I couldn't find my key. I searched in my bag; it wasn't there. I knew for certain that I'd had the key with me that morning, since I was the one who had locked the door.

I searched my bag again, but still no key. I went back to my car, hoping it was there, but nothing. After 15 minutes of searching, I almost gave up.

I knew it would be dark pretty soon, and it would be more difficult for me to search in the dark. I also knew I could not wait for my landlady to open the door because she was out of town and wouldn't be back until the following day.

I started to feel tired and a little bit frustrated. *Where will I sleep for the night?* I began to worry. Trying to find a place was not a pleasant task. What could I do?

Then I remembered to pray. *God, help me to find my key. You know that without this key I won't be able to enter the house. I believe, God, You have so many ways to help me. In Jesus' name I pray. Amen.*

As soon as I opened my eyes I walked to my car again. This time I saw that key right there, on the grass, next to the car's door. It must have dropped, falling down in the grass without my knowledge, when I climbed out of my car.

Praise the Lord! I knew God had answered my prayer. He opened my eyes to find my key in that grass. I had tried to find my key alone; I hadn't asked for God's help. But after I asked for God's help, He did help me. As it is written in Matthew 7:7: "Ask, and it shall be given you; seek, and ye shall find."

Thank You, Father, for answering my prayer. I praise You with my whole heart. I will praise You today and every day for Your help. Thank You for the assurance that You are always there for me.

I will remember to ask God for His help, seeking Him before I become tired and frustrated. How is it for you today? Ask and seek!

LANNY LYDIA PONGILATAN

Just Stay Pretty

You will keep in perfect peace all who trust in you, whose thoughts are fixed on you! Isa. 26:3, NLT.

THE NIGHT BEFORE HER surgery Trudy and I talked. "Deb, if you want to help me, help me by doing whatever you can for my children" were my aunt's words. I'll never forget those words. And I'll also never forget how, despite the ugly things that have happened in her life, Trudy has carried prettiness in her heart.

For 16 years Trudy has courageously fought horrendous brain tumors. With two successful surgeries behind her (both miracles), she was facing yet another intense surgery. Trudy knew the score—the possibility of death or major physical and/or mental deficits was a reality. She was the proud mother of three adult sons and two daughters, ages 12 and 11.

We saw another miracle. Trudy, age 48, survived the surgery, but was left lingering at death's door for several months. Now she has significant medical concerns. She is paralyzed on the right side, and her ability to speak has been greatly impaired. She is out of the hospital and perhaps will require much therapy in future months or years.

I've had time to meditate, reason, and act upon Trudy's request. My family believes in the power of intercessory prayer. In response to the Holy Spirit's guidance, our family has shared Trudy's story, requesting Christians of all faiths to uplift her in their prayers. This situation could easily become overwhelming if discouragement takes hold. Yet I know "the earnest prayer of a righteous person has great power and wonderful results" (James 5:16, NLT).

During times of great disappointment within my personal life, the Holy Spirit has impressed this upon my weary mind: "In the light of eternity, this is but a sad moment. No matter what happens, just stay pretty." I need pretty thoughts to keep me focused. Perhaps you do also. I need love that "binds us all together in perfect harmony" (Col. 3:14, NLT). It's a matter of the heart.

"Though we travel the world over to find the beautiful, we must carry it with us or we find it not" (Ralph Waldo Emerson).

Dear saints, just stay pretty!

DEBORAH SANDERS

God by Osmosis

But in your hearts set apart Christ as Lord. Always be prepared to give an answer to everyone who asks you to give the reason for the hope that you have. But do this with gentleness and respect. 1 Peter 3:15, NIV.

"YOU DO WHAT I'VE done for 24 years—then talk to me about God," Cheri quietly told me as she gently stroked the head of her severely retarded daughter. "People keep trying to get me to believe in God, so I tell them what I've just told you," she continued.

Devastated by her baby's condition and her own onset of Type I diabetes at the time of Stacey's birth, Cheri decided she wanted no part of a God who ignored her prayers for healing in either case. The ensuing years of battling her own disease and caring for Stacey only solidified her convictions.

We talked at length, but nothing I said made any impact. Her mind was made up against God for what He had done to her. Long after our visit, my mind churned with hurt for Cheri's lack of affection toward God. She needed Him so badly! I analyzed her reasoning, tried to "walk in her moccasins," and wondered what my own picture of God might be had my life paralleled hers. I had to come up with a witnessing technique that would not offend. I decided it would have to be "God by osmosis."

Every person has the privilege of believing as they wish about God, even though we may long for them to believe as we do. Their ideas may be different than ours; they may be wrong, but it's not our responsibility to convince them otherwise. That's the work of the Holy Spirit. We can help with gentleness and respect, but arguing the case only drives their nail of conviction deeper. Hopefully, my fervent prayers for Cheri, along with my Christian character and living witness, will soften her heart. When she brings up the subject, I will share. As scary as the responsibility is, I am, in part, her picture of God.

God by osmosis may be the only way some people absorb the love of Christ. Today's text says to give answers to those who ask and to do so with gentleness and respect, not forcing our beliefs on them. In this new year our lives reflecting God's character will hopefully encourage many to see God through us.

MARYBETH GESSELE

What If?

For you created my inmost being; you knit me together in my mother's womb. Ps. 139:13, NIV.

WHAT DO YOU WANT to be when you grow up?" I was asked, as all children are. And my answer was always the same: "A nurse." I thought of nothing else. I read books about nurses, played nurse, dreamed of being a nurse. While in high school I even worked as a nurse's aide. When I got to college I enrolled in nursing classes. I hated it, and soon changed majors. But I kept my course in anatomy and physiology.

One of the fascinating sections of physiology was the formation of the fetus and the changes that take place at birth. I learned that there is a hole between the two sides of the heart that normally closes at the time of birth. In those days, if it didn't, the baby died. Now these babies are often saved by surgery. It confirmed to me that we are fearfully and wonderfully made.

What if we had evolved, and the hole had not closed at exactly the right time? No one would have survived. What if the oxygen we need to breathe at birth had evolved later—or not at all? What if our lung air sacs were not elastic enough to hold air? What if our skin didn't grow but our bones did? What if our bodies had no way to purify our blood supply? Or what if we had been born without thumbs? Well, you get the idea. The what-if's could go on and on.

But each one of us is created in marvelous perfection. It is only sin that mars. And we're not mass-produced, either—God made each of us unique. There would be a loss if even one of us were not here. And if we do not have a relationship with our Creator, He feels the loss, because not only did He create us, He died to redeem us.

What if God had not foreseen the emergence of sin and provided the plan of redemption? What if Jesus had refused His part in the plan? What if God was not love? Fortunately, we don't have to worry about that. But there is something we do need to consider carefully, and that is whether or not we accept His offer of redemption and begin a relationship with our Creator. "For God so loved the world that he gave his one and only Son, that whoever believes in him shall not perish but have eternal life" (John 3:16, NIV).

ARDIS DICK STENBAKKEN

Looking on the Bright Side of Life

We know that in all things God works for the good of those who love him. Rom. 8:28, NIV.

WHEN I WAS A little girl my father made me a lovely dollhouse, complete with furniture. It even had lighting. I loved to play with it and my little doll family.

The dining room table was made of plastic and had four legs. When the first leg broke, I said to my mother, "Never mind. I can turn the table so that the missing leg is against the wall, and the table will still stand on its three legs." When a second leg broke, my comment was "Isn't it good that it broke on the same side as the first leg? This way, I can put a spool under that end of the table, and it will still stand." When the third leg broke, I snapped off the remaining one and said, "OK, I don't need this leg anymore. Now I can push the spool into the middle of the table, and it'll stand on that."

I was born with an optimistic attitude. When we moved to Africa and saw what our house was going to offer us in terms of comfort, I wrote in my first letter to my parents, "Actually, it's quite good that things are as they are. At least they can't get any worse, so they can only get better!" And, little by little, life did become more comfortable. But the experience was very valuable because it taught me that we can live with less and still be happy.

Life has been chipping away at my positive attitude, and there have been times when I haven't been able to recognize myself. I've even thought that I'd lost my optimistic side. But even in those dark times I've always known that there will be light again at the end of the tunnel, and that one day I'll get through to the bright side of life again. Life isn't always easy, but we don't have to make it more difficult.

Not everybody is born with an optimistic attitude, but we can still control how we look at life. We can learn to look for the positive side of things, and it will make our life so much easier. The only thing that cannot be taken from us is the freedom to choose our attitude, and that will make the difference.

One day soon we'll find out that because of Jesus everything did work out for our good, after all.

HANNELE OTTSCHOFSKI

My Passion for Words

As a dream comes when there are many cares, so the speech of a fool when there are many words. Eccl. 5.3, NIV.

I HAVE AN ABIDING LOVE affair with words. I love to read them, write them, hear them, speak them—even spell them and play with them. Crossword puzzles, Scrabble, Find the Word—anything like that entices me.

Of course, I'm a busy person, and I cannot—and do not—spend much time on the puzzles and word games, but sometimes while I'm riding my exercise bike I succumb to Target, from the back page of the newspaper. Target consists of a grid of nine letters from which you must construct a stated number of words, incorporating the central letter and at least three others. Then you crown your efforts by using all nine letters in one familiar word.

Easy? Usually it is. But some months ago I stumbled across a Target that I had cut out and tucked away. The grid letters were MEM, SEC, UNI. I quickly gained the required number of words, even adding a few. But that nine-letter word eluded me.

Every few days I'd make another attempt. Still no success. Eventually the word became an obsession. One night I couldn't sleep for puzzling over it. Just before midnight I decided I'd settle it once and for all. I crept out of bed and found my Scrabble set. Going into another room, I sat on the floor and sifted through 100 letters until I found the necessary nine. Then I arranged those nine letters into every word pattern that I could think of. Still no sensible word came out. My eyes burned and my head ached for lack of sleep. I gave up.

"Dear Lord," I prayed as I shoved the letters back into the bag, "I'm sorry. Forgive me for wasting Your precious gift of time. Humble me, and please take away this stupid obsession and let me go to sleep." I crept back to bed and slept soundly. When I awoke next morning, the first thought that came into my mind was the elusive word: ecumenism.

I learned many spiritual lessons from that small episode. Not the least of which was to marvel anew at God's blessings, His answers to prayer, and all the wonderful evidences of His love, custom-made for each of His erring children.

GOLDIE DOWN

God's Fingerprints

Great are the works of the Lord; they are pondered by all who delight in them. Glorious and majestic are his deeds, and his righteousness endures forever. He has caused his wonders to be remembered. Ps. 111:2-4, NIV.

ROOTING THROUGH BOXES, I came across some junior legal pads dated 1993 and 1994—my journals. I flipped through the pages and discovered fascinating things. I found jubilant answers to prayer. Honest expressions of spiritual stagnation. Neat insights to Scripture. Simple recounting of moments of joy. Heated words about an injustice. Warm reflections on a favorite book. Open-ended questions to God above.

One entry told about a belated Christmas present I had received in February. It was a daily calendar with wonderful quotes about coloring your life with joy. One said, "Do little things that you love on a regular basis." I mused on paper why I feel like I'm veering off my to-do list if I snatch bits of time to do something I enjoy.

"Should I be more deliberate in scheduling fun times?" I wrote. "Hey, why not add something fun to my to-do list? Why should my list just have work on it? Lord, You want me to be more balanced, and that includes the fun area."

The next day's entry in my journal listed moments of joy. In addition to scheduling regular fun times, I wanted to savor moments of joy.

"I stopped by the stream on my walk. I took joy in the moment, listening to the babbling and rippling of water, seeing the glaze of the snowy fields lighted by the bright sun, and trees silhouetted against the whitescape with a grain silo looking on. Water, surging from blankets of snow in the stream, or tagging along on the icy edge of a snow patch, coursing like blood cells in a vein. I took joy in that moment."

I'm not a daily journal keeper and feel no pressure to be. But I'm thankful that I've recorded some of my thoughts and feelings, because they show me where I've been and how far I've come. It's at once thrilling and humbling to trace God's hand in my life. Rereading my journals has inspired me to journal more—I don't want to miss any of God's fingerprints.

HEIDE FORD

A Tribute of Love

Inasmuch as ye have done it unto one of the least of these my brethren, ye have done it unto me. Matt. 25:40.

TODAY IT WAS MY task to send my condolences to the daughter of a dear friend. Jean was a bright, busy woman, who was always there, always helping, comforting, and counseling.

I had told Jean that she was a beautiful Christian. She was a wonderful example of selfless love and caring, the epitome of loving and benevolent deeds. How could anyone be so Christlike and not be a Christian?

"I think I'm an atheist," she had replied. "I don't like any of the religions I've studied or the churches I've attended. They just turned me off. I've given up on God."

I told her she was probably disappointed in the churches and their teachings but that she had not given up on God. "And I know God has not given up on you, Jean."

Jean's daughter wrote: "She will be remembered for her quiet, gentle spirit, her warmth and unconditional love, her courage and commitment to action, her listening skills, and her nonjudgmental approach to all people."

Oh, that we all would exhibit these positive qualities in our lives! Reaching out and touching an AIDS patient, a person of any race or belief, showing comfort and love. Helping a friend just home from the hospital and bringing food. There was no end to her generosity and compassion.

She took the time to take the training to become an expert, trustworthy volunteer in the Hand-to-Hand program carried out by the Sacramento AIDS Foundation. When she saw the need for a Mother's Support Group, Jean was right there to facilitate the group for many years.

In 1994 about 45 people got together for a "Jean Artman Appreciation Day," complete with a beautiful potluck dinner, music, flowers, and tributes given by many friends. Some thought she would be retiring, but she showed them! Why should she retire when she loved the work and the people so much? Besides, she was only 78 years old!

What a beautiful example for each of us! LILLIAN MUSGRAVE

God Can Restore Us

The Lord is my shepherd; I shall not want. . . . He restoreth my soul. Ps. 23:1-3.

FOR MORE THAN A year I have worked part-time at a local bed-and-breakfast as a laundry assistant. My duties include washing, drying, ironing, folding, and putting the clean laundry in drawers or on the linen-room shelves. Mending is another important part of what I do. Towels, washcloths, sheets, bedspreads, pillowcases, tablecloths, and scarves get tears or holes in them and need to be repaired. I have sewn and patched, stitched quilt pieces back together, and retied comforters.

But the most delicate sewing of all involves reworking lace or crocheted scarves, bedspreads, and tablecloths. When threads break, these items must be repaired quickly. It is interesting, challenging work. If it's properly reinforced, it's possible for a restored item to be stronger and in better condition than it may have been originally.

People are rather like these items that I restore. Life's storms can wreak havoc with tragedies such as abuse, illness, death, divorce, and disasters, both natural and man-made. Any of these can break the threads of what should be strong relationships with the most important people in our life and even cause us to question where we stand with God. We feel physically and emotionally frayed when the fabric of our life gets ripped apart.

At such times we need to remember that God not only exists, He also loves us and doesn't want us to stay "broken." He is more than willing to be the master mender, providing new threads to reinforce us. As the shepherd's psalm says, God restores our souls. Once our soul is restored, our body often follows suit. And with the passage of time, we begin to feel that life is worth living once more.

Isaiah 41:10 says, "Fear thou not; for I am with thee: be not dismayed; for I am thy God: I will strengthen thee; yea, I will help thee; yea, I will uphold thee with the right hand of my righteousness."

All we need to do is ask, claiming God's promises and believing we will receive. God's restoration work is much better than mine. Mine may last the lifetime of the mended item. His will stand the test of eternity.

BONNIE MOYERS

True Love Is From Above

Thou shalt love the Lord thy God with all thy heart, and with all thy soul, and with all thy strength, and with all thy mind; and thy neighbour as thyself. Luke 10:27.

TODAY'S VERSE WAS the first memory verse that our son learned when he was 2 years of age. I can still remember how he repeated it so well.

How do you express love to someone in words? When one of my sisters was small, she used to say, haltingly and with stutters but so endearingly, "I love you as much as the sand of the seashore." That is what our elders taught us to say when asked, "How much do you love me?"

We could say "I love you with all of my liver." It carries the same weight as heart because the liver is very important. I believe in some part of Africa they say, "I love you with all my stomach." Why not? Isn't the stomach important? So such love must be great, too.

Of course, most educated people worldwide have learned to say, "I love you with all my heart." We love to buy cards decorated with hearts. Yes, even the Lord wants us to love Him with all our heart, soul, strength, and mind.

These days we see so much sickness that affects important body organs. There are heart attacks, dead cells in the brain, diseased livers, and abused stomachs. Our way of eating and our lifestyle have added more problems to these organs. I wonder how effective or adequate is our expression of love with all these sick organs?

God's law is the very expression of His character, as He is the God of love. He lived among us in the person of Jesus, showing and inviting us to love Him with all our heart, strength, mind, and soul, and our neighbor as ourselves. It is the only love that will bear the fruit of obedience to His law. Humanly, it isn't possible to have such love. As all true love is from God, He alone can give us that love. He promised that He will give us a new heart in place of our old one and put His spirit within us that we may be able to walk in His statutes and keep His commandments (Eze. 36:26, 27).

Maybe you would like to join me in praying with David, "Create in me a clean heart, O God; and renew a right spirit within me" (Ps. 51:10).

BIRDIE PODDAR

Love Instead of Spears

A friend loveth at all times, and a brother is born for adversity. Prov. 17:17.

THE PLANE TOUCHED DOWN at the picturesque coastal outpost, and I eagerly looked forward to another challenging school term. This was years ago, and the Education Department was experimenting by taking some of the brighter, isolated, pre-high school students from the bush country and forming a school with just the one class, which consisted mainly of boys.

There were stark reminders of a fierce World War II battle that had raged in the area. The coconut trees bore bullet holes, barges lay rusting by the shore, trees were growing upward through abandoned vehicles, bullets exploded in the grass fires, and the boys dormitories were crumbling buildings left behind by the armed forces. In contrast to the surroundings, all the tribes blended and lived peacefully together, even with the small, warlike boys in their midst.

A somber atmosphere prevailed as I approached the school. No cheery greetings awaited me. To my dismay, I saw sick boys lying on their mats at the office.

During the short Easter break, the coastal boys had visited their villages and left their meager belongings in the care of some of the highland boys. On their return, the coastal boys showed their gratitude by sharing some food with their highland friends. It wasn't long before some students developed stomach pains, became nauseated, and began to pass blood. Many were taken to the nearby local hospital. Sadly, some passed away, and others were left mentally impaired. Despite investigations, a cause for the sad events could not be established. It was traced to the gifts of food, but which particular one remained a mystery.

In a land where the payback system was strongly adhered to, we fearfully wondered what would happen next. The local pastors visited the villages concerned and told them about the love of God. Their hearts responded to the appeal to put aside their payback customs.

It was with heavy hearts that classes resumed, but we felt joy and relief that the parents and villagers with Christ in their hearts put aside their traditional custom and extended the hand of love instead of spears. It is my desire that I too will always extend a hand of love to those who may cause me sorrow or grief. JOY DUSTOW

My Heavenly Father Knows Best

Delight yourself in the Lord and he will give you the desires of your heart.
Ps. 37:4, NIV.

TEARS RAN DOWN MY cheeks as I traveled home from the interview. I had looked forward to this day with much anticipation. I felt confident in my knowledge and experience. The ministry personnel who reviewed my application were impressed sufficiently to make it available even to other geographic areas.

I couldn't have anticipated that a routine annual medical checkup would result in my father being scheduled for lung cancer surgery on the very day of my interview. I discussed the matter with Dad, who encouraged me to go to the interview, since staying at the hospital during his surgery would benefit neither of us.

On entering the interview room, I immediately sensed that the interviewer was surprised, if not disappointed. She clearly found my physical appearance not to be what she had expected from my résumé. I felt the interview slipping away and could do nothing to stop the slide. Feeling dejected and utterly disappointed, I cried all the way home. What more could I have done? I thought I was fully prepared for what would have been an excellent job opportunity. But was I? Had I included reliance on God as part of the preparation? Maybe not as much as I should have. To add to my sorrow, my dad subsequently developed complications and succumbed to his illness.

When I reflected on this experience, the words of Solomon, recorded in Proverbs 3:5, 6, rang in my ears: "Trust in the Lord with all your heart, and do not rely on your own insight. In all your ways acknowledge him and he will make straight your paths" (NRSV). I have a tendency to be self-reliant. Had I been successful in that job interview, I would no doubt have credited myself for the success. The Lord was teaching me a much-needed lesson of dependence on Him, and only Him.

About a year later I received a lifetime judicial appointment—one beyond anything I had dreamed of or could have hoped for a year earlier. It's a position that I'm still enjoying some 14 years later.

We serve a mighty God, a God who has the capacity and compassion to bless us in spite of our shortcomings. He did just that for me, and I know He will do it for you. Just trust Him.

AVIS MAE RODNEY

When the String Breaks

I know what it is to be in need, and I know what it is to have plenty. I have learned the secret of being content in any and every situation, whether well fed or hungry, whether living in plenty or in want. Phil. 4:12, NIV.

ITZHAK PERLMAN, THE great violinist, performed one night at Lincoln Center in New York City. Since Perlman was stricken with polio as a child, getting onstage is no small achievement. He has braces on both legs and walks with the aid of two crutches. To see him walk across the stage, painfully yet majestically, is an awesome sight.

With effort he placed his crutches on the floor, undid the clasps on his legs, bent down to pick up the violin, placed it under his chin, nodded to the conductor, and proceeded to play. The audience was used to this ritual and remained silent. But now something went wrong. As he finished the first few bars, one of the strings on his violin broke. The snap of it sounded like gunfire. Everyone figured he would have to find another violin or another string.

He did neither. He waited a moment, closed his eyes, and signaled the conductor to begin again. Perlman played with a passion and power that the audience had never heard before! How could it be? Everyone knows that it is impossible to play a symphonic work with only three strings. But in his head he changed and recomposed the piece.

When he finished, there was an awesome silence in the room. Then came an extraordinary outburst of applause. Everyone was on their feet, screaming and cheering. Perlman smiled, wiped the sweat from his brow, raised his bow to quiet the audience, and then said in a quiet, pensive, reverent tone, "Sometimes it's the artist's task to find out how much music you can still make with what you have left."

Here's a man who prepared all his life to make music on four strings and, all of a sudden, finds himself with only three. So he makes music with three. And the music he made that night was more beautiful and more memorable than any he had made before.

Perhaps our task in this fast-changing, bewildering world is to make music with what we have left. Take whatever life has dealt you and make the best of it. Make today a happy day. NANCY L. VAN PELT

God Knows, God Hears, God Sees

For he will command his angels concerning you to guard you in all your ways. Ps. 91:11, NIV.

THAT NIGHT IN FEBRUARY seemed to have been made especially for us. We were leaving our congregation in São Paulo, where we had worked for three years. Now we were driving south, where we would assume a new church. In our car, along with dreams, we brought expectations, some precious personal belongings, and our two small children.

We had two days to spend on this long trip, but we were in a hurry and eager to arrive. I wanted to see my new house! So we decided that we would travel that night. We drove along the only highway that leads to the south of Brazil. A dangerous highway at any hour of the day, it is known by all as a "highway of death."

We were enthusiastic. As we sang to the children, it seemed as though we were the only people on that highway. A few miles later, however, a tropical storm came upon us. The truck traffic was intense. Bright lights and high speed hindered our vision. At one point we had to stop and wait for a while. However, the rain continued.

Finally, after midnight, we were unable to continue. When the car hit a hole and lost two tires, fear took hold of us. We were tired, hungry, and afraid. I thought, *No one will stop in rain like this, in total darkness.* With my fertile imagination I could see us being robbed, or something worse.

We prayed. Although we felt abandoned, God was there. My husband decided to look for help while I stayed locked inside the car with the children. But he returned without assistance.

Hours went by. Finally a small car, with an elderly man at the steering wheel, stopped. He knocked on the window and asked, "Do you need help?"

Minutes later this man led us to the nearest service station. We were safe. I got out of the car to thank the man, but couldn't find him. I looked around in the dim light, but he was no longer there. In my heart I knew that God had sent help.

That night I learned that God is aware of you and me; He is concerned for each and every one, and cares for us individually.

RAQUEL COSTA ARRAIS

Just a Speck

Why do you look at the speck of sawdust in your brother's eye and pay no attention to the plank in your own eye? Matt. 7:3, NIV.

IT'S MY FAVORITE SWEATER, so I keep hoping no one will notice the tiny speck that spoils its appearance. But someone always does. What's more, they always point it out to me.

I didn't see that I had brushed against some lily pollen while arranging the church flowers. Normally, some Scotch tape, turned sticky side out and dabbed against the stain, will lift the pollen, but it needs to be done immediately. Ignorant of the fact that I had pollen on my sweater, I washed it, and now the stain is permanent.

I use stain remover each time I wash it, but the speck is still visible. It is so tiny, and I love the sweater so much that I wear it in the vain hope that people will ignore the speck. They don't. Someone always says, "You have a little mark there," and tries to brush it off.

My sweater is spoiled; I know it and am sorry. Perhaps it's time for me to put it away and not wear it again—I know the stain will never go away. So why do I keep trying?

This experience reminds me of how much I owe to Jesus. My life is full of stains, stains as big as planks, but He doesn't keep pointing them out to me. Nor does He expect me to hide away and never come out. Instead, He applies His blood—His "stain remover"—and makes me clean. He covers me with the garment of His righteousness so that God will see me as pure and without spot.

Having someone point out the blemish on my sweater has sometimes made me feel resentful. Why can't people just ignore it? The lesson I've learned, however, is that just as that spot spoiled my sweater, so the tiniest sin mars my life. Ignoring the speck doesn't make it go away. All my efforts can't remove it. The sweater can't be made whole again. Nor can I wash away the stains in my life, in spite of all my efforts. Only Jesus can repair my life, but I need to invite Him to do so; I need to give my life to Him completely.

This experience has also taught me to be careful how I look at others and how I treat them. They don't like having their specks pointed out either—do you?

AUDREY BALDERSTONE

Looking for Love in All the Wrong Places

For God so loved the world, that he gave his only begotten Son, that whosoever believeth in him should not perish, but have everlasting life. John 3:16.

AS I SEARCHED FOR appropriate material for a Valentine's Day church program, I was surprised to find that material seemed scarce. I had articles on health, the Holy Spirit, faith, Sabbath—many topics—but nothing about love.

I found lots in the bookstores on New Age philosophy, but didn't find the type of love I was wanting to portray. I didn't want chocolates (as good as they may be), nor roses (as lovely as they smell), nor red hearts, nor cupid.

Next, I went to *Webster's Dictionary*. Most people use the dictionary for words such as latitudinarin, not love. Some of the love definitions include: passionate affection for; be in love; godly affection; to woo; a love of books; have a love for ice cream; in tennis, love means no score.

How can I have this love I say I have in my heart if I can't find anything relating to it? My eyes came to rest on the Bible. Love was there all the time—in the love letters of the Bible, from the beginning to the end. I do possess and own love. I have it in my husband, in the house of God when I worship in His cathedral of love. I have it in my children, grandchildren, brothers, sisters, mother, and friends.

I find love in my pets, my garden, the birds, the springtime, the food I have to eat, and a warm home. God gave these things to me because He loves me. The evidence is all around. Now I know I have love. I possess it. I own it.

Why didn't I go to God's Word first? Could it be we take love, given freely by Jesus, for granted? Do we look for Him only at prayer meeting, or when we are in trouble? Could we be looking for love in the wrong books, songs, or people? Could we be looking for love in all the wrong places?

What the dictionary does not say, the Bible does: "God so loved the world." Jesus bestowed (gave as a gift) all manner of love to us—His unconditional love. But the greatest of all loves is this: He laid down His life for you and for me.

VIDELLA McCLELLAN

Forget or Remember

I will not forget you! See, I have engraved you on the palms of my hands.
Isa. 49:15, 16, NIV.

PICTURES OF SOMEONE he loves. A stuffed tiger that his son gave him
13 years ago. A slip of advice from a fortune cookie. A handful of
American soil grabbed just before he boarded the plane. A coin engraved
with the Statue of Liberty. All of these are tiny remembrances treasured by
various soldiers who left to go to war. Perhaps you have a treasure chest of
remembrance too: a dried corsage or a ticket stub from a concert with
someone special, yellowed letters from someone now gone, a stone picked
up on a mountain peak or a riverbed, and, of course, albums full of pictures that have deep meaning for you.

As I was leaving to board the plane for Thailand, my 3-year-old granddaughter, Whitney, gave me a tiny candy heart "to remember me by." Then
both my granddaughters wanted me to give them something "to remember
you by." I was hard pressed to think what to give them, but then I looked
down at the bright orange and yellow bows I had tied on each suitcase to
help me quickly spot my luggage among the scores of similar suitcases in
the baggage claims.

"I'll give you a piece of my luggage tags," I said, and cut them each a
piece "to remember me by."

Later, while preaching in a thatched chapel in Cambodia, I showed the
people sitting on the floor my precious tiny candy heart and told how it reminded me of the love of someone very precious to me. I told them how
Jesus has scars on His hands to remember us by. The scars are imprints
from the cruel nails on the cross where Jesus poured out His supreme sacrifice to give us opportunity for salvation. He still carries the scars; He will
never forget us.

Jesus wants us to remember Him, too. Hundreds of texts in the Bible
speak of remembering, or not forgetting: His broken body, the Sabbath,
Lot's wife, the poor, our rulers, and what we have received. Jesus has given
us abundant remembrances of His love in His sacrifice, in nature, in His
Word, in His providences. Let's remember Him as He remembers us.

RUTH WATSON

Clothes That Fit

Do not store up for yourselves treasures on earth, where moth and rust destroy, and where thieves break in and steal. But store up for yourselves treasures in heaven. . . . For where your treasure is, there your heart will be also. Matt. 6:19-21, NIV.

EACH DAY MY MOTHER rushed through her daily morning cleaning routine. She knew she had to hurry if she wanted to have free time in the middle of the day when the sun was the brightest. When she was finally done she could sit at her beloved sewing machine for several hours. Mother had always had a difficult time finding ready-made clothes that fit her. With her sewing machine, though, she could create beautiful clothes that fit just right.

She had always made all her own clothes. As she grew older, she worried. She had noticed that her vision was becoming foggy, and the doctors told her that over time her eyes would become progressively worse. She would soon have to give up the pleasure of sewing. In several years she would probably be almost completely blind. There was nothing they could do.

Mother was always the kind of person who planned ahead. If she wouldn't be able to sew in the future, then she would sew as many dresses as possible while she could still see. She would save them so that she would have something to wear in the future. Dress after dress was carefully stitched and stored for a time when she would need it.

My mother is now almost completely blind. Her sewing machine sits in storage. The long days of sadness and failing health have left their mark on her. She has lost more than 100 pounds, and none of the beautiful dresses she so carefully made and stored up fit her at all. Her closet is full of beautiful dresses she will never be able to wear.

I look at my daily life. My work as a nurse is a path of constant work, meetings, phones, competency tests—trying to get ahead, trying to make ends meet. I realize this path is not fitting me with heavenly clothes.

Lord, let me spend the brightest times of my days with You. Let my clothes fit my life in heaven.

Will your clothes fit you in your future life?

BETTY WELCH

Be Watchful, Be Ready

He who trusts in his own heart is a fool, but whoever walks wisely will be delivered. Prov. 28:26, NIV.

A S I TRAVEL TO other countries I try very hard to make sure my valuables, passport, and money are secure. In one country my sister and I were enjoying the beautiful day as we walked around a small town in the former Eastern bloc. Having never been in this country before, we were delighted with the window-shopping and were looking over the interesting souvenirs and the beautiful crystal unique to that area. After examining a display, I checked my purse and was shocked to see the zipper half open. I scolded myself for being so careless.

We exited the store and stood on the corner, deciding where to go next. With amazement, I found the zipper on my purse half open again. I realized then that something or someone other than my own carelessness had caused this. I quickly turned around to see a small woman standing close by who had closely shadowed me in the store and then followed me outside. I blurted out, "She's trying to get in my purse!" as she hurried away and disappeared around the corner. A quick check of the contents of my purse assured me she hadn't been able to take anything, and I sent up a big thank-You to my heavenly Father for His protection that day.

I had always prided myself on my ability to prevent theft and other potential tragedies or mishaps when traveling internationally. I *knew* that being robbed could never happen to me! Through this experience I realized how easily we can be lulled into thinking we are prepared. I also learned to carry my purse in front so I could guard the zipper.

Just as this woman tried to sneak valuables from me, the devil tries to sneak up on us and is constantly trying to trap us in some unexpected way. In everyday life we can become deluded into thinking that we are self-sufficient in resisting the sneaky wiles of the devil, but it is only by placing our trust in God and through His strength that we are protected from evil.

Dear Lord, thank You for Your saving grace and for Your protection. Even though I am weak, You are strong, keeping me on Your path and protecting me in Your marvelous way. I praise You for guiding my steps, and I am longing to dwell with You forever.
GINGER SNARR

I Prayed to Pass the Test

I love them that love me; and those that seek me early shall find me. Prov. 8:17.

OUT OF A CLASS OF 38 girls, I considered myself to be the least smart. My classmates were extremely energetic and always seemed to have the right answers. I wondered if I would ever build up enough confidence to feel comfortable competing with my peers.

Daniel has always been one of my favorite Bible characters. Like Daniel, I prayed three times daily, listened attentively to my instructors, and put the greatest effort into my studies. One of my instructors never said much but paid attention to every move I made. She frequently paced around my desk in silence. I prayed for strength and understanding, and every day I knew the Lord was answering my prayers.

I was admitted to the hospital just prior to midterms. I didn't know how I was going to pass after missing two weeks of school. I never doubted God, but I wondered about myself. "Lord, I know You're going to work this out for me, but I don't know how. Please help me."

One of my classmates came to visit me. I was happy for her visit and to know what was going on in class. She told me they were studying the knee joint and told me all about it.

I returned to school in time for the midterm. As I turned the first page of the exam, there were instructions to draw, label, and explain the parts and function of the knee joint. I prayed silently as I continued to take the exam.

A few days later I met the instructor who had paced around my desk and peered over my shoulder. I asked her if I had passed the exam. She replied, "I don't think you did too badly. The grades are posted on the board in the hall."

I ran to the board but was so overwhelmed I couldn't find my name. One of my classmates pointed to the top of the list. "There's your name," she said. "You got the highest grade in the class."

I thanked her and ran to my room, fell on my knees, and thanked God for His blessings. Not only did I get the highest grade on the midterm, I got the highest grade in the finals.

I sought the Lord early. My confidence grew. He is still listening to and answering my prayers. He is worthy to be praised! He'll do the same for all who seek Him. He promised.

GERTRUDE E. BURKE

Forgive 70 Times 7

And forgive us our debts, as we forgive our debtors. Matt. 6:12.

QUOTES SUCH AS "turn the other cheek," "avenge not yourselves," or "if thine enemy hungers" are easier to read than to practice. Why do we find it so difficult? I used to be happy when somebody who did something against me fell into a problem. I used to think that God was justifying me. However, I was taught a bitter lesson about that sometime ago.

Somebody deliberately implicated me in something of which I was completely innocent. It was difficult for me to exonerate myself, so my husband and I prayed over it and left the matter in God's hands. On my own, however, I continued to pray that God would vindicate me.

A few years later the person in question got into trouble. I felt happy that she was now experiencing the sort of agony I had experienced at the time she implicated me.

My joy was short-lived. That evening in our family devotions we read Romans 12. By the time we got to verse 14, I felt some remorse. I am not to rejoice at the downfall of another person, no matter what, or who, that person is. Verse 20 says if my enemy hungers, I should give them food. I was not to allow evil to overcome me, but I could overcome evil with good. I was beginning to have a change of heart.

I can't say I became a saint from that day, but the Holy Spirit sowed the seed of righteous thinking. Whenever I feel like laughing at other people's misfortune, the Holy Spirit whispers these verses from Romans 12 into my ears. I needed to pray earnestly for a forgiving spirit, a forgiveness that does not look back, that does not want to know how many times I am offended. A forgiveness that does not whisper, "Serves her right!" Any time I am idle and my mind wanders to hurtful situations, I quickly whisper a prayer to God, and He helps me overcome.

Father, as I write this I still recognize my imperfection. I still see the unholy joy the devil wishes me to have at the expense of other people. Please, Father, give me the victory over this; help me to bless those who persecute me. Help me to pray for others when they fall so that they can rise. Amen.

BECKY DADA

Better Late Than Never

The end of a matter is better than its beginning, and patience is better than pride. Eccl. 7:8, NIV.

FOR NINE YEARS I worked in a junior high school in the inner city. As office manager, one of my many responsibilities was to give assignments from my superior to other office workers. At times I had to follow up to see if the tasks had been completed.

Recently, one of the workers to whom I had to give assignments called. It had been years since we had talked, and I was happy to hear from her. After about 30 minutes of reminiscing about our days at the school, she said she had one more thing to tell me.

"I didn't like the way you did things, and I hated it when you told me to do things. I stormed in the office one afternoon to confront you because I felt I had had enough. We talked, and you said you didn't know I felt that way. Then you said, 'Let's pray.' As evil as I felt, I was in no mood for prayer. It was 4:20, quitting time, and I told you that you could pray all you wanted, but I was leaving at 4:30."

This story astonished me, because to this day I do not remember the incident. I never knew she felt that way about me. She had some personal challenges and had confided in me, so this was shocking.

She continued, "You were very sincere, and that day I was an evil woman. But during your prayer something happened to me, and my whole attitude changed. From that moment on I never was angry with you again. I know prayer changes things."

She not only expressed appreciation for keeping her crisis confidential but said that she often relates this experience to her children as a lesson to them. It serves as a reminder to herself that nothing is so bad that you can't pray about it. She said she wanted to tell me so I could hear it myself, rather than wait to say it over my casket. A bit emotional, I thanked her.

I have no idea why, but I believe there was a reason that it took more than 25 years for me to learn about this incident. I thank God for the power of prayer and the gift of the Holy Spirit.

Truly, Lord, the end was better than the beginning. Once again, You are so good!   MARIE H. SEARD

Through God's Eyes

If anyone says, "I love God," yet hates his brother, he is a liar. For anyone who does not love his brother, whom he has seen, cannot love God, whom he has not seen. 1 John 4:20, NIV.

OUR TEXT CONTAINS hard words indeed! I do want to be a real Christian, but I just can't love everybody. To be honest, I don't always have only kind words about my neighbor. You see, it's more interesting to point out a person's bad characteristics. And then this text comes along, so I've been pondering it; I don't want to be a liar. Let me tell you what happened to me.

He was a coworker. He didn't know how he was getting on my nerves. As soon as he turned up, I would get irritated. But I wanted to be a real Christian, not just a so-called Christian. So I asked God to show me this person through His eyes. I was really serious about this.

A few days later a very nice coworker came to see me. As she worked closely with this man, I asked her how she got along with him. I suppose I expected her to slander him. Even now I have to smile when I think about what happened next. She did know his less lovable side, but she showed me a person who had many good qualities, qualities I wouldn't have discovered without her. I then told her about my attitude and the real reason I had asked her. And I thanked her and God for opening my eyes.

I often see this coworker. He hasn't changed, but my attitude toward him has. I've come to know the qualities that make him a valuable person to me. I meet him and his family not only during working hours, but in my private activities as well—not because I have to love and accept him, but because he has become important to me.

Maybe we often think that Christians have to be able to do everything, that the Christian life is hard and heavy. My experience is different. Because God opened my eyes I feel decidedly happier. I am free! And I love to be a Christian. I hope you do, too, and that you will get to know many people you can see through God's eyes.

You have made the daily Christian walk so practical. I want to thank You for this and for Your sustaining power each day. CHRISTEL SCHNEIDER

59

Guilty or Not Guilty?

I tell you the truth, whoever hears my word and believes him who sent me has eternal life and will not be condemned; he has crossed over from death to life. John 5:24, NIV.

THERE IT WAS IN my mail—the summons every citizen loves to receive: "Greetings. You are hereby notified that you have been selected to serve as a prospective juror, and you are therefore commanded to appear before . . ."

Some people dread receiving this notice. Others, like myself, may feel that the timing is not very convenient. But it's one of those duties that come with living in a country in which we are all equal citizens, and therefore asked to serve.

At the appointed date and time I made my way to the appointed place and eventually ended up in a courtroom. Now, courtrooms are solemn places; usually the people are not there by choice, especially in criminal cases. Someone has broken the law and has to answer for their actions. Since accused criminals in my country are entitled to a defense and are presumed innocent until they are proven guilty, they're usually represented by a lawyer who stands up to defend or represent them before the judge.

Judges tend to be solemn individuals, sworn to uphold the law and dispense justice. They must take the evidence and the testimony, keep order in the court, and instruct the jury. The jury listens carefully to the evidence and the testimony until they're able to deliberate and decide the verdict. Their decision is given to the judge, who then pronounces sentence upon the guilty.

This whole scenario started me thinking about the heavenly judgment. We will all have the opportunity to stand before the judge, but this time there is no question of guilt. We are all guilty as charged in the sight of God, and as judge He has no other choice than to declare us so and pass judgment. The wages of sin are death, and we all stand condemned.

Then my Lawyer steps in to intercede for me. "Father," He says, "this child is Mine. She is bought with My blood and has asked forgiveness for her sins. She has accepted My righteousness in place of her filthy rags. I have taken her punishment, and now she will live with Me forever."

What love! If God is for us, who can be against us?

FAUNA RANKIN DEAN

The Rest of the Story

So the king appointed a certain officer for her, saying, "Restore all that was hers." 2 Kings 8:6, NKJV.

I T'S EASY TO HAVE faith in God until the next setback blindsides us, slamming us against the proverbial wall. When tempted to wonder if your problem is bigger than God, remember the rest of the story—the Shunammite woman's story, that is.

You'll recall how the prophet Elisha prayed that she and her husband would have a son. God, through Elisha, restored life to this woman's little boy after the child had died of heatstroke.

Great stuff! Yet 2 Kings 8 tells us that the Shunammite woman had a series of late-life setbacks. A famine in Israel had forced her to relocate among the Philistines for seven years. The context suggests she was a widow at this point. Meanwhile, back at the Shunem ranch, opportunist home-steaders had usurped the absent woman's wealth and property.

Returning to Israel, the Shunammite widow decides to appeal her help-less plight to Israel's new king. Once again the manifestation of God's grace in her life begins to unfold with the dizzying speed of a novel's impossibly contrived denouement.

Gehazi, Elisha's servant, just *happens* to be in the throne room when the woman enters. The king just *happens* to be in the process of interview-ing Gehazi about a preposterous story he's heard concerning Elisha's restoring life to some woman's son. And that very woman just *happens* to walk in while Gehazi is retelling the story. Hearing her voice, Gehazi jumps to his feet and excitedly exclaims, "O king, this is the woman!"

Deeply impressed, the king quickly appoints an officer to ensure that the Shunammite be able to repossess her property and possessions. In addi-tion, the king tells the officer to collect, on behalf of the woman, every rightful penny due her from her land's last seven years of harvests!

The rest of the Shunammite's story reveals the good news that God is bigger than any problem His faithful daughters will ever suffer.

What is your latest heartbreak, fear, or setback? Without further delay, why not take it to the King? Not only can He restore loss, He'll also be happy—with His great pen of love—to write the rest of your story, too.

CAROLYN SUTTON

Who's in Charge?

I know whom I have believed, and am convinced that he is able to guard what I have entrusted to him for that day. 2 Tim. 1:12, NIV.

IT WAS A GRAY Sunday evening in eastern Pennsylvania. Two feet of snow lay on the ground, and freezing rain was beginning to fall. We had spent a cold, dreary day at my grandmother's funeral and now had two and a half hours to make the one-hour drive to the Newark Airport. The traffic wasn't heavy, and we talked about how good it would be to get back home to Florida. As we neared the airport we got off the expressway to find a gas station. Cities can be frightening, but on this night the streets all seemed to go nowhere, and there wasn't a gas station in sight. After 30 very tense minutes we found a gas station. Finally, one hour after we left the expressway, we darted up to the rental car desk. The clerk didn't have the proper numbers, said he'd have to verify the information, and promptly disappeared. We told the other attendant that we had only 30 minutes to catch our flight.

He said, "You better go on—we'll mail you your corrected paperwork."

Steve and I looked at each other, knowing we'd never see that paperwork again, but we had to get home. Thanking him, we grabbed our suitcases and dashed to the curb just as the shuttle pulled away. We dejectedly watched the bus disappear, knowing our chances of getting home that night were disappearing too. After 10 dismal minutes another shuttle bus came by, and we pulled up to Continental Airlines 10 minutes later. The ticket agent took our tickets and said, "You're at the wrong terminal."

"But our flight leaves in 10 minutes!" I protested.

"Well, honey, it ain't leaving from here! You're at terminal A, and that flight leaves from terminal C." She finally told us how to get to terminal C, three fourths of a mile away.

We ended up at the right ticket counter 20 minutes after our scheduled departure time. The attendant scolded, "You're late." We nodded, too tired and stressed to reply. The attendant sighed. "Your flight was delayed; I think you can still make it, but your luggage probably won't." We said we didn't care about our luggage; we just wanted to go home.

We made it home that night—and so did our luggage. Our rental car paperwork got to us two days later. We knew who was in charge—our incredibly thoughtful, awesome God!   SUSAN WOOLEY

Pardon

If we confess our sins, He is faithful and just to forgive us our sins and to cleanse us from all unrighteousness. 1 John 1:9, NKJV.

FORMER PRESIDENT CLINTON caused quite a stir with the presidential pardons that were granted in the last hours of his presidency. At the top of this controversy was Marc Rich, the billionaire fugitive who has been charged with tax evasion, among other things. To further complicate the matter, Hugh Rodham, the president's brother-in-law, received an exorbitant sum for helping two felons receive clemency. This resulted in an inquiry from two congressional committees and the U.S. Attorney's Office.

Amid all of this, I began thinking how fortunate we human beings are to be able to go directly to Jesus and ask for forgiveness for the sins we've committed. He intercedes on our behalf, and He doesn't have to be bribed with money to do so. Regardless of our socioeconomic status, social or political contacts, the magnitude of the crime, national origin, ethnicity, or religious beliefs, as long as we confess our sins to Him, He will forgive us. Christ makes us clean. There is no need for penances, offerings, or independent committee investigations. Isn't this wonderful to know?

I am also grateful that as long as I ask forgiveness, Christ grants it and remembers my sin no more. The very moment I confess I can start as a brand-new person.

Just as He forgives us, He requires us to forgive others when they have wronged us. Sometimes the magnitude of the offense causes us to withhold forgiveness from the individual who has wronged us, but no one is truly free without forgiveness. His love for us and the grace He extends to us are limitless. We must be willing to extend grace and forgiveness to the individuals who do us wrong. By so doing we will free ourselves of the hatred and pain that forever linger with an unforgiving spirit.

Thank You, Lord, for being so merciful to us when we don't deserve it. Thank You for forgiving us again and again. Help us to be willing to forgive other people when they do us wrong. Help us to be willing to accept their forgiveness.

ANDREA BUSSUE

A Truck and an Angel

Faith is the substance of things hoped for, the evidence of things not seen.
Heb. 11:1.

AFTER TEACHING MY FIRST year in California, I decided that summer to drive back to Michigan to see my parents. I laid out my route carefully. I was going to stay over a few days in Albuquerque, New Mexico, with the parents of my roommate from college. Then I was going to stay a few days in Claremore, Oklahoma, with the grandparents of some very good friends where I taught school.

I decided to start out on a Saturday night after sundown and drive all night and the next day into Albuquerque. All went well until I reached the mountains going into Needles, California. Suddenly a thick fog enveloped me, and I couldn't see anything at all. There were steep mountains on one side and drop-offs on the other. What to do? Well, of course I talked to God. I didn't dare pull off, and there were hairpin turns; I was barely able to see the road. So I just crept along. Suddenly, after I'd prayed, a huge truck came up behind me, then passed.

It was as if God told me, "Anne, step on the gas and follow that truck." Truck drivers don't like you to drive too close to them, but I kept right on his tail. I figured that if he went over a cliff perhaps I could stop before I followed him over! I was certain God was seeing me through the frightening experience.

The Lord is so good; He provides for our care even before we ask. That night He used a truck and an angel to get me through that frustrating time of need. I am so glad I have a heavenly Father to whom I can turn. No matter what happens, He can take care of it. Like the song says: "Nothing can touch me that doesn't pass through His hand. Nothing can touch me though life's billows may roll. Nothing can touch me; He's still in control. Nothing can happen unless He says it can, 'cause nothing can touch me that doesn't pass through His Hands."

Thank You, God, for being with us in every situation. Please be with me today; in everything I do, may I let You shine through to all the people with whom I come in contact.

ANNE ELAINE NELSON

My Little Evangelist

And when the chief priests and scribes saw the wonderful things that he did, and the children crying in the temple, and saying, Hosanna to the son of David; they were sore displeased, and said unto him, Hearest thou what these say? And Jesus saith unto them, Yea; have ye never read, Out of the mouth of babes and sucklings thou hast perfected praise? Matt. 21:15, 16.

MY 2-YEAR-OLD SON, Nathaniel, and I were waiting in the lobby of our apartment building for my husband to park the car after an afternoon of grocery shopping. While we were waiting, my son started singing different children's sing-along songs. One of our neighbors from the second floor came out of her apartment. I said hello to her as she walked by. Nathaniel stopped singing to say hi to the neighbor, also. She responded, and as she tried to converse with me, Nathaniel said, "Let's pray." She looked at him in amazement and asked me how old he was. I replied, and as she walked back down the hall he resumed singing "Jesus loves me, this I know."

Then he called out, "Let's pray; Jesus loves you," and ran up the three little steps on all fours, then ran down the hallway behind her, saying "Jesus loves you; let's pray." I realized that I'd better do something before he upset the neighbor, so I called him to come back. He stopped, turned around, and said, "Mommy, I'm in the Lord's army. OK?" With tears in my eyes I stared at him for a moment, realizing he had just witnessed to this neighbor.

On the elevator to the fourth floor I thought, *I'm in the Lord's army.* Yes, we're in the Lord's army—we are soldiers for Christ. We don't have to dress for battle or go to war, but we have a mission. Our mission isn't to fight but to share the good news of victory and everlasting life over death and God's righteousness over sin. Jesus Christ has already won the battle and given us the victory of hope, life, and free salvation.

Yes, it is very special to know that we are in the Lord's army, not fighting but sharing the victory. Jesus Christ came, died on the cross to redeem us from our sins, and rose from the dead. We have hope and the victory of everlasting life. Call someone today and share this precious and exciting victory that Jesus Christ has given us.

VELNA WRIGHT

Bread Pudding

Praise be to the God and Father of our Lord Jesus Christ! In his great mercy he has given us new birth into a living hope through the resurrection of Jesus Christ from the dead, and into an inheritance that can never perish, spoil or fade.1 Peter 1:3, 4, NIV.

I ENJOY BROWSING THROUGH magazines and recipe books, looking for new recipes to try out on my family. I recently ran across a recipe for bread pudding. As I read through the ingredients—butter, raisins, sugar, eggs, milk, cinnamon, brown sugar, etc.—I noticed something interesting. I don't know if every recipe for bread pudding calls for stale bread, but this one did. Right there at the top of the ingredients list, the recipe called for one loaf of stale French bread! If you have made bread pudding, maybe this doesn't sound strange to you, but it sounded strange to me. In fact, it didn't sound very appetizing at all. Stale bread? Who would want to eat that?

By now I was intrigued. So off to the bakery I went for a loaf of day-old bread. After a few days on the counter the loaf of bread seemed stale enough to try out my new recipe. I mixed the ingredients carefully and tore the stale bread into chunks that soaked up the egg-and-milk mixture. When it was baked to a golden brown, I presented the dish to my family. They ate it all up, never knowing that the bread had been stale. Even I couldn't taste the old bread. It had been transformed into something tasty enough to satisfy my picky 8-year-old.

Picture with me now the Master Chef: God in a pastry hat. He enters the kitchen of our life and looks around. From the breadbox He removes a large loaf of stale French bread. The Master Chef doesn't hesitate, breaking the stale bread into small chunks. He measures, mixes, and stirs in other ingredients. He sprinkles in seasonings. When He's satisfied that the ingredients are just right, He puts the mixture into the oven for baking. No longer does it matter that the bread was stale. The Master Chef has completed His recipe, added His ingredients, and the result is a complete transformation of a stale loaf of bread into something sweet and satisfying.

Master Chef, take what is stale and useless in my life today. Add Your ingredients. Work out Your recipe for my life. Refresh and renew me. Change me from a loaf of stale bread into bread pudding so that others may receive nourishment for their walk with You. Amen. SANDRA SIMANTON

Put God First

Trust in the Lord with all thine heart, and lean not unto thine own understanding. In all thy ways acknowledge him, and he shall direct thy paths. Prov. 3:5, 6.

THIS TEXT WAS WRITTEN in my autograph book by my father when I was a little girl. I tried to follow the instruction as I matured into adulthood. However, there are times when I just seem to deviate from the instruction given in this text.

If a situation presents itself that requires a decision to be made, I first ask God for His direction and leading in the matter and trust Him for the outcome. Experience has taught me that when I do this the outcome is usually a positive one.

I once had to make a decision between entering a college program in nursing or entering a refresher nurse midwifery program. I applied to both institutions. The response of acceptance from both came on the same day. What to do? I didn't want to make the wrong decision. The latter meant I would have to take a leave of absence from my job, meaning no money to cover my living expenses. The other choice would allow me to work and attend classes. I turned the whole scenario over in my mind. I'd been out of school for many years. Would I be able to make it through a college program?

Sometimes situations may overwhelm us, but if we trust the Lord and completely turn over our anxieties to Him, He will keep His promise to direct our paths by providing for us, helping us through situations of concern. These words kept ringing in my ears: "Trust in the Lord with all thine heart; and lean not unto thine own understanding."

So I entered the college program on faith and a great promise: "Be careful for nothing; but in every thing by prayer and supplication with thanksgiving let your requests be made known unto God" (Phil. 4:6).

Thanks be to God, I went through undergraduate and graduate school on full scholarships. His leading took me even further, and I became a nurse practitioner in obstetrics and a family life educator. I recognize that with God there is no failure. He can do for us more, so much more, than we can ever ask or think. To God be the glory!   DOLORES E. SMITH

Under His Wings

He will shield you with his wings! They will shelter you. His faithful promises are your armor. Ps. 91:4, TLB.

SOMETIMES GOD SENDS helpers as wings to cover us, and we don't even realize that until much later. I was on a trip through India on my way to Kenya. Reflecting on the incident later, I realized God's providence at work.

I had arrived in the Bombay airport in the middle of the night by myself. I was to change planes for the trip to Nairobi. My schedule indicated the wait would not be long, only a couple hours, but it was longer than that.

As I sat in the almost deserted terminal, I noticed a young family nearby who was also waiting. I moved closer and spoke to them. They were from England and were also on their way to Nairobi: a father, mother, and two small children. When I told them where I was going, the father said they had been waiting for many hours to get that same flight! He asked me to join them as the grandmother of their family and he would see that we got the attention we needed.

He disappeared for a while, and when he returned he motioned all of us to follow him along the hall to another room of the terminal where he saw some action happening. He spoke to the desk attendant there while we sat in that area.

Soon he returned to sit with us, saying we were next to board the flight. Whatever he said must have been forceful, because some local people were angrily shouting to the attendant, who apparently was not letting them go on this flight. It must have been overbooked, but we were going.

In a few minutes we were on the plane, a family together—with me as grandmother! After a successful flight, the arrival in Nairobi was closer to my original schedule by far than theirs!

God sends His helpers just when we need assistance! I now believe that is what happened for me that fearful night.

Lord, that was an awesome experience. Once again You sent help when I needed it. Truly, I felt Your loving wings around me, protecting and guiding.

BESSIE SIEMENS LOBSIEN

Go Home, and Everything Will Be All Right

Therefore I desire that the men pray everywhere, lifting up holy hands, without wrath and doubting. 1 Tim. 2:8, NKJV.

IT WAS THE SADDEST day of my life—the day when I was officially told that I was laid off. Though I knew that the downsizing was coming, its official announcement hit me hard. Because it was the first time I'd lost a job, it was difficult for me to accept. But the retrenchment couldn't be avoided. Our school was facing a great financial crisis, and the only thing that would prevent its closing was to lay off 10 staff members. I was one of those 10.

After I lost my job I began thinking about leaving South Africa and going back to my home in the Philippines. Some friends, though, urged me to wait until the situation at the college improved. My parents and my sister, however, suggested that I should go back home. I was in the valley of indecision for a long time. I had sleepless nights. When sleep did come, I'd wake up from a nightmare of being lost in a strange place.

When the church pastor visited me one day, I told him of my concerns, and he prayed for me. Nevertheless, that night I was still restless; I couldn't sleep. So I prayed and read a devotional message from *A Quiet Place*—a woman's devotional book. And there I found God's answer to my prayer: *Go home, and everything will be all right.* It seemed so clear I knew at once that God had sent this message for me. Nevertheless, I doubted the promise. So I paged through the book once more. To my amazement, I turned to a devotional message entitled "Homeward Bound." This time I firmly believed that God wanted me to go home.

I should not have doubted His answer to my prayer. Though I don't know what's waiting for me in my native land, I know God's promise is sure, that when I "go home, everything will be all right." And this promise I will never doubt.

Lord, I lift up my hands to You in praise. Forgive me for my lack of faith, for doubting Your promise. Help me, Lord, to have more faith in Your promises.

MINERVA M. ALINAYA

Let Go, and Let God

If any of you is lacking in wisdom, ask God, who gives to all generously and ungrudgingly, and it shall be given you. James 1:5, NRSV.

IT WAS LATE MONDAY evening when our phone rang. The voice on the line said, "We need your help urgently." When I asked what the problem was, the young mother said she was starting work the next morning and needed someone to care for their baby.

I was hesitant to commit myself, realizing that as a grandmother in my sunset years I was out-of-practice caring for an infant. I suggested other mothers who were younger than I, who helped to raise other babies besides their own children, but she pleaded with me, "Please say yes." It would be for three weeks until alternate arrangements could be made.

Jay was a healthy, chubby, 5-month-old baby. He had a hearty appetite and finished all his food. I would check and change his diaper, then spend time burping him. The moment I put him in his play seat or stroller, he'd scream louder and louder, without stopping. The minute I'd pick him up again, he'd smile and be quiet. I had household chores to do. This was stressing me out, and I developed tension headaches. The father admitted to spoiling him because he couldn't bear to hear his son crying, and always picked Jay up.

This baby isn't going to master me, I thought. I had to find a solution. I needed wisdom from on high. In utter desperation I cried to the Lord. I even prayed and pleaded through the hours of the night. Then I just let go, and let God take over.

God answered my prayers in a marvelous way! In the days that followed, Jay was the sweetest baby anyone could have. Once he was fed, diapered, and burped, I laid him in his stroller or sat him in his play seat, and he was so content! It was such a blessing, and I got through all my work.

I praised and thanked the Lord incessantly for answering my prayers. With Him at your side no burden is unbearable and no difficulty is insurmountable. God has promised that if you lack wisdom, ask Him, and it shall be given you—even for caring for a bonny baby boy!

PRISCILLA ADONIS

Angels in a Van

When you pass through deep waters, I will be with you; your troubles will not overwhelm you. Isa. 43:2, TEV.

WHAT A LOVELY DAY!" I said to myself while driving to church one sunny Sabbath morning. I glanced at my watch and noticed I had just enough time to get there and complete the last-minute details on my program. I was humming the familiar tunes coming from the tape player when, out of the corner of my eye, I saw a white van swerve into my lane. I slammed on the brakes and twisted the steering wheel, trying to dodge the van and avoid a collision, but my left front tire bumped into a low wall with a loud boom.

Shaking, I tried to get back on the road, but something was definitely wrong with that tire. I jumped out of the car to view the damage. My tire had exploded. Great! Here I was, all dressed up, dragging the spare out of the trunk, and obstructing traffic on a busy street. My mind went back to that time, many years before, when Dad had tried to interest me in the art of changing a tire.

By this time angry motorists were lined up behind me, honking frantically. Holding my head high, I ignored them. Eventually they figured out they would have to detour into the other lane. I threw the spare tire on the ground and bent down to figure out my next move. Suddenly a little white van with green letters painted on the side pulled up behind me, and four men jumped out. One grabbed the tire, another grabbed the jack, and a third man started prying off the hubcap. The fourth man just stood beside me silently. I wanted to tell him what had happened, but I was on the verge of tears by now. He smiled as if he already knew, though, and my anger melted away.

Suddenly remembering my manners, I thanked him for stopping. He kept on smiling. In less than five minutes they were finished. As I had no money to offer, I said, "Dios los bendiga" ("God bless you"). They smiled, waved, and jumped back into their little white van. As suddenly as they had come, they disappeared.

As I got back into my car, reality hit me. These had not been ordinary motorists—these were angels! I made it to church on time and shared my story.

DINORAH BLACKMAN

What Children Can Teach Us

Little children, . . . your sins are forgiven. 1 John 2:12.

IN GENESIS 5:21, 22 we read, "And Enoch lived sixty and five years, and begat Methuselah: And Enoch walked with God after he begat Methuselah." There's something about having a baby or being in a close relationship with a child that teaches us of God's love for us.

After teaching an art class at the church-sponsored elementary school, I decided not to leave the still-wet handprints on poster board on the table. "You don't know about them," I said to one of the teachers, referring to my rambunctious 6- to 9-year-olds. I wasn't saying anything negative about the kids. It's just that 6-year-olds don't always watch where they're running. And if I left the pan of water out on the table that was used to dip the finger-paint paper in, should I act surprised when I find them playing in it? They are acting predictably. That's what kids this age do. They're so lovable!

Is this how God thinks of us? Do you suppose that when He says "remember the Sabbath day" He tells an angel, "If I didn't remind them to keep the Sabbath, they would forget. They're so cute!" Maybe He adds, "My human children are so predictably unpredictable—you would love them!"

I'm not talking about deliberate defiance and disobedience, just the human things we often beat up on ourselves for. Birds don't feel guilty because they act like birds. Horses don't moan in a Mr. Ed voice, "I wish I could quit sinning!"

A child who barely remembers to clear his plate from the table at mealtime rushed to mop a whole kitchen floor when he thought his wiggly puppy, who tracked mud in, would get in trouble. When 3-year-old Hannah spilled milk on her sleeve and looked so helpless about it, I rushed to kiss her and laugh about it. Her weakness brought forth my strength to make it all right for her again. She didn't spend days thinking of herself as a wretched person.

Why can't we be as kind to ourselves? We love the child not in spite of his or her childlikeness, but because of it. When we see this is how God loves us, we, like Enoch, will walk with God too.

ALEAH IQBAL

How Sick Am I?

Trust in the Lord with all thine; heart and lean not unto thine own understanding. Prov. 3:5.

I WOKE UP FEELING TERRIBLE. I felt light-headed, and every movement left me breathless. A woman who usually raced around in her attempt to accomplish everything on her to-do list, I could barely function. Normally I travel 45 miles from Long Island into Manhattan each day. Today would be no exception—I had a full day scheduled with many patients. I was determined not to disappoint them. Besides, after a few swallows of medication I knew I would be just great.

I slowly dressed and finally managed to reach the train station. Arriving in Manhattan's Pennsylvania Station an hour later, I was just as short of breath as when I woke up, so I took a little more medication. I struggled toward the subway but had to find a bench and rest for 20 minutes before I could think of moving on. I began to wonder if this trip to work made sense or not. When I finally climbed the flight of stairs in front of the hospital where I worked, I couldn't deny I was sick, yet I still wanted to deny how serious my situation had become. Although I was at a hospital where I could receive excellent medical attention, I decided to go home and rest. I hoped that would make me feel better.

Eventually I arrived home, so weak from a lack of oxygen that I had to ask my mother to help me get undressed. She pleaded with me to go to the hospital. I had to admit I was having a severe allergic asthmatic attack, something that hadn't happened in more than 14 years.

By the time I arrived at the hospital my situation was a struggle for life. Insisting on being Miss Fix-it-herself, I had denied the situation, believing I could resolve it. I didn't seek expert advice until I'd attempted every self-remedy I could concoct. I knew I could handle it by myself.

How like my spiritual life! Often I don't seek the Expert until I've tried every other available source. I should know that self-medication causes more damage and/or pain. Why not ask the Great Physician? Why not trust Him to handle the problem, or even claim His promise in Proverbs 3:5? Why do I say "I can handle this" when what I should say is "Lord, take this"?

Thankfully, God is not like the berating emergency-room doctor who said, "Why did you wait so long?" God simply says, "Welcome home!"

TAMARA MARQUEZ DE SMITH

Disturbance in the Church

Train up a child in the way he should go: and when he is old, he will not depart from it. Prov. 22:6.

I GREW UP AS A "preacher's kid" back in the days of evangelistic meetings in tents with sawdust floors. I remember that at the church in our city each week we children received memory verse cards that illustrated the Bible lesson for that day. I treasured them and added them, week by week, to my collection. Church meant sitting beside my mother with my memory verse cards and my lesson paper to look at. It was a happy experience.

One particular Sabbath Mother was away, so my father instructed me to sit on the front pew during church. I had asked permission to invite my little friend to sit with me and, trusting me, Dad had consented. Alone on the front pew, with nothing to distract us, we sat listening to the sermon and looking at the memory verse cards we each had accumulated over the weeks. Occasionally we glanced at each other's cards, and soon we discovered there were some we'd like to trade.

As the service progressed, we became more involved in our cards than in the sermon. We began spreading them out between us, moving farther and farther apart, and whispering louder and louder.

"I'll trade you Gideon for David."

"No, I'd rather have Methuselah."

"OK, if you give me Rahab, too."

And so it went. Suddenly the church became painfully silent. Dad had stopped preaching. Then, like thunder from Mount Sinai, I heard his words: "Lorraine, sit up and listen to your daddy." A naturally shy child, I felt the immediate stares of hundreds of people behind me. It was an instant lesson, and as long as my dad lived and preached, I never talked in church again.

Through the intervening years I've come more and more to reverence the house of God and appreciate the peace and quiet I find as I dwell upon His Word. Someday, when we join that heavenly convocation, God willing, I will tell my devoted parents how grateful I've been for their consistent training and patient love. How I treasure the lessons they taught me!

LORRAINE HUDGINS-HIRSCH

He Who Laughs, Lasts

A merry heart doeth good like a medicine: but a broken spirit drieth the bones. Prov. 17:22.

FOR MANY YEARS I'VE worked with the psychotic, depressed, addicted, and maimed. I enjoy my work and the people I serve, although it's difficult to see the suffering and hopelessness. The psychiatric hospital where I work offers many classes to teach people alternative methods of dealing with their issues instead of relying solely on medication. I offered to do a therapeutic humor class.

I wasn't sure how this would be received, since most patients were fighting severe depression, hallucinations, suicidal thoughts, and overwhelming feelings of worthlessness. The benefits of humor, the patients learned, are that it reduces stress and anxiety, improves immunity, is a pain reliever, produces aerobic activity, increases creativity, increases self-esteem, and promotes hope. In addition, they were taught how to "humor up," as most adults can be humor-impaired at times. The lecture was usually given with the help of props—I would wear an elephant's trunk, pig's nose, flashing button, or a hat to develop the mood for the class.

I was pleasantly surprised by the response and the results. It was immediately obvious how a merry heart can benefit the mind and soul. The appearance of the patients changed. They seemed to have a better outlook on their treatment and hope for the future. Many started telling funny stories of stressful situations they had experienced. The biggest surprise was how it was also of benefit to the staff, including myself.

A poor spirit will dry up the bones, as it says in Proverbs 17:22, but the Lord has provided a merry alternative to that, if we will choose it. Nehemiah 8:10 reads, "The joy of the Lord is your strength," and I have found that to be true again and again. Many times I have relied on God to help me through tough situations. Most of the time He gives me a different, lighter perception of the situation. The peace that follows is priceless. The more I rely on Him to change my attitude, the more my "humor-muscle" is strengthened, leading to grace under pressure.

Lord, thank You for laughter and the benefits we reap from it. Please continue to fill my life with joy and help me to add to the joy of those around me.

MARY WAGONER ANGELIN

Needed Transportation

Be careful for nothing; but in every thing by prayer and supplication with thanksgiving let your requests be made known unto God. Phil. 4:6.

MY PRAYER PARTNER and I were both in desperate need of an automobile. Our cars were literally falling apart. Irma and I usually fast and pray at least one day a month. We make a list of things that we intend to talk to God about, then take our petitions to the throne of grace.

We asked for used cars that were in good condition. Irma prayed for a certain make, year, and color, and within a certain price range. My prayer requests were similar. For six months we prayed and fasted, convinced that we would receive good used automobiles if it was our Father's will.

Another month passed. A friend, who had purchased a car six years earlier, had told me she intended to trade it in in five years. I had replied, "Let me make you an offer before you decide to trade it in. I am almost sure I will need a car by that time."

When she said she was planning to purchase a new car, I reminded her of my offer. "I'm sorry," she said, "I didn't remember that you wanted to make me an offer, but if they should change their minds for any reason, I will definitely let you know."

On my way home I continued to pray. *Father, You know I need a car. If You see me having a difficult time keeping or maintaining that car, please don't give it to me, and I will accept whatever You give me. If it is Your will, please give it to me.* I thought no more about it.

About two weeks later Irma informed me that a friend had found a car they thought she would be interested in. It was the right make and color, and in the price range she requested in her prayer. A few days later the friend saw another car he thought she would like better that was in better shape.

Then one day my friend called to say her car had become available again. When I said it was a little more than I could afford to pay, she immediately deducted $500.

We didn't know how or when God was going to answer our prayers. We knew that God, in His own time, would answer.

God is able, and He is willing, to help you. He is listening. He is waiting. Won't you give Him a chance to prove Himself to you today? God loves you.

CORA A. WALKER

A God Who Eagerly Waits

Can a woman forget her nursing child, and not have compassion on the son of her womb? Surely they may forget, yet I will not forget you. Isa. 49:15, 16, NKJV.

THE BOY-SHAPED SHADOW stands statue-still in the darkness. Quietly, he had tiptoed into his mother's room. Surely she could bring him comfort. He hesitates. Should he awaken her? Could he awaken her? Tears fall quietly down his hot cheeks, yet no sound escapes his lips. He cries—from pain, fear, and despair.

Finally desperation takes over. A tiny, muffled voice escapes his lips. "Mama," he whispers. She stirs. "Mama!" A little hand thrusts forward and touches her shoulder. "Mama!" Instantly awake, she reaches for the pitiful form. Desperately she focuses on Tyler and the awful calamity that has caused him to slip so silently from his bed to seek hers. "Tyler, are you all right? Are you sick?"

"I don't feel good, Mama."

No other words are needed. Warm arms reach out. "How long have you been standing here?" she asks. "You're so cold. Why didn't you awaken me sooner? Oh, Tyler!"

We stand before our heavenly Parent. Heartsick and wretched, we long for a healing touch. Yet how often do we find ourselves overwhelmed with feelings of unworthiness and fear? Jesus says, "Can a woman forget her nursing child, and not have compassion on the son of her womb? Surely they may forget, yet I will not forget you."

That's our Father! He seeks out you and me and speaks with a voice so soft and tender, "O Jerusalem, Jerusalem, the one who kills the prophets and stones those who are sent to her! How often I wanted to gather your children together, as a hen gathers her chicks under her wings, but you were not willing!" (Matt. 23:37, NKJV). Hear Him calling to you with out-stretched arms, "I love you so much that I gave My Son to die for you" (see John 3:16).

Searching for forgiveness? He promises "I will forgive their iniquity, and their sin I will remember no more" (Jer. 31:34, NKJV).

Don't just stand there today, silently in need, alone and helpless. Reach out. He will not turn you away.   GINGER CHURCH

His Watch Care

I will instruct you and teach you in the way which you should go; I will counsel you with My eye upon you. Ps. 32:8, NASB.

MY HUSBAND AND I were reminiscing about God's blessings. "I've had at least six miracles in my life," Marvin remarked, naming his spectacular rescues. His last miracle we'd shared together. A huge logging truck, directly in our lane, bore down on us as we traveled a narrow hairpin curve. A split second of terror, a blink of an eye, and it was in its own lane, passing us on our left.

I thought back over my life, appreciating God's tender care. I'd had miracles, too, although most were not as dramatic as Marvin's. One experience stands out, perhaps because it was somewhat of a turning point for me. I was 18 years old and needed a job. My mother was on disability, and money was tight. Scanning the newspaper want ads, I saw one that interested me: "Dancing girls wanted." I decided to check it out, never mind that I was a recently baptized Christian, had no experience as a dancer of any kind, and that a job like this might lead down a dangerous path. I was young, adventurous, and possessed the eternal optimism of youth.

The next day I made the tedious journey across the city—a long streetcar ride, then a bus change, and finally the last few blocks on foot—dressed in my best blue dress. Map in hand, I walked past one building after another, with never a doubt that I was doing the right thing. Just one more block.

Then it happened. Nothing earthshaking—just words spoken lovingly to my heart. "Don't go! Turn back; go home!" Without a moment's hesitation, without a qualm, I did just that. I can only imagine the troubles that might have been mine had I not turned back.

It's sometimes fun to go over various stages of life and see how God has been helper, guide, and protector. I've heard we should have no fear for the future except as we forget how the Lord has led us in the past.

I'll never forget that quiet, loving voice I heard that day. I've heard it a few other times, and I'm so grateful. I know He's there for each of us, and our children, as we are open to Him.

Thank You, Father.

MARILYN KING

God Was Leading

Yea, though I walk through the valley of the shadow of death, I will fear no evil: for thou art with me; thy rod and thy staff they comfort me. Ps. 23:4.

MOVING FROM BETHEL to Cape Town was not easy. I had to stay with friends for the first month, and then they moved. I had difficulty finding an apartment, as apartments were so expensive in Cape Town. There was a time when I slept in a stranger's house. The next day she told me that her brother was coming, so I must leave. I thanked her for her generosity, but I was heartbroken. Where was I going to sleep the next night? I'll never forget the day I had to go to work by public transport for the first time—I used four taxis. When I calculated the cost for the month, I wanted to cry. Sometimes I asked myself, "Lord, did I make the right choice by coming here?"

I prayed *so* hard, and I even fasted. Then a new teacher arrived in my school; to my surprise, she belonged to my church. Stella and her husband were so kind—they gave me a place to stay for a week while I looked for an apartment. Fortunately, by God's mercy, I got one before the week was over.

Then another disaster struck. The Mila family would take me to work, because they lived quite close, but Stella and I would have to travel back home by taxi. One day in October Stella and I were in the taxi, both seated in front. We were aware of the taxi violence in Cape Town, but what we didn't know was that the problem had moved out to us in Brackenfell. I don't know exactly what happened, but we saw a taxi blocking us in front. Our taxi tried to pass through, in the process hitting other cars and causing accidents. Gunshots were being fired at our taxi. The blocking taxi hit our taxi again. The front window shattered in my face. Although I didn't feel a thing, I wanted to jump from the moving taxi, but Stella stopped me.

We finally did manage to get out, then we and the taxi driver ran. When we arrived at my apartment, the first thing Stella and I did was pray. Actually, I was the only one injured; Stella was only very shocked. I soon discovered the train—it was near the apartment, and it was cheaper.

Life hasn't been easy, but I still see God's leading in my life. I know He is there for me, and I won't give up—I've come too far to give up now.

DEBORAH MATSHAYA

Sent Back to Moab

All Scripture is God-breathed and is useful for teaching, rebuking, correcting and training in righteousness. 2 Tim. 3:16, NIV.

A FRIEND SHARED THAT she felt like Naomi, who sent her daughter-in-law back to Moab. When I asked her how that could be, she explained. "I was reading the book of Ruth one night and came to the place where Naomi and her daughters-in-law, Ruth and Orpah, were leaving Moab and going back to Judah. I found myself reading again and again the verses that tell of their journey on the road to Judah. Naomi suddenly stops and tells both of them to go back. They refuse, but she insists. Finally Orpah goes back. I wondered why it worried me so much that Naomi had insisted they go home. Moab was an idolatrous nation, while Judah offered salvation."

I was still wondering about Naomi's daughter-in-law when my friend continued. "I had a teaching, rebuking, correcting experience with God. It was a revealing moment and not very comfortable. God asked me why I should be condemning Naomi when my own slate was less than clean. I too have daughters-in-law from 'Moab.' They aren't practicing Christians.

"God reminded me of an incident about 10 years ago. It was my husband's birthday, and we planned a party. We were all in a happy mood and determined to enjoy the event. One son and his wife had had a disagreement, and it spilled over into the party. She was sullen and resentful, and generally started making everyone near her uncomfortable. Finally, I got angry with her and told her if she couldn't allow us to enjoy the party, I'd rather she wasn't there." There was a stunned silence, and then she left the room. Our daughter said to me, 'I can't believe you said that, Mother,' to which I replied, 'I can't believe I said it either.' But I had said it, and nothing could take it back. I apologized later, but our relationship was never the same after that."

"In effect," my friend concluded, "I had sent her back to Moab. Instead of showing her a Christlike character and giving her a welcoming invitation to Judah, I had turned her steps back to Moab. She and my son have since divorced, and I have no contact with her, no further chance of inviting her to Judah."

My friend learned a hard lesson. Every word in the Bible has a lesson for us, if we will allow ourselves to be taught.   ARDIS DICK STENBAKKEN

"Slow Down Children"

O Lord, you have examined my heart and know everything about me. You know when I sit or stand. When far away you know my every thought. You chart the path ahead of me, and tell me where to stop and rest. Every moment, you know where I am. You know what I am going to say before I even say it. You both precede and follow me, and place your hand of blessing on my head. Ps.139:1-5, TLB.

AS I DRIVE TO my friend Christie's house, on a pretty country lane near a quaint cottage, I pass a sign: "Slow Down Children." I smiled the first time I saw it—the absence of punctuation seemed to make it into a direct command from God.

Like most people, I have a busy life. I want to spend more time in prayer and Bible study, but I'm so busy. I want to prepare my weekly Bible study lessons more thoroughly, but I'm so busy. I want to bake bread for my family and make my garden into something that looks like a slice out of Eden, but I'm so busy. The mundane but necessary tasks of life—the cooking, the cleaning, the washing, the ferrying of children to their activities, the career, the study—all take their toll. I'm tired and stressed.

God loves us and wants us not only to look forward to heaven but to enjoy and experience the here and now. If I'm rushing heedlessly about, He whispers, "Slow down." If I'm wishing that my 2-year-old and 4-year-old were older and less difficult and dreaming of a time when we can reason with them better, He laughs and says, "Slow down." If I'm feeling as though I'm a failure and that I'm doing everything badly, He shakes His head and says, "Slow down."

I'm His child. He looks on me with love and care, even when I rebel and stamp my foot and tell Him that I just don't understand. He enjoys my delight when I admire beauty, embrace a friend, cuddle a child, stroke a cat. He is my all-wise, all-loving, all-just Father.

Although I aspire to be a Mary and sit at His feet, resting in His goodness, I act more like a Martha, trying to get everyone and everything organized. It's a hard lesson for me to let go of my cares and to let God care for me.

Slow down, children; slow down.   HEATHER HANNA

Getting Things Ready

I am going there to prepare a place for you. John 14:2, NIV.

A T THE LIBRARY WHERE I work there's a lot of preparation behind the scenes before we're ready to open each day. The janitor arrives at 6:00 a.m. He scrubs all the bathrooms, vacuums the floors, and dusts the tables. My job starts with a thorough inspection of the public areas. I pick up loose books and magazines from their hiding places. Sometimes I wonder why people expend so much energy messing up the library. One day someone put acorns all over the library. Many people find it an ideal picnic spot, judging from the soda bottles and food wrappers we pick up.

While I'm busy picking up, a small army of librarians, clerks, and volunteers are getting other things ready. Current newspapers and magazines are put out. Videotapes are rewound. All the computers are turned on and set up for public use. The cash register is emptied and the money counted. The copy machines are freshly loaded with paper. Circulation figures are tabulated, and memos regarding policy changes are read. When the library opens promptly at 9:30, workers are staffing the desks and ready to serve the public.

Some people can't wait for us to open. Through the glass doors they can see people walking around inside, and they become frustrated and angry when we don't let them in. Sometimes they pound on the glass and shout through the book drop to get our attention. When unlocked, the electronic doors can be forced open by hand, and on several occasions overeager people have pushed them open and come inside. Once inside, however, all they see is people rushing around. There are no people at the reference desk to answer their questions, and no people at the circulation desk to check out their books.

When I think about how eager I am to see heaven, I can relate to those people who push through our doors. I don't want to get there before everyone and everything's ready and find no one waiting to meet me! I have to remind myself that my time is not the same as God's time. When everything's ready, I know Jesus will come. Until then, I must wait in the knowledge that preparations are taking place. GINA LEE

A Miracle!

Many believed in his name, when they saw the miracles which he did.
John 2:23.

I T WAS ONLY TWO weeks before I was to leave my home in Indonesia to
move to the United States that my mom discovered a lump on her breast.
Naturally she became quite alarmed and consulted our physician immediately.
Based on the result of the mammogram, the doctor suspected there might be a
cancer. To make sure, he suggested she have a second mammogram.

Our family was shocked. Meanwhile, my mom was experiencing her
own fluctuations in her faith. "Well, then, if this is really cancer, just leave
me in peace," she said. "I don't want to have further treatment and an operation." I encouraged her to trust God and believe in His power to take
care of the troublesome lump.

Our family had many prayers for my mom, the most difficult petitions
we ever sent to the Father. We weren't only asking for my mom's healing;
we were asking that the Lord's will be done. Even though it would be hard
for us, we had to accept whatever plan God had for us.

Time went so fast; soon it was only two more days before I had to
leave. I wished I could change my departure date so that I'd have more days
with Mom, especially during this difficult time. But I had a ticket that had
been issued long before, and there was no way for me to change the date—
it was a nonchangeable, nonrefundable ticket.

Finally we got the results of the second mammogram and took them to
the doctor. The lump wasn't there! A miracle! There was no need for
surgery. We couldn't believe it!

God had tested our faith. He had given us a demonstration of His power
at the right time. A sense of our awesome God surrounded us, and right
there at the doctor's office we offered a prayer of praise and thanksgiving.
Soon we were on our way home again, still awestruck by the love of God.

Sometimes God answers yes, and sometimes no. Although we might
never know the reason, we can still trust Him to do what is best for us because He is our God. And He alone knows what the future holds. He is in
control of everything in our lives.   LANNY LYDIA PONGILATAN

How Do You Fold?

Though it cost all you have, get understanding. Prov. 4:7, NIV.

THE CHILD PAINSTAKINGLY folded her tiny, dimpled hands. "See; see?" she cried. "You do it!" Her mother complied graciously. The child looked carefully from her hands to her mother's, then back again. Her face was a puzzle.

"I know," her mother said, smiling. "They don't look the same. God made us different. That's OK. It's fun!"

The child's body relaxed. Her face beamed. "I wuv you, Mom!" she said and leaned her tousled, curly, red head close.

It was my turn to smile. I folded my hands automatically. Did someone teach me this skill? I don't know. It just happened. I'll fold and unfold them thousands of times during my lifespan. There are similarities and differences in the way people fold their hands. No style is right or wrong, good or bad. Just "unlike."

Although we rarely stop to think about it, even these small habits represent personal preference. Fold your hands. Which thumb is on top? Refold your hands so the opposite thumb is on top, paying close attention to the sensations you experience. The first time I consciously folded my hands the opposite way, I actually looked down to see whose hand it belonged to! It felt awkward and uncomfortable, and one hand felt unaccountably smaller.

Now fold your arms. Which arm is on top—the left or the right? Refold your arms the opposite way. How does that feel? With practice, we can increase our comfort level. The new style will likely never become as automatic, however. Unless we make a conscious choice to override natural preference, we'll usually be most comfortable with our own preferred folding style. Hand folding could be called a form of eccentricity. Eccentricity, as Oliver Sacks points out, is like having an accent—it's what *other* people have.

The subway we were riding on clicked and swayed. The underground stations flew by. The child continued to practice hand folding. Her skill increased with each repetition. Her young mother was so wise, affirming the child for her innate preferences. Part of honoring one another (Rom. 12:10) comes from enjoying our differences!

ARLENE TAYLOR

No More Illness

And God will wipe every tear from their eyes; there shall be no more death, nor sorrow, nor crying, and there shall be no more pain, for the former things have passed away. Rev. 21:4, NKJV.

FAITH AND I WERE always close. Although we grew up 1,600 miles apart, we got to see each other about once a year when our mothers, who were sisters, would visit back and forth. When Faith was 18 she came to live near us, much to my mom's chagrin. By this time, Faith was smoking, drinking, and wanting to run around. My mother didn't want that life for her children, and she knew how much we liked Faith. My brothers and sisters did tend to follow in her footsteps, but I just enjoyed her company and having general fun.

Soon, however, things seemed to change. Faith was not the same girl we had played with when we were younger. She thought people were following her. She was beginning to hear voices and seemed to be more violent than usual. She had married and, while continuing to work, was more "strange" than ever.

I went to visit her once in the small trailer where she lived. She had hung her clothes on the fence by her house and was spraying them with a water hose.

"What are you doing?" I asked Faith.

"My laundry," she said.

"Oh, Faith, I can't believe they'll get clean just by hosing them down," I objected.

"Soap's bad for the environment," she answered, "so I want to help the environment."

So went her life. After one bizarre incident the medical personnel requested that my mother take Faith to the local mental hospital to be evaluated. Eventually Faith ended up at the place where they could best help her.

It has been a horrible eight years since that first diagnosis, and it's very hard for me to understand mental illness. I can see bruises, sore throats, and cancer—all that I can understand. It's simple. But when a person hears voices, or chooses to gather supper from a local Dumpster, I have a hard time. Praise God! Soon He will return and wipe all illness from the earth. I can't wait.

CHARLOTTE ROBINSON

Running To and Fro

Seal the book, even to the time of the end: many shall run to and fro, and knowledge shall be increased. Dan. 12:4.

MULTITUDES OF PEOPLE waited with us for the delayed flight at Logan Airport in Boston. I looked out the window, watching the jets come in and take off. I called out to my husband all the different countries they were from—Britain, Canada, Italy, and so on. I remember the days long ago when we would go out to the airport to watch the planes. There weren't many then, but it was exciting to us to watch this fast-growing phenomenon.

I remember, too, my first flight from California to New York. I thought I would never afford another flight. And now I fly several times a year to visit my children, and have even flown to Russia and China. I would have never believed that would be a part of my life. And now, almost everyone appears to take planes. Somehow money to purchase tickets is found.

When we finally left Boston and got to Switzerland, I saw many more planes from such countries as Israel, Bahrain, Yemen, and Cyprus. I was amazed that these little countries had their own airlines. It seems that everyone is going somewhere. It used to be exciting to take the bus or train. These are left far behind today. Everybody is going somewhere, and fast is what they want.

What did Daniel say? He talked of spiritual knowledge, but all knowledge is increasing. Is that not true with our vast technological age? I can't comprehend it all. And he adds that many will run to and fro. Technology has produced our immense jets. As I watched them land and take off that day, pouring out people of every ethnic group imaginable, I thought, *Everyone is going somewhere—maybe to the ends of the earth. Surely this is a sign of the Lord's soon coming. We must keep Christ in what we are doing.*

The gospel of Christ is still the simple story we find in the Bible. But our new technology can help us to spread that story quickly throughout the earth. And we ourselves can travel quickly to other cities and countries, where people are eagerly awaiting the good news of Jesus. They have been oppressed so long, and their lives are so empty of Christ. We have a wonderful opportunity now as we can run to and fro quickly with the message of the gospel of Jesus.

DESSA WEISZ HARDIN

I Want Out of Here

Let your eyes look straight ahead, fix your gaze directly before you. Prov. 4:25, NIV.

WITH TEARS IN HIS eyes, 3-year-old Eric said, "I want out of here." Freeze-frame. Go back in time 24 hours. It was Monday morning, and the day began at 6:45 with Eric saying, "Mom, it's daytime. Let's play." I'm not, by any stretch of the imagination, a morning person. So being awakened at 6:45 was not my idea of a good start to the day. After putting on my housecoat and turning off the heater, I ventured downstairs. There the reality of the day hit me—this was packing day. Tomorrow we would fly to Texas.

By the time 8:00 p.m. rolled around, Eric had gotten his bath, and finally we had him worn out. All day he was talking about Texas, telling everyone he saw about his vacation.

We were up early the next morning, too. We were on the way to catch our plane in Chicago, two and a half hours away. We arrived at Chicago's O'Hare Airport with an hour to spare. After parking the car, we checked in and were ready to board the plane. But so were many others. We got stuck waiting on the walkway, an enclosed area connecting the airport and airplane. Neither Eric nor I are fond of close quarters, and Eric began to panic.

End freeze-frame. Back to "I want out of here." Rick and I quickly assured Eric that we would move soon and be able to enter the plane and find our seats. It wasn't until we found our seats and got settled for the two-hour flight that I began to think of the depth of Eric's words. He wanted out of the walkway because he was afraid. I too want out—out of this world and into heaven. I'm tired of feeling cramped by sin all around me. I want to be surrounded by the love, peace, and kindness that heaven has to offer.

As our text says: "Let your eyes look straight ahead, fix your gaze directly before you." This life is not where we should focus. Do you want to say with Eric, "I want out of here"?

Lord, help us keep our eyes straight ahead until that great morning.

MARSHA CLAUS

A Case of Mistaken Identity

Be diligent to present yourself approved to God, a worker who does not need to be ashamed. 2 Tim. 2:15, NKJV.

WHEN SMALL FOREIGN CARS were quite new back in the early 1960s, to save on gasoline we traded our beautiful green-and-cream 1957 Ford for a little red Renault. It had its share of problems, and it sometimes had to go to the shop. One day I went to pick it up and found it on the lot with the keys in it. I got in and headed home, but had an uneasy feeling that something was not quite right. Sure enough, though it was a red Renault, it was not *our* red Renault! I was so embarrassed that my husband drove it back. He was able to return it and get the right one without even being detected.

Another time I wore a black coat to church and hung it at the end of the rack so I could find it easily when church was over. The day had warmed considerably, so I didn't put the coat on when we went home. When we were going out that evening I put the coat on and stuck my hands in the pockets. To my dismay, I found a large pair of men's gloves in the pocket! Again, I enlisted my patient husband's help in returning what I'd taken by mistake and asked him to retrieve my coat. The owner of the other black coat had pushed mine back from the end so he could hang his coat there. Later he mentioned to us that there were honest people in our church, as someone had taken his coat but had returned it. I confessed that I was the culprit, and we had a good laugh.

One winter Sabbath day after the last amen had been said and the congregation dismissed, I found one of the older women putting my coat on. I gently pointed out her mistake, and we found her coat, which was the same beige color as mine.

Some mistakes are much more serious and not so easily made right. Jesus warned that in the last days there would be those who would come in His name, saying they were Christ, and deceiving many—if possible, even the very elect. The only way to avoid falling prey to the deceivers is to know what to look for, and that knowledge is found in God's Word. I'm sometimes ashamed of my lack of knowledge; I want to follow Paul's advice that I might be "approved unto God." How about you?   MARY JANE GRAVES

Who Are You?

Not everyone who says to me, "Lord, Lord," will enter the kingdom of heaven, but only the one who does the will of my Father in heaven. Matt. 7:21, NRSV.

FOUR OF US FLEW from Michigan to California just as spring was blowing farewell kisses to winter. With an eye to protecting the budget, we formed pairs and shared rooms in an old historic inn. Because we each had different roles at the conference—organizing, presenting, and participating—we needed two cars.

Exhausted at the end of the third day, I loaded my belongings into our car and waited for my roommate. When she mentioned that she was going to be delayed by at least another hour, I hitched a ride with my other travel partners. We zoomed off into the starry night. It was then I remembered: my room key was in a bag in the other car!

"No problem," my girlfriends reassured me. "The desk will give you a replacement key."

I sallied forth, secure in the knowledge that all I needed to do was explain my predicament to the front-desk attendant. Checking his computer, the concierge could see that a person with my name was indeed registered at the inn.

"I'll just need to see some ID," he told me, smiling. But that was a problem. I had none with me. "What's the address of the sponsoring conference?" I had no clue. "Their phone number?" I didn't know that, either.

"Well, how do I know that you are who you say you are?" he asked, his patience now thinning.

Then a girlfriend stepped up. "I know her. I can vouch for her." With that she slapped her own ID and room key on the counter.

Shaking his head, the man couldn't help smiling. "Then I guess it's all right. This time."

But it won't be that simple on the day of judgment. My records will have to be more intact than they were that night. I pray that I can hear the language of heaven when my heavenly Brother steps in with grace-filled words I long to hear: "Father, I know her; My blood is sufficient to give her access to heaven." That will be such joyful music to my soul!

GLENDA-MAE GREENE

Growing Like a Tree

Like a tree planted by streams of water, which yields its fruit in season. Ps. 1:3, NIV.

WITH A MIXTURE OF sadness and elation, I viewed the plum tree last spring. Its stark, bony branches reached skyward, as straggly branches poked earthward.

I guess it didn't make it through the winter, I thought as I surveyed the tree against a backdrop of a colorful lemon tree and a stately palm. Both of them had made it through winter—and Southern California winters aren't all that bad.

The plum tree didn't belong to me. It stood just across the block wall that divided my front yard from my neighbor's. The tree was an ugly, crispy black. I wished they'd cut it down. During its lifetime it spewed plums in my flower bed, and I had to pick them out, which didn't endear the tree to me. My attitude toward it softened when my neighbor shared some plum butter. She emphasized that the plums came from that tree.

Then one morning several weeks later I saw the plum tree again. It wasn't dead. Like a porcupine awakening from a nap, it bristled all over with little blossoms. I just hadn't gotten close enough to see it grow.

Sometimes people—even ourselves—are like the plum tree. They are growing deep inside. We can't see it yet. We aren't close enough. We see no change, so we think there's no hope. We think the prayers aren't being answered, when all the time God is working behind the scenes. At the right time, things happen.

As I look out my window this year and see a "dead" plum tree, when the other trees are blooming, I remember last spring and look forward to seeing a plum tree full of blossoms one morning.

Lord, keep me growing on the inside, even when I may look dead and dry on the outside. And help me get close to those around me so that I may see that they too, are growing and ready to bloom. EDNA MAYE GALLINGTON

Butterfly Kiss

He has made everything beautiful in its time. Eccl. 3:11, NIV.

IT HAD BEEN A very difficult week. All my hopes and plans had been crushed in seven days. I was working two part-time jobs and had a major writing project to complete. I needed some quiet space in my life to finish the writing. I had asked for reduced hours at the rehabilitation center where I worked. But now the senior therapist had decided to take another job. Two of my most promising patients had died unexpectedly, and I was refused the funding for a desperately needed major piece of equipment that I'd been promised for more than a year.

In my other job, a project that I'd planned and dreamed about for years was turned down. In both areas of my life I felt overwhelmed with challenges. Everything I was looking forward to in both jobs had disappeared in a couple of days. I needed to take stock of my life, to admit that two demanding jobs were too much for me. I was in grief, discouraged and numb.

I was trying to work on the writing project, but my mind and heart were so heavy I couldn't think straight. I went out into the garden. *Father-God, please give me a hug!* I prayed. *I just need to feel Your love and Your comfort right now. I know everything will be OK because You've never let me down, but I just need to feel Your hug around my heart.*

I wandered around the garden with tears in my eyes, pulling halfheartedly at the odd weed and snapping off a stray creeper. Finally, I turned around to go back toward the house. There on the wall was a beautiful red admiral butterfly, brilliant in the sunshine.

"There's your hug," I almost heard God whisper.

"A butterfly. What did a butterfly have to do with anything?" I wondered.

"You're feeling really dark and shriveled right now, just like a chrysalis, but this isn't wasted time. One day there'll be a butterfly. You just need to be a little more patient. I'll make everything beautiful in My time. Just wait and see."

I put my son to bed. "Mommy, please give me a butterfly kiss!" I fluttered my eyelashes against his soft cheek. He smiled. "I don't always need a hug," he said. "I just need one of your butterfly kisses." I knew exactly what he meant.

KAREN HOLFORD

Thank You, Lord

Oh, give thanks to the Lord, for He is good! For His mercy endures forever. Ps. 136:1, NKJV.

IT WAS ONE OF those moments in life when the 24-hour Sabbath that the Lord gave was not enough. There were too many tasks and responsibilities. The cares of life were just too much, entangling me. It was getting harder for me to spare my precious time with anybody. I was scared, because it seemed my days were always like that. Sad to say, I was lagging behind on my time with the Lord. Bible reading was hurriedly done, or sometimes I even reasoned, "Oh, well, if I miss it today, I'll read more chapters on Sabbath."

One afternoon, for no reason at all, I found myself picking up the phone and dialing Aida's number. Aida is a quiet lady in our local church who works as a private-duty nurse. She is not one you'll always find up front or leading out. But I always see her at all the church programs, quiet and smiling, in her little corner.

"Hello, Aida? How's everything with you?" I didn't even know what to ask or what to say to her. I was surprised that I had dialed her number.

She began to tell me about her good visit with her daughter in Florida, of the fun she had with her granddaughter, how cute her new grandson was, and how thankful she is for a good son-in-law. But these were not the words that woke me up that day. It's what she said after that.

"Jem," she said, "I'm so sad, though, because my daughter doesn't spend time reading her Bible. I told her that it shouldn't be like that, that we should spend time with the Lord, just as we enjoy His blessings every moment."

She was doubly right. I breathe every moment; I have food on the table, a loving family and friends, wonderful work, and a healthy body. I'm enjoying God's blessings every hour of the day and don't even have minutes to spend with Him?

Lord, help me to spend as much time with You as I do enjoying Your blessings. Thank You for leading me to call Aida and reminding me of Your greatness and love.

Today, may we be like the psalmist and thank God for His goodness to us. May our prayer be "Oh, give thanks to the Lord, for He is good! For His mercy endures forever."

JEMIMA D. ORILLOSA

When the Angels Pushed

The angel of the Lord encampeth round about them that fear him, and delivereth them. Ps. 34:7.

WHILE DRIVING ON A narrow stretch of paved road, I came upon a boulder blocking half the road. I decided to stop to try to roll it into the ditch. While bending over to give it a try, I looked up and noticed that my car was rolling slowly backward. I ran toward it and pushed on the back of the car as hard as I could. It slowed down some but soon began to roll again. I was pushing with everything I had when my feet started to slide on the pavement. The car was crossing the centerline and backing toward the drop-off into the lake on the opposite side of the road. The only alternative I had was to make myself an obstruction. So I flopped down behind the rear wheel.

What a sight I must have been—white pants all dirty, skinned-up elbows; pinned under my own car and blocking the road. I looked around for something to put under the tire in place of my leg, but there were only tiny pebbles and grasses, none of which would hold the car. There I lay, looking up and down the road, silently praying for someone to come.

As I helplessly lay there, I struggled to turn around and look behind me once more, and my eyes fell upon a fist-sized rock. Quickly, I jammed it under the tire and released my leg. I was shaking badly and held on to the car for support. Finally I was able to get behind the wheel.

The Lord sent His angels to help me hold back the car, but the most amazing thing is that on that stretch of road there are no rocks on the shoulder. The angels had placed one just the right size within my reach. I know He did.

That afternoon as I drove back over the road, I stopped the car and got out to relive my experience of that morning. I looked around for the rock that had helped me, but it was nowhere to be seen. There were still only the grasses and small pebbles. For a moment I felt as if I were standing on holy ground, and in my heart I knew the angels had been there, and that they can carry rocks. "The angel of the Lord encampeth round about them that fear him, and delivereth them."

VIDELLA MCCLELLAN

It Took 51 Years

Do for others what you want them to do for you. Matt. 7:12, TEV.

THE SCHOOL SPRING banquet was coming, and my roommate and I had just broken up with our boyfriends. We vowed that we'd go with the first guy who asked us to the banquet.

The next morning during assembly it was announced that the fellows could now ask the girls to the banquet. The minute we were dismissed a certain young man asked me to be his date. Because I had been the victim of so much unkindness in my life, I was determined to never cause anyone pain. I never considered myself superior to anyone; in fact, I tended to feel inferior, but some folks just seemed so crude to me that I preferred to stay away from them. This young man fit into that category.

The night of the banquet he told everyone at our table that I really did love him and that we were going to "E-lope right after the bankwit." I was horrified and embarrassed, even though my friends understood. I wasted no time in returning to the dorm when the evening was over. Over the years I've chuckled about that evening and wondered what had become of that young man.

Recently, while attending my 50-year class reunion, I looked up to see an elderly man walking with a crutch, his overalls rolled up about six inches above his ankles. He walked up to me and said he was looking for Anna May Radke. I told him that I was Anna May. He then proceeded to ask whom I had attended the junior banquet with, and I knew instinctively it was he.

"You!" I responded.

With tears in his eyes he shook my hand and thanked me sincerely for having gone to that banquet with him. He said he appreciated my kindness to him so much. Then he asked if I knew where the other girl was who had gone with us that evening. I told him I had no idea. He said he needed to apologize to her for the awful way he ignored her that evening.

I suddenly felt good all over. I was so thankful that God had impressed me 51 years before to show kindness to everyone, even when I didn't feel like it. I was now genuinely happy to see this man again, and I was truly glad I had attended my junior banquet with him.

ANNA MAY RADKE WATERS

Look at That Ticket in Your Hand

Then the Lord said . . . , "What is that in your hand?" Ex. 4:2, NIV.

I'M A CHRISTIAN who married a Christian of another denomination, but neither of us went to church. He'd been married before, and his first wife was also a Christian. I really didn't know her except what he told me about her. But I hated her. I had so much hate and anger toward her that I'd go into a rage when her name was mentioned.

About seven years after my marriage I decided to go back to my church. This made my husband very upset with me. So in my morning devotions I asked the Lord to show me what I needed to do that would convince him that my religion could make a difference.

I got one of those impressions from God that showed me a part of my uglier side. I didn't hear an audible voice; it was just a thought process that crossed my mind. But it came to me as though someone were talking to me. "Joyce, I want you to take a look at that ticket in your hand."

Startled, I said, "Ticket? What ticket are You talking about?"

"You know. You think you have a first-class ticket to heaven, and your husband has a third-class—or maybe only a standby."

I said, "OK, Lord, I know what You are talking about. Go on."

He said, "You know how you feel about his ex-wife. Do you think your husband sees Christ in you when you express those thoughts and feelings? She has the same first-class ticket as you do. And when you do get to heaven, you may find that your mansion is next to hers. Then as you get to know her, she might turn out to be the best friend you've ever had. How are you going to feel when you think of the way you talked about her and treated her on earth?"

Friend, words can't describe how I felt. I knew I was in the presence of the Judge of the universe. It was one of the most humbling feelings I've ever had. I was convicted of my sin and asked God's forgiveness. I gave all the hate I had toward her to Jesus.

About five years later she attended a revival at her church and also had a change of heart. After that we did become friends. We truly are sisters in Christ.

JOYCE MAPLES

And Then There Were Four

God created . . . every winged fowl . . . : and God saw that it was good.
Gen. 1:21.

THEY ARE MANY wild ducks in the canal suburb where I live—such
pretty birds with gray plumage. There's also a resident pelican that
swims past, followed by his flotilla of seagulls; and a blue heron, a very elegant slim bird. About a year ago two domestic ducks appeared in our canal.
Where they came from nobody knows. We wondered if someone dumped
them here because the brown female has a broken wing and can't fly. She
more than makes up for this lack of mobility with her loud, continuous
quack. Her mate, a sleek black duck, is so protective of her. As they swim
around, he is always there, chasing the wild ducks away from food thrown
to them. Everyone keeps spare bread for "our" ducks.

Then the brown duck disappeared for a couple months. We'd see the
black male from time to time and wonder what had happened to his mate.
Then early one morning as we were getting ready for work, I heard such a
quacking. When the noise continued, I ran outside to see what was going
on. There were mother and father duck, as proud as punch, with nine
beautiful black balls of fluff swimming along behind them. The ducklings'
legs were going "ninety to the dozen" as they furiously paddled to keep up
with their parents.

Sadly, by the evening of day one there were only eight ducklings.
Someone thought a crow or a sea hawk might have taken the ninth baby. A
second duckling disappeared on day two, another on day three and another
on day four. A week passed, and suddenly there were only four ducklings
left. Those four are daily growing so fast and are so adventuresome. We
watch as they wander away up the beach until squawks from Mother bring
them running back. Perhaps whatever fate befell the five missing ducklings
happened because they didn't keep up with their parents.

Whenever I fail to ask my heavenly Father for His protective care and
wander away, Satan is always right there, waiting to snare me. I, too, fall behind when I fail to keep up with my daily worship. My prayer is to grow
daily with God.   LEONIE DONALD

My Meadow

And we know that all things work together for good to them that love God, to them who are called according to his purpose. Rom. 8:28.

MY HUSBAND USED TO tease me about my dream of one day having my very own meadow, where I could run barefoot through acres of tall grass and look out at rows of lofty trees instead of highways and cars. I almost envied folks who were fortunate enough to live on the farms we'd pass by on our rides in the country. *What is it like,* I wondered, *behind those garden gates where everything appears so picture-perfect?*

I lived in town most of my life. When I was a child, our house was hemmed in by other houses, all with very small yards. After I married and had children, we wound up in the same mode—in the city, close to jobs and school. Before long our children had married and moved away to homes of their own, and our house no longer served the same purpose as it once had.

Eventually we built a small house in the country, but because of several detours along the way it was five years before we could move in, and then it was short lived. Changes in management and circumstances at the shop where my husband worked made it seem more practical for us to move back to the city.

As retirement time came, old dreams of having my own meadow once again came to mind, so I began to scan the "For Sale" signs on small farms and acreages in the area. But it was not to be. My husband became very ill, and we decided to remain in the old homeplace in the city. And I've never been sorry. Even though the traffic and noise are worse than ever, living in town has its merits, especially as I get older and am now living alone. There's something to be said for having family, friends, church, and stores so accessible.

It's disappointing to have to give up dreams, but I've learned to put my faith and trust in God. He'll direct my paths. He promises, "I will instruct thee and teach thee in the way thou shalt go" (Ps. 32:8).

It may not always be the direction I'd choose, but I've trusted Him thus far, and He'll take me the rest of the way. And if I stay with Him, someday I will have my meadow.

CLAREEN COLCLESSER

Let Not the Enemy Triumph Over Me

Did not our heart burn within us while He talked with us on the road, and while He opened the Scriptures to us? Luke 24:32, NKJV.

THE TWO DISCIPLES were totally engrossed in the weekend's happenings when a Stranger joined them on their way to Emmaus. Their hearts were truly heavy, for they had hoped that the Man who was crucified was the very one who would free them and their people from the Roman bondage. Oh, how disappointed they were! They were crushed to despair. All their flickering hope of being freed from the yoke of the oppressors vanished like a bubble.

All of us at one time or another undergo disappointments and discouragements. Many of us experience crushed hopes. Beautiful dreams for ourselves and our families become elusive as family problems, financial difficulties, or trying relationships burden us. Maybe we have experienced separation or divorce. Perhaps our children, whom we reared in the fear of the Lord, have left the church. Or it could be a bout with an incurable disease or a financial setback.

Whatever trial or hardship we encounter, when we agonize about the sad episode our tendency is to focus on the difficulty. We concentrate on the dark side of life. Seemingly, we are overwhelmed with the happenings in our lives or our loved ones' lives, just like the two disciples. We forget that Someone who overcame the world and all the trials hurled by the enemy can aid us. Why do we dwell on the dark side of life? Why do we so easily succumb to the enemy's trap?

Jesus Himself invites us to "come to Me, all you who labor and are heavy laden, and I will give you rest. Take My yoke upon you and learn from Me, for I am gentle and lowly in heart, and you will find rest for your souls. For My yoke is easy and My burden is light" (Matt. 11:28-30, NKJV). O that our eyes may be opened to behold Jesus, who can rescue us from all the vicissitudes of life. Our faith, tested through the crucible of life, may come out victorious because He cares. We may have our lapses, our ups and downs, but thanks be to God, who never gives up on us.

Dear Jesus, help us to trust You, no matter what assails us in this day and age. We know You will carry us through, in spite of all the difficulties we may experience.

OFELIA A. PANGAN

A Seed Planted

As newborn babes, desire the sincere milk of the word, that ye may grow thereby. 1 Peter 2:2.

WHAT A WONDERFUL time spring is with all the varied colored flowers and beautiful new foliage. I can't help thinking of the many seeds that have been planted and the care it takes to produce such beauty.

As I reflect on the beauty I remember the seed that was planted in the small town of Bethel, Pennsylvania. There was a family who held meetings in our town and shared the wonderful message of Jesus with us. They planted the seed, but didn't stop there. They shared themselves and their home with us. As a result, we shared many wonderful times together and learned of and became closer to our Lord.

One of the very special moments was when my brother and I watched our parents being baptized. Several years later my brother gave his heart to the Lord and was baptized. When I was 13 years old I was baptized, and it was a wonderful experience as I stood in the outdoor swimming pool that was filled with the cool mountain water. The day was cool, but the love of Jesus filled my heart and gave me warmth.

The definition of a seed is the start of a new plant—a source from an original. I think of the many times I've tried growing plants from seeds and how many times I've been unsuccessful. Or the times I tried taking care of a plant, and the many times I'd forget to water it—or would overwater it—and the plant would die.

We can plant the seed of God and His love, but it doesn't stop there. I've learned through my walk with God that there must be a constant connection with the original source—Jesus. Yes, Jesus must be the root in our lives, a root that goes deep into the rich soil of His life.

Thank You, Jesus, for the seed that was planted in my life and for the growth I have experienced in knowing You. I need You to be the root of my life, a root that goes so deep and is so strong that nothing can break that connection.

KAREN EDRIS

Don't Be a Fool!

Only fools say in their hearts, "There is no God." . . . The Lord looks down from heaven on the entire human race; he looks to see if there is even one with real understanding, one who seeks for God. Ps. 14:1, 2, NLT.

IN THE UNITED STATES the first day of April is called April Fools' Day, and it's a day when young and old often play practical jokes on each other—from something so simple as "Your shoes are untied" to something as troubling as "I wrecked the car today." No one particularly likes to be thought a fool, but on April Fools' Day, well, they kind of make an exception because things are usually done in fun, and aren't meant to cause harm, humiliation, or anxiety. People take great pains to trick each other, to get someone to believe a crazy prank, to make another person look like a fool. And often they succeed when people unknowingly fall into the trap that's been laid. I'm sure we can all think of at least one trick that was played on us either as a child, or as an adult (on April Fools' Day or any other day), and we might even relish the thought that we had a family member, friend, or coworker believe some ridiculously silly or untrue thing.

So what is a fool? *Webster's* says a fool is "lacking in judgment or prudence; a harmlessly deranged person or one lacking in common powers of understanding." H'mmm. Seems like a fool is someone who just doesn't get it, even when evidence backs it up.

The Bible has given us so much evidence and proof that there is a God, that He rules the universe, and that He cares deeply about each and every one of us. Nevertheless, every day millions of people deny His existence and live in fear, despair, sadness, desperation, helplessness, and hopelessness. For them, life just isn't worth it. They lack good judgment or understanding! Are you one of those people?

"Child," the Master of the universe cries out, "I see you—unhappy, unfulfilled, unknowingly living as though you have nothing to look forward to! And oh, how My heart aches for you. Are you really seeking Me? Do you really understand how very much I love you? My Word is true! It's not a practical joke. I'm here with you! I'm real! Please, don't be a fool! I am your God—today, tomorrow, and always. I am your God. Come to Me and have life eternal."

IRIS L. STOVALL

My Social Butterfly

And endurance develops strength of character in us, and character strengthens our confident expectation of salvation. And this expectation will not disappoint. . . . God . . . has given us the Holy Spirit to fill our hearts with his love. Rom. 5:4, 5, NLT.

SOCIAL BUTTERFLY. THESE words kept resurfacing in my thoughts. This is how Sonny's special-needs teacher recently described him in his communication booklet. My heart is bursting with pride for Sonny, because what was written is true. It's Sonny's time to shine! The road Sonny travels (severe mental retardation with autism) can be so ugly, scary, and cruel.

Sonny has attended the same public school for 12 years. Since day one Jesus was—and still is—uplifted at Sonny's school for His glory, not mine. This mission has been accomplished via inspirational sharing letters. I celebrate life in harmony with those "special days" acknowledged by society as indicated on our calendars. I write and/or find inspirational material to share in the hope of encouraging others to develop a personal relationship with Jesus while there is yet time. Sonny then personally hand-delivers these letters at school. Blessings flow; our sharing territory has increased to include many others who have somehow touched our lives. In hindsight I can see that Jesus has given Sonny and me "the ministry of presence."

We are His witnesses wherever we are. I sincerely believe that we are "chosen vessels." For an Easter gift this year I gave Sonny a briefcase filled with paper, scissors, glue stick, and stickers so that he can continue to make personalized greeting cards, just as we've done together for many years. I'll keep Sonny supplied with inspirational material to share.

God spoke to me through Scripture. I was given my flying orders, which in reality is my personal mission statement: "Today I have given you the choice between life and death, between blessings and curses. I call on heaven and earth to witness the choice you make. Oh, that you would choose life, that you and your descendants might live!" (Deut. 30:19, NLT).

Choose to love the Lord your God and to obey Him and commit yourself to Him, for He is your life. I have no regrets, nor am I ashamed for the way I share, for I'm also a social butterfly. DEBORAH SANDERS

Joy in the Morning

Weeping may endure for a night, but joy cometh in the morning. Ps. 30:5.

I HAD TAKEN A BIG financial leap, and not with my dad's hearty blessing. But he wouldn't interfere. I had bought a lot in town, had blueprints in hand, and had a contractor ready to erect my dream home. My parents had come through the Hungry Thirties and feared their single daughter would not be able to pay off a hefty mortgage by herself. But bless my dad, he helped me pick out the lot.

A short time later I was informed that a major developer was negotiating with the town to build a large shopping mall adjacent to my lot. I wanted out of my contract, and fortunately, the developer wanted my lot for a buffer zone. There would be no problem buying another piece of property, so I sold it to him for a 67 percent profit. I was on cloud nine for days. The extra money would go a long way toward meeting expenses that come with buying a home, such as landscaping and fencing the backyard.

One evening a phone call shattered my excitement. The real estate agent, who had sold me the lot in the first place, demanded a commission on the resale price for reasons that didn't seem logical—he had had no part in the transaction with the developer, but this burly man intimidated me. I didn't have a husband to face this guy man to man, and he knew it. I refused to promise him anything, saying I needed time to think about it and get some advice. I detected his annoyance, bordering on anger, when he hung up. My mouth went dry, and like Belshazzar in Daniel 5:6, the joints of my loins were loosed, and my knees smote one against another.

I couldn't sleep that night. I prayed for help, but the night grew darker and my anxiety mounted. *Is this the beginning of headaches I'll have to face as a homeowner?*

I eventually dozed off and awakened to the sun streaming through my bedroom window. *Where is the gloom of last night?* I couldn't believe the happiness and relaxation I felt. Indeed, it was a good day! I received encouragement from the school board chair, and the real estate agent never called me again. Since then my motto has been "This is the day the Lord has made. I will rejoice and be glad in it" (see Ps. 118:24). EDITH FITCH

Jumping Hurdles

We have courage in God's presence, because we are sure that he hears us if we ask him for anything that is according to his will. 1 John 5:14, TEV.

I AM LIGHT-SKINNED, small-boned, and of early European heritage, which makes me a candidate for osteoporosis. I always thought that was a problem of "other people" until one day I discovered that I was one of the "other people."

One of the things needed for strong bones is exercise. I laugh when I tell people I have plenty of exercise—most of it jumping hurdles. We have four dogs, and my 97-year-old mother-in-law lives with us. She has a heart condition and short-term memory problems. In order to accommodate her needs and those of our dogs, we have walk gates and other gates to ensure that she is safe but that the dogs can still exercise. Rather than take the gates down each time I want to enter or leave a room, I hurdle them.

We encounter many spiritual hurdles as we go through life. There is the hurdle of accepting the sacrifice of Christ for each one of us. There is the hurdle of accepting the life that God plans for each of us. Most people would not plan to lose a mother when they were 5, a stepmother when they were 10, a brother when they were 14, a baby when they were 22, a daughter when they were 46, or a father when they were 47. Yet God permitted me to lose all of them. Nevertheless, I know that He is in charge and will always see me through each hurdle.

The Lord has been good to me in many ways. He has allowed me to do many fun things along with my spiritual hurdles. He allowed me to teach a church-related school for 14 years. I still have contact with some of the students I taught in first and second grades years ago; I cherish their continuing friendship. He allowed me to work in libraries for another 20 years. Part of that work was in a special library for my denomination. I even had the privilege of planning a new library for the world headquarters of the denomination. That was a real fun thing to do.

The Lord has led me in paths I never dreamed possible. My prayer today for you and me is that we will be willing to jump the spiritual hurdles that come our way.   LORAINE F. SWEETLAND

Moving but Going Nowhere

There is a way that seemeth right unto a man; but the end thereof are the ways of death. Prov. 16:25.

EVERY MORNING, WITHOUT fail, a bird flies to my office window, looks at its reflection, and begins hitting its beak against the darkened glass again and again. This task appears to have become its obsession, and it seems so deliberate and determined in its efforts. Again and again, every day; moving but going nowhere.

As I watch this bird I think how ridiculous it is to return to the same spot, do the same thing, and get the same results—essentially nothing. There are darkened windows in our lives that we continue to revisit. We too are deliberate and determined. The task before us has become our obsession.

Again and again, every day, we are moving and going nowhere. We return to the same spot, do the same thing, and get the same results—essentially nothing. We often are living our lives in the comfort zone or in a holding pattern. Waiting. Motionless. Wasting time. Our fears forfeit the blessing we could be to others. God is challenging us to move confidently for Him.

I recently stepped out in faith and moved for my Master. I'd been praying for my coworker Wendy. I felt impressed to ask her about doing a Bible study together. Initially I ignored the impression, fearing I might offend her or feel rejected if she said no. I finally spoke with her and asked her if she would join me in a Bible study. She was elated! She said that she had been wanting more Bible study and a study partner. I kept thinking how close I came to a missed opportunity to move for the Master because of my own fears that could have interfered with my ability to move for Him. Praise the Lord for the courage He gave me to move in obedience to His call! I'm learning that the only way our movement can have meaning and our plans have purpose is to stop moving on our own and listen for God's directions.

"Trust in the Lord with all thine heart; and lean not unto thine own understanding. In all thy ways acknowledge him, and he shall direct thy paths" (Prov. 3:5, 6). Let's commit ourselves to move only at God's leading. We'll finally be moving and going somewhere.   TERRIE RUFF

Sentinels

Be alert, be on watch! Your enemy, the Devil, roams around like a roaring lion, looking for someone to devour. 1 Peter 5:8, TEV.

MY SON, HIS WIFE, and children were visiting from another state. Now on this glorious summer's day, we decided to visit the Monarto Open Range Zoo, situated in a semiarid mallee tree environment east of Adelaide in South Australia. The zoo was created some years ago because of a need for breeding programs for endangered species. Only recently was it opened to the public.

From the safe haven of the tour coach, we enjoyed seeing zebras, Mongolian horses, impalas, a 2½-month-old baby giraffe with its mom, and the spotted shadows on the horizon that were the newly acquired cheetahs.

As we alighted from the coach, our attention was drawn to an enclosure that was encircled by people. We made our way over and were completely fascinated by the colony of meerkats the enclosure held. These tiny animals were a spiritual inspiration. Three sentinels were on duty at strategic points. They seemed to be very still, but close observation showed that their alert and watchful eyes took in every detail in every direction. Not once did they drop their vigilance for an instant. Then I watched as they swapped sentry duty. The new guard ran and sat next to the one on duty, gently touched him, then while both of them remained on alert, they communicated together before the now off-duty meerkat returned to the depths of the earth.

What a lesson for us humans! The meerkats were ever on the lookout for the enemy. They communicated and cooperated together for the best good of the whole colony, much like the experience of the Israelites in Numbers 10. God directed Moses to make trumpets; then He gave instruction for how they were to be used as a warning sound and for the protection of the community. But to be effective, the people had to be totally united with one another and God, just as the meerkats were.

Satan is seeking to devour me in an off-guard moment. Many times I have remembered the colony of meerkats, their alertness and attention to details. I, too, must be alert, on guard, and united with God and my church for the spiritual safety of us all.

MAY SANDY

Multicolored Plant

He hath made his wonderful works to be remembered: the Lord is gracious and full of compassion. Ps. 111:4.

LAST YEAR I PLANTED but two coleuses. They both grew well, and my friends admired them. The plants looked robust and colorful. This spring I planted six of them, three in each pot. They looked healthy for a few days, so I continued to nurture them. When the freezing weather was over, I took them out to the patio for sunlight.

One morning I noticed that one of them was shrinking and drooping. The following day another one looked sick. I watered and fed them. Then a third one looked like it was wilting too. Soon only one of the six was standing tall and firm.

I showed a friend what was happening. "The plant chilled," she said. "It's just too cold for that kind of plant."

I had thought I was a "plant wizard," that I knew all about the plants I had because I had bought, fed, watered, and nurtured them. But now I knew better! I wasn't aware that those plants had been chilled. At first they just looked like they sagged; then they slowly withered, in spite of the food, water, and sunshine they were provided. I had neglected to keep them warm enough. Just a little more attention would have made a difference.

How often do we neglect someone who could have benefited from the full blessing God had intended for them to receive? We either forget or don't put enough effort into making something happen. It saddens my heart to see suffering, especially when I think of my negligence. However, in God's mercy, He gave me a lesson to help me learn of His wisdom and to follow up on His plans.

The Father gave the Son, the best that He could give us. The Son gave all He had, His ultimate, His maximum, love—His own life. He died that we may have life more abundantly.

God, You are so good. Thank You for everything. I pray that You will give me the power to do Your will so that I can do what needs to be done.

ESPERANZA AQUINO MOPERA

A Question of Time

The men of Judah came [to Hebron] and there they anointed David king over the house of Judah. 2 Sam. 2:4.

I'D BEEN ASKED TO speak about time management. Because of this topic I too began to place a greater value on time. I feel as though it's a present from God. I realize that God's time doesn't correspond to our human way of understanding. This leads us to develop patience, faith, meekness, and so many other virtues.

The Bible tells us that before David made any decision he asked the Lord what path he should take. Only after a positive response from God did he "pack up" and go to Hebron, a village in the territory of the tribe of Judah. "And the men of Judah came, and there they anointed David king over the house of Judah." From the time that Samuel anointed David, he waited seven more years until all of Israel anointed him king. David learned to wait on the time of the Lord.

Our generation is "high-speed." People want solutions, by yesterday, and they have difficulty waiting. I'm not referring to those who don't know the Lord, but to those of us who love Him. We want promises fulfilled with dispatch. For this reason many churches exist that promise rapid success, instant service, prosperity now, as if the agreement with God were a business, a deal, a quick transaction at the automatic teller.

The Bible suggests that there is another way. It invites us to enter into the school of God, where we learn to wait patiently for what we still don't see (Rom. 8:25). Invest your time in permanent relationships so that the instant ones don't steal time from the true ones.

Time used for the acquisition of goods is well spent, but better still is the time we devote to Christ in eternal values and permanent blessed relationships. It's time to learn to love and wisely put priorities on God's time. For the things we want, we always find time.

Teach us how to wait on the Lord as David did, respecting and valuing the precious moments with those who are important to us. CASSANDRA MARTINS

Mountains Into Molehills

If you have faith as small as a mustard seed, you can say to this mountain, "Move from here to there" and it will move. Nothing will be impossible for you. Matt. 17:20, NIV.

SEVERAL TIMES A WEEK I would have to drive on a rather formidable stretch of State Route 460 which runs between Princeton, West Virginia, and Bluefield, Virginia. It winds its way around the side of a hill that looks more like a mountain to me. As mountains go, it isn't Mount Everest; the elevation is only 3,000 feet, but it caused me to sit upright and pay attention as I drove along. In the winter it could get rather treacherous, and at night it was somewhat eerie, but I didn't have much choice.

One day I noticed a lot of heavy earth-moving equipment and signs indicating roadwork ahead. *What are they planning on doing?* I wondered.

I rolled down my window and asked one of the men directing the roadwork detour, "What's happening?"

"We're evening out the road," he replied.

"What?" I chuckled, rather surprised.

"We're making the road not as steep, kinda moving a mountain," he quipped.

As I drove away, prompted by the driver behind me, who thought that he had been patient long enough, I shook my head in disbelief. "Never!" I snickered with a know-it-all attitude.

Scoopful by scoopful, they proceeded. There were some days I'd drive by and, except for the irritating traffic flow interruptions, not notice a thing. As time went by I noted the gradual change in the landscape as they worked to level that stretch of roadway. Then one day I came upon that familiar stretch and, amazingly, they had done it!

If construction workers could think to move a mountain, why do I doubt that God can move problems that, real or imagined, appear as mountains in my life? Whether He chooses to eliminate them miraculously in an instant or bit by bit, I know He's able.

Lord, help me to remember this day that You still move mountains. Give me the faith and patience that I need. MAXINE WILLIAMS ALLEN

Kelly

A little child shall lead them. Isa.11:6.

IN THE TYPICAL STYLE of a proud 3-year-old, our young niece, Kelly, ran to the door to meet my husband as he walked into my sister and brother-in-law's home to join us for dinner and an evening visit.

"Uncle Mike, Uncle Mike, look at my owie!" she said, proudly displaying not one but two Band-Aids on her lower left arm, the result of a minor mishap earlier in the day.

Picking her up from the middle of a collection of dolls and teddy bears she'd been playing with and giving the owies the admiration they deserved, Mike responded, "Kelly, would you like to see *my* owies?"

Intrigued with this shift of attention from herself to the idea that adults could have owies too, Kelly climbed down from Uncle Mike's lap as she began a thorough search of his exposed face, arms, and legs to see where these supposed Band-Aids might have been placed.

My husband has been a building contractor for many years, frequently spending several hours a day kneeling as he installs intricately designed ceramic tile floors. As a result he's acquired several layers of rather tough calluses on his knees. It was these calluses to which he was referring rather than a newly acquired cut or scrape, as Kelly was anticipating.

She was duly impressed with these owies, but quickly lost interest as her two big brothers came home, dinner was served, bedtime baths were given, and stories were read. Kelly seemed to have lost all interest in both Uncle Mike and his owies, and the subject had apparently been forgotten.

Just before bedtime, however, I watched as she returned for another quick but silent inspection. Finally, after nighttime prayers had been said, Kelly came out of her bedroom for one last round of good-night hugs and kisses.

Purposefully saving Uncle Mike's hug till last, Kelly, smelling sweetly of scented bubble bath and clad head to toe in fuzzy pink pajamas, sat on the floor in front of Mike, her recent bedtime prayers fresh in her mind as she earnestly studied, then carefully touched, the calluses one last time and asked quietly, "Uncle Mike, is that from praying so much?"

PAULETTA COX JOHNSON

Easter Vacation

"For My thoughts are not your thoughts, nor are your ways My ways," says the Lord. Isa. 55:8, NKJV.

I WANTED TO RETURN TO Washington, D.C., on Easter Monday. The Easter weekend was three weeks away, and I had waited too late to book my flight. I prayed; I called. I prayed, and I called again to get the dates I wanted but to no avail. I even awoke at 2:00 a.m. on several mornings to see if I could get a flight on Thursday and return on Monday. I didn't want to spend any money on extra nights at the hotel. I was disappointed each time I called. I wasn't getting the answer I wanted, so I finally gave up and consoled myself that it wasn't God's will for me to get a flight on Thursday and return on Monday. Suddenly, I was at peace.

I arrived one day earlier at the hotel and checked in. After taking my luggage to my room, I noticed that my hotel key said that I had a complimentary gift at the front desk. I took the elevator downstairs to the lobby, went right over to the front desk, and asked about my complimentary gift. I was given a stress ball, asked a few questions, and asked to complete a survey sheet. The marketing director then told me that the information I'd given had qualified me for a presentation at another facility. She asked if I could spare two hours the following morning to listen to a presentation, informing me that the incentive for my time would be breakfast and a $75 gift certificate that could be applied to my hotel bill. Of course! I needed that money. I quickly told her yes. I had made no plans for that day. Remember, I didn't want to pay for extra nights at the hotel. What an interesting answer to my prayer.

Our text for today came to mind as I returned to my room and thanked God for the answer. When I checked back, the incentive for listening to the presentation was no longer $75.

No, He didn't allow me to get the days I wanted, but He provided the means for me to pay for the extra day. What a mighty God we serve! I am convinced again and again that God has a thousand ways in which He can answer our prayers. I just need to leave the matter to Him.

ANDREA BUSSUE

Changes

I am the Lord, and I do not change. Mal. 3:6, NLT.

I RECENTLY WENT THROUGH a time when life held more changes than I felt able to deal with. Our daughter had recently married, problems had forced us to change our church membership, my husband's parents had come to live with us, and our son was away doing ministry work. That meant we had to set aside our family music ministry.

These changes, along with an early change of life at age 42, became overwhelming, and I began to see these changes as losses. I felt bad for feeling down about my problems when others around me had serious problems of their own, yet I couldn't help how I was feeling. I didn't like these changes; I certainly couldn't control these changes.

Quite by accident I discovered a diversion that made me forget these changes for a few minutes. It was a puzzle called Tetris on my husband's electronic organizer. The computer sends seven geometric shapes in random order, and you manipulate them into rows, trying not to leave holes. I played Tetris as a stress reliever, a challenge, and a time to think about an inanimate problem for just a few minutes.

As I played the game, falteringly at the beginning, I found myself laughing at the circumstances of the puzzle and forgetting those concerns that seemed so big only a few minutes before. Before long, I was able to look ahead to the next piece and place the current piece so the next piece would fit. I learned that the purpose of Tetris is to make the most of the piece the computer sends you.

As I applied this to life I realized that successfully meeting change is making the best of what life hands you. Changes happen whether we like it or not. The mark of success and peace of mind is what we decide to do with change.

Yes, life changes. But, thankfully, we have a God who does not. Even in the midst of our most stressful times we can always depend on Him.

Great God, who changes not, guide and direct me this day. Help me to look ahead to the next piece of my life, placing it according to Your direction.

JUDY MUSGRAVE SHEWMAKE

Walking Where Jesus Walked

Stand at the crossroads and look; ask for the ancient paths, ask where the good way is, and walk in it, and you will find rest for your souls. Jer. 6:16, NIV.

Then Jesus said to his disciples, "If anyone would come after me, he must deny himself and take up his cross and follow me. Matt. 16:24, NIV.

FULTON COLLEGE, SITUATED in Fiji, is a Christian training institution of the South Pacific that provides numerous workers for the mission field. The Fulton family consists of students and staff from 14 island nations of the Pacific. Friday evenings at Fulton College are always a memorable time for any former Fultonian. It's when every member of the college family comes together for song service and vespers. As members of the Fulton family, we make it a point to be at vespers for the fellowship, friendship, and keeping this Fulton tradition alive. Burdens and worries are put aside as we all sing praises to the Lord.

The special song service had ended. A special message was presented from Luke, the story of Jesus' crucifixion. Christ was being led out of the city to Golgotha for His crucifixion. When He could no longer carry His cross, the people seized Simon of Cyrene and "put the cross on him and made him carry it behind Jesus" (Luke 23:26, NIV).

Simon had just returned from the country. He hadn't had much time to do the physical preparation for a typical Friday night vespers, song service, or fellowship. He'd had no time to prepare for the comforts of being in a city. He had followed Jesus and showed pity. As a result, he was seized and forced to share Jesus' load—the cross. The road to Golgotha was out of the city. Out of the comfort zone for spectators. The road Jesus walked. The right road.

I need to come out of that city. To stand on that crossroad of decision and look for the ancient path. To ask where the good path is, the path where Jesus suffered. I must endeavor to walk in it to experience His agony.

Let's pray that the Holy Spirit will influence our thoughts and decisions. To choose to come out of our spectatorship and participate actively in ministry for the Lord. To share one another's burdens as we look forward to that city Jesus has prepared for you and me.   FULORI BOLA

God's Lifeboat

For God so loved the world that he gave his one and only Son, that whoever believes in him shall not perish but have eternal life. John 3:16, NIV.

DESPITE THE LAPSE OF more than 90 years since the event, I found reading about the tragedy of the sinking of the *Titanic* to be an emotionally compelling experience. Not only is the story intensely sad; it's unspeakably frustrating! The outcome could have been so very different—if only.

The list of "if only's" is a long one, but I'll pick out just a few: If only the designs for *Titanic's* hull and watertight compartments had been as good as they were boasted to be. If only the ship had been fitted with sufficient lifeboats for all those on board; and if only lifeboat drills had been held for both passengers and crew. If only the ship's officers had taken more notice of the ice warnings and proceeded more cautiously. If only the radio operator of the nearby *Californian* had remained on duty just a little longer and had heard *Titanic's* distress signals. The list goes on.

The most haunting circumstance for me, however, is the fact that all but one of the lifeboats had rowed away from the ship with empty seats for fear of suction pulling them under as the *Titanic* sank. They refused to return to the aid of those in the water for fear of being swamped. The lifeboat passengers could hear the cries of the dying but did nothing to help.

The story set me to wondering. Could history repeat itself on a much grander scale? God's Word warns us that Planet Titanic is on course for disaster. The good news is that there is space in God's lifeboat of salvation for everyone who chooses Him—but people need to know that! It can be tempting to sit by silently while others struggle in the waves of ignorance or sin. I need to be constantly calling out words of hope and encouragement, proclaiming that rescue is at hand. I need to be always ready to reach out in love to help a weary swimmer into the boat.

Dear Lord, let me never forget that You died to bring salvation to everyone. Help me to be a voice of hope, a hand of love, to someone else today.

JENNIFER M. BALDWIN

Childlike Trust

Pray one for another, that ye may be healed. James 5:16.

I VISITED IVANI, A lady from the city of Americana, who was a Radio Novo Tempo listener. I didn't know her personally, but I was familiar with her handwriting and her voice because of her letters and her voice on the telephone.

I presented a daily radio program on prayer and committed myself to praying regularly at 5:30 a.m. for my listeners who requested it. I had a notebook full of names; Ivani was one of them.

While we talked, she told me how much she suffered with her illness, at times at home, at times in the hospital. She also told me of the nights without sleep, when her pain kept her awake. During these nights she got up from her bed and went into another room, where she prayed and cried in silence so she wouldn't awaken her husband. Then, suddenly, she made a surprising statement to me: "After I spend the whole night awake, as day begins to dawn about 5:00 I lie down and sleep peacefully because I know that you are praying for me."

At that moment I felt affirmed and amazed. She believed in the effectiveness of my prayers!

The apostle James commands us to pray one for another, but I'd never been able to understand the reach and influence of these prayers. In fact, I'd imagined that the value of intercessory prayer was to produce in me empathy for those who suffer. I also thought that this type of prayer helped us to celebrate together prayers that had been answered. As I saw prayers being answered in favor of my brothers and sisters, I thought this contributed to greater development and strengthening of my faith.

Prayer is a fantastic means from God for my direct communication with His throne of grace! If I can trust that He hears me, just as Ivani believed that I prayed for her, if I can believe that the Holy Spirit intercedes for me today, if I can believe that Jesus is more willing to give to me than I can imagine, all the treasures of heaven can be mine!

Help me, Lord, to have faith as simple as that of Ivani. Faith that doesn't need proof but that believes in Your Word and in Your promises!

SÔNIA RIGOLI SANTOS

My Assurance of the Iris

Now glory be to God who by his mighty power at work within us is able to do far more than we would ever dare to ask or even dream of—infinitely beyond our highest prayers, desires, thoughts, or hopes. Eph. 3:20, TLB.

LYING IN BED EARLY one morning, I had little energy and was in a great deal of pain. Some worrying concerns were tossing back and forth in my mind as I glanced toward the bay window. Suddenly I spied the brave spore of an iris with its unfolding bud of deep-purple beauty. I remember planting that iris a few months before, and now the vibrant color of the promised flower brings a surge of joy to my heart.

The brilliance and beauty of the flower mesmerize me, impressing me that the Creator God can make my life full of beauty and allow me to reach skyward like this iris. The euphoria of this gift of God's love carries me through many days.

Then a new morning dawns. As I look again at the symbol of hope and happiness, I'm distressed to see that the purple petals of the iris are turning brown, crumpling and shrinking. How I mourn the loss! While I know the flowers don't last forever in this sin-struck world, my heart longs for the assurance of the miracle of confidence and joy that the iris first brought.

The next day I walk over to the window, saddened at the passing of my beautiful gift. But what is this? Below the shriveled flower are two more flowers in full bloom, their petals glorious banners moving gracefully in the breeze. How I thrill at God's extravagant love for me! While I'd been sad about losing things I treasure, God had planned and delivered multiple new joys!

Days pass. Now, however, I know better than to mourn for my lost flowers. As I look expectantly lower down the stem of the plant, I see with delight that the plant has produced four more irises! Here are exponentially expanding blessings!

Dear Father, I am awed by how You overwhelm me with tokens of Your love, Your assurance, and Your eternal promise of everlasting care. How can I ever be discouraged or doubt, when I am surrounded with symbols of beauty from the Creator's hand? Please recreate me to reflect the beauty and attractiveness of Your love. And thank You.   URSULA M. HEDGES

An Encounter in Spring

Anxiety weighs down the human heart, but a good word cheers it up. Prov. 12:25, NRSV.

IT WAS ONE OF those beautiful spring mornings. The sun was shining, and the birds were singing. I had to go to the shop to get some things for lunch, so I chose to walk through a little green park across the road from our house.

Nobody was around, but as I turned around a corner I saw a woman who was crouching to pick green grass and dandelion leaves for some hungry pet. When she stood up again, I recognized her. It was Mrs. S. She lives not far from our house, on the other side of the street, and is a patient of one of the doctors I work for.

"Good morning, Mrs. S!" I called to her.

We had a short, friendly conversation about the lovely morning and the turtles for whom she had been picking the fresh greens. In the middle of the conversation she suddenly asked, "How can you be so friendly and balanced? You are always so radiant when we meet."

I was a bit stunned at her question and considered a few seconds what I should answer. Then I said, "You know, Mrs. S, maybe it's because I'm a Christian."

"Yes, maybe" was her prompt reply.

Then I told her about my church. She knew where it is, because her daughter lives just down the street from our church.

We often long for a chance to share our faith and to tell others about You, Father—even pray for the opportunity, asking You to send someone. I pray that my life is a constant witness to others. I hope that this experience will help me to be ready to share my faith whenever there's an opportunity. I want to take advantage of every occasion to let You use me to tell others about Your love. May You continue to give each of us a friendly and balanced attitude so that You, Lord, can use us.   GUNDULA ZAHALKA

What a Difference a Day Makes

Since God chose you to be the holy people whom he loves, you must clothe yourselves with tenderhearted mercy, kindness, humility, gentleness, and patience. Col. 3:12, NLT.

MY LIFE WAS IN chaos. I had no job and was living with one of my children on a temporary basis. My body was racked with pain, and I had been told it would probably take months before it would subside. My father and I had bonded during his last six months of life more closely than ever before. This only made my grief more intense following his memorial service.

I was in God's waiting room, listening for His voice in spite of my physical and emotional pain. I longed for Him to tell me which way I should go. I kept reaching up for His victorious right hand to give me courage and strength. He tells me, "So do not fear, for I am with you; do not be dismayed, for I am your God. I will strengthen you and help you" (Isa. 41:10, NIV). But so often God's hand seemed just out of reach.

It was a beautiful, clear day, but my mind was anything but clear. In a troubled state, I drove across a very lengthy toll bridge. To my horror, as the tollbooth loomed into view I rolled up and hit the car in front of me. *Now I've really messed up,* I thought. *That woman will jump out of her car, come back to assess the damage, and undoubtedly give me a piece of her mind.*

What a relief when she moved on through the gate and out on the freeway. Then came one of the most rewarding surprises of my life. As I handed my dollar to the toll taker, he smiled and said, "Your toll has already been paid."

At that moment I felt I had been touched by God's right hand. He did care about me and my future. He impressed that kind, tenderhearted woman in front of me to change my outlook by her random act of kindness.

Dear Jesus, give me wisdom to reach out to hurting people around me. Clothe me with Your attributes of kindness, patience, and love. Show me how to change the day for anyone who is struggling, just as my unknown benefactor did for me.   DONNA LEE SHARP

On Folding Clothes

Then Simon Peter . . . arrived and went into the tomb. He saw the strips of linen lying there, as well as the burial cloth that had been around Jesus' head. The cloth was folded up by itself, separate from the linen. John 20:6, 7, NIV.

WHAT WAS JESUS thinking as He folded the graveclothes on Resurrection morning? He didn't have to fold the burial cloth that had covered His face or the linen strips that had bound His body—the angels would have willingly done this for Him. When we fold clothing or bedding, it's because it is clean and ready to be used again. Jesus' graveclothes would have been blood-stained and dirty. Why fold them? He would never need them again.

I like to think Jesus paused to fold the graveclothes while rejoicing that through His death and resurrection such signs of death were now only temporary, already superseded. He paused before going out into the world that would never be the same again, though its inhabitants didn't know it yet. He paused before going to His Father and before looking for His sad and bewildered disciples. He paused to fold the symbols of humanity's fall and redemption.

Truly,

"Thine is the glory, risen, conquering Son;
  Endless is the victory Thou o'er death hast won.
  Angels in bright raiment rolled the stone away,
  Kept the folded grave clothes where Thy body lay.
  Thine is the glory, risen, conquering Son;
  Endless is the victory Thou o'er death hast won."

—Edmond Budry, 1884

One writer says, "It was the Savior's hand that folded each [of the grave cloths], and laid it in its place. In His sight who guides alike the star and the atom, there is nothing unimportant" (Ellen White, *The Desire of Ages*, p. 789).

Not even folding clothes. Gwen Pascoe

The Picture

We know that God will make everything that happens to us in this life come out to our eventual good, as long as we trust Him and remain true to the purpose for which He called us. Rom. 8:28, Clear Word.

HIS BRUSH STROKES WERE swift and sure as the artist began his work on the canvas in front of him. The palette he held in his hand contained many colors. He loaded his brushes with the wet paint that he used generously. My family and I watched in fascination as, little by little, the picture unfolded. At the top of the canvas he applied not blue, as we expected, but rosy red with some touches of brown.

"What do you suppose he's doing?" we questioned one another.

"Just watch and see" was the only reply we knew to give.

Soon some mountain peaks appeared, then trees and bushes materialized at their base along the shoreline of a river. As he applied the strokes to make the river, we could see that the color of the river was a reflection of the sky. The finished product was breathtakingly beautiful.

But what caused the beauty? There was no blue in the sky or the river. It was then I realized it was the clouds with their pink hues tinted with brown that made the picture so outstanding.

When my day starts out with beautiful blue skies and everything is going smoothly, I'm happy. Then a problem comes up, a cloud of sorts, and my day is changed. However, I can choose to look on the bright side, to search the promises of God to find a solution to the problem. Sometimes a friend's encouraging words may change the dark problem cloud and give it a tinge of pink.

Father God, help me today to look for the bright side of the cloud, to help others with their problem clouds, and to reflect the colors of love back to others. I need to remember that the most beautiful sunsets come at the end of a cloudy day.

BETTY J. ADAMS

Buried Under the Blood

Casting all your care upon him; for he careth for you. 1 Peter 5:7.

THERE IS A STORY set during World War II of a woman who has taught me to cast my burden on the Lord.

At night when bombs were falling and sirens wailing, people rushed into the basement shelter. There in the shelter was this woman with her pillows. As soon as she got to the basement, she put her pillows down in a corner and went right to sleep. Night after night, while others were worried and fidgety, this woman slept peacefully. There was a peace about her that passed the understanding of those around her.

One night one of her neighbors couldn't help asking her how she always managed to sleep every night, in spite of the noise and fear that surrounded her. She answered by referring to Psalm 121:4: "Behold, he that keepeth Israel shall neither slumber nor sleep." She said that if God was watching—and she believed He was—why should two people be keeping watch when only one needed to do so?

If I believe the words of the Scripture, then I should never negate what God has clearly stated.

A man was carrying a heavy load, trekking home, when a truck pulled up to offer him a lift. The driver of the truck knew the man, so he made him comfortable in the back of the truck. As he got back in the driver's seat and started the engine, he looked in the side mirror and was surprised to see the man was still carrying his load. He continued to carry his load until he got to his destination.

Before the man left, the driver asked him why he was carrying his load, even when he was already in the vehicle and was no longer walking. The man answered that he didn't want to make the vehicle carry the extra load.

How ignorant, you may say. But how many times do we continue to carry our burdens when they are supposed to be buried underneath the blood at the cross at Calvary?

BECKY DADA

The Day That Changed My Life

The Spirit of the Lord will come upon you in power, and you will prophesy with them; and you will be changed into a different person. 1 Sam. 10:6, NIV.

MY HUSBAND HAD BEEN sick for two days, and I desperately needed his help on the computer. He told me to bring my laptop, and he would help me from his sick bed. Our conversation was interrupted by a phone call from his best friend, so I wandered off.

Within minutes my husband's friend was at our front door, explaining that he was rushing Harry to the hospital. "Why?" I asked in confusion.

"I suspect by our phone conversation that he's had a stroke," he replied hastily.

The next five days passed in a blur as I visited my husband in the hospital, where he was hooked up to monitors and endless tubes and wires. Five days later he was home, his left side still affected. He couldn't dress himself or walk without the aid of a walker.

What were we going to do to rehabilitate him? Friends and family had endless suggestions. Soon Harry entered a lifestyle rehabilitation program with me as a companion. His exercise therapist revealed that he was expected to walk every day.

"You've got your work cut out for you," I quipped to the therapist. "He argues about walking around the block when he could drive around it!" His carotid artery was measured by ultrasound, and I learned that he had the arteries of a man 130 years old. "Doctor," I exclaimed, "I'm married to a dead man!"

"If he walks several miles daily and switches to a vegan diet, he'll have a second chance at life," the doctor explained. They expected me to learn how to cook vegan-style, using no animal products or oil.

Eleven months later both Harry and I have proved to ourselves and others that change is possible. He has lost 50 pounds and walks two or three miles faithfully every day, and I prepare three vegan meals daily.

What about you? Are there some changes you need to make in your life? Are you putting it off because you think that you can't do it, or that it's too difficult, or that the time isn't right? My prayer for you today is that you'll relinquish your will to God and let Him do for you what you think you're too weak to accomplish.   NANCY L. VAN PELT

Out of the Mouth of Babes

And that, knowing the time, that now it is high time to awake out of sleep: for now is our salvation nearer than when we believed. Rom. 13:11.

DURING A SABBATH WORSHIP service in our church in Charlotte, North Carolina, the elder assigned to lead the morning prayer asked the congregation to kneel and join him in a season of silent prayer. As everyone in the pews began kneeling, I decided to remain seated to avoid disturbing Riley, my 2-year-old granddaughter, who was comfortably snuggled in my lap with her eyes closed and her favorite pink pacifier in her mouth.

All went well for a few seconds. Then the sudden absence of sound in the sanctuary as the congregation prayed silently caused her little eyes to snap open in puzzlement. She listened intently for a moment. Then, in the continuing stillness, she sat bolt upright. For several moments she gazed at the people whose heads were bowed and eyes closed. Then, jerking the pacifier out of her mouth, she startled everyone around us by yelling at the top of her lungs, "WAKE UP!"

Riley was confused by the unexpected laughter of the worshiping saints. Looking up at me, she innocently asked, "Why is everybody laughing at me?"

I hugged her to muffle my own giggles and said, "They're laughing because you just preached the best sermon I've ever heard. And *you* did it in just two words!"

Riley's advice is biblical, you know. You'll find it in Romans 13:11: "And that, knowing the time, that now it is high time to awake out of sleep: for now is our salvation nearer than when we believed." Jesus is coming soon. The signs are all around us. The world is in turmoil. The celestial clock is ticking the final countdown of the ages. This is not the time to be spiritually lethargic and apathetic! It's not the time to have our spiritual eyes closed. Jesus is coming very soon. And sometime when we least expect it, out of the mouth of a babe and straight to our hearts comes a vital message: "WAKE UP!"

Thank you, Riley. And thank You, Jesus. We are so glad Your coming is near.

ELLIE GREEN

The Mourning Card

Do not judge, or you too will be judged. Matt. 7:1, NIV.

WE ARRIVED HOME FROM a weekend visit, tired and exhausted. In our mailbox was a card with a black mourning border. We looked at each other with questioning eyes; both of us had a presentiment as to who might have died. During our trip we had tried to reach our old friend several times by cell phone, but each time we only reached his answering machine. My husband opened the envelope. Yes, it was he!

Old memories flooded my mind as if they had happened only yesterday. I didn't have to search for memories; images just came up: My daughter's first day in high school. His friendly welcome as principal. The kindness and warmth he radiated. His personal way of dealing with the young people entrusted to him. He called them his "buttons." He understood their little sorrows. He took them seriously. And we parents were simply spellbound.

He had suffered personal tragedies during the past few years. He wasn't the same anymore. He was a broken man with a big vacuum in his life.

Suddenly I broke down in tears. My husband tried to calm me. But the more he tried to soothe me, the worse I felt. I was shaking. My insides were freezing, and my heart would not work as usual. My friend had been a convinced humanist. I had spoken to him on the telephone six months earlier. We'd been talking about this and that when suddenly he wanted to speak about Jesus. He wanted to convince me that my Jesus is just a lot of nonsense. He couldn't believe in that rubbish. This last conversation filled my mind. The unerasable mourning border seemed to constrict my heart. Now he had really died. A second time. Without hope of resurrection in Christ.

But did I know his last days, hours, and seconds before his death? Did I have a right to know them? They were hidden from me. Only my heavenly Father, who can see into the hidden, knows each heart. I became calmer. I laid my heart into the hands of Jesus and fell into His arms.

Lord Jesus, only You really knew my friend or knew his problems. You shed Your blood for him. You are the gracious and just judge. Thank You for Your love and kindness. Even today.   CHRISTEL MEY

Orange Blossoms

His great faithfulness is new every morning, as refreshing as the dew and as sure as the sunrise. Lam. 3:23, Clear Word.

THEY WERE NOT THERE yesterday, but this morning they are out in perfusion. Marigold centers cupped in milky white, delicate petals. Their fragrance mingled with the crisp morning air. Tiny white flowers adorned the orange trees. The days that followed were fascinating.

Slowly the tiny white petals fell off, leaving small green studs and, eventually, miniature oranges. It's interesting how we welcome oranges but rarely think of the blossoms that prepare the way for the succulent fruit we enjoy so much.

Our lives are like those blossoms. The orange blossoms signify new beginnings—a new day, a new month, a new year, and new opportunities. Each new day affords us the opportunity to begin again with God. He grants us enough time to do the things that were not accomplished the day before. Time to restore a damaged relationship. Time to mend a broken heart. Time to ask forgiveness.

I'm reminded of the opportunity I have each new day to start over again. The old fruits of yesterday are gone—the mistakes, the wrong decisions, the ills and hurts, leaving me today with a new chance to begin again with God.

Orange blossoms remind me of the day when this earth will shed sin. There will be renewal after the devastation of sin. The old fruits of this world will be renewed with the freshness of a new era, fresh and sweet as the orange blossoms.

In the words of the songwriter: "New every morning is the love our wakening and uprising prove; through sleep and darkness safely brought, restored to life and power and thought. New mercies, each returning day . . . ; new perils past, new sins forgiven, new thoughts of God, new hopes of heaven."

Dear Father, thank You for taking away the ills of yesterday. Thank You for a brand-new start today. Thank You for the courage to face today knowing that I need not face any challenge without You by my side.

GLORIA GREGORY

Flying Roaches

Turn to me and be saved, all the ends of the earth! For I am God, and there is no other. Isa. 45:22, RSV.

MANY YEARS AGO MY husband and I were transferred to a new town and began the task of finding a place that was large enough for our growing family of three kids and two dogs to call home. The town's population was only 2,100, and there were no three-bedroom apartments or houses available. After much inquiry and negotiations we were able to rent a lovely old house and proceeded to move in. It had been vacant for some time, as the owner was an elderly lady who had moved into a nursing home. The house had beautiful wooden floors and 12-foot ceilings. The kitchen was huge, with a lovely bay window and a walk-in pantry. I was delighted and thought my dream had come true.

Our second day there I started discovering some unpleasant things about the house. It was home to creatures I detest—flying roaches! It seemed that the walls had so many layers of old glue and wallpaper that the roaches thought it was a perfect place to call home. They could eat the glue and be protected from intruders by the wallpaper. I learned that before I opened a door or drawer it was best to make a lot of noise, stamping my feet and banging on the door. That way the roaches would scatter, and I could avoid a confrontation. All our food had to be stored in plastic containers with lids, and all the eating utensils, pots and pans, and dishes had to be washed before they could be used, even if they appeared clean.

One night I was talking on the telephone when a roach came flying right at me. I screamed and ducked as it whizzed past my face. Needless to say, as soon as we found other housing, we gave our notice and moved.

The roaches we found in that lovely old house remind me that this world may look attractive, but in the end it is full of roaches. May we each determine by the grace of God to run from evil, trying to avoid it, as I did the roaches. And may we remember that God always has something better for us than the world can offer.

CELIA MEJIA CRUZ

Through a Glass, Darkly

For now we see through a glass, darkly; but then face to face. 1 Cor. 13:12.

I'D HAD SURGERY ON my right eye. My cloudy lens had been removed, and a new artificial lens had been put in the eye. For the rest of that day I had to wear sunglasses all the time, even when in the house. When I could do without those glasses, I found that the colors of the flowers on my window shelf were so much brighter when seen with my operated-on eye than with the other eye. I could see almost as well without eyeglasses at all with my right eye as I could with a strong lens for my left eye. I was delighted.

Then it happened. Quite suddenly my eye was painful, and the vision clouded over. I was worse off than before the operation, because "the cloud" was now in my cornea, the front part of the eye, and I was aware of it whenever my eye was open. Over the next seven weeks I saw a corneal specialist and had intense medical treatment, but the vision deteriorated. I considered giving up women's ministries because driving was difficult. We were planning to go to Nepal as relief physicians for two months. How would I cope with that?

I was told by the corneal specialist that this would almost certainly be permanent and that a corneal-transplant operation would be necessary to restore vision in that eye. It was during this time that I really appreciated vision and the gift that it is.

I became very discouraged, but my family, friends, and church family prayed for me. Then as suddenly as the cloud had come, it left.

I was humbled that God would answer prayers for my one eye when there are so many with worse vision in both eyes. I was very grateful that I was not now seeing as "through a glass, darkly."

The experience reminded me of that verse in 1 Corinthians 13:12 and how our view of heaven is like looking through a clouded glass, but one day we will see Him "face to face." One day the flowers will be brighter in color; there will be no more sickness or dying or terror, and we will understand and see clearly why things have happened to us here in this life. But the greatest result of our transformed bodies will be that we will be able to see Jesus face to face.

Come soon, Lord Jesus. I long for that day.   RUTH LENNOX

Weeds or Beauty?

And the earth brought forth grass, the herb that yields seed according to its kind, and the tree that yields fruit, whose seed is in itself according to its kind. And God saw that it was good. Gen. 1:12, NKJV.

I'VE ALWAYS HATED DANDELIONS. Well, maybe not always. I can remember being a kid and having fun blowing the puffs of seeds into the air. But certainly I've detested those weeds ever since I've had a lawn to care for. They're hard to get rid of. If you've ever tried to pull one up by the roots, you'll understand what I'm talking about. And besides, they're ugly.

Or are they?

We moved to northern New Hampshire in late winter. By the end of April the snow was about gone and the wildflowers made an appearance. How pretty they looked, like a carpet on the hillsides. Then I discovered that most of the wildflowers I had admired from a distance were dandelions. And they were starting to make an appearance in our yard. My 5-year-old son loved them and picked me bouquet after bouquet of the yellow flowers.

During the first week in May we went on vacation for a week. It was dark when we got back. The first thing my young son did the next morning was to look out his bedroom window. He was beside himself at the sight that greeted him. So was I! I hadn't realized that so many dandelions could grow in such a small space. But as I watched my son staring out the window in awe, mentally going over his bouquet list, I began to wonder if I hadn't been too harsh. After all, roses have thorns, yet they're a prized garden plant. I wouldn't dream of getting rid of my roses simply because one pricked my finger. I had learned to work around the unpleasantness and see only the beauty. I began to see dandelions through a child's eyes again.

Suddenly it became about more than just weeds and flowers. How many times do I harshly plan to remove someone who gets in the way of my idea of a perfect picture? Perhaps that person is just the one to add the final touch of beauty I was looking for all along. Jesus said that we should be as little children if we want to get into the kingdom of heaven. I guess that means looking for beauty, even the weeds.

Dear Lord, please take me back to the days when my eyes were untouched by cynicism, when I could look at Your creation and say with You, "It is good."

RACHEL ATWOOD

Sing the Clouds Away

Sing aloud unto God our strength: Make a joyful noise unto the God of Jacob. Ps. 81:1.

TODAY'S TEXT SEEMS TO tell me not only to sing to myself but to sing loudly. And in case we don't know how to sing (for there are people who can't carry a tune), then we should make a joyful noise unto the Lord. Why not? The Lord will know that you're praising Him, and He will be pleased.

Have you ever seen sad birds? No! They always sing from morning until they go to bed. In fact, they wake up before we do and begin to sing. It's not that they don't have problems. They face danger every day. They live out in the open in all kinds of weather, and they have to hunt for food every day. Have you ever watched a magpie robin? Here in India it usually perches in its favorite treetop or post, and from there it sings lustily. It's also a very good mimic of other birds' calls, even trying to imitate the music coming from your window.

When we were small we learned the song, "Sing the clouds away, night will turn to day; if we sing and sing and sing, we'll sing the clouds away." As we grow older we seem to forget to sing these beautiful songs. David says in Psalm 33:3, "Sing unto him a new song." Yes, as we meet new victories we should have new songs to sing.

My mother had taught us early to sing, as she was a lover of music. As a young girl, I would go about my home duties singing. I seemed to accomplish more when I sang while working. Very often while my mother was making garments she would join me, singing the same song. Many times we sang in parts while working. Work became a pleasure when we sang.

Jehoshaphat led his army in singing. Imagine singing at such a time as this. Jehoshaphat defeated the Ammonites and Moabites with songs of praise to God. Deborah sang songs of victory, and so did Miriam. Hezekiah and his people sang praises over the repaired Temple. David sang songs of praise his entire life, which proves a great blessing to us now.

We, too, shall be overcomers through songs of praise, believing He will help us even while we are facing the enemy. Only as we learn to praise Him now shall we get to join the great company singing the Song of Moses and the Lamb (Rev. 15:3).   BIRDIE PODDAR

You Are With Me

Even though I walk through the valley of the shadow of death, I will fear no evil. Ps. 23:4, NIV.

M Y FATHER SUFFERED A massive heart attack and remained in a coma for many, many months before he died. It was a very painful experience for my three brothers and me to see how his body declined more and more from one visit to the next. Often I would stand by his bed and think of the twenty-third psalm.

We meet suffering in so many forms and are always touched by it, particularly when it reaches the boundaries of life and death. David knew what he was talking about in this psalm. He was being chased by Saul, and at the precipice of death he often experienced God's saving hand.

Why was David able to say, "I will fear no evil"? Did he think of the God who had said to Moses, "Do not be afraid, for I am with you" (Gen. 26:24, NIV)? Our paths on this earth are not only bathed in pure sunshine; we also have to cross dark ravines and valleys, where we will experience fear and pain. These dangers are very real and not easily overcome.

There is but one thing that will give peace to our hearts, and that is the presence of Jesus our Shepherd. "For you are with me; your rod and your staff, they comfort me" (Ps. 23:4, NIV). Jesus our Shepherd, God with us, brings us God's presence. He lifts His rod up as a sign of authority. We belong to Him, and He will drive away the enemy with His rod.

The shepherd's rod is like Jesus' parting words of comfort: "All authority in heaven and earth has been given to me" (Matt. 28:18, NIV). The Christian who accepts God's leading in their life knows that they can trust in God, even in the border situations of life.

My daddy found peace and rest in God, and we can look forward to the wonderful promise found in John 14:27, 28: "Do not let your hearts be troubled and do not be afraid. You have heard me say, 'I am going away and I am coming back to you.' If you loved me, you would be glad."

Do you love Jesus? Then you can say with David, "I will fear no evil, for you are with me" (Ps. 23:4, NIV).   INGRID NAUMANN

The Arum Lily

[She] shall grow like the lily. Hosea 14:5, NKJV.

THE BEAUTY OF THE arum lily has always attracted me. It grows in dirty, muddy soil but gives a tall, white bloom. Scientifically named *Zantedeschia aethiopica,* it's a fleshy-rooted, bulbous plant with arrow-shaped leaves. Flowers consist of a decorative spathe surrounding a bright-yellow spadix. Flowering times depend on rainfall region. For best growing conditions, it needs a sunny location (with light shade in hot inland areas) in rich, well-composted, moist soil. You have to water it well during the growing season, and it must not be allowed to dry out during its dormant period either. They grow from 14 to 60 inches (35 to 150 centimeters) tall. Arum lilies can be found mainly in the southwestern Cape of South Africa.

I have some arum lily plants at the entrance to our house. Some have withered away because we had very little rain this winter. Because of water restrictions, I've had to keep these plants moist with used water from the kitchen. A few weeks back we had a refreshing downpour of rain overnight. This worked wonders for my withering arum lily plants. Before long, I noticed a bud pushing up. I gave it extra water and watched it daily until it bloomed into a very large and beautiful flower. How I admired it—so tall, upright, and white.

Then one day I was horrified when I came to admire my one and only precious arum lily. It had a large, black deposit on it, dropped by a passing bird! I tried to clean it from the defilement, but the stain was a stubborn one. How my heart ached!

I thought of my heavenly Father, who has given me a spotless white robe to wear (Rev. 19:8). I must try to keep it from becoming stained by sin. Although I live in the mud of this sin-cursed world, I want to be like the arum lily, pure and white.

"What good could come out of Nazareth?" (John 1:46) Nathanael asked; but Jesus grew up in Nazareth. He is our perfect example. He will help us to have a good character.

I don't want any deposits from Satan to defile and ruin the beautiful white robe You have given me. Help me to stay pure and clean like the arum lily, even though I live in the mud of sin, and to grow each day, as Jesus did in Nazareth.

PRISCILLA ADONIS

Slow Down

Do you now know that in a race all the runners run, but only one gets the prize? Run in such a way as to get the prize. 1 Cor. 9:24, NIV.

TWO CARS. ONE DESTINATION. One driver takes the smooth highway, the high road, while the other takes the proverbial low road—a stony shortcut. This is a weekly race between fellow coworkers, Randi and Brad, as they leave the office. When they reach their mutual destination, usually in close succession, one is the dejected loser for the day, while the winning driver grins. (We find creative forms of amusement in our small town.)

Unaware of my coworkers' ritual, I caught a ride one day with Randi. I wondered why Randi and Brad seemed to be in such a hurry to get to their cars, but it became plain to me what was happening when Brad sped by us, and Randi turned down the gravel "road less traveled." As she put the pedal to the metal I forced myself to relax so I could enjoy my last few moments alive. With eyes wide and brows determined, we laughed between moments of terror as we tackled each twist and turn of the road.

Suddenly we stopped laughing.

A truck pulled out onto the rocky, one lane road, drastically slowing us down and ruining our chances of winning the race. Although sad that we would not be arriving first, I was relieved that my life was no longer flashing before my eyes.

Our frowns turned back to smiles at the sight of a beautiful deer scurrying across the road about 100 feet in front of the truck. After the deer dashed out of sight and the dust around our halted car had settled, we were humbled by what had happened. God, whose timing is always perfect, used a big red pickup truck to slow us down so we could see and, more importantly, avoid hitting a beautiful deer. We were awestruck. Time seemed to stand still. The truck driver was totally unaware of how God had used him. We won't know until we get to heaven how often God has placed us on someone's rocky road or painful path to bring a blessing or help avoid disaster.

Have you ever grumbled under your breath when something doesn't go exactly as you planned? Randi and I had a race to win—but God had a better plan. So we won in a different way. If we learn to slow down and trust God, we can all win this race called life. CLARISSA MARSHALL

God's Creation

And God saw every thing that he had made, and, behold, it was very good.
Gen. 1:31.

THERE ARE SO MANY beautiful things God created. What a multitude of colors, shapes, and perfumes! I love the sunlight and the moonlight, the heavenly bodies that govern our night and day. And what woman doesn't love flowers? I never fail to be in awe of what beauty there is to be seen in sunsets and sunrises.

I drive over a two-mile-long (three-kilometer-long) bridge every day going to and from work. The bridge connects a heavily populated peninsula to the mainland. This is a time that's so special to me as I observe the splendor of the sky. The water of the bay adds to the beauty of the picture.

The sunrises are so lovely—sometimes pale-pink fluffy clouds float around the early-morning sun; sometimes large white majestic clouds fill the eastern sky; and sometimes it's just the golden sun, rising in a clear blue sky. Like snowflakes, no two sunrises are the same.

And in the evening the sunsets are just as spectacular. Sometimes the sky seems to be on fire with red clouds that look like a ball of fire behind distant hills, reflecting in the water. Sometimes the clouds are tinged with a gold of such brilliance that no artist could ever capture the color with paints.

There are calm days when the bay is like a millpond. Then come stormy days when the sun hides behind great gray clouds, reflected in an equally gray sea. The wind whips up the waves with whitecaps that are visible for miles.

One afternoon a storm raged around me. I drove onto the bridge with some trepidation as the wind and rain were ferocious. But God heard my prayer for His safekeeping, and as I drove over I felt cocooned in His love. There was a patch of sunlight surrounding me as the sun peeped through the dark clouds that stayed with me for the entire two miles.

A real bonus is crossing the bridge at nighttime. If the moon is just rising in a clear sky, it casts a silvery path across the sea. Yes, there is so much beauty in God's creation—it is very, very good. Give God the praise as you, too, enjoy it.

LEONIE DONALD

Who Is the Greatest?

I tell you the truth, unless you change and become like little children, you will never enter the kingdom of heaven. Matt. 18:3, NIV.

A S PEOPLE AROUND THE United States celebrate Asian Pacific week in May, my thoughts reflect on how I landed in the U.S. and what I've accomplished as a Christian. In 1988 I embarked upon a scary journey of seeking education in the "land of milk and honey." I enjoyed the freedoms and the luxuries of the Western world, the bubble baths and candlelit dinners. At the same time, I noted the nation's high crime rate, teenage pregnancy, and missing children. Without realizing it, I froze into a state of inaction—I became a nominal Christian. I didn't think I could do much among the talented, educated, and affluent.

It has taken me a while to realize that in a world of 6 billion there is no one like me—my fingerprints, my story, and my experiences are unique. And God's people, whether White, Brown, Yellow, or Black, all experience the same discouragements, hurts, and temptations in this world of sin and pain.

Matthew 18 tells the story of the disciples asking Jesus, "Who is the greatest in the kingdom of heaven?" (verse 1). Who is the greatest among us? It has nothing to do with ethnicity. Jesus responded, "Unless you change and become like little children, you will never enter the kingdom of heaven" (verse 3). I've learned so much from my own children: honesty, faith, and acceptance. My kids can strike up a conversation with a total stranger at the playground, and pretty soon they're playing together; they see no color. Another boy simply means someone to kick ball with. No wonder Jesus made reference to children!

In the end it doesn't matter that I'm an Asian living in a Western culture. I don't have a tag that says I'm made in Malaysia, but I want a tag that says I'm a Christian, a Christian with the same goals as my African, Mexican, or Irish brothers and sisters.

It doesn't matter to my Christian family that we're so diverse. I rather like that! I used to say I hope we have spring rolls in heaven. Now I want spring rolls and burritos. As Christians, we have a job to do; we'd better do it fast.   VIOLA POEY HUGHES

My Computer

Blot out all mine iniquities. Ps. 51:9.

GOD CREATED PEOPLE WITH a wonderful instrument—the human brain. Humans, in turn, have made many marvelous tools, including my computer.

When I first graduated from the commercial course at high school, I found a job as secretary to the president of a publishing company and used a manual typewriter. Later, I worked for several court reporters. One of them encouraged me to learn to operate an electric typewriter. What a struggle! In the "good old days" we used stencils (if you're old enough to know what they are!). All the stencils I typed looked as though they had chicken pox as a result of my dabs of correction fluid. Unconsciously dragging my fingers put a J or K in every other word.

Later, I was introduced to that outstanding invention, the computer. I've often expressed the feeling that I'm standing at the edge of a vast ocean of knowledge, but my toes are barely touching the water. With what little I do know, however, I've typed thousands of pages of manuscripts, letters, tests, financial statements, and books. My computer has so many marvelous functions! With one stroke of a key I can erase my mistake and put in the correct word. I can search the entire manuscript and command that the incorrect word be replaced with the correct one. My misspelled words are underlined in red to catch my attention. Each new version of the computer introduces new features.

Whenever I'm inclined to feel impatient with my computer, I'm reminded what a marvelous invention it is and how it reminds me of some of God's promises and admonitions. "O Lord, search my heart for me. . . . Let me know if there is any wicked way in me, and then help me walk the way I should" (Ps. 139:23, 24, Clear Word). "Don't look at my sins; blot out my iniquities. Create in me a clean heart, O God, and put a right spirit within me" (Ps. 51:9, 10, Clear Word).

Every day I thank Jesus for blotting out my sins of yesterday and giving me a clean page for today. And I pray that I will allow Him to control the input of my life so that what is produced will be a blessing to others and bring honor to Him.

RUBYE SUE

What's a Mother to Do?

You are the God of miracles and the God of all power. Ps. 77:14, Clear Word.

OUR 19-YEAR-OLD DAUGHTER was finished with high school, living at home, and working. She had no plans, no goals—just life, one day at a time. Her friends were loser types whom she worked with. My husband and I watched her routine with interest, wondering when she was going to tire of her current life and get on with an education. We worried when she stayed out late and lost interest in spiritual things.

It was as though a bombshell fell the day she announced that she was going to move out and share an apartment with non-Christian acquaintances who had many problems. My insides exploded as I tried to remain calm and reason with her.

I was sure there was a place she could afford by herself, so I found myself looking at ads and driving around trying to spot a For Rent sign. I got more panicky as the days went by, because she had showed me where the apartment was.

I felt as if I had to solve this problem, that it was up to me to intervene, to turn the situation around. I'm sure I prayed about it, but I never turned her completely over to God and His able hands. Instead, I came up with a plan I thought was God-inspired.

Without my husband's knowledge, I made arrangements with the business office of a Christian college to write my daughter a letter. It said that an anonymous donor was giving her $7,000 toward her education if she enrolled for the next semester. (That was the amount I thought I'd have in savings by the time she started.)

Finally the letter came. You can't imagine my disappointment when, after reading it, she tossed it aside, not showing any interest. My heart was in the offer, but apparently God wasn't. It's taking me a long time to learn that God can do anything, and without Him I can do nothing.

God works in mysterious ways, because it wasn't long afterward that the apartment idea vanished, and she felt a strong need to get away from the influences around her. One turn of events was followed by another. She volunteered to work at a boys' orphanage in Bolivia for almost a year. I had the privilege of spending some of my savings to visit her there! Allowing God to take control makes life so much better!   DONNA MEYER VOTH

Take My Life and Let It Be

Except the Lord build the house, they labour in vain that build it: except the Lord keep the city, the watchman waketh but in vain. Ps. 127:1.

THE OCCASION WAS THE dedicatory service for our two grandsons, who had been born six weeks apart. Several friends of our daughters traveled from around the country for this special ceremony. We gathered on the platform, and the pastor signaled to Dwaune, a family friend, to sing the dedicatory song. What melodious music filled the sanctuary and our hearts as he sang a beautiful and familiar hymn: "Take my life, and let it be consecrated, Lord, to Thee. . . . Take my will and make it Thine; it shall be no longer mine; take my heart, it is Thine own! It shall be Thy royal throne."

As he sang, a hushed silence filled the sanctuary. I had heard and sung this hymn on several occasions, but never had it impacted me like this. The Holy Spirit's presence could be felt in the sanctuary as if speaking to each of us to give our lives anew to God. It was obvious from the expressions on the faces of the congregation that their hearts had been touched and drawn closer to the Savior.

As I listened to the words I offered up a prayer for our two little innocent grandsons, asleep in the arms of the officiating elders, unaware of what was taking place. I wondered what the future would bring them. Would they grow up to be loving, kind, Christian young men? We are surrounded by so much evil every day. It makes me shudder when I think of what this world will become if Jesus doesn't come soon. I prayed that God would bless them and their parents, and that He would give their parents wisdom, understanding, and patience to train these precious jewels in the right way, and that whatever the future holds, He will keep them in His loving care. I know they will encounter difficulties and hardships as they travel life's rugged road, but I am confident that my God is able to uphold and protect them from the evil one.

Yes, Lord, take our lives and use them ever, always for You. Thank You, heavenly Father, for the privilege of "grandparenthood" and for the opportunity and wonderful privilege of helping to teach these little ones to love and obey You. May we always be good examples to them.

Today I humbly reconsecrate my life to You, the giver of life.

SHIRLEY C. IHEANACHO

Waking Up With God

If you wake me each morning with the sound of your loving voice, I'll go to sleep each night trusting you. Ps. 143:8, Message.

ONE OF THE STRANGEST dichotomies of motherhood for me was that I'd spend much time and effort trying to get my baby to go to sleep, then, after a few hours, find myself standing over the crib, longing for my little one to wake up again!

More than once I picked up a sleeping child to awaken her so I could delight in her smile, or to rouse him so he would nuzzle his face into my cheek. It did seem crazy, but I couldn't help it—I loved them so much that I longed to be with them every minute of their day.

How does God respond when you wake up each morning? How does He look at you? What does He say to greet you? How does He feel about you?

God loves us so much! We are His children. I'm sure, with so many of us to care for, it must be almost something of a relief for Him when we sleep. Still, He is more than delighted when we wake up again to start another new day with Him.

Sometimes our picture of God may be blurred. We may think that God isn't interested in the moment we wake up, or that He doesn't even notice we've opened our eyes, or that He groans when He sees us, wondering if we'll wreck yet another beautiful day.

But God delights in us each day, just as we delight in our own little children. Maybe He hovers over us to catch the very minute we stir into wakefulness. Just as I plan fresh and creative ways to show my love to my children each day, so He is planning creative ways to love me, too.

Do I get excited about another day to spend with God? Do I smile at Him as I wake and feel safe because Daddy's there? Do I nuzzle my face into His cheek to show how much I love Him, too?

How do you wake up with God, and what does that do to your day? Greet Him joyfully. Sense His wonderful love for you, and experience His anticipation of your new day, another new start with Him. He is there, longing to startle you with His love. Look for His love each day. Write down how you experience that love, then find new ways to startle those around you with the startling love of God.

KAREN HOLFORD

I Am Grateful . . . and You?

Praise the Lord, O my soul, and forget not all his benefits. Ps.103:2, NIV.

EVERY DAY WE MEET marvelous people who support us and help us in different ways. We are immensely grateful to these individuals who are so special in our lives.

I like to remember the person who cared for me, nursed me, taught me to read, showed me the value of studying, disciplined me with love, established limits, and transmitted lessons on ethics, values, and moral standards. She taught me, through her example as she exercised her profession as a teacher, that it's important to carry out one's work faithfully and to seek to improve one's professional career.

Her breath was always a prayer. In the silent hours of the night, alone with her children, she was always praying. When I saw her in her bed, she was speaking with the Father. At daybreak she gathered her children in the living room for the family altar. In the evening she once again gathered everyone for evening worship. This woman had thick calluses on her knees from so much praying, and she is, without a doubt, the most special woman in my life. She brought me into this world; she deserves all my gratitude. She was the one who gave me my faith and the certainty of salvation in Jesus Christ.

Above all, I am grateful to God for giving me the privilege of being her daughter. She gave me a happy home, in spite of losing my father early in my childhood. She knew how to carry out, with great ability, the double task of being both father and mother.

Life passes rapidly. Opportunities go by, and we don't express our gratitude—gratitude for even simple things that take place daily, or for more complicated and difficult things that give us the opportunity to grow, to overcome obstacles.

Gratitude is not natural for some people. Once Jesus cured 10 lepers, but only one remembered to give glory to God. His gratitude didn't go unnoticed by the Master. It isn't enough to feel gratitude; it's necessary to express this feeling.

Today—not tomorrow—think of someone that you would like to thank for some reason. Don't put off the moment. Express your gratitude.

MEIBEL MELLO GUEDES

The Rainbow of Promise

And I seal this promise with this sign: I have placed my rainbow in the clouds as a sign of my promise until the end of time, to you and to all the earth. Gen. 9:12, 13, TLB.

IT WAS ONE OF those blue Mondays. As I went for my usual morning walk, I was discouraged and full of gloom. I'd been praying about something for a long time, and the Lord seemed so silent. I walked with my head down, talking to Him, telling Him how I felt, and asking Him if He was listening.

The chirping of two weaverbirds on the telephone wire broke into my reverie and forced me to look up. When I did, I saw a beautiful double rainbow, bright and clear, even though there was no sign of rain. It was as though God was saying, "How could you doubt Me? Of course I've heard your prayers! You must be patient, and in My time I shall answer, and you'll not be disappointed. Have I ever let you down in the past?"

My mood changed dramatically. I felt pangs of remorse and asked for forgiveness. I had behaved like a spoiled child. Once the barrier between us had been removed, I felt joy in my heart and walked with a spring in my step.

I recalled the many times the Lord had answered my prayers—some promptly, some after a long wait, and sometimes He said no. In retrospect, I would not have had Him answer any other way. His way has always been best.

I followed that rainbow during the 45 minutes of my walk. I thought about Noah and his family in the ark and tried to imagine how they must have felt. Would the rain ever stop? Had the Lord abandoned them?

What joy must have been theirs when God sealed His covenant with them with a rainbow. A rainbow is beautiful, with its colors in perfect harmony, an apt symbol of God's relationship with us. Revelation 4:3 tells us that there is a rainbow encircling God's throne. There is a message of hope and comfort in the rainbow, especially after we have experienced storms in our lives. God has promised to be with us in all our trials.

The next time I'm tempted to doubt Him I'm going to remember the rainbow. I also want to see His rainbow in heaven; don't you?

FRANCES CHARLES

Unforgettable Experience

Call unto me, and I will answer thee, and shew thee great and mighty things, which thou knowest not. Jer. 33:3.

IT WAS 1976. My daughter, Angela, was graduating from nursing school at Loma Linda University, but I was in Michigan. I wanted so much to attend the service. I couldn't see the possibility of having my dream fulfilled. My sick husband, aging mother, and 11-year-old daughter depended on me to take care of them. Our financial situation was tight. I prayed about it, but not clinging to hope, I went on with my duties.

Early one Sunday morning my niece in California called. "Aunt Marge, how would you like to come to Angela's graduation?"

I swallowed. I could say nothing but "Thelda, that's an answer to my prayer."

"That will be my graduation gift to Angela. But you must keep it a secret," Thelda urged.

The ticket came, and I flew to California. My niece picked me up at the airport. She had sent Angela on an errand, telling her that she was going to get her graduation gift. "I hope you'll like it, because I can't return it," she had warned.

When we got to Angela's, Thelda tucked me into Angela's closet. When Angela returned, Thelda called, "Angie, look in your room. I hope you like your present." Excitedly, Angela searched her room but could find nothing new.

"I don't see anything," she reported. Disappointment tinged her words.

"Look again," her cousin advised.

When Angela came back into the room, I opened her closet door and stepped out. My daughter screamed, jumping up and down. We hugged and kissed, tears of joy streaming down our cheeks. Angela couldn't believe that I was actually there.

This was a moment I shall never forget. It brings to mind today's text, which shows God's interest in the minutest details of our lives. I called. He heard my prayer and answered it in a grand and mighty and wonderful way. I thought, too, of how excited we shall be when Jesus comes. Like my daughter, we shall shout and praise God. What a day of rejoicing that will be!

MARJORIE BOYCE

Driven by the Wind

But ask in faith, never doubting, for the one who doubts is like a wave of the sea, driven and tossed by the wind. James 1:6, NRSV.

THE NORTHWESTERN SKY was dark, and the clouds looked ominous. A cold front was moving through, soon to replace the heat wave we'd been experiencing. Unfortunately, when weather fronts move through in these conditions, the outcome is often a storm. It was as though we could feel the approaching storm. I turned on the television at 9:00 p.m. to see what was predicted. There was a possibility of 100-mile-per-hour winds and heavy rains that could cause flash flooding in our area. At 9:12 the television screen went blank—all power was cut off.

The winds hit with full force. I watched our century-old willows wave and bow with each gust. The rain came in sheets. The force of the storm was tremendous. I felt a sense of awe as I observed the demonstration of its power. Darkness descended, and the temperature dropped 30 degrees or more in just a few minutes. I later learned that many of our neighbors sought shelter in their basements. My husband had gone to bed earlier and peacefully slept through the tempest, trusting that God was in charge.

I went to the cupboard for candleholders and candles so I would have a little light. As the winds subsided, I peacefully enjoyed a quiet time reading, a moment of calm after the storm.

In the morning we found our major loss was that of the willows and other trees. Our son and his family, who live next door, lost shingles and had other minor damage. With the grandchildren helping, my husband cleared the driveway and restored order. By midafternoon our electrical power was back, and the telephone repairman came to repair broken and corroded phone wires. We began to learn of the extensive damage throughout the community. Fortunately, no one was injured or killed.

Our kind heavenly Father, we praise You for the protection You provide as we face the storms of life. Your arms of love have given us a security that even the worst of storms cannot remove. We thank You for the assurance we have that You are ever present in our lives to shelter us from the winds that seek to destroy. EVELYN GLASS

Grandma's Picture

However, as it is written: "No eye has seen, no ear has heard, no mind has conceived what God has prepared for those who love him"—but God has revealed it to us by his Spirit. 1 Cor. 2:9, 10, NIV.

THE PICTURE HUNG ON the wall above my maternal grandmother's sofa. It was 1948, and I often visited Grandma while my new husband, Warren, was at work, and after I had put our little cottage to rights. She usually stretched out on the sofa, a small blanket over her legs. As I sat across from her, my eyes would stray to the picture. It fascinated me!

I could see myself strolling down the path through the woods. I might touch the rough bark of the trees, and maybe pick a bouquet of colorful flowers for whoever lived in the small cabin at the end of the meandering path.

Could there be a grandmother living there who would give me fresh-baked cookies and a glass of cold milk? Or was it a grandpa, who whistled and whittled? What sort of toy might he make for me? Maybe one of them would go over to the edge of the little lake with me, so I could dip my toes in the water. Ohhh! Brrr!

"Grandma," I said one day, "I just love that picture!"

She sat up, removed the blanket, picked up a pencil, and stood up. Removing the picture from the wall, she turned it over, upside down, and wrote something on it. I later learned she'd written "For Patsie" (the way she spelled my nickname). "This is for you when I'm gone."

"Thank you, Grandma! Thank you!"

In 1957 the picture came to hang on my living room wall. It has moved east, west, north, and south with my family, and now, for some years, is with just me.

I've read that if you feel stressed you should sit down, close your eyes, and imagine the most peaceful setting you've been in—the beach, mountains, wherever. As for me, I don't close my eyes. I look at Grandma's picture and am comforted.

Dear Jesus, I praise You for all the beauty You've placed in our sin-sick world. May we be ready for that future perfect state—heaven in all its glory, and with You to glorify!

PATSY MURDOCH MEEKER

From Sunset to Sunset

O Lord, how manifold are thy works! in wisdom hast thou made them all: the earth is full of thy riches. Ps. 104:24.

THE SKY WAS AGLOW with color and atmosphere. I couldn't take my eyes off the delightful scene. Walking in the nearby park one evening, I turned a corner and faced one of the most beautiful sunsets I had seen for many years. I kept staring at and selecting the colors as if painting a picture. Gradually I felt as if I were actually in this picture. I sat on a bench and let the sun's comforting warmth spread over me. I closed my eyes and whispered, "Thank You, Lord, for the beauty of this world You have created."

After meditating on the glorious sunsets I had experienced in the past, I was a child again, walking through our garden where there was summer year-round. The sunsets were vivid and alive with color, and then gone within a few short moments.

This led me in thought to a new day in our garden, looking at the varieties of hibiscus flowers in several shades of softest pinks and brightest reds and oranges. In the middle of the lawn was a large date palm, with its thick bark and broad, waxy green branches. At the side of the house were two flamboyant trees, giving welcome shade with vivid flame-colored blooms. It never ceases to amaze me how our brains retain so much detail after all those years, especially as I took the view of the garden for granted at that early age. Yet I was remembering the feel of soft grass under my feet, and the smell of the roses in big white tubs, and bougainvillea placed along the edge of the driveway. I even remembered the sound of a donkey braying in the field.

Now I know how all these memories come together: our Creator has designed the beauty of nature and created our minds to absorb and retain far more than any man-made computer can ever achieve.

Once again I travel back in time to my park bench as the sunset is slipping away in the twilight. Once again I whisper, "Thank You, Lord, for Your glorious handiwork."

"One day speaks to another, night with night shares its knowledge, and this without speech or language or sound of any voice" (Ps. 19:2, 3, NEB).

PHILIPPA MARSHALL

Pretty Things Aren't Always So

On the outside you appear righteous, but inside you're full of hypocrisy and evil. Matt. 23:28, Clear Word.

ATTRACTION. SOME THINGS we are naturally drawn to. For a woman, it's pretty things, such as flowers, candles, art, crafts, china, and crystal.

It was the cut-glass crystal bottle that caught my eye. It held a lovely, pastel green-colored lotion. Invitingly placed by the sink, the bottle was handy. I was excited when I first saw it. Someone has been so thoughtful. *Some just know how to add those extra little touches,* I thought.

A fragrant lotion is always a treat. It not only makes my hands feel smooth, it also speaks to my psyche. I feel more feminine when I use lotion, more pampered. Aren't we drawn to the perfumes and lotions in a store? We want to try them all to find our favorite. Sometimes it's the color that draws us, or the pretty-shaped bottle. But there's a sense of excitement in trying the various fragrances. It's like you're going to give your nose a treat!

Being a practical person, the fragrant lotions are my choice over perfume. They serve three purposes: soften my skin, relieve the dryness, and leave a pleasant scent.

Isn't this the way we want to be as Christians? Having a gentleness to our spirit so people are drawn to us. Being attractive in our appearance, realizing we are daughters of Christ—His representatives of what a Christian woman should be. Having His fragrance of love penetrating our soul so as to smooth our disposition—put an end to our "dryness," our irritation, so that others will want to "try us out" and get to know us.

I tried the pretty green lotion in the cut-crystal bottle, only to discover the fragrance was awful! I was shocked; my senses were startled. It was repulsive, like some type of medicine. It still had the smoothness lotion offers, but the smell was a complete turnoff.

I never touched the bottle again. That's not to say I wasn't tempted, though. I wanted what the attractive bottle had to offer. Then I remembered the terrible smell and refrained.

Lord, help me always to have a pleasant fragrance about my spirit that I might be consistent inside and out. May those who come in contact with me be blessed and not disappointed. Amen. LOUISE DRIVER

Locked Out

Wherefore the rather, brethren, give diligence to make your calling and election sure: for if ye do these things, ye shall never fall. 2 Peter 1:10.

I KNEW THE MINUTE I closed the car door that I'd made a big mistake. It was a Friday afternoon. There were errands to run, groceries to buy, and food to prepare before sunset. I was in a hurry, and now everything had come to a sudden halt.

Looking through the window of the car, I saw them—my car keys—lying on the seat, inside the locked car. How could I have done that? One of my biggest fears had just become a reality. I was locked out! My husband was out of town. I felt so helpless and alone. I had no one to call—except the Lord. "O Lord, help me!" I cried to myself.

Fast-forward in your mind to another event—past the end of earth's history, past the millennium of happiness in heaven to the day when the New Jerusalem descends to this earth. The resurrected sinners are marshaled together by Satan in one last attempt to overthrow the government of God. This sinful sea of humanity surrounds the city, intending to conquer it. Suddenly their eyes are raised and then riveted on Jesus, with all His redeemed saints, standing on the walls of the Holy City. The faces of the saints, whom they recognize as some of their own friends and family, are so full of happiness and serenity that they stand out in stark contrast to the sea of angry faces surrounding the city. Immediately the conviction comes over the sinners that they are lost, locked out of heaven forever. There's no locksmith who can open that door. Even Jesus cannot reverse the final decision they made during their probationary period in this life.

Now rewind the scenario. You're back in your own fast-paced life. You're so busy, perhaps so filled with things to do that they've crowded out your time with God. Resist the temptation to let otherwise important things take the time you need to get ready for heaven. Hold fast the "keys" to the kingdom—study and prayer. Don't lay them down for anything. Pray for the Holy Spirit to help you hold fast your faith until the end. That way you'll avoid that terrible experience of being "locked out" of heaven.

NANCY CACHERO VASQUEZ

Tiny Miracles, Huge Blessings

O Lord, you are my God; I will exalt you and praise your name, for in perfect faithfulness you have done marvelous things, things planned long ago. Isa. 25:1, NIV.

SPRING IS A TIME of rebirth and new beginnings. The spring of 1997 was just that for my husband and me when our grandson was born.

Our home is situated close to a bird sanctuary and conservation area. We've always been blessed to live in areas where we're surrounded by the sights and sounds of nature. I've heard birds sing and doves coo before, but in the spring of 1997 I listened to the doves with different ears. Their cooing sounded very much like the cooing sounds my grandson made when he lay playing in his crib. What a melodious sound!

I have since been blessed with three more adorable grandchildren. Each has unique beauty and special gifts. How can I ever forget Omari at age 2 announcing with pride, "Grandma, I'm *caming* down the stairs," or almost-3-year-old Naomi, on a recent Caribbean vacation, imitating the crowing of the rooster for her grandpa as "Cock-a-doodle-*moo*"?

Many grandmothers these days are pursuing careers or are in professions that require them to work long hours outside the home. For me, being a grandmother provides a wonderful distraction from the pressures of a busy life. Tiny hands, tiny feet, and trusting eyes have brought me so much closer to my heavenly Father. I am reminded each day that God loves me even more than I can begin to love these tiny miracles He has brought into my life. Never a day goes by that I don't give thanks for the special blessings of being a grandparent.

I'm most grateful that God has granted me another opportunity to influence young lives for eternity. For this I count my blessings and say "Thank You, Lord!"

*Please help me today, dear Lord, to count all my blessings. Help me to name them, one by one. I know I'll be surprised to see just how much God has done for me.**

AVIS MAE RODNEY

---

* Modified from the song "Count Your Blessings," found in the songbook *Praise—Our Songs and Hymns*. Published by Singspiration Music.

Another Day—What a Difference!

The Lord is near to those who are discouraged: he saves those who have lost all hope. Ps. 34:18, TEV.

AS SHE BREATHED ON the puffed corn, watching it move and bounce up and down, I almost thought I saw her grin she was so full of joy. Was this a child? No, it was one of my little dogs, a Boston terrier named Sweetie. She has a stress immune disease called "red mange." Some dogs outgrow it, and others have to be treated for the rest of their lives. Every time she gets her yearly shots, she has a few days when she's feeling poorly and isn't very happy about anything. This was the second day after her shots, and she had begun to feel a little better. When she realized that she could just breathe on the corn and it would move, she almost danced for joy. She continued to breathe on it with a purpose, and I knew that she really was feeling better. What a difference a day can make!

And what a difference a day can make in our lives. One day we may have a loved one, and the next day that loved one may be gone. One day we may have a difficult, unsolved problem, and the next day the Lord may have helped us find a solution.

Sometimes we have an illness that we feel will never end or go away, then another day and the illness may begin to disappear. Every day we get better, and finally it's gone. Or we may be discouraged and depressed about a perplexing situation. Then another day, and when the sun is shining bright—who can stay discouraged? It is another day that the Lord has made, and all is right again.

Our vet tells us that we can put little Sweetie to sleep or let her die slowly as the mites take over her little body, or we can continue to treat her and ask the Lord to finally heal her. I can't consider the first two options as long as she is healthy in all other ways. The only option I can consider is to treat her, love her, and ask the Lord to do the rest.

My prayer today is that God will give us wisdom to know how to care for our pets, our loved ones, and ourselves, and that we will be a witness for Him in all we do and say.

LORAINE F. SWEETLAND

The Heavenly View

I have set before you life and death, blessing and cursing; therefore choose life, that both you and your descendants may live. Deut. 30:19, NKJV.

I LIKE PLAYING GAMES such as Chinese checkers, Draft, and dominoes. These mind games require quite a bit of concentration, skill, and the ability to read your opponent's move so that you can win the game. Sometimes I play with people who are masters of the game, and it's very difficult for me to read their minds and guess their next move. I discovered that it's much easier to read the board and the players' moves when I'm an observer rather than an active player. However, an observer must remain silent. I can't give any hints to the players. That is forbidden and would be considered cheating.

In the game of life God is the onlooker. He has the heavenly point of view because not only does He have the "height advantage," He is omniscient and knows exactly what moves we're going to make. He'll orchestrate our moves if only we'll invite Him to do so. Unlike the silent observer in the game who's never allowed to give hints, He will come to our aid and point us in the right direction if only we'll ask. He will guide us if we listen to and obey His voice. He also tells us in His Word what we should do.

In the game of life we're faced with issues every day and have to make choices. Some of these issues are more important than others. Even though we have the freedom of choice in the decision-making process, we should cultivate the habit of seeking His advice. The most important decision we can make is to choose to follow Him. Eternal life is guaranteed.

Not only did God create us with a free will, but our text for today says He makes it easier for us as we weigh the options between life and death, blessing and cursing. He tells us what is the best choice. Choose life, He says, that your descendants and you may live.

I pray today that we would invite Him into our lives so that we can make wise choices regarding our salvation.

ANDREA BUSSUE

Dreams Become Realities

But as it is written, Eye hath not seen, nor ear heard, neither have entered into the heart of man, the things which God hath prepared for them that love him. 1 Cor. 2:9.

NORWAY . . . A DREAM come true! I could hardly believe it! Today we really docked in Norway. I remember reading about Norway back in grade school readers. The stories seemed so real that I used to imagine being there, walking along the docks, looking at the ships of all sizes as they came in on this beautiful body of water—even talking to the fisherman with his fresh fish.

Fifty years later my dream became a reality. I was truly in Norway, walking along the docks, seeing for myself the different ships as they came in on the beautiful blue North Sea.

I have another reader now. This book is called the Holy Bible. I get even more excited when I read it than I did when I read about Norway in the third grade. In my Bible John the revelator talks about a new city that he calls the New Jerusalem. According to my reader, the walls of the new city are made of jasper, and its foundation is garnished with all kinds of precious stones. Can you imagine a floor made of sapphire, emerald, sardonyx, amethyst, or topaz?

My Book also says the gates of that city are made of pearls. "Every several gate was of one pearl: and the street of the city was pure gold, as it were transparent glass" (Rev. 21:21). The city won't need the sun or the moon because the Lamb of God will be our light, "and the gates of it shall not be shut at all by day: for there shall be no night there" (verse 25).

What I like most about my current reader Book is that I know its Author, and I have a personal relationship with Him. He has assured me that "eye hath not seen, nor ear heard, neither have entered into the heart of man, the things which God hath prepared for them that love him." I dream this dream every day, and, by God's grace and mercy, in time this dream will also become a reality.

CORA A. WALKER

The Important Children

Suffer little children, and forbid them not, to come unto me; for of such is the kingdom of heaven. Matt. 19:14.

I SAW THE CHILDREN FILING into their classrooms as I stepped into the school building. In loud voices they clamored and waved. "Mrs. Hardin is here! Mrs. Hardin is here!" I returned their waves with a big smile as I quickly walked down to the office to sign in. I've been coming for some years to volunteer in first grade for reading enrichment.

I went to Mrs. Gress's classroom first. The children were excited as they found places to sit on the carpet around my rocking chair. Mrs. Gress greeted me with a smile, and we took a moment to chat. The children and I had a chat, too. They had important things to share, such as "I lost my tooth," "My mom is expecting," and even "I'm moving."

Then we settled down, and I opened my basket. Some days I have stories from countries to which I've traveled and objects I've brought back to show them. Other days we just read stories that we all enjoy and can talk about. They're eager for information, and I enjoy their questions and eagerness for learning.

I have four classrooms to do. And always, as I come in, someone is happy to see me and cries out, "Mrs. Hardin is here!" Of course, it sounds good to hear your name being called out, but more important is what I'm sharing and leaving with them.

Now the end of the school year is here, and I must say goodbye to this group of children, as they'll be in second grade next year. The children have written me goodbye letters. Lauren wrote, "Thank you for all the stuff you showed us." Zoe said, "Thank you for giving time just for us. I feel so special. I wish you could come to second grade." Dylan declared, "I learned a lot."

I cherish their letters, smiles, and hugs. Did I give them a little more love on their way in life? These are Jesus' little children, and He said "of such is the kingdom of heaven." How important it is for us to love and care for them!

DESSA WEISZ HARDIN

Berries and the Bible

All scripture is inspired by God and is useful for teaching, for reproof, for correction, and for training in righteousness, so that everyone who belongs to God may be proficient, equipped for every good work. 2 Tim. 3:16, 17, NRSV.

THE RASPBERRY CANES were full of fruit, and I picked rapidly. We'd need many berries to feed 11 family members at breakfast. While my husband, Larry, and his father, Ted, picked in the row next to me and chatted together, I thought of the plans we'd made for the day.

"Don't leave any ripe berries, Denise," Larry admonished.

"Yes," chimed in Ted, "it's important to the U-pick owners that we do a thorough job."

When our baskets were full, I joined the two men as we walked back to the car. Though friends might describe Larry as "fun-loving," many others think of him as "methodical." So I was surprised to note many ripe, luscious berries still on the stalks that had just been picked by Larry and his dad.

"Look at these," I cried, picking several berries and balancing them on top of the laden baskets. "And these . . . And these. You've left lots here!"

"So we have," they laughed. "We thought we were getting every one, but when you look from a different angle, you find many more."

The same idea is true with Bible study. Ted, a retired pastor, reads the Scriptures for devotional inspiration and discovers promises that stir his soul. My mother-in-law, June, a musician and homemaker, looks at the teachings of the Bible pragmatically and notes things that her husband didn't see. Larry, an archaeologist, studies the Bible from the vantage point of history and finds other insights. I, an English teacher, analyze the stories and poetry of the Bible from a literary perspective and discover additional understanding. Each of us, coming from a different angle, can add food for thought as we discuss the Bible together.

I looked forward to returning home, eating raspberries and cream, and studying the Bible. With 11 different viewpoints from three generations, our time together promised to be exciting. And very sweet.

DENISE DICK HERR

Not Alone

For the Lord your God goes with you; he will never leave you nor forsake you. Deut. 31:6, NIV.

M Y HUSBAND WAS TRAVELING, and I was alone again. As I sat down for my breakfast and prayed before I ate, on a whim I suddenly added, "Why don't you come sit with me, Jesus?" Then I sat there to think about what I had said. I liked the idea. Then the thought came: *What are we going to talk about?*

I looked out the window at my bird feeder. That would be a good topic—He could tell me all about the birds. I didn't even know most of their names, but I wanted to learn. I'd like to talk to Him, too, about the fact that winter would be coming on, and lots of things would be dying. In fact, a young woman, only 24, who taught sixth grade at our church's elementary school, had died two days before. The services were going to be that afternoon. I would like to talk to Him about that. "How long, O Lord, is this stuff going to go on?" I would ask Him.

"And what about Curtis? I just met him. He claims that after he read Greek mythology he doesn't believe in You anymore. What do I say to him? Do things like that bother You?"

There were so many topics I'd like to talk to Him about: sickness, war, AIDS, domestic and sexual abuse, women in poverty, sharing the good news of the gospel with all those women in the 10/40 window—really, so many topics and so little time.

I might talk to Him, too, about my plans for the day. It was Sabbath, and I didn't have to worry about work or bills or cleaning. Such a great feeling! Suddenly a radical thought struck me: If He were really sitting here at the table with me, wouldn't it be nice to ask Him, "And what would You like to see happen today? Just what would You like for us to talk about and what would You like to say to me?"

As I crunched my cereal and enjoyed my bagel, I thought about what had just happened. It had been a bit of a one-sided conversation, but He had listened patiently. Now breakfast was over, and it was time to clear the table and get on with the day.

Why don't You just stay and spend the day with me? There's so much we could do together. I would really enjoy the time.   ARDIS DICK STENBAKKEN

With High Honors

Man looketh on the outward appearance, but the Lord looketh on the heart.
1 Sam. 16:7.

WOULD YOU WRITE UNCLE Dan's tribute?" my brother asked. Dan had passed away at the veterans' home. He had no wife, children, or siblings nearby. I was stumped. What could I say? He'd been with us on holidays and at weekend dinners, but he'd made a habit of criticizing and complaining. Most of the time he was depressed, discouraged, and broke. He came to us when he was lonely or needing money. Often he called the house and went into a tirade. Then there were the times he called at 2:00 a.m., afraid to be alone, and came to sleep on the couch. We loved our uncle; however, we knew he was troubled, and how could I tell that in a tribute?

I had to pray and ask God what to say. Then my brother picked up our uncle's personal belongings at the veterans' home. Among them were documents of bravery and valor in combat for which he'd been given medals. Our uncle was a war hero! What a shock! We never even knew it. He'd been in the battle of Normandy, helping to march the Nazis all the way back to Germany.

Realization came now. War had taken its toll on Dan. That was why he'd had such a hard time with life. He kept things to himself because it was painful to talk about them. Now I was able to write the tribute and say our uncle was a war hero. Although we didn't see him as that kind of person, God knew his heart. It broke my heart to think about it, and I wept and wished we'd taken time to put our arms around him more often, to understand Uncle Dan. I wish we could have seen him as God saw him. Dan did come to Christ again in later years, but God knew all the time where he was.

The day before the funeral a surprise letter came from a large business owner in the city. He sent a donation to the church in Dan's name. This man had had our uncle take care of his yard, and then given him lunch afterward. He claimed Dan was his most dependable worker and praised him. We were able to add that to the tribute as well. Dan's military honors didn't mean much to him, but he'll receive high honors from Jesus.

Lord, change our hearts so we can better understand those around us.

DARLENE YTREDAL BURGESON

Reunion

I heard a loud shout from the throne, saying, "Look, the home of God is now among his people. He will live with them, and they will be his people. God himself will be among them. He will remove all their sorrows, and there will be no more death or sorrow or crying or pain." Rev. 21:3, 4, NLT.

ONE OF MY FAVORITE activities as a child was going to Grandpa and Grandma's "little house on the prairie"—especially when the whole extended family was having a reunion. My great-grandparents came from Norway and settled on a farm in central Nebraska. They had 17 children, 14 of whom grew to be adults. Every year all the aunts and uncles and cousins gathered at the tiny Elm Creek church. Their talents combined to make it overflow with praise and worship. Old hymns such as "Shall We Gather at the River?" and "The Old Rugged Cross" would echo from the rafters.

Afterward, everyone would adjourn to the little town park for a fellowship lunch and lots of laughter, hugs, and delicious food. We'd gather around my great-grandmother, who still baked bread every day except Saturday, and who could still touch her toes when she was 100 years old. We'd stuff ourselves with casseroles, fresh-baked bread, farm-fresh produce, cool lemonade, and Great-aunt Grace's burnt-sugar cake.

Then the adults would sit in the shade and visit or doze while the children played on the swings or ran and shrieked with delight in childish games of tag or hide-and-seek. All too soon it ended, and everyone packed up to go home, promising to return the next year.

As the years went by and the older members of the family passed away, the reunions came to an end. But I'm looking forward to one last great reunion.

Imagine with me, if you will, the reunion to end all reunions. Friends and loved ones who have fallen asleep in Jesus will be there to greet us. There'll be laughter, hugs, tears of joy, and lots of catching up. The food will be heavenly! Maybe the children will play tag around our feet. Maybe we'll join in the game. But best of all, Jesus will be there to welcome us to a home where there will be no more crying and no more separations. Pray that we all will be there.   FAUNA RANKIN DEAN

Master Designer

Woe to him who strives with his Maker! . . . Does the clay say to him who fashions it, "What are you making"? or "Your work has no handles"? Isa. 45:9, RSV.

TRAVELING WITH A CHRISTIAN group of 38 in May of 1990, shortly after the Berlin Wall fell, we visited London, Berlin, Warsaw, Moscow, Helsinki, and Stockholm. On our way to Copenhagen I was grateful to pass Linköping, Sweden, the birthplace of my grandmother. Then we stopped for a tour of a glass factory in the small village of Granna.

Standing on a balcony in his shop, we looked down at the owner-creator of beautiful, handcrafted glass on display in his showroom. He addressed us from his workplace below. "What would you like me to make for you?"

There was a chorus of voices, but somehow mine penetrated his ears. "I would like you to make a vase with handles," I requested.

"All right," he replied. Motioning with his arm, he invited, "Come on down and help me."

Surprised, I went down to his work area. Handing me a long, hollow tube with a glob of molten glass on the end, he instructed me how to blow. "Carefully . . . Blow a little harder . . . Not so hard . . . That's enough." With that, he severed the just-blown vase from the tube and stood it on the table, a fragile globe-shaped vase with a long, elegant neck—something I would treasure.

But it had no handles. Then I realized that he knew it would be too much for this inexperienced, first-time glassblower to attempt. I wasn't disappointed. When he presented it to me, I was overwhelmed and grateful. It was without handles, but original, and mine! The passage from Isaiah 45 came to my mind, and it seemed to have been written just for me.

With our limited judgment we can't always understand the reasons why our lives take on a pattern far different from the one we choose. But then God, in His perfect wisdom, makes of us something precious—a treasure for His kingdom, uniquely designed for His special purpose.

I displayed my vase proudly in my china cabinet. It wasn't perfect, but it was a beautiful memento of an experience that brought me in touch with my Master Designer. What a privilege to have a one-on-one relationship with Him!

LORRAINE HUDGINS-HIRSCH

A Child's Miracle

I will praise you, my God and King, and bless your name each day and forever. Ps. 145:1, 2, TLB.

I GREW UP RECOGNIZING happenings as blessings and miracles from God.

One day, when I was 9 years old and was riding home from school, I was sitting in the back seat. My brother was with Dad in the front. The bright, shiny handle on the car door caught my attention, and I kept running my hands over it. I kept on touching the handle until the door swung open. The next thing I knew, I was waking up in a strange bed in a strange place and it was the next morning. Not only did I feel very ill; I was very frightened. Although my family had been there the night before, they weren't there when I woke up, and I felt very alone. When I asked where I was, the nurse told me that I was in the hospital and that it was important to keep calm and to stay in bed.

When Friday night came, I told one of the nurses that I needed to go home because the next day was the day I went to church. She told me that I was too ill to go home. I was so upset that I cried and cried. The nurses tried playing different games with me, but I remained upset.

I was told that I had fallen out of the car onto the highway. I was knocked unconscious when my head hit the cement as I fell. A truck driver heading in the opposite direction stopped his big semi and then stopped the other traffic. The police and the ambulance were called. The police arrived, but the ambulance was taking a long time, so the police picked me up and put me in the police car, along with my brother and my dad. They met the ambulance on the way to the hospital. My dad went home to tell my mother what had happened. I was told that I had a serious, extensive fractured skull, and that I could have died or been paralyzed for life. The doctor told my parents that the collar on my winter coat helped save me because of the protection it gave over my spine, but I know that it was a miracle from God.

Thank You, dear Jesus, for coming into my life and my heart. I will praise Your name each day and forever!

KAREN EDRIS

God's Concern

Beloved, I pray that you may prosper in all things and be in health, just as your soul prospers. 3 John 2, NKJV.

WHAT MUST BE WRONG with me? I've never been dizzy like this before. I thought I needed to see my family physician, so I set up an appointment.

My doctor told me that I had high blood pressure. I was quite concerned because my father and oldest brother had died of stroke, even though they were of good old age when they passed away. My doctor gave me a diuretic prescription, and all of a sudden my weight decreased remarkably from 118 to 108 pounds in a very short time. I was happy, because I am five feet two inches tall, and I really wanted to be lighter.

Shortly after this loss of weight, my daughter-in-law from Dallas, Texas, called. In the course of our conversation I mentioned how happy I was about losing some pounds in a short time. Instead of congratulating me, she expressed concern. She is a nutritionist-dietitian and advised me to see my doctor right away to ask why I was losing weight so fast. And now instead of being happy, I became alarmed.

My earthly relative, my daughter-in-law, had expressed concern about my health. She urged me not to wait any longer in seeing my doctor. She knew something must be wrong with my health, and I understood she didn't want me to suffer. She cared enough to urge me to go back and see my doctor.

I also have a heavenly relative, my Father above, who cared enough that He sent the message in 3 John 2: "Beloved, I pray that you may prosper in all things and be in health, just as your soul prospers." My daughter-in-law was concerned about my physical health, but my heavenly Father is concerned not only about my health but also my spiritual condition. As a matter of fact, He is concerned about all phases of my life, because God said He wanted me to prosper in all things.

What a wonderful God we serve! I will certainly praise and worship Him as long as I live. He is wonderfully good to me always.

OFELIA A. PANGAN

Got a Purim?

These days of Purim should never cease to be celebrated. Esther 9:28, NIV.

I'M BEING DISCHARGED on Wednesday!" Her voice was full of hope and joy. It was a miracle. At least her doctors had no other explanation for her recovery after weeks of being locked in a coma. Caught in the middle of a high-speed drunken chase, a sports utility vehicle had rammed her VW off the highway and squashed it like a bug against the utility pole.

My heart leaped as I replied, "I'm so happy for you, for all of us!" But her next sentence stopped me cold.

"So, can you help me put together a Purim for Thursday?"

"Thursday!" I exclaimed. "That's tomorrow. Won't you need some recovery time?"

She laughed. How wonderful to hear that melodious sound. "Of course it's the next day," she replied. "I heard about Purim in one of your seminars!"

I agreed to help. Instantly! The concept of Purim had slid to the back burner of my mind. I got it out, dusted it off metaphorically, and reread the book of Esther.

My dear friend was correct. True recovery includes celebration, and the Jews of the Medo-Persian Empire celebrated the day after they were delivered from nearly being "done in." We held her Purim on Thursday, complete with food, singing, conversation, rejoicing, and thanks to God for having given her relief from her enemy, death. She plans to celebrate annually.

We all have enemies. Every one of us! Enemies such as abuse, dysfunctional behaviors, and painful memories. Recovery and healing strategies help us to rid ourselves of these enemies, to distance ourselves from abusive situations, to free ourselves from the potential harm of dysfunctional behaviors, and to remove the sting of painful memories. Emotionally, we often choose at some level how deeply we'll hurt and for how long we'll remain at the heartbreak level. Many of us forget to rejoice, however. The Jews immediately created a celebration—Purim—the day after their deliverance!

Do you need to create a Purim in your life? It can inspire you to remember your deliverance, help you to pass on lessons you've learned, or encourage you to celebrate your restoration.   ARLENE TAYLOR

God's Measurements

Until we all reach unity in the faith and in the knowledge of the Son of God and become mature, attaining to the whole measure of the fullness of Christ. Eph. 4:13, NIV.

AT THIS WRITING I am sewing together a "Sunbonnet Sue" quilt for my 20-year-old granddaughter. I think it will take 56 blocks to reach the queen size she wants. This quilt will probably be finished by the time she gets married, which could be years. She says she has no current interest in matrimony. Time will tell.

I know that I must follow the exact measurements given in the description guidebook for this quilt to finish properly. If the measurements of the blocks and borders are one-eighth inch off, the quilt blocks will not fit evenly at the corners. So I must carefully follow directions.

Here in the United States we have standard measurements, though most of the world uses the metric system. Thankfully, we can all depend on our consistent standards for any assembled thing to be put together correctly.

God, too, has His standards of measurement that we can depend on to be consistent. I'm very thankful for that consistency. He is "the same yesterday and today and forever" (Heb. 13:8, NIV). I can, if I study, know where I stand with God's measurements.

Sometimes I don't "measure up," so I must again consult the guidebook, God's Word, to see where I went wrong. And the Holy Spirit guides me in my search when I ask for His guidance.

I want my life to follow my Lord's standards of measurement, and I am so thankful for His forgiveness when I don't measure up. I confess, He covers me with His righteousness, and I can continue in my walk with Him.

My granddaughter's quilt is coming together nicely so far, and I can proudly present it to her when it's finished. I pray I'll be able to present myself to Jesus, my Savior, when He comes, "a living sacrifice, holy, acceptable to God" (Rom. 12:1, NKJV). I'm still working on that one!

Dear Lord, please help me to keep focused on Your acceptance guidelines and daily bring to You my failures for Your blessed forgiveness.

BESSIE SIEMENS LOBSIEN

The Gift Bible

I will put my trust in God. Heb. 2:13, TLB.

I RECENTLY VISITED MY FRIEND'S church in Silver Spring, Maryland. It is a nice church with about 200 members. When the service was over, I went to my friend's house to have a fellowship lunch. On the way, I realized that I had left my Bible in the church.

When I arrived at my friend's house I tried to call the church, but no one picked up the telephone. It seemed everybody had already left. I told my friend about what happened, and she promised she would check to see if someone had found my Bible.

As I went home, my mind was preoccupied with my Bible. That Bible had special meaning for me. Five years before, my sister, Daicy, had given it to me as a birthday gift. Since that time that Bible was always with me, wherever I went. It became my "best friend." It was with me when I was sick, desperate, and in doubt. It also had my dried tears on it. It not only became my best friend during the down periods in my life but also during my happy times, when most of my prayers were answered. I knew it would be easy for me to buy another Bible, but deep in my heart I wanted my Bible back.

For the next three days I prayed that someone would find and keep my Bible. I realized there was only a small possibility of getting it back, since I hadn't written my name on it. Besides, the church building was used by another church on Sundays.

On Wednesday I again went to the church to attend prayer meeting and Bible study. I asked a deaconess if anyone had found my Bible, but no one had. Knowing that I had lost my Bible, my landlady lent me her Bible. I used it for several days and told myself to accept the fact that I'd lost my Bible forever. But it wasn't easy.

The next week, however, my friend told me that someone had, in fact, found my Bible. I was overjoyed at God's help. I know that He will never let me down. If only we put our trust in Him, we can be sure that He will take care of the rest. I want to put my trust in God, don't you?

LANNY LYDIA PONGILATAN

Locust Training

I will repay you for the years the locusts have eaten—the great locust and the young locust, the other locusts and the locust swarm. Joel 2:25, NIV.

IT FINALLY HAPPENED. Rumors of downsizing that had been flying through the office for months were now a reality. I received two months' pay, giving me plenty of time to find another job—or so I thought.

Six months later reality struck even harder. Bills had eaten up our savings, and I was still without a job. I cried to the Lord in frustration. Hadn't He promised to supply all of our needs? We were out of savings, and the budget revealed we were $500 short of meeting the bills every month. Things went from bad to worse. The IRS said we owed more money, and penalties were growing. It seemed that every time I turned around something else went wrong. Where was God when I really needed Him? Faithfully, I wrote out checks for our tithe and offerings, but it seemed God was not holding up His end of the bargain. I wasn't even asking for more than I could store, I simply wanted to meet the budget!

Over the next six months the Lord took me through a training ground such as I'd never been on before. Every month was a test of faith, yet He taught me valuable lessons. I learned to focus on—and trust in—His promises rather than looking at my circumstances. I learned that God can turn the worst of events into blessings.

One year to the day, I was employed again, and within a year our savings were restored and multiplied. We purchased a larger home and were out of debt and blessed beyond imagination. God was faithful to His word. He did supply all our needs during the year of the locust, just not in the way we thought He should. When the "training" was over, He not only replaced what the "locust" had eaten, He gave us much more than we'd had before. The greatest blessing of all, though, was learning to trust in His words rather than focusing on the circumstances around me.

Father, You have brought me to this very place in my life for Your purposes. Fill me with the desire to trust in Your decisions and to allow You first place in my life.
JUDY NEAL

Birthday Blues and Blessings

The faithful will abound with blessings. Prov. 28:20, NRSV.
Stand up and bless the Lord your God from everlasting to everlasting.
Blessed be your glorious name, which is exalted above all blessing and praise.
Neh. 9:5, NRSV.

MY HUSBAND WAS SCHEDULED to attend a week of church meetings. Again. I hadn't minded his going before, as the children were nearby, but this time I would be alone. Furthermore, he was leaving the morning before my birthday. The more I thought about it, the bluer I became.

The morning he left turned out to be sweltering hot, like a furnace, so I couldn't go out. The prayer band group was coming over, so I ventured out toward evening to buy some cakes. I made a wrong turn and stopped at a café for directions. A waitress told me the cake shop was very far up the road. She said I couldn't walk that distance in the hot sun and offered to take me to the shop in her car. What a blessing—and from a stranger! I even got two cakes at a reasonable price. Another blessing!

The meteorologist had forecast very hot conditions for the rest of the week. I prayed, "Please, Lord, send rain. Will You please answer this sinner's payer?" The next day it was cool and overcast.

Then another "blue" cropped up. On my birthday some thugs cut and stole the telephone cable, and our whole area suffered. No one could phone in or out. I questioned, *Why today?* I knew many folks were trying to contact me from overseas, as well as locally. For two days there was no connection.

Two days later I left early to walk to church. At the halfway point it started drizzling, and I prayed again. Just then my nephew stopped and gave me a lift to church—an instant answer. At church everybody crowded around me to find out why they hadn't been able to contact me, so I tried to explain. I was showered with good wishes, cards, and gifts.

The whole week the blessings just flowed, far outnumbering the blues, so I just kept praising the Lord! There's so much to be thankful for every day of our lives.

PRISCILLA ADONIS

Ten Ants and a Cashew

Bear ye one another's burdens, and so fulfil the law of Christ. Gal. 6:2.

ONE MORNING AS I was setting the table for breakfast I noticed a bustle of activity around a piece of cashew on the floor. Many tiny black ants were clustered around the nut. "Enjoy your breakfast!" I said.

By the time I had finished setting the table, the cashew and the ants were gone from the kitchen. I discovered they had taken the nut through the kitchen, through the dining room, and were just entering the front hallway.

As I prepared breakfast I kept checking on them every minute or two. I watched as they climbed with the cashew over the doorjamb and through a crack where the screen door didn't quite meet the doorframe.

I called my husband to watch as the procession took the nut across the front porch to the far wall. They climbed up the wall until they reached a small hole in the corner. It took them some maneuvering, but they finally found a way to get the cashew inside the hole.

I counted the ants. There were always 10 on the job. Two ants pulled, two pushed from behind, and three pushed from each side. Other ants scurried back and forth. As soon as one ant let go, another quickly rushed in to take up the load. During the course of 10 minutes most worker ants had been relieved. At one point I saw two ants nudging another ant who was pushing. Evidently the one pushing didn't want to quit. However, those two ants finally pulled the one away, and one of them took its place. All seemed eager to help. Now, that is cooperation for you! What one cannot do alone, we can all do when we work together to get a job done.

I immediately thought of the secretaries who work in our church's country headquarters office. Sometimes one of the secretaries gets sick or goes on leave or the work just gets piled up. It is then I've seen secretaries leave their own desk for a few hours to help lift the load of another. When I've had to face the inevitable backlog of work after a trip, it's meant the world to have someone come along and say, "May I help? I have time today."

Father, help me to remember the lesson of the ants. Show me someone whose burden I can bear today.   DOROTHY EATON WATTS

The Award Ceremony

For the Son of Man is to come with his angels, in the glory of his Father, and then he will repay everyone for what has been done. Matt. 16:27, NRSV.

IT WAS A BEAUTIFUL sunny day in early June. The sun glistened brightly on the dark-blue water of the lake. What a day to enjoy the best of God's creation! We docked our ski boat close to a picnic table by the shore. A few yards from us, on a small grassy hill, a large group was gathered under a shelter. Most of them were young boys, around 6 or 7 years of age.

As we were eating our lunch, every few minutes a loud clapping and cheering erupted from the shelter. At first we thought the children must be performing in some way. Then I saw a young boy proudly holding up a shiny brass trophy. It was obvious to all that he had received some kind of reward. As the clapping and cheering continued, we realized that every one of the boys, about 15 in all, were the proud recipients of trophies.

Later, I saw one of the mothers down by the water. She told me they were a Little League softball team. I asked if they had won the league championship. "Oh no," she said. "Actually, we came in next to last. But the boys all love their coach and have devoted their time and their very best effort to him. They all deserved recognition and praise for trying. They may not have won first prize, but they each played the game to the best of their abilities. Their hearts were in it, and they were filled with the desire to please him, so he said that in his eyes they were all winners."

God is our coach, loving us and giving us guidance and encouragement in the game of life. If we are filled with His Spirit, if we are committed to doing our very best to play by His rules, in His eyes we are winners. And His reward of eternal life, provided by His gift of redemption, is available for everyone who is committed to His team.   BARBARA SMITH MORRIS

The Other Side of the World

And the Lord will take away from thee all sickness. Deut. 7:15.

THE PHONE RANG JUST before 5:00 a.m. that Sunday, a sound very obtrusive in the still of the morning. *Nobody—not even my family—rings this early,* I thought. *I hope it's not bad news.*

It was worse than bad—it was terrible news. Our son had taken ill and was in a hospital in Italy, on the other side of the world. No, they didn't know any more. What a nightmare the next few days turned out to be! Should I fly over to Italy? I knew absolutely no one there. All I could do was pray. Eventually more details were filled in, thanks to our son's Belgian girl-friend, whose brother speaks Italian.

Our son is a mechanic on a race team based in France, and he'd been working incredibly long hours. There was no time to eat properly, no time to sleep very long at a stretch, and his body had said, "Enough is enough!" Tony had collapsed, and instead of being at a race circuit near Monza, he'd ended up in a hospital in Monza with a serious case of pneumonia. It felt isolating to be with people but to be unable to speak their language. And Tony was very ill.

I prayed; how I prayed! God heard and answered my prayers. He sent a doctor to my son's ward, an Italian doctor who had lived and worked for some time in America and spoke English with ease. The doctor hadn't been on the original roster, but was filling in for someone else. With the communication barrier broken, Tony said the relief was instant. There had recently been a huge yachting event in Auckland, New Zealand, between the countries of Italy and New Zealand. This formed a common bond between our Auckland-born son and the doctor, as both were keen "boaties."

Yes, God heard and answered my prayers, and after only five days Tony was well enough to leave the hospital to recuperate.

There will be no more sickness when Jesus comes and takes us home to heaven. And there will be no communication problems. It won't matter if we are Brown, Black, Yellow, or White. It won't matter if we speak German, Italian, French, or English. We will all have a common bond, a bond with our Savior Jesus Christ.

LEONIE DONALD

Ebenezer

Then Samuel took a stone and set it between Mizpah and Shen, and named it Ebenezer, saying, "Thus far the Lord has helped us." 1 Sam. 7:12, NASB.

ISRAEL, IN THE TIME of Samuel the prophet, was steeped in idolatry and sin, suffering oppression by the Philistines. But the nation responded to Samuel's call to return to God, repent of their sins, and put away their idols.

Their enemies heard of this and marched against them, causing great fear for Israel. They entreated the prophet to pray for them, and the Lord answered Samuel's prayer by thundering and confusing the Philistines, and they were routed. Samuel commemorated this wonderful victory by setting up a stone pillar he named Ebenezer—"thus far the Lord has helped us." This story has always intrigued me.

A few years ago my daughter, Judy, experienced a series of wonderful events in her life that brought her out of a debilitating depression. She then had an opportunity to go to a special computer college. However, there was no suitable public transportation, and she had no car. We managed to get a car for her for $750.

As we were discussing the car's need to perform well, I related the story of Samuel's pillar. Judy too was inspired, so much so that she promptly christened the car Ebenezer. We both felt that our God had been there for her every step of the way. Thus far, the Lord had helped her.

Throughout Judy's schooling and subsequent job search, Ebenezer performed acceptably. In time, Judy found just the right job only nine miles from her home. This is a job she has come to love, and again Ebenezer provided the needed transportation.

Recently my husband constructed a concrete block pillar at the top of the walkway going down to our river. Naturally, I named it Ebenezer. I walk down to the river every day for prayertime, and I find I can't pass this pillar without resting my hands on top and thanking God for His goodness. This daily time of gratitude and praise is a blessed way to begin my day.

Are there problems, worries, and concerns? Praise God, He has invited us to cast all our cares upon Him, for He cares for us! I know He has never failed me nor forsaken me. Ebenezer—thus far the Lord has helped us.

Thank You, dearest Father. MARILYN KING

How Possible?

Jesus looked at them and said, "With man this is impossible, but with God all things are possible." Matt. 19:26, NIV.

I FOUND MY DAUGHTER sleeping when I got to the children's ward of the Heatherwood Hospital. As I looked at her pale face and her bandaged wrist, I became very low-spirited; but I gathered courage and whispered, "Father, in times like this You are the only one I can call on for help; so let Your will be done, for our Marian is Your daughter, too."

Suddenly she woke up and said feebly, "Mommy, you came; I knew you would come. I'm very hungry, Mom, but the nurses are being mean to me. They refused to give me some of the lunch."

I checked and found out that her bed had a "Nil by mouth" sign on it. Then I was told that her fracture was so bad they needed to operate, but she had to wait her turn.

By 8:00 p.m. Marian had cried herself to sleep. An hour later two nurses came and took her to a side ward. My husband and I were invited to be there while they prepared her for the operation. When we got there, we were shocked to see that the nurses were our neighbors. All I could say was "How is this possible?" Then one of them explained. "Two night nurses are off with the flu, so Mrs. Waite and I were called in to cover, and we are going to help fix Marian's wrist." After they prepared her for the surgery, my husband prayed, and we left.

I thought of a phrase from Psalm 124:1: "If it had not been the Lord who was on our side." My 9-year-old girl had broken her wrist, and though I was disturbed, I trusted everything to God's hands. He had sent His angels in the form of Christian nurses, our neighbors and friends. Then I realized that with God all things are possible. My fear was replaced with joy, and I praised Him.

Then I thought, *Why did two nurses get the flu? And how is it that out of the hundreds of nurses in such a big hospital, God made it possible for these two surgery nurses to be called?* I can't tell, can you?

Loving Father, please give me hope, teach me to remember that You are always close, and with You everything is possible. MABEL KWEI

Our House—An Example

Live a life filled with love for others, following the example of Christ, who loved you and gave himself as a sacrifice to take away your sins. And God was pleased, because that sacrifice was like sweet perfume to him. Eph. 5:2, NLT.

ALMOST 30 YEARS WOULD pass before I'd meet again one of the three evangelists who came to our home church in 1965 to share the gospel of Jesus Christ. It was good seeing this pastor after so many years. During that series of meetings I had been baptized at age 15. My younger sister, Beth, had also been baptized, and my mom had been re-baptized.

As we reminisced, the pastor said two things that struck love chords deep within my heart. He said, "On my first visit to your house, I didn't know whether to stay or run. There were beer bottles stacked up outside the front door. When I entered the house, the air was blue from cigarette smoke."

His description was accurate. Soon, however, Daddy saw Jesus living in the hearts of his wife, Lila, and daughters, Debbie, Beth, and Janet. We prayed that Daddy would start going to church. He did, and was baptized. Daddy won the victory over his bad habits. Still I shout, "Amen! Thank You, Jesus!" Soon after that, he was in a horrific accident; and it was a miracle that he survived. Less than three years later, at age 44, Daddy passed away with stomach cancer. My daddy died with dignity, and in watching I sincerely believe that I became a better person.

Sonny was still quite young when our pastor-friend met him. It's always been obvious that Sonny is a special-needs child. The pastor said, "We'll just have to wait until we get to heaven to see who Sonny really is." I look forward to that day!

I have so many questions and concerns about mental retardation and autism that I don't know where to begin, Father. I was told, when I was still just a child, that if I believed in Jesus and trusted Him, even though I couldn't see the end from the beginning, I wouldn't want to change a single thing that's happened in my life. I guess this is the essence of my faith! Oh, how tightly I've clung to You since becoming Sonny's mommy. Therefore, I praise and trust You always.

It is my prayer that you trust the Lord in whatever you face this day. He is worthy of trust.

DEBORAH SANDERS

The Life-in-Review Thing

"For I know the plans I have for you," says the Lord. "They are plans for good and not for disaster, to give you a future and a hope." Jer. 29:11, NLT.

AS I APPROACHED MY fortieth birthday, I realized I had accomplished very little compared to what my former classmates had. I recently attended my twentieth high school reunion. To my dismay, I discovered that I had remained the same height—I'm still five inches shorter than all the other girls in my class. They had all finished college, and some had graduate degrees as well. It seemed they all had beautiful homes, successful jobs, exciting stories to tell, perfect children, and not a hair out of place. H'mmmm!

It's funny what we do to ourselves when we do the life-in-review thing. It usually starts like this: "Well, I didn't finish college because, well . . ."

For many reasons I have yet to finish my college degree; but make no mistake—I will! I chose instead the get-married route. I must admit I do love it. Motherhood has given me an edge on life that I would have never had if I had just gone to college. I understand now without any doubt the love God must have for me. I understand how He must feel and react when I'm in pain or go through times of disappointment. Parenthood, as many of you know, can alter your reality.

It dawned on me recently how God works with us as His children. It doesn't matter how tall we are or what degree we hold or don't hold. It doesn't matter how successful the job or how beautiful the home. It has taken me 40 years to realize that He is interested in my character, and that alone. What a discovery! This has changed my life and how I view everything. Now I wake each morning renewed, waiting to see how God's plan will test my character. I no longer see challenges as "Oh, brother, here we go again!" Now I say, "OK, Lord, what are we going to work on this week? Show me how this problem can improve my character."

As I head into this new life phase, I can only pray that the Lord will reveal more and more of what He has in mind for my life. Now I can see more clearly my accomplishments and how God has gently led me through many life experiences into a better understanding of His plans for me.

CATHY L. SANCHEZ

169

An Amazing Month

Call upon me in the day of trouble: I will deliver thee, and thou shalt glorify me. Ps. 50:15.

THE MONTH OF JUNE 2000 proved to be an amazing one for me. Early in the month I was traveling one morning to a nearby town to attend a church function. My route followed the Mississippi River, and the traffic was moderately heavy. While keeping an eye on the cars in front of me, I had the opportunity to admire the beautiful scenery God had created along the peaceful river.

Midway in my journey a car suddenly passed me, traveling at a high and reckless rate of speed. To my horror, I saw a car coming over a small hill ahead, straight toward this passing car. A crash seemed inevitable, with me situated somewhere in between them! Quickly I prayed for God's help. Incredibly an opening mysteriously appeared in front of my car where another automobile had been just seconds before. Checking to see that no one was behind me, I slowed my car and steered to the right. Halfway off the pavement and on the nearby grass, I was able to stop. The speeding driver was able to slip into the opening, and the accident was avoided. Miracle number one had occurred. Shaken, I thanked God for His protection and intervention, then continued safely on to my destination.

One sunny morning later in the month I decided to finish painting my cement driveway. Upon opening the paint can that I had previously used, I discovered I didn't have enough paint to complete the job. I decided to go ahead and paint as much as I could while I had the opportunity.

As time went by, I noticed that the paint level in the can never seemed to go down. Thanks to God, the paint lasted the whole job with some left over for touch-ups! Then the paint can became empty! It was miracle number two for which to thank God. June was certainly a month to remember with a grateful heart.

Dear heavenly Father, I am so grateful for the love and protection You bestow upon Your family daily. You constantly amaze us with Your goodness. Please enable us to always be willing to help others, as You are always willing to help us.
ROSEMARY BAKER

The Ultimate

Behold, what manner of love the Father hath bestowed upon us, that we should be called the sons of God. 1 John 3:1.

THERE IT WAS IN a little out-of-the-way shop on a back street! Black ink on silk, depicting the rudiments of landscape painting our art appreciation teacher had enumerated for us. The landscape components included a distinct foreground: the bent-over willow-tree branches touched the clear waters of a lake. A simple pier extended into the lake to accommodate the fragile fishing boat. Low hills extended from the lake's opposite shore, partly obscured by vapor and fog. Massive peaks penetrated the cloud cover and stretched heavenward.

How would my classmates with their varied cultural and philosophical backgrounds interpret these elements? As a Christian, I envisioned the foreground with its graceful willow and simple pier as today, tomorrow, and perhaps next month. Present activities on life's lake are generally quite well defined and relatively predictable. The fisherman was small, faintly visible from the shore. In size, humanity is insignificant in the immense universe.

Thinking of the fisherman, I admitted to myself that in God's great universe I am even smaller than a period on this paper. Although I'm so minute in His amazing creation, I've learned that God is aware of me and has plans for me. He has told me, "I will be a Father unto you, and ye shall be my sons and daughters" (2 Cor. 6:18), and "I have loved thee with an everlasting love" (Jer. 31:3). He has sent His Son to take the punishment for my sins (John 3:16).

And His Son explains to me that He came that I might "have life" and "have it more abundantly" (John 10:10). Furthermore, His Son promises to come back to take me to be with Him (John 14:2, 3). And there is a hint of more to come: He is preparing a place for me. I haven't seen or heard, nor can I even imagine what it will be like (1 Cor. 2:9)!

I visualized the foothills, partially obscured by clouds, as next year and the next and the next after that. What involvements, achievements, and joys might I encounter in my lifetime? And those massive peaks penetrating the fog suggested the ultimate—an eternity with God.

Ah, the ultimate! A daughter of God living eternally amid the majestic mountains of His creation! What love my Father bestows on us!

LOIS E. JOHANNES

I Am With You

Fear thou not; for I am with thee: be not dismayed; for I am thy God: I will strengthen thee; yea, I will help thee; yea, I will uphold thee with the right hand of my righteousness. Isa. 41:10.

I WAS PREPARING TO attend a graduation ceremony early one Sunday morning when suddenly my thoughts drifted to the following day. I would be leaving my husband behind to return to my home and work. This was the first time that we would be separated by 1,000 miles for medical reasons. I dreaded the thought of leaving him behind. I wondered how he'd manage. I'd gotten used to accompanying him to his treatments. I felt sad and alone.

Suddenly—out of nowhere, it seemed—I heard an old familiar hymn playing on the Christian station: "Thou wilt keep him in perfect peace, whose mind is stayed on Thee." I listened as several other familiar hymns began to soothe my sad heart: "I am weak but Thou art strong," "Peace, be still!" "Just a closer walk with Thee," "All the way my Savior leads me." I began to hum along as I meditated on the words.

The hymn that brought the greatest feeling of solace and peace of mind was "Under His wings I am safely abiding; though the night deepens and tempests are wild, still I can trust Him; I know He will keep me; He has redeemed me, and I am His child." What beautiful words! As I listened I felt as though God was speaking directly to me through these hymns of assurance and comfort. My faith was strengthened to know that He who holds tomorrow would take care of my husband and me. A wonderful feeling saturated my body. What a great God we serve! It was amazing how these hymns seemed custom-made for me at a time when I needed them most.

My anxiety and worry vanished, replaced by hymns that God had sent my way to dispel my moments of anxiety. The next day as I sat on the plane I found myself humming these hymns as I traveled my long journey home alone—well, not really alone, because I had the assurance that God was with me.

Friend, I am here to tell you that when your burdens are too heavy to bear and life seems to hit you with hard blows, don't grow weary or be discouraged. God is able to see you through. He has promised never to leave us nor forsake us. He is a keeper of promises. SHIRLEY C. IHEANACHO

The Gray Cat

God is our refuge and strength, a very present help in trouble. Ps. 46:1.

THERE WASN'T A CLOUD in the azure-blue sky that Sunday morning. It was a perfect day for cycling, so my husband and I started out on our regular route in minimal traffic. Everything seemed peaceful.

As we rounded the corner and turned off onto a side road, I saw the cat. He was just sitting there, looking on as my husband rode slowly by. *OK, kitty,* I thought as I glanced at the gray brindled creature. *Stay right there, little cat. Here I come.* I expected the cat to remain still, but he had a different idea. Just as my bike drew up beside him, across the street he darted, directly toward me. I felt a soft thump as my front wheel slapped his side. The cat sped away, apparently unhurt, but I went hurtling to the ground, the bicycle almost on top of me. "Lord, have mercy on me," I prayed as I sprawled, dirty and bruised, on the wet, muddy shoulder of the road in a dazed heap. My husband rushed over. Gently, he pulled me up, brushed off the mud, and straightened my bike. Shaken, we rode slowly home.

When I set out on my journey I never expected to fall or be hurt, but God uses troubles to educate His children. He used that jarring incident to teach me a precious lesson. He helped me customize Psalm 91:15: "I will be with her in trouble. I will deliver her and honor her."

Putting ice on my swelling shin and the reddening bruises, I remembered an old adage: "The oak is not only threatened by the storms but toughened by them." I realized afresh that I was strengthened by the painful situation. I knew I could have broken a bone or been more badly bruised, but He gave me instead the opportunity to praise Him.

There's a quote in an old book that brought me comfort: "God takes a thousand times more pains with us than the artist with his picture, by many touches of sorrow, and by many colors of circumstance, to bring us into the form which is the highest and noblest in His sight."*

Thank You, God, for rescuing and strengthening me through the bruises of my circumstance. You are indeed a present help in my time of trouble, and You never turn away.

LEILA FAY GREENE

---

* Mrs. Charles E. Cowman, comp. *Streams in the Desert* (Grand Rapids, Mich.: Zondervan Publishing, 1925), p. 152.

Hiding in the Secret Place

Oh, how great is Your goodness, which You have laid up for those who fear You, which You have prepared for those who trust in You in the presence of the sons of men! You shall hide them in the secret place of Your presence. Ps. 31:19, 20, NKJV.

I WAS ENJOYING THE beauty of the early hours of a June morning working in my flower garden. I reached over to remove a Johnny-jump-up that had grown too close to another choice plant. Imagine my surprise when I felt the soft warm fur of a living creature under the foliage. Lifting the leaves, I looked into the eyes of a tiny little rabbit, calmly sitting in its hiding place. Thinking a mother had left her baby there for protection while she went to eat, I covered the little animal with the plants and weeds I had pulled out.

Several hours later I again went to the garden to see if the mother had come to take her baby home. When I lifted the greenery, the little bunny was still patiently waiting for its mother. I knew now that mother would not be returning, and baby needed help. I called Tiffany, my granddaughter, and told her to come see what I'd found. When she and her mother came, they watched in awe as the bunny remained quietly hidden in its secret place.

Of course, Tiffany was eager to take the bunny home and keep it as a pet. As with all wild animals, great consideration must be taken when deciding to keep a rabbit in captivity. Her mother agreed to care for the bunny if Tiffany was willing to return it to the wild when it was old enough to care for itself. So the bunny spent the next few weeks in a cage, growing to maturity as it was well cared for and loved. When the day came that it could survive on its own, the bunny was taken to a wooded area where it could find its natural habitat, and released.

When we face challenges in our life we can put our trust in the Lord. He will hide us in the secret place of His presence. There we can calmly wait, rest, and trust in His goodness, His protection, and His deliverance from the evils that assail us.

Lord, when trials and troubles come, help me to remember that You will hide me in the secret of Your presence. You will cover me and protect me from the evils that plague my soul. Thank You for this precious promise.

EVELYN GLASS

Encapsulated by His Arms

Those who wait on the Lord shall renew their strength; they shall mount up with wings like eagles, they shall run and not be weary, they shall walk and not faint. Isa. 40:31, NKJV.

WHILE ON SUMMER VACATION in Aberdaron, North Wales, my husband and I purchased a painting of the Lleyn Peninsula depicting its wonderful picturesque coastline and surrounding hillsides. This year we decided to find that same view and to sit where the artist sat and to admire it firsthand. We headed off, following the coastal road and passing many a tiny cottage nestled in along the road and hillsides. We saw a sign that said "Tea Shop." *Great*, we thought, *afternoon tea!* After all, vacations are for those lovely treats—homemade scones, jam, and cream.

However, we soon realized that we'd taken the wrong road as we approached a V junction. As we were studying the map, we both looked up toward the sea. Yes, there it was, the view, the treasure that we had been in search of. The sight was so breathtaking that we couldn't believe our eyes: magnificent coastline. Shimmering sea. Bardsey Island in the distance, and two islands off the Aberdaron Bay that have become bird sanctuaries. Encapsulating all of the Lleyn Peninsula in one magnificent sight was breathtaking. As we sat in our car taking in the view, our favorite song, "The Power of Your Love," by Geoff Bullock, played on the car stereo.

"Lord, I come to You. Let my heart be changed, renewed. Flowing from the grace that I've found in You."

The moment was captured. The view—a tiny piece of land almost surrounded by water—reminded me of how God daily stretches out His arms and encapsulates us in His arms of unconditional love and offers us instant forgiveness and peace that can be found only in Him.

I should like to thank You, Lord, for the privilege of allowing us to find such places that encapsulate Your love and beauty. Hold me close; let Your love surround me; bring me near. Draw me to Your side; and as I wait I'll rise up like an eagle and I will soar with You. Your Spirit leads me on in the power of Your love.

ANNETTE KOWARIN

Lost in Lucerne

All we like sheep have gone astray; we have turned every one to his own way. Isa. 53:6.

WHAT A GORGEOUS SUNNY day it was as we left the hotel that morning to tour the Swiss Alps. The views of the mountains and lakes were spectacular, and we enjoyed every minute.

On the schedule that day was a two-hour shopping stop at Lucerne in the late afternoon. We eagerly looked forward to visiting the quaint shops. Before we left the bus, our driver, Hans, told us to note our route so we could find our way back to the bus at exactly the set time.

My friend, Lois, and I set out for the shops. I had wanted to find a Heidi doll as a gift to our daughter, Heidi. None of the places we checked had one. I then noticed a street going uphill, a little apart from the area we were in. Although the time was short, we went anyway. We weren't able to find the Heidi doll, and, on top of that, as we left the last store we got disoriented and went the wrong direction.

It's OK, I thought. *Everyone here knows English.* I was wrong. We asked several people, and no one understood us, not even the Swiss police. Such a dilemma! Lost in a foreign country where we didn't know the language, and a bus was waiting.

Then we spied a familiar building and knew we needed to turn left. We made it back to the bus 20 minutes late, and the whole group booed us as we climbed aboard. It was embarrassing to have kept everyone waiting.

Why had I insisted on more shopping when Lois reminded me that our time was running out? It was one of those stubborn little characteristics that led me on, forgetting about the inconvenience it might cause.

Isn't that how we often get in trouble? Perhaps we put our prayer and Bible study off and something else comes up, so we delay our appointment with God while He waits. Then sometimes we do feel as if we're lost, as if we are in a foreign country. Many of our non-Christian friends don't understand our language either.

How important it is to stay on the right path; but if we do get lost, Jesus doesn't boo us when we come back. Instead, He waits for us with open arms.

DARLENE YTREDAL BURGESON

An Earnest Prayer Answered

O give thanks unto the Lord, for he is good: for his mercy endureth for ever.
Ps. 107:1.

I TOOK FOUR BARRELS of clothing and other articles to share while on vacation to visit my family in Jamaica. When I arrived in the country, I had to clear customs and shipping and pay $8,600 in Jamaican currency for the release of documents. I was told I'd also be required to pay $7,500 to customs. All I had left was $5,500 in Jamaican dollars.

After opening the barrels for inspection, a female customs officer refused to inspect them. So I prayed silently, *Lord, please send a male customs inspector to help me. Thank You. Amen.* As I opened my eyes, a male customs inspector walked in my direction. I approached him and asked, "Sir, will you please inspect the contents of these barrels?" He consented with a smile and proceeded to check the barrels. He then informed me I would have to pay $7,500.

"Sir, I have only $5,500," I said. He told me to go to the cashier and purchase a form for $50. As I followed his instructions, my heart beat twice its normal pace. I had just spent $50 of the money I so badly needed. I continued to pray, filled out the form, and took it back to the cashier, only to have her confirm my insufficient funds. I would have to travel 46 miles to get the balance of the money and return the next day.

The barrels would remain open, with no guarantee I would find them as I left them. I returned to the officer to see if he could assist, though he had done all he was required to do. "Follow me," he said, heading toward his office. He stopped at the door, looked into his shirt pocket, and handed me $500. I was in total shock. I tried to say thank you, but a big lump rose in my throat. Before I could get the words out, he said, "By the way, you're going to need bus fare." He reached back into his pocket and handed me another $500. With tears streaming down my face, I managed to ask for his telephone number. I have since had the opportunity to witness to his family and interact with them on a regular basis.

I cried all the way home, "God is good! God is good!" My family couldn't imagine why I was still shouting and crying "God is good!" when I got home. I'm sure it was the hand of God that used that officer to deliver me from that situation. When you cry unto Him, He will answer.

GERTRUDE E. BURKE

The Solid Rock

The Lord is my rock, and my fortress, and my deliverer; my God, my strength, in whom I will trust; my buckler, and the horn of my salvation, and my high tower. Ps. 18:2.

TODAY AS I START out on my usual leisurely walk along the pathway adjacent to the shoreline of the bay near where I live, my feet seem to have a mind of their own as they lead me closer and closer to the water's edge. There I stand, transfixed, gazing in awesome wonder across the vast expanse of seemingly endless ocean, shimmering brightly as silver sunbeams dance merrily on the calm surface, as if performing just for me. The reflection of the blue sky, puffy white clouds, and surrounding hillside paints the most beautiful picture my eyes have ever beheld.

The ocean seems unusually calm for this time of day and reluctant to send any of its waves my direction. I remain motionless, filled with tranquillity and peace, as the gentle breeze caresses my face. God's presence is so very real. I can almost feel His hand holding mine. I softly whisper prayers of praise and thanksgiving to the Master Designer. Oh, how I wish that I could be caught up in the clouds today to be with Him forever! It would be a perfect day for traveling—barely any wind! But no, it's not to be. Not today.

Without warning the scene before me changes drastically. The angry north wind seems to have been awakened from its slumber, sending the lazy waves crashing to the shore with such violence and speed that I quickly scramble for safety. I take my cue from an experienced feathered friend who has both feet planted firmly on a nearby rock. He doesn't seem to mind at all the sudden intrusion as I frantically take my hold upon the rock, clinging for dear life lest I be swept out to sea and lost forever.

I am again reminded that when the angry waves from the storms of life threaten to overcome and drown me I can have confidence as I stand firmly on the Rock of Ages, Jesus Christ. I need not fear, for He will rescue and save me.

I will praise Your name forever, Lord, my rock and my salvation.

VIRGINIA CASEY

All Are Invited

And the Spirit and the bride say, Come. Rev. 22:17.

I WAS IN A QUANDARY. The time for the wedding was almost here, and we hadn't been invited! Anticipating a shower for the bride, whom we'd known all her life, we'd checked the bridal registry at a department store and selected a nice gift. Then I agreed to help host the shower and spent several hours working on the refreshments. In thanking the guests for the gifts, the honoree said she hoped each one could be at the wedding; however, I was aware that we still hadn't received an invitation. The wedding was in our church, so I thought perhaps there would be an announcement in the church bulletin with a general invitation. It didn't happen, so I reluctantly concluded that we wouldn't go.

There have been other times when we were invited to a wedding but not the reception. We learned after one wedding in our church that it was intended that all the guests be included. Years ago we drove for several hours to attend the wedding of the son of a coworker. Our invitation hadn't mentioned the reception, so we left immediately after the wedding ceremony for the long drive home. They had assumed that no one from so far away would leave before the reception, so they hadn't invited us. They were most apologetic when they realized what had happened. Such an oversight had sad results at one wedding when not one person went to the reception! The beautiful bride, an only child, had grown up in a multigenerational home. Her adoring grandfather was so disappointed and upset that there were no guests that he cried.

We do have an invitation to a very special wedding, and you're invited too, when the Lamb of God comes to claim His chosen bride. This is the one wedding, above all others, that I don't want to miss! We're all invited to the reception, too, which will be everlasting and more wonderful than the most lavish ever seen on this earth.

Matthew 22 tells us that there were people who were invited to the wedding of a king's son who made excuses not to be there. The king was angry and sent his servants into the highways and byways to find others to take their places. I don't want anyone to take my place, do you? Send in your acceptance today!

MARY JANE GRAVES

I Wasn't Afraid

There is no fear in love; but perfect love casteth out fear. 1 John 4:18.

I SAW HIM STANDING on my front porch as I pulled my car into the drive. I almost panicked. All the old fear engulfed me until I thought I couldn't breathe. Just one look took me back to my early childhood.

I don't remember a time when I wasn't afraid of him. I was afraid when he hit me, when he touched me, and made me touch him, in all the wrong places. I was even afraid when he looked at me. I was around 8 when my mother noticed that I had too many bruises after a visit to his house. She never made me go back. I never had the courage to tell her the other things he'd done to me; I was just happy I didn't have to see him anymore.

As the years went on, I thought I'd forget, but I didn't. I was afraid of all the men around me, though I tried not to let it show. Then I met God, and slowly, more than 14 years of hate and fear began to seep away, and peace filled the void.

Then, after all those years, there he was, waiting for me to get out of the safety of my car and go to meet him. "God, help me not to hate him for what he did to me," I breathed as I picked up my purse and opened the car door. With confidence on my face that was only skin-deep, I walked up to the house. He hadn't moved since I'd driven up. I smiled and said hello. He smiled back. Looking at him, I realized I'd never noticed before how short he was. All my life I'd thought of him as the biggest, scariest person I knew. Then it hit me—he wasn't the biggest anymore because I had met Someone bigger.

I smiled again, this time for real. We talked for a while; then he left. As I watched him go I discovered that I wasn't sad he'd come; I was happy. I never saw him again, never found out if he'd changed or if the only thing that changed was the way I saw him. I don't think it really matters, because I found out that day that I never need to be afraid of anything, because God is with me. His love surrounds me, and in that love there is no room for fear. Where there is no fear, there is no hate.

SALOME MARKS

The Jilted Bride

When one of those at the table with him heard this, he said to Jesus, "Blessed is the man who will eat at the feast in the kingdom of God." Luke 14:15, NIV.

ACCORDING TO A STORY in the Boston *Globe* (June 1990), a woman and her fiancé planned a $13,000 catered hotel wedding banquet. They made the required down payment for half of the total bill. The day the announcements were to be mailed, the groom got cold feet and backed out. His angry fiancé returned to the hotel to cancel the banquet but learned the contract was binding. She had two choices: forfeit the down payment, or go ahead with the banquet.

The jilted bride thought it over and decided to go ahead with the banquet—not a wedding banquet, but a big bash for her friends. A few years before, she'd been penniless and lived in a homeless shelter. During the next few years she'd done well financially. So instead of a wedding banquet, she changed the menu to "boneless chicken"—in honor of the groom. A new party was planned and invitations sent to rescue missions and homeless shelters. On the evening of the banquet, those who were accustomed to begging and gleaning from garbage cans dined on gourmet foods. Bag ladies, vagrants, and addicts were served in style by tuxedoed waiters.

As I read this story I thought of the parable of the great banquet recorded in Luke 14. Jesus wanted to correct our notions about who God is and whom God loves. Jesus often hung out with women of ill repute, foreigners, and outcasts. And when He did so, the Pharisees often stood at the edge of the crowd, muttering and grinding their teeth. Who would waste money throwing an expensive banquet for the outcasts of society? What would people think? Who in their right mind would honor the homeless before the educated wealthy?

But Jesus said He came to save the sick, not the well; the unrighteous, not the righteous. "There will be more rejoicing in heaven over one sinner who repents than over ninety-nine righteous persons who do not need to repent" (Luke 15:7, NIV).

Lord, may I always be willing to accept Your invitation to dine with You at Your banquet table. I am aware of my unworthiness but trust You to make me acceptable to be a guest at the table You have prepared for me.

NANCY L. VAN PELT

Proving the Lord

And it shall come to pass, that before they call, I will answer; and while they are yet speaking, I will hear. Isa. 65:24.

I WAS A SECOND-YEAR teacher who received my summer pay in a lump sum early in the summer vacation. After receiving my lump sum that summer, I cashed it at a local bank and returned home. I was faced with a dilemma. My husband of three years was missing. He'd been part of a crew sailing a boat from Florida to our home island; they had failed to make radio contact at the expected time and were now two weeks overdue. All efforts to locate them had been unsuccessful.

I had a 20-month-old son, a missing husband, and a small lump sum to last for six weeks until I'd receive another paycheck. Should I pay tithe under these circumstances? I'd grown up paying tithe whenever I worked, but I'd never been in such a difficult situation. It was a real struggle because the enemy made his case for not bothering with it this time.

On arriving home, I entered my bedroom and closed the door. I counted out the tithe and offering and placed them in an envelope. Then I fell on my knees and told the Lord what He already knew. I didn't know how I'd manage, but I was giving Him the tithe and an offering. In tears, I lingered on my knees.

Then I heard the telephone ringing. It was wonderful news! My husband was alive! The boat had been found in Cuba. Words are inadequate to express my joy at the news and my awe at the goodness of God.

How quickly He had responded to my commitment! Truly, while I was yet speaking to Him in prayer He was moving the wheels of the Cuban government to reveal the whereabouts of that boat and its crew.

Would I ever neglect to return tithe to Him? By His grace, I won't, for I have proved His faithfulness and know that His promises are sure. His children can always depend on Him to come through on their behalf when they call on Him.

CANDACE SPRAUVE

God's Mirror

Love never fails. . . . Now we see but a poor reflection as in a mirror; then we shall see face to face. Now I know in part; then I shall know fully, even as I am fully known. 1 Cor. 13:8-12, NIV.

RECENTLY I HAD THE wonderful experience of getting married for the last time in my life. How do I know this? There is but One whom I love more than this man, and He is the Lord. I am ultimately addicted to the love of God. My feelings are accepted by my heavenly Father as they are. When I'm ready, He lovingly holds a spiritual mirror before my soul.

During those times when God is stretching my point of view, I may cry, laugh, or feel either humiliated (though embraced) or apologetic. The Lord's ability to show me who I really am inside the human mask I wear is not always appreciated, though His honesty is necessary for my spiritual growth. Eventually the image I hope to reflect is that of His heart to the world.

Because I'm a stubborn—at moments arrogant and at other times self-pitying—bratty human woman, God has to veil the mirror of my heart. It's not an image I can view full force and exist. He is my consolation in my hours of need, nurturing me with strength and kindness. We're not shown something awful about ourselves without the gift of God's presence beside us to make our effort a positive experience.

There are others who are always willing to tell us what to do, overly insistent that what they think is best for us is the only way. Even after years they'll tell us they knew it would never work out, or that they knew we should have listened to them. And then there is the evil angel working against us by twisting the truth, most often showing us our soul's mirror through the tainted eyes of one lost from grace. Or if we already have low self-esteem it makes us feel bad about ourselves. It leads us away from the Lord's wings of love, those wings wanting so desperately to surround us with love and peace and joy.

When praying and giving God time in conversation, I am gifted with the enjoyment of His response. Not just by feeling, but by hearing Him and relaxing in His ancient eternal existence where I am allowed to just be. I am given the confidence that what I hear and what I feel are indeed the positive gifts of the Lord. Those moments are precious and, yes, very necessary.

SALLY J. AKEN-LINKE

Give Me Another Chance

I am the rose of Sharon and the lily of the valleys. S. of Sol. 2:1.

I AM A NATURE LOVER—I enjoy watching the formation of the clouds, the sparkling raindrops, beautiful sunsets, the different shades of green carpeting the earth. But above all, I love flowers. I take pleasure in watching the formation of a bud as it gets bigger and a full flower bursts forth in all its beauty. Because of my love of nature I found myself specializing in growing roses. It gave me great joy as I tended them, talked to them, and watched as they came forth so beautifully.

Because of the sandy soil of Florida, my roses started dwindling after a few years, so I started raising orchids, which were even more fascinating. I had as many as 30 plants. Oh, the beauty and fragrance! I had them for years, but when we moved to a condo I had to get rid of some. In making the selection as to the ones I would take, there was one plant that I'd had for about three years, and although it was petted and cared for like the rest, it never bloomed. One morning I told it I was very disappointed and maybe I shouldn't take it. After sorting those I was taking, I looked at this particular plant, and it looked so lonely that I decided to take it with me.

Every morning I talked to the plants and reminded that nonbloomer that if there were no blooms it would be thrown out. To my surprise, one morning I saw a little green thing coming up from one of the leaves. I watched each day, and finally it was a bud. I was so excited, and started praising it. After a few days I saw a small petal, and one morning there was a beautiful flower, a lacy, embroidered white flower, the most delicate of all the orchids. I praised and petted it every day. This bloom lasted for nearly three weeks, and its fragrance perfumed the entire room.

Then one morning while admiring the plant, I remembered that I'd planned to throw it out. Then I thought of our lives. So many times we go our own way instead of God's way, and then we're left looking lonely and forlorn. But our loving and merciful Father never leaves us. Instead He carefully and lovingly cares for us, watching, protecting, and guiding us until we eventually bloom into beautiful flowers, full blooms for His heavenly garden.

PEARL MANDERSON

The Father

Now may our Lord Jesus Christ himself, and God our Father, who loved us and gave us eternal comfort and good hope through grace, comfort your hearts and establish them in every good work and word. 2 Thess. 2:16, 17, RSV.

RECITALS, GRADUATION, AWARD ceremonies, plays, concerts, games—I went to many of these functions when my girls were little, and I still continue to go to these things even though the girls are now in college. I enjoy watching parents and grandparents, aunties and uncles, applauding the little ones. Many times I've heard mothers say, "That's my girl!" or "That's my boy!" The pride is in their faces, the joy in their voices. I've seen, for example, a 5-year-old child performing a very simple or common piano piece. The applause of the parents and grandparents is not less than the applause when their child is called to receive a doctorate degree or a valedictorian award.

When my daughters first sang in church or when they first recited a Bible verse, the joy that I felt is the same joy I feel now when they make a graduation speech or sing the song they composed or read articles they themselves wrote.

I remember when I surprised my youngest daughter, Cristine, during her eighth-grade graduation in Kenya, Africa. I made the trip from Washington, D.C., to Africa, just to witness my little girl's graduation. I was so proud to see her march! Even when finances were low, I flew to California just to see my daughter, Susan, perform in a musical drama. You should have seen the beam in my eyes as I watched her perform!

God, looking at His children—some veterans in the faith, others just little children, performing their best for the Master—feels the same joy.

We may be a church elder or a clerk, a treasurer or a deaconess, a chorister or a pianist—whatever we do for the Lord is great, and the Lord is proud of us just as our earthly parents are proud of even the little things we do. We may not be a Moses, but we can be an Aaron, holding up the hands of a Moses; God is pleased with us.

Just remember that every time we lift a name in prayer or lend a helping hand or offer a shoulder to lean on, the Lord is proud of us. He smiles as He sees us do things for Him.   JEMIMA D. ORILLOSA

Like Little Children

And he said: "I tell you the truth, unless you change and become like little children, you will never enter the kingdom of heaven." Matt.18:3, NIV.

I LOVE SPENDING TIME with my 8-month-old granddaughter, Bianca. She marvels at the simple things of life: a silly face, a funny sound, a tickle, a quick-moving graphic on the computer, the gentle breeze, the neighbor's dog barking, voices on the radio. She finds pleasure in these things. Her toys bring a smile to her face, and even everyday things that we adults think are mundane are stimulating and challenging for her. It's fun watching her.

It's a great experience, too, listening to her make new sounds. "Maaaa-maaaa. B-r-r-r-r-r-. Ooooooh!" They come out without her even trying, it seems, and oh, how cute they are! She'll make them again and again, slowly adding more complex ones. I like listening to her and have even made a tape, as I did with my children, so she can listen to herself when she is older. By then she won't remember her exciting learning-to-talk phase.

My moments with Bianca are precious to me and bring countless hours of happiness. And yes, she keeps me young (not that I'm old yet!). I seek opportunities to help her discover life because I love seeing her reactions. Each stage of her life will bring its own discoveries, yet they won't compare to the wonder of these first experiences when she doesn't know what to expect and anything is potential pleasure for her.

What a change from the adult world! We take much for granted, expect more than we should, and are dissatisfied most of the time. We find no pleasure in simple things and therefore often miss out on life's unexpected pleasures. We drive ourselves to do more, have more, be more. How different from little children! No wonder Jesus said we must become as little children. Oh, just to go back for a day and joyfully take everything at face value!

Lord, help us to be like little children, accepting all the simple yet wonderful blessings You send our way, without feeling the need to add to Your already perfect plan for us. Amen. IRIS L. STOVALL

Water From the Source

Come to me, all you who are weary and burdened, and I will give you rest.
Matt. 11:28, NIV.

I HAD NEVER LIKED to drink water because I didn't like the taste of it. It would take a mighty thirst to make me drink water. But during a hike in the mountains I learned to appreciate water.

It was so hot during our picnic lunch that we rested and drank and bathed our feet in an icy mountain brook. After lunch we hiked through a gorge; the sun was very hot! We'd almost reached the end of the gorge when we needed to climb up a steep path. But I couldn't go on. I was exhausted. And I was terribly thirsty. Unfortunately, we'd left the water in the car.

We'd already seen the most beautiful part of the gorge, so we turned back. And then we came to a waterfall. If I didn't want to die of thirst, I would have to drink that water. Pure, cold water from the source splashed into my hands as I stretched them to the waterfall. What a delight! I couldn't drink very much, but I felt refreshed and strengthened for the next few steps. A few mouthfuls of water at every source we came upon made our way back a pure delight. (And by the way, the bottled water never tasted as good as the water directly from the source.)

This experience opened my eyes to an important truth. Jesus invites, "Come to me . . . and I will give you rest." Rest refreshes us. How I needed such refreshment! At that time my life was like a ride on a roller coaster.

Jesus: the source of life. His word: the water of life. It's not enough to drink just once and then go on through life without a reserve of water. It's not enough to hear a sermon, experience companionship with believers, and talk about spiritual things once a week, only to forget and neglect prayer and personal devotions in the hassle of our work week. If I'm not refreshed by the water of life on a regular basis, I'll only be able to complain when painful situations and difficulties arise. They'll test my faith and make me lose all the joy of living.

I can come to the source of life, Jesus, in prayer every day, and read His word, which "is living and active. . . . It penetrates even to dividing soul and spirit, . . . It judges the thoughts and attitudes of the heart" (Heb. 4:12, NIV). Refreshment from the source—I love that taste! What about you?

SABINE SCHLICKE

Houdini Ducks

I am not saying this because I am in need, for I have learned to be content whatever the circumstances. Phil. 4:11, NIV.

THE VARIETY AND NUMBER of beautiful Australian birds that fly through the eucalyptus trees on our property give us continual delight. One day as I was pulling some weeds from beneath the camellia bushes along our driveway, there was a sudden flurry of wings and small bird cries as at least a hundred gorgeously colored lorikeets swooped low to zoom in on a flowering gum tree. There they partied on nectar for at least a half hour.

We've seen kookaburras and magpies, butcher-birds, galah parrots, native yellow-beaked mynas, and other species enjoying the birdbath. Many wood ducks make this area their home and fly down from the trees to waddle importantly in groups around our grounds. Amazingly, one black-and-white magpie will decide to round them up and send them packing, if it suits him, and a dozen wood ducks move off obediently.

These wood ducks are really very greedy creatures, eating everything in sight. This has caused a mini tactical war between my husband and the ducks. Oh, he's quite fond of them, but they gulp down all the birdseed he has for the beautiful redheads he is in love with. These eastern rosella parrots have brilliant red plumage on their heads, complemented by yellow and iridescent blues and greens. They are jewel-colored and much smaller than ducks.

You'd be intrigued by my husband's ingenuity in providing a feeding station that is solely for the eastern rosellas. For every model he's produced, the greedy ducks have managed to do Houdini contortions and gobble up the seed while the rosellas hover like shadows in the nearby trees. At last he produced a feeding station with four high wire loops to dissuade the ducks, but there they were, one at a time, their webbed feet at contortionist angles and their heads twisted so that the greedy beaks could gobble as usual.

I guess the Houdini ducks don't know about the tenth commandment as we humans do, although we often go on coveting our neighbor's something or other and twisting ourselves into uncomfortable and unsustainable knots just the same.

May God give me contentment with what He has provided for me today.

URSULA M. HEDGES

About Mosquitoes and Faith

The apostles said to the Lord, "Increase our faith!" Luke 17:5, NIV.

SUMMERTIME ARRIVED, AND IT was time for my vacation, for which I had longed so much! I accompanied my friend, who lives in Europe, to her home in Martinique and spent two weeks with her family.

It was the rainy season when we arrived, and I had a hard time adapting to the hot and humid climate. Eventually it became easier, but in addition to the climate there was a second problem that hindered me from enjoying my holidays—mosquitoes that seemed to love my blood! Shortly after my arrival I had more than 60 bites on my legs. We tried many different products and approaches to lessen my agony—sprays, electronic appliances, long trousers, socks—but nothing worked. One night was particularly terrible, and I could no longer stand the pain and the itching. I cried, and the only thing I wanted was to return to Europe.

The next morning my friend and I read together a devotional on Luke 17:5. The author quoted several texts from Matthew, and his conclusion was that it's not the amount of faith that counts but the quality. As I reflected on my mosquito problem, the devotional came back to my mind. I realized this was sort of a test to reveal the quality of my faith, so I prayed, "Lord, You are all-powerful. Even the mosquitoes obey You, and I know and believe that You can prevent them from biting me. Please help me. I thank You, because You hear my prayer and because You have already started to act on my behalf."

Then my friend's neighbor, who saw my despair, offered me a place to sleep at her apartment under a mosquito net. I was so grateful for the care of my friends and this neighbor. It took several days until the itching sensations got better, but at the new sleeping place I received no new bites. I praised God for His intervention. With relief from the mosquito bites, I gratefully stayed through my vacation. I went home with plenty of nice memories: hospitality I had experienced, family worships, excursions, beautiful nature, and lively church services.

Thank You, Lord. Please help each one of us to increase the quality of our faith, to believe that You are all-powerful, and to trust You completely.

HEIKE EULITZ

What Do You Treasure?

For where your treasure is, there your heart will be also. Matt. 6:21, NIV.

WHEN I WAS ON a backpacking trip with my family in a wilderness area, we had one item that we hadn't brought enough of. It was carefully rationed out, but there were still considerable doubts as to whether it would last our entire trip. This valuable commodity was a single roll of toilet paper.

I've never enjoyed backpacking, and that trip was my farewell performance. I enjoy pretty scenery, but I can enjoy it watching television from my favorite couch. I've never understood why someone would purposely want to leave their comforts behind to rough it in the woods and call it a vacation. Enthusiastic backpackers tell me that getting back to nature helps them to appreciate all the modern conveniences, such as plumbing and electricity. I can only respond that doing without these things isn't called going on vacation but being poor.

Somewhere along the last mile to civilization my sister dropped the roll. At this point it didn't matter all that much, because we soon would be in a town where we could have both toilet paper and plumbing! Nevertheless, we backtracked and picked it up. I don't know what we were thinking, but we'd been guarding that last roll for so long we had no intention of leaving it behind.

We all value things. There's something very satisfying about surrounding oneself with things we love. For me, it's my book collection. But when my apartment caught fire several years ago, I didn't give my books a second thought. Fortunately, the fire was confined to my bedroom, so I didn't lose all my things. When confronted with the fire, all I was worried about was getting my animals and myself out in one piece.

What do you value? For many people it's a nice home, fancy car, or designer wardrobe. Some people like having money in the bank because it makes them feel secure. Jesus didn't have a home or a savings account. He knew that treasure doesn't consist of things you can buy. Treasure is found in your heart, not in your house. The person who is richest is not the person with the most money but the person with the most love. Cars, clothes, books, antiques—even your last roll of toilet paper—are all worthless compared to love.

GINA LEE

Trading Spaces

But God demonstrates his own love for us in this: While we were still sinners, Christ died for us. Rom. 5:8, NIV.

WHEN I'M WORKING FULL-TIME (and more), I don't have time to watch television (which may be a blessing). While I was recuperating from a recent illness, though, I watched some daytime programs. One that I discovered rather accidentally was *Trading Spaces*. If you've not seen it, it's a program in which two sets of neighbors trade houses for 48 hours. During that time each couple, a professional decorator, and a carpenter have $1,000 to redecorate a room in the other neighbor's home.

They remove everything from the room, often even the carpeting. They paint, change furniture as much as the budget allows, add different window treatments, perhaps paint the floor or add tiles—anything they think the neighbor might like, or even tolerate. Sometimes they take down ceiling fans or add fans, repaint or recover furniture. In one show they painted what I thought was a nice varnished wood bedroom suite with white paint. I was horrified, but the room really did look nice when they were done.

When the 48 hours is up, each couple returns to their own home, blindfolded, and is led into the room. The host says, "Open your eyes," and there is usually astonishment, giggling, squealing—or stunned silence. It was interesting to me how many men were more accepting of the drastic changes than were their wives.

Trading spaces, trading places. Have you ever wished you could change places with someone else? Maybe you thought they had it better than you and that if you could only change places, everything would be all right, and all your problems and challenges would disappear.

It can happen. It has happened. Jesus traded places when He came down to this sick earth to change everything about it, especially you and me. He died so that we'd have no more fear of death, so that we'd never have to bear the eternal consequences of our sins. "God made him who had no sin to be sin for us, so that in him we might become the righteousness of God" (2 Cor. 5:21, NIV). Now, that's really trading places!

ARDIS DICK STENBAKKEN

Forgiveness Brings Strength

The Lord will give strength unto his people; the Lord will bless his people with peace. Ps. 29:11.

ONE DAY IN 1995 my daughter invited my husband and me over for a barbecue. Many smokers and drinkers were there. Seventeen years before, I had quit smoking. Everyone there knew about my recent rebirth experience and that I'd been attending church for nearly two months.

I was able to say no to the first few offers of a drink. My husband, who doesn't share my beliefs, said, "Have one; they're good." Soon I found myself taking "one tiny sip." Later I graduated to a whole bottle, as well as a cigarette later in the evening. I thought no one would notice, as it had been my pattern in the past to "be one of the crowd."

That night I asked my Lord for help. He impressed me to make it right with each person. I knew it wouldn't be hard to face my son and daughter, but my husband would be tough.

The next day over lunch I told my daughter how important it was for me to overcome this thing. Reaching across the table to hold my hand, she said, "Yes, I forgive you, Mom, and I'm proud of you." My heart soared with assurance.

It was a quick visit to my son's place, and as I explained things he gave me a big hug and said he forgave me but it hadn't been necessary to explain. He also said he was proud of me. That evening I thanked my Lord for success.

A week later I told my husband of my feelings; I was right—he didn't understand. He accepted my explanation but didn't support me.

All in all, I felt good for speaking out. As a new Christian, I was amazed at how my Lord gave me power to tackle each step as I was going through this growing process.

That was nearly eight years ago, and I'm around many who smoke, but I haven't been tempted to take even one tiny puff. I feel that by righting a wrong, even if it was only as I saw it, I was able to have strength and to overcome.

My Lord hands me some things on a silver platter, but I'm finding out that I have to work harder, reach higher, strive longer, and pray more intensely for others.

VIDELLA MCCLELLAN

Almost Home

But he that shall endure unto the end, the same shall be saved. Matt. 24:13.

MY LEGS FELT LIKE lead as the hot sun beat down on my head. Beads of perspiration trickled down my forehead and down my back. My friend made several attempts to turn back.

"How much farther is it to the head of the river?" she asked each passerby.

"Oh, a little while yet; you've come too far to turn back now. Keep going. It's worth it!"

"Are you sure we're going in the right direction?" she pressed for assurance.

The graffiti on the trees and rocks indicated the right direction. We walked along the riverbank, wishing we could dip our sweltering feet in the cool water, but the embankment was too steep for us to climb down.

"How much farther?" my friend whined again.

"Just five minutes more. It's worth it. Keep going."

This last comment was encouraging. We quickened our steps with renewed vigor. Finally we reached the head of the river. Crystal waters gushed from the rocks, forming their own fountain. We plunged into the refreshing water up to our knees. What a wonderful relief! The delicious sight and feel of the water rewarded us for the agonizing trek.

Sometimes our Christian experience seems like the events of that day. Life is so difficult, but we are encouraged not to give up now—it's too near to His coming. The graffiti on the trees and the rocks, like the signs of the times, tell us it can't be long now. His coming is much nearer than when we first began.

How refreshing and rewarding will be our experience when He comes to take us home!

My dear sister and friend, your spiritual legs are weary, and you may feel as if you want to give up now. Today, be rejuvenated by the thought of His soon coming—just a little while longer. In the words of John R. Sweeney's song: "Just over the mountains in the Promised Land. . . . As our weary footsteps gain the mountain's crest, we can view our homeland of eternal rest. We are nearing home! We are nearing home!" Maranatha.

GLORIA GREGORY

Freedom

And ye shall know the truth, and the truth shall make you free. John 8:32.

THE NEWS HAD SPREAD quickly that Mr. Gorbachev had been taken captive, and now was the time to fight for freedom from Communism in Russia. Mr. Yeltsin was the big hero. The year 2001 was the tenth anniversary, but Mr. Yeltsin was too sick to attend the celebration. Ten years before had been his greatest day, and he was hailed as a savior who freed the country.

I was in St. Petersburg (then called Leningrad), studying the Russian language and living in a Russian home. Our group was nervous, as we knew our city would be next if Moscow fell. We were told that Finnair would fly us out. But my teacher, Vadim, encouraged me to stay. He said, "The American Marines will come and get you if it gets really unsafe." He then added, "I may die, but my little girl will live in freedom." The young people were desperate for freedom, capitalism, and Western-style democracy.

The fighting was contained in Moscow. By the third day it was all over, and Yeltsin had won. And now on that day the new flag—white, blue, and red—was flying bravely over many buildings, replacing the red Communist flag with its hammer and sickle. And the city name was changed back to St. Petersburg. They were now ready to also tear down Mr. Lenin's statues; they were ready to give up their 70 years of Communism.

The evening of the conflict I was invited to a birthday party. Lovely cakes had been prepared. Then the phone rang, and we foreigners were warned to go to our own homes. I rushed out, saying no, I didn't need any help. I knew my way. But that evening I somehow got on the wrong bus— on one going out of the city, where the tanks were supposed to be. A man who spoke a little English rushed me onto the right bus. There were no lights in the bus, even though it was now dark. I stumbled on the steps and hit my cheekbone. I still have the scar. This is my memory of those brave people's desire for freedom.

We, too, would like freedom from living in a sin-sick world. We know we have our hero, Jesus, who will come to free us. And the name of our city will be changed, too; the name will be "the New Jerusalem."

DESSA WEISZ HARDIN

What About Me?

The Lord will watch over your coming and going both now and forevermore.
Ps. 121:8, NIV.

IT WAS GOING TO take some time to get used to being single again. After being married to the love of my life for 53 wonderful years, I'd taken having somebody in the house with me almost for granted. Now my husband was gone, but my life had to go on. There were thank you cards to write, people to visit, and repairs to complete.

A repairman arranged to come the following Monday. It suddenly dawned on me that I didn't really know this stranger. The cowboy outfit he wore, complete with boots and broad brimmed hat, was neither businesslike nor reassuring. I decided to ask one of my brothers-in-law to pay me a visit around the time the man would be at work in my home.

The first one was not there when I called. So I called my second brother-in-law. Could he come?

"Oh, Carol," he responded, "I have several appointments that I just can't cancel. I'm so sorry."

I was in a quandary. What should I do? Then I heard a still small voice ask clearly, "What about Me?"

I was embarrassed at my lack of trust. Lifting my thoughts in thankfulness to God, I thought of a passage about Jesus calming the storm. "It was in faith—faith in God's love and care—that Jesus rested. . . . As Jesus rested by faith in the Father's care, so we are to rest in the care of our Saviour" (*The Desire of Ages*, p. 336). Where was my faith?

My failing memory had placed my assurance of protection on the back burner. Today's text was the one my loving Savior and Friend had brought to my attention the day after my husband died. I hope and pray that I never forget His promise again.

Thank You, dear Lord. You helped me learn to shun the darkness of doubt and put my hand in Yours. You taught me patience, and You gave me the desire of my heart. I trust You.
CAROL JOY GREENE

Just Waiting for You to Call

In my distress I called to the Lord; I cried to my God for help. From his temple he heard my voice; my cry came before him, into his ears. Ps. 18:6, NIV.
In the day of trouble I will call to you, for you will answer me. Ps. 86:7, NIV.

I WAS DRIVING TO summer school on the freeway one fine morning, thinking about getting to class on time. I suddenly felt my car begin to jerk and shake. I knew instantly something was wrong with my passenger-side front tire. I was in the passing lane at the time, traveling at more than 70 miles per hour, and had to maneuver carefully over to the other lane and onto the shoulder. Shaking, I called my dad at work on my cell phone.

"Oh, Dad, it's me!" I said. "I've done something to my car. I think I've blown a tire."

Dad told me to calm down; he'd be there as soon as he could. About 20 minutes later he pulled up. He looked at the damage and said he didn't think it was bad—just a tire. He told me to take his car and go to school. He'd deal with the problem.

So off to school I went, but all day I couldn't stop thinking how my earthly and heavenly fathers are so much alike. So often I go barreling down life's freeway, when something suddenly blows. Instantly I put out a cry for help to heaven. "O Father, it's me. I've done something to myself. I think I've blown my life big-time." I assess the damage and begin to cry. My heavenly Father gently tells me to calm down; He's on His way. He comes and looks at the damage, says He doesn't think it's that bad—just a bruised ego—and tells me to take His grace and go on with my life, gently reminding me to stick close to Him. How thankful I am for His love, help, and guiding hand!

Later that evening as I thanked my earthly father for being there for me, he said something I will never forget: "I was sitting at my desk, just waiting for you to call." How many times does my heavenly Father say the same words: "I am here, just waiting for you to call."

Thank You, heavenly Father, for always waiting for me to call You and for coming to rescue this daughter of Yours so many times.   RISA STORLIE

Late

Trust in the Lord with all thine heart; and lean not unto thine own understanding. In all thy ways acknowledge him, and he shall direct thy paths. Prov. 3:5, 6.

SINCE MY RETIREMENT I occasionally get an opportunity to reflect on the days of my nursing career. Each day it was essential for me to leave home no later than 6:30 a.m. to get to work on time.

One morning I knew I'd be late; I had overslept. I dashed out the door and jumped in the car, praying, "Father, please take me to work and back home safely today without any accidents or incidents. Please help me to get to work on time. Thank You; in Jesus' name I pray. Amen."

My adrenaline was pumping fast and hard. Traffic on the service road was bumper-to-bumper and barely moving. How I hated the idea of being late! After carefully evaluating the situation, I decided to take the back streets that run parallel to the service road—there were fewer lights. All went well until it was time for me to return to the service road again.

Ironically, I was then facing the same traffic I had just done all within my power to escape. Cars passed by that had been behind me, in front of me, and all around me prior to my turning off the service road about two miles back, moving at moderate speeds.

Oh, how I wished I had stayed on the service road! I immediately acknowledged the fact that I had prayed, asking God to help me get to work on time, then proceeded to detour on my way to work.

Proverbs 3:5 and 6 are two of my favorite verses in that they have touched my life in so many ways so many times. How many times have I detoured after asking God's guidance? How many times has He put me back on the right path?

Father, please help me to put all my trust in You and lean not toward my own understanding. Help me not to stray. Help me to wait for You to direct me and help me to follow Your directions in all that I do is my constant prayer.

CORA A. WALKER

Taught by a Cat

Remember the words of the Lord Jesus, how he said, It is more blessed to give than to receive. Acts 20:35.

CHOCKY, OUR PRECIOUS CHOCOLATE-POINT Himalayan tabby cat, is one of the most loving pets I've ever seen. As most cat owners know, cats like to please the "big cats"—their masters or mistresses—by bringing them presents from time to time. The present may be a mouse or some other game that the cat has hunted and brought to their master's feet, or some other interesting or unusual object the feline has found.

Chocky is a house cat and doesn't hunt outdoors, nor do we have mice indoors. But Chocky decided he would give me something, anyway. I was setting the table and preparing supper when I saw Chocky standing on the chair I always sit in when I eat. Gently he placed his little purple ball onto my empty plate, then looked at me. His blue eyes were shining with love and pride. I was very touched by his gesture, for I knew that the fuzzy purple ball that he presented to me was his dearest treasure. He played with it more than any of his other toys.

How could I properly show my appreciation and yet give him the ball back without hurting his feelings? Savoring the moment, I picked him up, stroked him, kissed the top of his head, and said, "Thank you! It's so sweet of you to give me your ball! Would you like to play a game of fetch with me?" He purred happily, and we played. I threw the ball a number of times, and he retrieved it for me to throw again.

Later, I resumed supper preparations and got myself a clean plate. But his kindly deed made me wonder about how giving I am, and how well I share with others. Do I do it willingly? Chocky did. And if I give somebody something, do I offer them my best? My cat did. He probably didn't know that he was demonstrating a couple of biblical principles about giving cheerfully and about it being better to give than to receive.

But what a gentle way to be reminded—by one of God's special creatures—that life should involve sharing and giving, as well as getting. And how easy to remember, since each time I look at him I think of what he did.

BONNIE MOYERS

Gasoline in the Diesel Engine

There is a way that seems right to a person, but its end is the way to death.
Prov. 14:12 , NRSV.

ONE BEAUTIFUL SUMMER DAY I picked up my kids from school and stopped for groceries on the way home. When we got back in the car and I cranked the engine, I looked at the fuel gauge and realized I needed fuel. My car had a diesel engine, and my husband always told me to be sure I kept enough fuel in it. My sons liked to take turns pumping the fuel, so I told the next in turn that he could get out to fill the tank. He pumped $10 worth, paid the attendant, and we continued on our way home.

About two miles down the road the car started acting funny. It sputtered and jerked, but we couldn't figure out why. I continued driving, hoping we would make it home, where my husband could figure out what was wrong and fix it.

We finally rounded a familiar curve in the road and could see the house sitting up on a hill in the distance. Then the car slowed to a crawl, and the engine quit. I managed to coast to the shoulder of the road. We got out, and one of my sons volunteered to run the last quarter mile home to get my husband.

He appeared in his car a few minutes later with our son by his side. We transferred all the groceries to his car while he looked under the hood and asked me questions. When I told him we had stopped for fuel, he decided to check something else. He then announced his findings to us: the tank held gasoline instead of diesel fuel! We could have ruined the engine.

We towed the car home, and my husband drained the fuel tank. Fortunately, the car wasn't ruined, and we all learned a valuable lesson. Even though our intentions were good, the outcome could have been very bad. We must pay attention to what we do, and think through what the consequences might be.

Yes, there is a way that seems right to a man or a woman, but in the end it can lead to death or disaster. We do need to pay attention.

CELIA MEJIA CRUZ

Who Is the Mole?

Be sober, be vigilant; because your adversary the devil walks about like a roaring lion seeking whom he may devour. 1 Peter 5:8, NKJV.

THE AMERICAN BROADCASTING CORPORATION (ABC) ran a six-week television series called *The Mole*. The objective of the game was to identify the mole. Each day the players were faced with a different challenge, and if they were successful in that segment, the value of the pot increases. At the end of the game the player who answered the least number of questions regarding the mole's identity was eliminated. It's a rather challenging game that requires keen observation and great distrust among a group of strangers who must cohabit. Each participant wants the prize of approximately $1 million. The difficulty lies in being teamed with someone during one of the challenges who could possibly be the mole, making your efforts to add to the pot open to sabotage.

This series brings a different situation to my mind. We're all players on the stage of life. Each day we're faced with situations, some more challenging than others. At times we're deceived because we may think that we're on the right path when, in fact, we're really in enemy territory. Sometimes we can't trust family members or even friends with decisions because they may inadvertently misread a sign.

While watching the game, on numerous occasions I tried to identify the mole, but each time a player was eliminated I was confused by the real identity of the mole. The Bible has identified the "mole" for us. It is Satan. He's like a roaring lion, cunning and cruel, and sometimes his devices aren't easily detected and the test seems very difficult.

The best thing to do is to trust our heavenly Father and let Him take control. Jeremiah 29:13 says, "And if you will seek Me, you will find Me when you search for Me with all your heart" (NKJV). Jesus has promised that He will come to our aid and help us discern right from wrong.

Lord, please help me today to let You take control of my life because You know what is best for me.   ANDREA BUSSUE

Lessons From Broken Bricks

The heart is deceitful above all things, and desperately wicked: who can know it? Jer. 17:9.

YEARS AGO WE LIVED in an outer suburb of Calcutta in a rented house that stood in a walled compound beside a slum. There was no grass, no flowers—nothing but parched, rocky earth littered with broken bricks. We didn't plan on being there long enough to hire a gardener and try to wrest some life out of the barren soil, but I decided it would look better if the rocks were cleared away.

So I gathered up bucketfuls of rocks and broken bricks and piled them in one corner by the wall. A few days later I found time for another attack and added more rock and bits of brick to the pile. I didn't have time to gather rubble every day, though, and a week or more elapsed before I went out again with my bucket.

There seemed to be just as many bits of broken brick as before, and I complained to my husband that the bustee (slum) dwellers must be deliberately throwing stones into our compound. We knew they disliked living in close proximity with Christians.

I still kept picking up stones, even though every time I did it there seemed to be just as many as before. One day, as I emptied my bucket into the corner, I noticed that these stones and bits of brick were smaller than the first ones I had collected. Then it dawned on me. As I removed all the large stones and half bricks that littered the compound, the smaller ones became more visible.

Isn't that like our Christian walk? There's no end to it. With the Lord's help, we eliminate the bigger sins, and the smaller ones become more apparent.

Thank You, God, for Your grace and forgiveness. Help me to get rid of all the stones in my character. Amen.   GOLDIE DOWN

An Answered Prayer in St.-Malo

"Because he loves me," says the Lord, "I will rescue him: I will protect him, for he acknowledges my name. He will call upon me, and I will answer him; I will be with him in trouble, I will deliver him and honor him." Ps. 91:14, 15, NIV.

IT WAS REALLY MY own fault; I should have known better. I often travel without an alarm clock, and only on rare occasions does this cause problems. This was one of them.

The hectic schedule of the previous day included an overnight train trip from Strasbourg in northeast France to St.-Malo in the northwest, a return bus trip to the spectacular Mont-St.-Michel in Normandy, and a walk around the walls of St.-Malo at sunset. Knowing that I had an early departure the next day, I went to bed shortly after the sun's disappearance. After the exhausting pace of the previous day, though, I woke up 15 minutes behind schedule. I quickly gathered up my things, dropped off my key, and headed out into the predawn darkness. The town was still in a deep sleep. The train station was a 45-minute brisk walk away, and no taxi was in sight. The only sign of life was the milkman far off in the distance.

Luggage in tow and a train leaving in 30 minutes, I hobbled as fast as I could, praying, asking God to help me. Five minutes before my train was scheduled to leave, I was in the middle of a long causeway that stretched between the walled city and the train station. I was ready to give up.

Just then a large tour bus stopped by my side. The driver opened the door. "I'm heading to the train station. Would you like a lift?" he shouted.

I quickly scrambled on the bus with my suitcase, not even taking time to sit down. We arrived at the train station with one minute to spare. I spent a few seconds thanking the driver profusely, then raced into the station. As I ran by a man in a uniform, I shouted, "Where is the train for Paris?" He pointed and told me to hurry. I clambered on board seconds before the train pulled out.

Maybe French tour bus drivers picking up desperate travelers running through town in the middle of the night is an everyday occurrence, but for me it was another sign that my God does care about me, down to the little details of getting me to the train station on time. CHRISTINE HWANG

A Taste of Forgiveness

Be ye therefore merciful, as your Father also is merciful. Luke 6:36.

A BIG SIGN ON the wall of the ice-cream shop boasted more flavors than I'd ever seen in all of my nine years. "Let's have some," Aunt Ann said to me. I didn't argue. "What flavor would you like?"

"Licorice," I replied, ignoring the funny look on her face. I liked licorice but had never tasted it in ice cream. I could hardly wait for my order. At last it came—a long sugar cone with a big scoop of smooth, ebony sweetness on top. In went my teeth, and out went my euphoria! It was bitter and stung my mouth and tongue. Two thoughts terrified me. First, I had made a horrible choice. Second, I knew I had to eat it. I looked around at other children who were enjoying their ice cream and felt even worse when I realized what I was missing.

I walked over to my aunt with my ice-cream cone in one hand and tears in my eyes. She took one look at me and understood. "You don't like it, do you?"

I shook my head.

"Then I'll take yours," she said. "You can start over again." She bent down, gently took it from me, and bit into it. I knew it tasted bitter. I'll always remember her act of love.

I'm older now. The choices I make today often have greater consequences than those of my childhood days. Unfortunately, I still make some bad decisions. Some I deeply regret. When I sin I like to remember that licorice ice-cream cone, because I find hidden in it a glimpse of the cost of God's forgiveness.

Just as I came to my aunt years ago with my poor choice, I can take today's blunders to Jesus. He'll bend down and gently take away my sin, bitter as it is, and make it His. Just as my aunt gave me a chance to start over, my Lord does the same, only with much more significance. And He does it out of His magnanimous love for me. Because of Jesus I will cherish the assurance that where His love is, there is forgiveness, even when my sins are as black as licorice ice cream.

MARCIA MOLLENKOPF

The Queen Visits

But we are all as an unclean thing, and all our righteousnesses are as filthy rags. Isa. 64:6.

THE SUMMER OF 1970 was an exciting one for my friend Marion and me as we helped Henry and Anna Bartsch with Vacation Bible School in Yellowknife, Northwest Territories (NWT). Working with Native American Indian children was a new experience for both of us. Eager not to miss any activity, many children came still munching on their breakfast of bannock or an apple. With black-eyed wonder they watched as we arranged our props for the morning session. Their enthusiastic participation in all the activities thrilled us.

But the summer offered another highlight. This was the summer the royal family visited the Territories. Their visit coincided with the centennial celebrations of the NWT and Manitoba.

The *News of the North* had posted their itinerary in 5-, 10-, and 15-minute segments. We smiled at the tight schedule and wondered how punctually they would meet their appointments. The event we were most interested in was their arrival at Petitot Park at 3:55 p.m.

There was time to do some preparations for the next day's Vacation Bible School and tidy up our room before dashing off to the park. Yellowknife's population of only 6,000 meant we had a good chance of having a close view of the royal family. However, we allowed plenty of time to get a front-row seat to hear the queen's message.

Marion collected the garbage to drop in the barrel in the back alley as we hastened through a shortcut to the park. Although it was a short walk, we weren't about to waste any time by following the streets. We chose the bleachers closest to the roped-off area and sat on the third level, catching our breath. Few people had gathered, so we needn't have rushed.

"Look here!" Marion exclaimed as she elbowed me.

We burst out laughing. She held up the bag of trash that she had forgotten to drop off. We stealthily hid it under the bleachers, vowing to take it home later and place it where it belonged.

When my heavenly King arrives, it's my prayer that I won't be found carrying verbal garbage, character flaws, an unforgiving spirit, or filthy righteousness rags. Through His grace I want to be found cleansed of all unrighteousness.

EDITH FITCH

Airbrushed Vapor

I will sing your praises among the nations. For your unfailing love is higher than the heavens. Your faithfulness reaches to the clouds. . . . May your glory shine over all the earth. Ps. 108:3-5, NLT.

TODAY I CAME TO the conclusion that over this patch of England where I live there will never ever be an absolutely completely cloudless, clear, azure-blue sky! And that isn't because of our unpredictable mild, damp climate. There are glorious sunny days that lift the spirits and warm the body while we enjoy an expansive heaven—but not a cloudless sky.

You see, my corner of this green and pleasant land lies in the flight path of hundreds of aircraft leaving and arriving at one of the world's busiest airports. So from the first glow of dawn to the last pastel shades of twilight the sky is crisscrossed with vapor trails.

I love to watch the slithers of silver crawling along way up high, leaving a clean, neat double white line behind. Slowly the two trails merge into one. Then an unseen Artist begins His work. He breaks the misty trail into various lengths, and with just the right size brush teases the upper edges of that straight line. Sometimes the strokes are gentle and finish with a flourish. Sometimes they are bold and elongated. Or perhaps the Artist swishes His brush from side to side, leaving behind an unruly mass of creamy tendrils. My favorites are the airbrush strokes lifting soft, curly lines from the vapor, scattering white feathers against that ethereal blue.

Sometimes two silver birds cross each other's path at such an angle as to leave a big cross in the sky. I smile to myself, imagining that God is sending us a big kiss just to show us in yet another way that He still loves us. I wonder, if I blow a kiss into the air, will it soar up, up, and up until it brushes against the cheek of God? Will He smile and say, "I'm so glad that you love Me. I'm looking forward to the time when we can be together for always. But until then, I'm going to send you My love every day. Please share some with everyone you meet"?

What a fancy! Yet I'm glad that God uses His airbrushes to turn vapor pollution into images of beauty. It increases my confidence in His ability to take the vapor trail I call my life and change it into something beautiful. Won't it be wonderful when we can fly with Jesus way above the clouds, sharing the Father's love together for always? JOYCE HILL

I Do Set My Bow

Like the appearance of a rainbow in the clouds on a rainy day, so was the radiance around him. Ezek. 1:28, NIV.

A BEAUTIFUL SPECTACLE WAS given to us in the clouds one mid-July night. The day had been sweltering and muggy. Immediately after sundown the sky was suddenly filled with what seemed to be one large threatening cloud of darkness. Turbulent winds blew to and fro, and streaks of lightning flashed across the middle of the cloud. It was truly a frightening sight of an impending storm. Outside I noticed our horses beginning to run back and forth along the fence line. They too sensed nature's turbulence with fear.

And then, like a miracle, the most beautiful rainbow appeared. Not just a faint, partial streak of color, but one etched perfectly in clear, vibrant color. Often we may see sketches of a rainbow, but this was only the second time in my life I remember seeing a complete rainbow, bowed perfectly, touching the ground from one side of the horizon to the other. Truly, a statement of divine creation spanned the night sky. More than the beauty, though, it delivered a message straight from God to me.

A feeling of total awe engulfed me. It was as if God had come into our personal presence, so revealing and yet untouchable, just like the rainbow. The storm clouds were still there, but we didn't even notice them as we beheld the radiance of the rainbow. As I continued to take in the scene before me, I received a message. Though the storm clouds of life are ever present and the turbulent winds of strife continue to blow, if we fix our eyes upon the radiance of Christ, we can have peace in the middle of the storm.

I have one text written in the front of my Bible. It reads: "Whenever I bring clouds over the earth and the rainbow appears in the clouds, I will remember my covenant between me and you and all living creatures of every kind" (Gen. 9:14, 15, NIV).

BARBARA SMITH MORRIS

Our Private Chauffeur

I can do everything through him who gives me strength. Phil. 4:13, NIV.

I GREW UP IN A large northern city. I wasn't eager to learn how to drive because there were buses, taxis, rapid transit, family, and friends to take me wherever I wanted to go. When I married, my husband became my chauffeur.

I decided to go to college while our four children were in school. During this time my husband lovingly assisted with the children, and I chose to use public transportation to and from school. After my graduation I started working, and my husband continued as chauffeur. Family and friends encouraged me to learn how to drive, and my husband would say, "Sweets, let me teach you how to drive!"

"No," I'd say. "It's difficult for a husband to teach his wife to drive. I'm not ready yet!"

No one knew that I had had a secret fear of driving. One summer when I was a child I stayed with an aunt who lived in the country. My mom was on her way to visit us when she had an automobile accident. The shock of the accident caused me not to want to drive.

One day the Lord gave me a desire to at least learn how to drive. My husband taught me, knowing nothing about my fear. Even though I got my license, my husband continued as my chauffeur. When he'd say "You wanna drive home?" I'd answer emphatically, "No!"

After the children were grown and gone from home, my husband and I decided to move south to the country. In the country you need to drive! We were miles from stores, work, and hospitals. I remembered that fear is not of God but our enemy the devil. Trust in the Lord with all your heart. Love conquers all fears. With God all things are possible. I finally began to drive. My husband beamed with pride. "I knew you could do it!" He was surprised, because I have weak eyes and overcame the challenge of driving at night on country roads without street lights.

I never thought about the Lord preparing me for a day when I would have to drive, but recently my husband began having visual problems. He's been diagnosed with a hereditary eye disease that could leave him sightless. With my whole heart I thank God for helping me overcome fear and for my strong, patient, persevering husband. God never loses sight of our needs when we travel the highways of life with Him.   ELAINE J. JOHNSON

Clouds

In the clouds, to meet the Lord in the air. 1 Thess. 4:17.

WHEN I WAS A little girl I spent a lot of time lying on the grass, looking up at the sky. With my childhood imagination, the clouds became all sorts of things. There were animals—elephants with long trunks and horses with their manes flying. Then there were castles. The clouds could become anything I imagined.

I still love looking at the clouds. Clouds can be majestic. Clouds can be beautiful—and frightening. One can literally fly above the clouds in an aircraft, looking down at a thick white layer between you and the earth.

Clouds make a sunrise so pleasing. This morning I saw a truly spectacular sunrise. Enormous dark clouds filled the eastern sky, then as the sun came up, the color of the clouds changed. They became orange—not the usual red or pink, but a frothy shade of orange as the sun shone through them. Ever-changing rays of light shone out above the clouds in the sky. Just beautiful!

I thought about how our lives can be dark with sin, but if we allow Jesus to come into our hearts His love can shine through. We become changed because of Him. As the clouds lightened with the sun shining through them, we too can change. The choice is ours.

A friend, traveling home by train, was watching a superb sunset through the window. When she got off at her station, so did the young man sitting opposite her. She couldn't help saying to him, "Wasn't that sunset beautiful?"

"What sunset?" he replied.

What sunset! He'd been gazing out the same window, but wasn't aware of the beauty before him.

Psalm 46:10 tells us to "Be still, and know that I am God." I often think of this Bible text as I sit and watch the sun sinking in the west. My husband is used to me calling, "Oh, just come and look at *this* sunset! You've never seen anything like it!"

One day soon, when Jesus comes, we'll be caught up in the clouds to meet the Lord Himself. I can't think of anything more beautiful than that will be!

LEONIE DONALD

Always Check the Manual

The whole Bible was given to us by inspiration from God and is useful to teach us what is true and to make us realize what is wrong in our lives; it straightens us out and helps us do what is right. It is God's way of making us well prepared at every point, fully equipped to do good to everyone. 2 Tim. 3:16, 17, TLB.

I CAME OUT OF church and started my old car one very hot day in July, and as I drove away I noticed that the air conditioner was not working properly. I finally switched it off and opened the windows. *What could be wrong?* I wondered. I tried to set the controls again, but finally I decided that it was truly broken.

For several days I did my errands around town with my windows down and took very short trips. At last I decided that I must call the mechanic. The clerk told me that a new law had been passed and now they would have to check all the systems of a car when they fixed the air conditioner, and that it would cost more than $200! I was devastated. I couldn't afford that much. I prayed that somehow God would help me find a way to fix it. I decided to trust and wait.

In a day or so I wanted to go to the grocery store. As I started the car, I felt impressed to check the car's manual, which I keep in the glove box. I looked carefully at the diagrams of the control board, and my eyes popped open as I looked at the controls and discovered that I had forgotten to push the center button that lets the air conditioner work! I had set all the other controls but that one. I went on my way, thanking God for prompting me to check the manual. The cool air was a great relief.

Our Maker's manual is the Holy Bible, and I sometimes forget to check it when I run into trouble. It's our guidebook for living. I want to be more attentive to its precepts before I get into trouble, instead of regretting afterward that I hadn't checked the manual.

Dear Lord, forgive me for neglecting Your Holy Word. Help me to always check Your Maker's Manual first. BESSIE SIEMENS LOBSIEN

The Cream Roses

Thanks be unto God for his unspeakable gift. 2 Cor. 9:15.

IF YOU HAD A special friend, would you give her roses? Roses seem to be the favorite flower for expressing love. But there are other ways to express your love—a card, a note or letter, a gift, or even a call. There are so many ways to say you care.

I've met many wonderful people over the years, and many of them still keep in contact, even if it's only to send a birthday card.

I met Winnifred when I started working at the publishing company. She seemed to take an instant liking to me, and we've been friends for many years. After I got married, we moved to other provinces, but I continued to receive my birthday card regularly. Then three years ago I didn't receive my card and sensed something was wrong. I made inquiries, but couldn't trace her. So I prayed about it.

Two months later I received a card from her niece. Pam had found my card with my address on it in her aunt's belongings. She told about the trauma of the stroke Winnifred had suffered and how she had landed in a nursing home. I was able to contact her again. How happy she was to see me after all those years!

On her birthday I try to show my love to her by visiting her and taking her favorite flowers—pink roses. Unfortunately, this year I couldn't find pink roses, so I bought cream roses. I conditioned the roses, and picked bracken, sword, and other ferns from our garden and gave them all a long drink overnight. The next day I arranged the roses and ferns and put on a cream bow to match. I was already anticipating her smile and her face lit up with joy.

Then I noticed first two roses drooping, then another. My heart sank! I couldn't present her roses in that condition. My love gift had to be disposed of, and I told her about my disappointment.

What about the gift I am to my Friend? Are my "petals" drooping because of pride? (Prov. 16:18). Have my "leaves" withered because of selfishness or impatience or some bad habit? I have to dispose of bad habits but cannot do that on my own. My sinful life is an unworthy gift to my Friend.

Thank God for His unspeakable gift of grace! PRISCILLA ADONIS

Inside and Out

You clean the outside of the cup and dish, but inside they are full of greed and self-indulgence. Matt. 23:25, NIV.

WAIT A SEC," Melissa said, flinging open the car door and running toward the pantry. "I'll check!" We were on our way to the store. Her favorite cousins would soon be arriving for the weekend, and she wanted to be certain there was plenty of her favorite breakfast cereal.

"Three boxes on the pantry shelf," she said on her return, slightly out of breath. "We can scratch cereal off our shopping list."

It was a busy afternoon, and I forgot all about the three boxes. Early the next morning Melissa's wail summoned me to the kitchen. "It can't be," she moaned. "They'll be down to eat any minute."

"And?" I prompted.

"And," she explained dramatically, "the three boxes of cereal are nearly empty. There's hardly one bowlful among them!" There were plenty of other things to eat, of course, but that wasn't the issue. This was a definite catastrophe. Her shoulders sagged; her lips drooped. "I looked to see if the boxes were there," she explained ruefully. "I didn't look to see if there was anything in them."

Actually, it made for thought-provoking conversation at breakfast. We talked about things—and even people—who look good on the outside but are either empty or filled with disagreeableness on the inside. But there was another lesson—for me, this time.

Dishwasher loaded and the kitchen cleaned, we all piled into the car and headed for the grocery store. Melissa wanted to be sure her favorite cereal was on the menu for the following morning. In a hurry because of an already tight schedule, I raced to the cereal aisle, grabbed three boxes of the preferred food, and headed for the checkout.

"Wait a minute!" Melissa cried. "Not that one. There's a brown stain on one corner."

"We're in a hurry, Melissa," I responded. "I doubt the stain has affected the contents."

"Oh, please wait!" Melissa pulled on my sleeve in desperation. "I want the outside to look as good as the inside."

We exchanged cereal boxes. Inside and outside. They're both important!

ARLENE TAYLOR

Crisis in the Air

When anxiety was great within me, your consolation brought joy to my soul.
Ps. 94:19, NIV.

IT'S HARD FOR ME to empathize with people who fear flying. From planning the trip until developing the pictures, I enjoy all the components of air travel. The only one thing I'm afraid of are the small airplane seats. Because I'm overweight and can't afford first-class tickets, my prayer is not so much for safety as for a child or a skinny person to sit next to me. And my prayer is not so much for my own comfort as for my neighbor to be comfortable. Whenever possible, I sit by the window, squeeze myself as much as I can, and get up only on long trips.

One time I was going to a convention in Florida. The plane was full, but the man next to me was skinny, and I got my window seat—5A. Everything seemed fine until I tried to fasten the seat belt. It was too short! When I finally asked for an extension, even though I was almost whispering, I felt as if I were screaming to the whole airplane. "I'm so fat that I don't fit in the seat," I told the flight attendant.

She looked but couldn't find an extension. It seemed as if all the passengers knew my problem and blamed me for delaying the plane. Finally I was handed the piece of strap. One of the sides fitted perfectly, but the other didn't. I tried again. Same result. Now I was desperate. The man next to me tried to help. I had to call the attendant again. By now I was sweating and on the verge of tears. The attendant belatedly realized she'd given me the small safety demonstration belt. When I finally I got the correct strap, everything was well. Until the return trip.

At the airport I looked at my boarding pass for my seat number—5A. It had to be the same seat, and probably the same plane, that made the New York round-trip. While I was trying to think how to unobtrusively ask the flight attendant for the extension, I found out that one of my friends was going to sit next to me. I knew better than to promise the Lord that if He would shield me from embarrassment I'd start dieting immediately. I simply asked God for serenity and grace. When I got to seat 5A and tried on the notorious belt, it clicked perfectly!

I imagined Jesus smiling even more broadly than I.

Thank You, Lord, for loving me so much and for taking care of even the smaller things.   ALICIA MARQUEZ

Walking in the Light

Jesus answered, "Are there not twelve hours of daylight? Those who walk during the day do not stumble, because they see the light of this world. And those who walk at night stumble, because the light is not in them." John 11:9, 10, NRSV.

CAMP CEDAR FALLS IS nestled high in California's San Bernardino Mountains. I call it Camp Vertical. From the abrupt descent of the main road to the hike from the lodge to the dining room, it should be billed as a fitness camp. As a camp counselor, sunrise would find me hiking down to the falls for a private worshiptime. The old trail was incredibly steep. A rappelling rope had been installed to assist in the descent over a veritable cliff. What followed was a dizzying myriad of switchback turns, ending at the beautiful falls in a serenely wooded ravine. The morning sun rays filtered through the huge evergreens and danced on dewdrops hugging the low ferns. Sitting by the gurgling water and watching the skittish wildlife made the rigors of the journey melt away.

Late in July three adolescent boys tiptoed out of their cabin in search of adventure and headed for the old trail. What promised to be great fun turned into a hair-raising night of terror and pain. As soon as the boys went over the edge, their screams alerted the entire camp of their midnight escapade. They began to tumble head over heels until they landed in heaps at the bottom of the falls. Those of us who knew the area chose the much longer but safer trail. We soon found the boys, whimpering in a huddle, humbled, bruised, and frightened but, miraculously, not seriously injured.

When I feel overwhelmed by my schedule and deadlines, I remember my sanctuary. Too frequently I find an excuse to work long, crazy hours. The path to the waterfalls was precarious, but in daylight the dangers could be plainly anticipated, negotiated, or even avoided. During Jesus' short ministry He could have worked day and night. He could have exhausted Himself mentally, physically, and spiritually. Instead, He showed us how to manage our lives. Every night Jesus renewed Himself with sleep and prayer. By morning He had a clear vision of His daily mission.

I've learned that in this busy world I need to take time for renewal. Working in the light encourages confidence in the next step. Strength, vision, and direction are restored through the sunlight of prayer, study, and rest.

SHIRLEY KIMBROUGH GREAR

Speed Bumps

Whether you turn to the right or to the left, your ears will hear a voice behind you, saying, "This is the way; walk in it." Isa. 30:21, NIV.

I'M AN EARLY RISER. Four o'clock is my normal waking time, so I make the most of it in my quiet time with God. After a quick shower and preparation for the day, I'm outdoors by 6:30, ready for a brisk, two-mile trek that takes me through the lovely grounds of the veterans' hospital next door, and beyond.

Part of my jaunt is along the tree-lined one-way traffic lane that borders the hospital parking lots. Large, elegant ducks keep me company as they amble over the green lawn or swim in the delightful ponds. A picturesque water fountain spouts high in the air. At that hour few cars are in the parking spaces, so it's a great place to walk. I round the wide, sweeping curve and pass honeysuckle bushes filled with lovely, heavenly perfume.

Ahead of me is a yellow-painted speed bump, designed to keep hospital traffic at a moderate pace. It is that yellow speed bump that intrigues me. Some vehicles slow down appropriately. Others seem not to notice and heedlessly bounce over it to their destination. A few, however, driving at a much-too-high speed, swing to the right around it, through the empty parking spaces, and I fear for the jogger who isn't alert to such a driver. That's dangerous! I observe almost audibly, and move quickly out of their way.

Then I remember a "speed bump" story Jesus told in Luke 10:30-37. A man on his way to Jericho had been attacked and wounded. It was a biblical "speed bump," to be sure. A priest deliberately ignored it as though it wasn't there. A Levite observed it, then purposely swerved around it and went on his way. A Samaritan heeded it and carefully honored it, as God's love-thy-neighbor law indicated. And then Jesus said, "Go, and do thou likewise."

Our speed bumps are always in plain sight. The way we relate to them depends on how we relate to God.

So as I take my walk each morning that yellow speed bump is my daily reminder to listen to His voice as He seeks to direct me through each new day. His blessings are too precious to miss! LORRAINE HUDGINS-HIRSCH

No Broken Bones

Many are the afflictions of the righteous, but the Lord rescues them from them all. He keeps all their bones; not one of them will be broken. Ps. 34:19, 10, NRSV.

TEREAPII, MY 10-YEAR-OLD daughter, and I were busy with house-cleaning and food preparation when we heard a banging noise, a thud, a painful wail, and then silence. We raced simultaneously for the door. Out on the lawn my 8-year-old son lay sprawled and motionless. There were signs of agony written all over his face. I called to him, but there was no response.

My mind raced back six years to the time his father had died instantly in a road accident. Was this another tragedy? Prayer after prayer flashed through my mind. An urgent, direct connection with God had to be established. "My God, Father, lover of my soul, the great healer and refuge—work a miracle today. I'm now going ahead in faith to raise my son to his feet. I know You can, and that You will protect all his bones that not one will be broken, just as Your Word says."

Tereapii had run ahead. She felt Joshua's wrist for a heartbeat, then his collarbone. I was still at the doorway, too stunned to move. With a slight tone of urgency in her voice, she called for me to hurry. I advised her not to move Joshua, as we were not quite sure if he had internal injuries.

She called back, "Joshua is OK! Just come quick and help him up. Bring some water."

I'm so thankful. A very responsible daughter commanded actions and bravely took on the role of big sister. With renewed strength and hope in our great God, I knelt by his side and conducted a quick check for any fractures or swellings. He asked for water. Tereapii poured him a glass, and he emptied it. We poured him another, and he drank half. I asked him if he felt any pain. He said that he had landed on his belly and felt aches on the muscles. His left foot had a little scratch. He added, "I'm not hurt; my angel was very busy looking after me, and I'm grateful to the Lord for him."

We sat there for a moment, thanking our heavenly Father. The God you and I pray to and worship and listen to is such a wonderful deliverer. We are to taste and see that this Lord is good. He is attentive to our cry. Let's wait in hope for the Lord. He is our help and our shield.

FULORI BOLA

What's Behind Our Smiles?

Peace I leave with you, My peace I give to you; not as the world gives do I give to you. Let not your heart be troubled, neither let it be afraid. John 14:27, NKJV.

IT WAS OUR FIFTIETH anniversary party, and our children had almost gone overboard in their preparations for a grand time. There were friends and family whom we hadn't seen in a long time, and we were just bubbling over with happiness. To look at our smiles you would have thought we didn't have a care in the world. But our smiles might have been deceiving.

Our hearts were aching that day because our oldest son had passed away 17 years before. His children and widow weren't able to attend because one son was working at a youth camp, where they desperately needed him. And there was no way the younger one and her mother could attend, either. Two of our children were going through divorces, so, of course, their soon-to-be-ex-spouses weren't there. My husband had just lost one of his sisters two weeks earlier, and her memorial service had been the day before our party. We hadn't been able to attend because it was 2,000 miles away.

No heartaches? We had plenty of them. But we also remembered the joy of having been together for 50 years and being able to share our joys and our sorrows with our best friend, Jesus. We knew He was in control of everything around us. We shared the joy of the four wonderful children we still had with us, and the very special seven grandchildren we could enjoy. When we returned home that evening, there was a message on our answering machine saying that my husband had lost another sister. While there was pain in our hearts, we still had the peace that Jesus gives. We were able to smile.

Sometimes we meet people who don't seem to have a care in the world. They are smiling and happy, and seem to have good health and no financial or relationship problems. We're quick to judge, and perhaps even a little envious. To paraphrase one of my favorite songs by Flo Price: "No one knows what a smile can conceal; only God knows what your heart truly feels."

I don't understand how it works, but I know we can safely place our heartaches in God's care and know that He will bring us peace in the midst of our pain.

ANNA MAY RADKE WATERS

God's Ways

"For my thoughts are not your thoughts, neither are your ways my ways,"
declares the Lord. Isa. 55:8, NIV.

IT HAD BEEN AN inspiring mission trip to southern Mexico, where we'd
been part of a group who went into a remote mountain village to do
medical and dental work. We'd also taken gifts to the schoolchildren, and
we all felt the reality of the Bible verse that says "it is more blessed to give
than to receive." All had gone well. Now it was time to go home.

We arrived at the airport in plenty of time to catch our flight to Mexico
City. However, as soon as we got to the check-in counter we saw there was
a problem. Our flight had been delayed because of fog in Mexico City.
There was nothing that could be done about that but wait. Four hours later
we were headed on another flight to Mexico City, but it was already too late
to connect with our flight to Los Angeles. We had originally planned to
make several connections that would get us home the same day, but now all
that was changed.

We were thankful when we finally arrived in the United States in time
to catch the last flight to our final destination. And we were thankful for
good friends who would put us up overnight, as it was now too late to drive
on home that night.

The next morning we found that a snowstorm had been raging in the
area of our mountain home at the time we had originally planned to arrive.
The roads had been impassable so that even if we had arrived as we intended, we still wouldn't have been able to drive on home. Though our
plans hadn't worked out as we thought they should have, God knew what
was best for us all the time.

Thank You, God, for guiding our steps. When there is fog and we cannot
discern the future, help us to realize that You do see the future and that always
Your ways are better than our ways.   BETTY J. ADAMS

Camp Mom

Yet I considered it necessary to send to you Epaphroditus . . . the one who ministered to my need. Phil. 2:25, NKJV.

WHILE I WAS ASSISTANT youth camp director one summer, I cautiously approached the phone booth. I could hear the hysterical pleas of 11-year-old Wendy inside: "Mom, please let me come home! I *need* you!"

Later that day the camp director handed me a candy bar. "Wendy needs a 'mom' here at camp. This might help you start meeting the need of your new camp daughter."

Thanks a lot! I thought. When I heard Wendy's now-familiar whine a few minutes later, I mustered a smile and called out, "Wendy, is that you? I've been missing my camp daughter. How about sitting together at campfire tonight?"

She eyed me with suspicion—until I held out the candy bar. By the end of campfire Wendy's head was on my shoulder and her arms were about my waist. The rest of the week Wendy shadowed me whenever her cabin wasn't assigned a specific activity. Her counselor told me the girl had become a model camper instead of the impossible whiner she'd been the first few days.

On the last day of camp Wendy's counselor came to me with disturbing news. "Wendy has done nothing all morning except cry. She refuses to come to line call or even to pack to go home."

I found the girl on her bunk, crying. "What's the matter, camp daughter?" I asked.

She looked at me through swollen eyes before wailing, "I don't *wanna* go home!"

"Why not? You can see your family—especially your mom."

"But if I go home," she sobbed, "I'll have to leave my *camp* mom!"

I stifled my near-laugh and gently reminded her, "But your camp mom can write you."

Oh," she said, wiping her eyes. "I never thought of that." She threw her arms around me and said, "And when you write me could you also, uh, send me another candy bar?"

Dear Lord, just as Epaphroditus ministered to Paul's need, help me see the specific needs of those around me. Please give me wisdom to minister to these needs. I ask these things in the name of the One who has promised to supply all my needs through His riches in glory. Amen. CAROLYN SUTTON

Not Guilty!

The Lord is compassionate and gracious, slow to anger, abounding in love.
Ps. 103:8, NIV.

THE TWO YOUNG MEN stood in the dock in front of me, accused of being part of a gang who had physically assaulted another young man, causing grievous bodily harm. I was part of a jury of 12 people who would decide the final verdict. For two weeks we had listened to all the witnesses, heard their cross-examinations, listened to their barristers, and, finally, to the judge himself. All kinds of details complicated the picture. But these two young men had their lives—promising lives—ahead of them. I prayed, wanting to have a clear picture of how I should vote for them on the jury. By the last day I knew that I would come down on the side of "not guilty." There wasn't enough evidence to convict them with the certainty required by English law.

It took us only one hour to decide their fate. We filed back into the courtroom for the final time. The entire court was hushed. This was a deep and solemn moment for everyone there, especially the young men and their families.

I thought that our spokesperson would declare the verdict and that would be the end of it. We would just leave. But it wasn't that easy. As we declared the two men not guilty, there was a tremendous surge of emotion. Joy and exhilaration exploded in the room, tears of relief rolled down many cheeks, including those of us in the jury. I sat there with tears in my eyes, so happy for such a positive outcome. I longed to go over and hug the young men.

As I left the room my emotions were so intense, more than I could have ever imagined. It felt so wonderful to give these young men the gift of their normal lives back again with hope for the future, freedom from anxiety, a new beginning, an experience of grace.

We were told we were free to go, but for a while I couldn't go home. I needed to wander through the local park and reorient my feelings. For a few minutes I wanted to continue to feel how good it was to declare someone not guilty and taste something of how it must feel to be a God of grace and love and forgiveness.

Thank You, God, for declaring me "not guilty," even when I make mistakes.

KAREN HOLFORD

A Day Trip

Therefore, since we are surrounded by such a great cloud of witnesses, let us throw off everything that hinders and the sin that so easily entangles, and let us run with perseverance the race marked out for us. Let us fix our eyes on Jesus. Heb. 12:1, 2, NIV.

IT WAS A DAY like any other—sunny and cloudless, simply wonderful. We'd moved to the Turkish Riviera and had planned a trip to visit a little town.

Arriving at our destination, we got out to explore the old village, the houses, and their inhabitants, the numerous fruit trees, and the little rough paths. We felt transported back into our childhood! We became thirsty, so we found a place to get a drink. We waited awhile for the owner, but he never showed up. We got more and more thirsty and went looking for someone.

We found the villagers gathered in groups, watching a TV that was turned up to high volume. Everybody was intently watching, spellbound. We came closer and saw two high towers and planes crashing into them, one after the other. At first we thought it was a horror movie, but the scenes were repeated. Something was wrong! We asked the people what had happened. "America," they said. "Great catastrophe."

We got more detailed information when we got back to our rooms that evening. As long as we live we'll probably never be able to erase the pictures from our memory. The World Trade Center in the heart of New York had been reduced to a heap of debris. Thousands of people were buried under the ruins, people who had been full of hope and the joy of living a few moments earlier.

Muslims and Christians prayed together for America and the grieving. They gathered together in the Christian church in Antalya's old town, unified in their tears of grief.

Hundreds of Americans and other nationalities left Turkey the next day and returned home. We looked at each other. We felt devastated. But to run away now? Where to? There is no safe place in the world anymore where we could hide. Terror can reach us anywhere. It is only in Jesus that we are safe. Only in Him can we find peace and rest. He will return very soon in the clouds of heaven. That is His promise. We believe it.

Dear Lord Jesus, help us to look up to You more. Only You can save us with Your power and consolation. That is Your promise.   CHRISTEL MEY

Flowers in the Desert

The desert and the parched land will be glad; the wilderness will rejoice and blossom. Water will gush forth in the wilderness and streams in the desert. Isa. 35:1-6, NIV.

WHILE VISITING CHILE I received an illustrated calendar as a present. It was filled with beautiful and picturesque scenes of that country. Each page made me feel part of the landscape, and I imagined how wonderful it would be to visit all those locations.

In the midst of these thoughts I came across a figure that caught my attention. Within the various landscapes with crystalline lakes, leafy green trees, and even magnificent volcanoes, I had run across a desert. But it was a different type of desert. A carpet of colorful flowers decorated the arid floor of that desert. The photographer purposely portrayed the magic of life, even in that inhospitable place.

I stopped for an instant and looked at the end of the calendar to find more information about that location. I discovered that it was the Atacama Desert in northern Chile that is one of the most arid deserts in the world. It rains occasionally to the south of the city of Copiapó, and when it does, the flowers blossom several weeks later, bringing life to that dry land.

Sometimes I feel like the Atacama Desert. Arid, struggling in my own strength before the difficulties and concerns of life, forgetting that I have a fountain of water that can send rain when I ask, making colorful flowers bud in my garden in the hope of better days.

It's possible that today you're living in the desert of your spiritual, emotional, or physical life, thinking that you can have happiness and a long life far from the Source. Remember, God promises showers of abundant blessings to all who rest in His promises and seek power at the Source. "Ask and you will receive, and your joy will be complete" (John 16:24, NIV).

Rest in Him, and the source of all joy will flow in your life, and through each one of us it will reach others. Today God wants to send you showers of blessings in addition to many flowers. Accept them!

Lord! Teach me to seek from Your fountain the power that I need to be able to go on. During this day may I blossom by Your grace and mercy, which is renewed each morning. Amen! RAQUEL COSTA ARRAIS

Unexpected Rest!

Come to me, all you who are weary and burdened, and I will give you rest.
Matt. 11:28, NIV.

I WAS TIRED. AGAIN. Very tired. We had worked most of the summer at family and teen adventure camps, and now I was exhausted. I thought of all that would need to be done back in the office. There didn't seem any way to have a break from it all.

After the last camp ended, we got home late in the evening and needed to catch a plane early the next morning. I shuffled through the mail to check for anything urgent and found a brown manila envelope from the local courthouse—a summons for jury service. I couldn't believe it! Didn't I have enough to do? Why now, of all times? Another ton dropped on my shoulders. The last thing I needed was another two weeks out of the office. And what if the case was disturbing? I didn't feel as if I had the emotional resources to deal with all the details of a violent or sexual crime.

The jury form had to be mailed right away. I knew that my employers could make a case for me to postpone the jury service, but I couldn't contact them before I had to return the form. Miserably, I filled out the details and mailed the form on the way to the airport.

On the plane I prayed that the case would be short and not traumatic in any way. Little by little I began to feel a sense of peace and reassurance. My feelings of frustration began to be transformed as God gave me a new picture of the jury service. This was His gift to me. A gift of some time and space when I could feel free of all my responsibilities at work—a time to be passive, to sit and just listen in the court and rest my exhausted body. To wander around a picturesque ancient town during lunch breaks. To enrich my experience of life by having a chance to see how the English legal system worked.

Within a few days my distress had turned to a peaceful and happy anticipation, even a sense of excitement about the jury service.

Thank You, God, for finding a way to give me just what I needed, even if I didn't recognize the gift to begin with. Help me not to miss any of the gifts You have for me today.   KAREN HOLFORD

Let Go My Toe!

If God is for us, who can be against us? Rom. 8:31, NIV.

HELP! HE'S GOT MY toe," I yelled to my husband.

People who know us also know about our love for animals, especially dogs. We're on our eleventh and twelfth Boston terriers, and our fourteenth, fifteenth, sixteenth, and seventeenth dogs since the 1950s. Our latest dog, a toy poodle, was now attached to my big toe, and I was trying frantically to shake him off. It's funny now, when I look back at the incident, but at the time I wasn't the least bit happy about it.

It was Friday evening, and I was preparing to take my bath. I wandered into the kitchen in my bare feet. Muffin, the new poodle, apparently thought my toe was either food or a threat in some way to him. I finally shook him off.

Muffin weighs only eight pounds, is more than 10 years old, and has only one front tooth, but he knows how to use that one tooth. He was rescued from the humane society, as were all our dogs. He had slight cataracts, which meant he wasn't sure what he had latched on to, but he wasn't willing to let go without a fight. Even though he wasn't really hurting me, he surely was scaring me into believing that he could, and I'm a real coward when it comes to pain.

Perhaps that's the way Satan works on us. We wander onto his turf, not really realizing it, and when he latches on to us we aren't sure just how to shake him off. We're told that he knows the Bible better than we do; he's had years of experience enticing people, and when we forget that we're in a real spiritual battle with him, he takes the advantage and takes us unaware.

Let's try to be like Christ and use a "thus says the Lord" whenever we're caught. Let's be faithful, study our Bible, put its words into practice daily, and learn with Christ's help to become Christlike. "If Christ be for us, who can be against us?"

My prayer for today is to be aware of Satan's snares and to be on guard. With the Lord's help and Christ's love we can escape his snares. Remember Muffin, and don't let Satan get your toe!   LORAINE F. SWEETLAND

Calm in the Storm

Do not be anxious, saying, "What will we eat?" or "What will we drink?" or "What will we wear?" Matt. 6:31, RSV.

OCCASIONALLY TORNADOES rip through the parkland of central Alberta, so when my husband, Larry, and I heard a tornado warning on the radio, we took it seriously. Often, in the midst of summer storms, we like to look out our living-room windows or stand on the porch and feel the freshness of newly washed air rush past us. But this time we hurriedly went to Garrick's room.

It wasn't hard to get our 6-year-old son up, since he'd been watching the torrents of rain and the leaning trees from his window. He untangled himself from a sheet and made his way down the ladder, clad in his black pajamas, which had glow-in-the-dark skeleton bones decorating them from neck to ankle (an appropriate gift from his aunt who worked in a physician's office).

Our adrenaline pumping, the three of us clattered down the stairs, made up some beds on the floor far from any window, and settled down.

"What will happen, Dad?" asked Garrick.

"Well," explained Larry, "there's some danger with a tornado. They don't come by here often, but we need to be careful. That's why we're downstairs, far from the windows."

"Have you ever seen a tornado, Mom?" he asked, eyes round with excitement—and fear.

"I didn't see one, but we were very close to one. There was lots and lots of rain and trees were torn up, but we didn't get hurt. And some of your grandpa's family had a tornado, but—"

Before I could complete the sentence with words of comfort, he interrupted. "At least," he said resolutely, "I'm wearing my favorite jammies."

Larry and I smiled at each other over his head: our young son had faced the possibility of having the house torn from above him some time in the night, his toys and Legos scattered across the neighboring fields, and his bike twisted around a tree. But if he was wrapped in the comforting folds of his favorite pajamas, he felt secure, unafraid of what tomorrow would bring.

He wasn't worrying—and neither would we, because Jesus Himself had said, "Do not be anxious, saying, "What will we eat?" or "What will we drink?" or "What will we wear?"   DENISE DICK HERR

Makiel's Unconditional Love

Let them bring their little ones, because the kingdom of God belongs to those with childlike faith. To tell you the truth, unless you are open to the kingdom of God as these little children are, you'll never enter it. Luke 18:16, 17, Clear Word.

I CALLED MY NEPHEW to wish him a happy birthday. Makiel was finally 12 years old! He shared about his activities and wonderful gifts of the day. Before our conversation ended, he became quiet. He told me everyone had called or sent a special gift for his birthday except a very special person in his life. I asked Makiel if he felt hurt about this. "Sometimes," he replied.

Did he feel angry? I asked.

"I try not to," he said.

I continued in amazement. "Makiel, what do you do to not feel angry?" I'm still in awe at his 12-year-old response: "I pray for him."

I immediately thought of acts of betrayal toward me by supposed friends. Quite frankly, my first response had not been to pray for them. I wanted so badly to confront the betrayal. I wanted to defend myself and take care of the matter in *my* way and in *my* own time. Yet it seemed that every devotional read, every sermon preached, and every conversation shared pointed me toward forgiveness and prayer. As I began to pray for them, my hurt healed, my disappointment disappeared, absorbed by God's love.

I continue to pray for them and, as a result, I'm set free.

We grown-ups would do well to follow Makiel's example. Instead of responding in an irrational or emotional way, pray. Pray for him. Pray for her. My little conversation with Makiel has left an indelible impression upon my life. I, like Makiel, want to pray for those in my life who have hurt and disappointed me. Prayer, after all, is the answer.

It's amazing. I called Makiel on his special day and came away from the conversation having received such a powerful and life-changing gift; a life lesson from a child.

Pray for him. Pray for her. Now, that's unconditional love. Thank you, Makiel.

TERRIE RUFF

The Saved Refrigerator

Casting all your care upon Him, for He cares for you. 1 Peter 5:7, NKJV.

M Y COUSIN FAITH HAD just moved into a small house trailer, one with few furnishings. But it was better than living in her van, which she had previously done. Since her landlord would allow her to keep her dogs, she wanted to keep the trailer as long as possible.

Faith had been under the care of the local mental-health provider, and while she still worked, she wasn't in a financial position to purchase much furniture or furnishings.

Soon after she moved in, her refrigerator quit working. We had a plumber check it out; he said the refrigerator was shot—completely. So David, who was Faith's care provider, approached the landlord on her behalf.

"I am not putting any more money into that trailer," the landlord responded rudely. "If she doesn't want to get her own refrigerator, she can just move. I rented the trailer as is, and as far as I'm concerned, that's 'as is.'"

Faith asked me how we could get another refrigerator. "I really don't even need one," she continued. "I've lived without one for about eight years; I can keep living like that."

"No, we will look for a refrigerator," I assured her. I know I'm used to the luxuries of this life when I see how Faith lives. I couldn't go eight days without a refrigerator in my life, let alone eight years.

Returning home from school one day, the kids and I saw a yard sale, and a refrigerator stood in the yard. I questioned the young girl tending the sale. "This fridge says $175. Do you think you would take $100?" I asked.

"Well," the girl responded, "it's our neighbor's, and he put it in our sale. I did hear him tell someone earlier that he wouldn't take $125."

"Please ask him if he'll take a hundred-dollar check, and if so, it'll be gone today," I told her. I left her my phone number and prayed all the way home. The owner called and said he wanted to get rid of it, so $100 was fine. By 5:00 that afternoon Faith had a working, clean, wonderful refrigerator. Truly God had saved the refrigerator for us. CHARLOTTE ROBINSON

Friendship and God

A true friend sticks closer than one's nearest kin. Prov. 18:24, NRSV.

MY FRIENDSHIP WITH DORIS started when I was 4 and she was 3. We made mud pies together, played dress-up in old clothes left in an abandoned trailer, attended yearly Easter services, jumped double dutch, played hide-and-seek, and skipped hopscotch in the streets. In high school our lifestyles took us in different directions, but during my college years our friendship was renewed. We had missed our fun times together!

Then I married and moved to a different state, and being day-to-day friends was impossible. Doris and I kept in contact by phone. On birthdays and holidays one of us would always call the other. We shared ups and downs, offered insight and advice and comfort. Woman-to-woman. Heart-to-heart. And no matter what, I could always count on Doris to look on the bright side, despite her own difficulties.

During my yearly visit to see my mother, Doris was the first person I'd call. We'd talk for hours, and sometimes order a pizza or some carryout. We became real chums during those visits, and I eagerly looked forward to the next visit. On one trip about nine years ago we spent more hours than usual, laughing and sharing. I promised her that on my next trip—forget the kids and the husbands—*we* were going to go out to dinner and spend a lot of time together, just the two of us! She agreed, and as I left she gave me such a big hug she almost choked me. She told me she loved me, and I said the same. We'd never said it before, but somehow it seemed right because I'd come to realize what a special friend Doris was. I couldn't wait until I returned in just two months!

Less than a week later I got a call from my mother. Doris had had a massive stroke a few days before, at 43 years of age. She never regained consciousness and had passed away.

My bosom buddy, my lifelong friend—gone? I knew that no earthly friend would ever take her place; her death left a gaping hole in my heart. It's not been easy, but my heavenly friend, Jesus, has helped heal my hurt and loneliness. My day-to-day Friend, He's there even when I move away. He shares my ups and downs, offers insight and advice and comfort. He wants to spend more time with me. And He always tells me He loves me. I look forward to the day when I will see Him and my friend Doris again.

IRIS L. STOVALL

Growing Within

I will praise thee; for I am fearfully and wonderfully made: marvelous are thy works; and that my soul knoweth right well. Ps. 139:14.

A FRIEND ONCE ASKED me why pregnant women always touch their belly. I've had quite a lot of time to think on that subject since this is my fifth pregnancy. And it's still hard to describe.

There's a tiny miracle growing inside. She wriggles and kicks. When she gets the hiccups, I feel it. I know when she's asleep and when she's awake. Every movement becomes a part of me. When I touch my belly, I'm letting her know that I care. That touch says, "I felt that." That touch says, "You are loved."

While my belly is swelling to an enormous size, I feel each turn or somersault. Other mothers start to realize that I'm carrying an extra person, and they want to touch my belly and coo to the little one growing within, too. And they do—whether stranger or friend.

When a pregnant woman doesn't feel movement, she gets worried. She will rub, pet, and talk to her little one just to feel the special movement inside.

I'm carrying this extra person within me. She's a part of me, but she's already becoming her own person—extremely unique! For you see, God put her there from the love my husband and I share. What a miracle and honor to have created within my very own body a part of our love and promise to each other. And our trust and love in God makes it even more special.

Even though there's a lot of pain during labor, you can't remember feeling it, or how much it hurt, after that first embrace. When the doctor lays your baby across your chest, it was worth every hour of pain. Jesus suffered hour after hour in pain and humiliation on that cross for us, to save us from our sins.

God gives us blessings in a world of so much sin because He never meant for us to suffer. He wants so much better for us. And if we stay close to God, we will get to see how He meant this world to be. Until then, let's give God thanks for everything, whether small or large, joyous or sorrowful. God is right by our side through all the pain, just as He was with Jesus.

Thank You, God, for Jesus, Your Son, and for the privilege and miracle to reproduce. You are our all powerful yet tenderhearted Father, and we give You all the praise.

TAMMY BARNES TAYLOR

Deliverance in His Time

For we wrestle not against flesh and blood, but against principalities, against powers, against the rulers of the darkness of this world, against spiritual wickedness in high places. Eph. 6:12.

MANY TIMES WE FIND ourselves in situations for which there seems to be no way out except by divine intervention. I was in such a situation on my job. By nature I'm not a fighter. Although I've learned to trust God to fight my battles, I internalized my anger. I found myself hating my oppressors, which didn't help me, since I was developing medical problems as a result. After giving prayerful thought to my dilemma, I thought, *Why not turn hate into love?* It made a difference in the way I felt. I saw my oppressors, not as enemies but as individuals to love.

Having gained that victory, I was faced with another situation. Satan never gives up. He stops at nothing to try to defeat a child of God. He was trying his best to get me discouraged and to give up my job. I didn't. So he tried another scheme. I remember driving to work many days crying, "O Lord, how long, how long, how long?"

One day I was told that a meeting was scheduled for me to meet with the supervisor and staff members. The evening before the meeting, a staff member told me, "Dolores, in all fairness I have to tell you that this meeting is a conspiracy." I had already suspected as much.

I phoned my pastor so that he could pray with me, but he wasn't available. I phoned the Bible worker. She wasn't available either. Then I went directly to God, who is always available.

After my encounter with God in prayer was over, the phone rang. On the line was my sister, asking me to pray for her. We were able to pray about both of our situations.

I went to the meeting, confident that God would see me through. Another challenge was presented. Nothing tests our character more than having something untrue said or done about us. The end result was that I received a promotion.

Surely Jesus never fails. Adversity will ultimately become an advantage for those doing what is right—if we're willing to wait for Him patiently.

DOLORES E. SMITH

The Surprises of Ministry

And we know that all things work together for good to them that love God, to them who are the called according to his purpose. Rom. 8:28.

BEING A PASTOR'S DAUGHTER, I always thought being married to a pastor couldn't be a big deal. After all, I was already used to the many visitors who thronged our house. My father was pastor, teacher, and medicine dispenser in the little village where I grew up. I was used to transfers. In my father's days, transfers meant traveling partly by truck and partly by foot.

I thought I was well equipped to become a pastor's wife and that there couldn't be many surprises. However, when my husband was transferred four times in four years I realized there were still new surprises left in the ministry. I enjoyed all four churches with their differences and approaches to life. But there were surprising disappointments, too, especially at the unspoken disapprovals from church members.

There was still another surprise when we moved to our next station. God wonderfully confirmed our transfer in a miraculous way. My husband and I were more than 125 miles (200 kilometers) apart and had no telephone; we could not communicate. We wanted to worship together the first Sabbath in a new station, but I wasn't sure whether he had moved or not. I was confused. With a fuel scarcity I doubted whether I should travel to the new place with the children, because it would be a wasted effort if we should miss him.

Before we left we put ourselves into the hands of our Maker and prayed for His guidance. I thought that if we didn't meet, I'd just leave a note and travel back immediately so as to spend the Sabbath with our old members. Surprise! We arrived about five minutes after my husband arrived!

Romans 8:28 says, "We know that all things work together for good to them that love God, to them who are the called according to his purpose."

What other evidence do I need from God? Surely He has sent us to our new station, and He confirmed our ministry there by showing us that He could move us from different places and bring us together without missing each other. The Lord truly is good.

BECKY DADA

The Waiting Room

Wait on the Lord: be of good courage, and he shall strengthen thine heart: wait, I say, on the Lord. Ps. 27:14.

I RUSHED THROUGH THE door to my appointment like an Olympian in those last crucial seconds in which it is still possible to lose the entire race. I checked the clock and triumphantly signed in. I had made it, and on time. Those who know me, and my nearly legendary status of "always late," would have applauded.

"Please have a seat," the receptionist said automatically and all too cheerfully, the result no doubt of having said it a million times before. "Someone will be with you shortly." I knew that could mean minutes or what could seem like days. Wait. God knows I hate to wait. That's an amazing confession from one who has caused others to wait by running consistently late for years. I would half jokingly blame it on my dad, who seemed to think it was OK to be "fashionably" late.

I realized I hated to wait after a few occasions when, though I was late, there was someone who was even later than I was. I realized that what I didn't like was the sense of not being in control of the situation inherent in just waiting. Instantly you're on someone else's schedule, and you have no clue of the timing of events. Time is so precious; it's one of the gifts from God, like good health, that we take for granted. So after a lifetime of being fashionably late, I've endeavored to be on time.

But I've still had to wait. Not only for appointments and for others who run late, when I'm behind a slower driver, or when once again I've managed to choose the wrong checkout line, but to wait on the Lord. Wait—for His direction, His timing, and His answer. He's always on time. And sometimes He just wants me to wait because I'm not ready yet for what He knows is best for me.

And me? I'm still late more times than I care to admit, but I will not be deterred from my mission. I've made remarkable progress.

Dear Jesus, help me to wait patiently on You.   MAXINE WILLIAMS ALLEN

The Crowns of a Dreamer

The Holy One says this: "I live in that high and holy place with those whose spirits are contrite and humble." Isa. 57:15, NLT.

HEAVEN SENT US SONNY just before my thirty-fifth birthday. Since his birth I've literally lived on energy coming directly from the throne of God. Being the primary caregiver of a mentally challenged child can be overwhelming. Jokingly I tell my friends, "I don't know if the Lord gave me Sonny to wear me out or to keep me young!" The same applies to Sonny's dad.

I'm so thankful for our daughter, Andrea, 14 years older than Sonny. Watching her become a responsible adult is affirmation of our good parenting skills. For Ron and me, those parenting skills are continuing to be transformed into survival skills. To survive, we must stay mentally healthy. So we're a family on the go, in the strength of the Lord. Repeatedly jumping through the hoops that government policies dictate, plus other unavoidable stressful issues encompassing our special-needs child, drains us of precious energy. Without faith and hope in a loving and caring God we could easily become discouraged or even devastated.

I listen when other "special" parents give advice. This tidbit stuck: "You must make time for yourself, even during times of utter chaos and total confusion." The recommendation? "Sit down in a comfortable chair with a nice drink and 'think of Paradise'—away from your children."

It's fun and rewarding to think of Paradise. I'm a dreamer who writes. Jesus knows my pain. Years ago, while scrubbing the toilet and floor, I felt the Holy Spirit speak to my heart: "For every tear that you've cried because of unkind things people have said and done there will be a gem in your crown." Recently I told the Lord, "If I don't stop crying, my crown will be too big to wear!" In a whisper He replied, "Who said you'll have only one?"

Jesus makes me smile. Proudly I'll wear my crowns when I worship Him in celebrations across the universe throughout eternity. I hope and pray that those who have done hurtful things will be there, celebrating, too. Jesus has taught me how to guard my spirit: By not allowing others to become stumbling blocks, I'm actually inviting God to bless those who have, or will, hurt me. God works in mysterious ways. DEBORAH SANDERS

The Difference

Ask, and it shall be given you; seek, and ye shall find; knock, and it shall be opened unto you. Matt. 7:7.

RECENTLY, I WAS SEEN by my physician for a routine physical examination. I was given three cards and was to return a stool specimen on each in a special envelope. Specific instructions were also given for the collection over a period of three days. Having completed the collection, I couldn't find the required envelope with which to mail the specimens to a specific laboratory.

I remembered placing the envelope on my dressing table, but it wasn't there when I looked. Frantically, I started to search every possible place in the house. I became quite anxious and was upset with myself for being so careless. I thought, *Maybe I tore it in pieces and threw it out* (I am good at that, you know). I searched every garbage pail, my handbag, my jacket and dress pockets.

All through my anxious search I kept repeating, "Seek, and ye shall find." What made the difference was that I was seeking on my own. I didn't ask the Lord to help me seek. I remembered reading about a conversation between a robin and a sparrow. Said the robin to the sparrow, "I would really like to know why those anxious human beings rush about and worry so." Said the sparrow to the robin, "I think it must be that they have no heavenly Father such as cares for you and me."

I thought, *How silly of me. I must look to Jesus.* He was probably standing in a corner of the house with His arms folded, watching me as I was frantically running around the house, wondering when I would seek His help.

I then stopped everything I was doing and sought God's help. I was less anxious, and a miraculous thing happened. It was as if I were led by a hand. I went into my bedroom, and there was the envelope on the dresser where I had left it. I had looked there several times before and not seen it. *Why did God not help me sooner?* I thought.

The reply came back to me, "My child, you did not ask."

DOLORES E. SMITH

Envy Is a Dangerous Thing!

Speaking to yourselves in psalms and hymns and spiritual songs, singing and making melody in your heart to the Lord. Eph. 5:19.

PROVERBS 14:30 STATES that "a sound heart is the life of the flesh: but envy the rottenness of the bones." I remember a time at church that if you said amen too loudly people would look at you funny and have words for you. There was also a time that if you didn't sing classical songs it was frowned upon. When I was a new believer, someone once told me, "You should pray and ask the Lord for forgiveness because you sing with too much feeling, and the Lord is not pleased with you."

You know what? I believed them. I was young and gullible, and I thought that what was said to me was the truth because it was from a "saint." So I didn't sing for a couple years. People would ask me to sing, and I would say No. I found out later that the "saint" was jealous because singing was not her gift.

When the Lord gives you a talent, use it. Go to Him for guidance. I read, "Also their love, and their hatred, and their envy, is now perished; neither have they any more a portion for ever in any thing that is done under the sun" (Eccl. 9:6). From that day I vowed to use my voice and talents for Him and have been doing so ever since, exactly the way the Lord gave them to me.

Music is nature's melody. Psalm 89:1 says, "I will sing of the mercies of the Lord for ever: with my mouth will I make known thy faithfulness to all generations." Don't let someone else's shortcomings or envy stop you from growing stronger in faith and putting your trust in the Lord. He will give you a song to sing—maybe not with a voice, but with witnessing, speaking, Bible work, hospitality. Envy is a dangerous thing!

Lord, help me to have unwavering faith so that I will believe Your promises regardless of what I see or hear, knowing You are absolutely faithful to fulfill Your word to me. "The Lord is my strength and my shield; my heart trusted in him, and I am helped: therefore my heart greatly rejoiceth; and with my song will I praise him" (Ps. 28:7). The Bible says, "Envy is the rottenness of the bones." Help me to grow stronger in faith and trust each day. In Jesus' name, amen.

HATTIE R. LOGAN

Of Grass and Dandelions

If that is how God clothes the grass of the field, which is here today and tomorrow is thrown into the fire, will he not much more clothe you, O you of little faith? Matt. 6:30, NIV.

AFTER TOO MANY COLD seasons in Michigan, we retired in California. We exchanged raking leaves and shoveling snow for year-round dandelions. Every week we inspect our handkerchief-sized yard for tiny leaves. These baby dandelions are easily removed. Last summer, after a four-week absence, there was more to the usual search-and-destroy mission. As I went about my task I noticed that where the grass was lush and green there were very few intruders. Where the watering system had failed, there were no dandelions—and very little grass. In the in-between sections, where the grass was growing but not thriving, the number of dandelions was much greater. Obviously, the lawn would need better watering, fertilizing, and mowing.

My mind turned to spiritual intruders—those pesky reminders that I'm still living in enemy territory, that life is a constant battle. Mostly they are negative thoughts about myself, others, or even my Lord. These are the tares sown in the wheat field by the enemy (Matt. 13:25). These mental dandelions are of no concern to those who make no profession, who never turn to God. There's no lawn to disfigure.

The person who is spiritually alive, constantly fed by the Word of God, irrigated by the water of life, and rooted in the Lord abounds in good works and loving attitudes. Weeds can't penetrate the thick green carpet. If they do begin to grow, they are easy to eradicate.

While the lush, thick grass is my ideal, I often find myself in that intermediate situation—neither good nor bad, with weeds easily taking root. Honestly, I don't like my position. However, unlike my yard, I can do something about it.

I can choose to turn over my life to the Master Gardener. He knows exactly when to irrigate and how to fertilize. My task is to accept divine help and grow. Good soil, plenty of water, and adequate fertilizer in the spiritual realm are pleasant experiences.

Yes, I want my life to be a cool, green carpet, strong and thick, free from spiritual dandelions. And since God cares about the grass, how much more will He care for me! NANCY JEAN VYHMEISTER

Sleeping Sickness

*I know thy works, that thou hast a name that thou livest, and art dead.
Rev. 3:1.*

I MET EMILIA FROM the Dominican Republic. We were both special friends of Norma from Jordan, from my church, but we didn't know that when we moved to apartments across the hall from each other. Emilia belongs to a different denomination than mine. Out of curiosity I attended a prayer meeting with her. The service was in Spanish, but the pastor and some of the members were somewhat bilingual.

A local American woman, speaking only English, sat in front of me but turned often to Emilia and me. She had just gotten out of the hospital that day. She'd been suffering with sleeping sickness, she said, and the doctor told her not to be alone for 24 hours because she might die if she fell asleep. I became alarmed.

The room barely held a dozen chairs. I tried to cover my mouth so I wouldn't breathe her germs, in case she was contagious. I silently prayed during her coughs, "O God, I don't want to die." Near the end of the service she handed a wrapped piece of candy to Emilia, who took it unsuspectingly. Then she handed one to me. I took it, not wanting to offend her, yet thinking my whole family could die if I was a carrier of the disease.

Once in the car, I explained my thoughts to Emilia. She panicked also. Then, for some reason, we both started laughing. I confessed that I used to tell people that I never wanted to die in pain, that I wanted to die in my sleep. Now I was sorry I had ever said that. At our apartment parking lot I dumped the candy out of my purse. Emilia was looking for hers so she could do the same. We were both doubled over in laughter as she screamed, "I don't want to die!"

As I thought more seriously about this woman and the conversation, I realized she couldn't really have had sleeping sickness. And a doctor certainly wouldn't have sent her home alone to die in 24 hours. I decided the woman must have been exaggerating to get attention or sympathy. But she did have me alarmed for a while.

Shouldn't we Christians be more alarmed that we can get spiritual sleeping sickness that leads to eternal death?

ALEAH IQBAL

Willow

We live within the shadow of the Almighty, sheltered by the God who is above all gods. This I declare, that he alone is my refuge, my place of safety; he is my God, and I am trusting him. Ps. 91:1, 2, TLB.

WHEN WE BROUGHT WILLOW the cat home from the shelter, it was pretty obvious that he was damaged goods. His antisocial behaviors began to stress my husband, so within a week of bringing the cat home, he began to feel that maybe we'd made a big mistake.

I defended my pet. I had fallen in love with him from the start, a shy cat with definite Maine coon tendencies: a luxurious thick coat, huge paws, and a beautiful, intelligent face. But whatever experiences he'd been through had left him terrified of being touched to the point that he'd shake if you tried to hold him. Now that he was mine, I couldn't bear to lose him. I wanted for him to be happy and to feel loved. Slowly, with months of patient love, he began to respond and became much less timid with us and even began to purr, ever so softly. He even began to respond to our friends when it suited him.

Then after the birth of our first child he felt threatened and afraid again. He "marked" his territory when he felt intimidated or if we did anything to offend him. I was devastated. I wanted love to be enough to save him from his fear. I wanted him to understand that nothing he could do would stop me from loving him, even when his behavior was exasperating. I wanted him to trust us that everything would work out OK.

It made me think about how it must be for God. He wants so badly to let us know we are loved. He wants us to know that no matter how much we mess up, He will still love and care for us. He wants us to know that all this earthly trauma is temporary and that it will all be fine, if we can just hang on. He sees our potential, not just our behavior. His capacity to forgive is boundless and will always exceed our capacity to sin. He wants us with Him, no matter what.

Willow made me experience (on a far lesser scale, of course) how God must feel. Multiply that by everyone in the world and think how God's heart must break every day over us, and yet He never gives up. Thank God!

HEATHER HANNA

Independence Day

Then Jesus said to the disciples, "If anyone wants to be a follower of mine, let him deny himself and take up his cross and follow me." Matt. 16:24, TLB.

AUGUST 17 IS INDONESIA'S Independence Day. Recently I received an invitation from the Indonesian Embassy to celebrate the Independence Day in the Indonesian ambassador's home in Washington, D.C. I received the invitation the day of the dinner.

I was enthusiastic about attending this dinner party. It's always nice to meet people who are from the same country and who speak the same language, especially when you're away from your own country. I printed out the driving directions from the Internet—it was only six miles away, about 20 minutes of driving.

I hurried home to prepare myself to go. When I was ready to leave, my housemate advised me to call a friend to accompany me. She was afraid I'd get lost, especially after dark, since I wasn't familiar with the streets in the city. But I assured her I'd be all right. After all, it was only six miles, and I had the directions.

For about two miles I was OK, but when the directions told me to turn right, I wasn't sure it was the right street because I couldn't clearly see the name of the street. So I decided to go straight. Then I realized it had been the right street and decided to make a U-turn but couldn't find a place to do it. After driving for about a mile, I finally was able to make a left turn. But this time the road was a one-way street. It took about 10 minutes to get back to the main road. Then I realized I was hopelessly lost. Since it was getting dark, I decided to give up and go home.

I now know I can get lost even if I have directions to follow. But I also know we will never get lost if we follow Jesus in our lives. As Jesus said in Matthew 16:24: "Follow me."

Thank You, Lord, for the assurance that I have You to follow in my life. I can depend on You to direct my path so I know where to go in this life. Amen.

LANNY LYDIA PONGILATAN

Walk in the Light

Walk while ye have the light, lest darkness come upon you: for he that walketh in darkness knoweth not whither he goeth. While ye have the light, believe in light, that ye may be the children of light. John 12:35, 36.

SOME NIGHTS I LIE awake in bed and gaze at the silhouetted trees outside my window. Occasionally the reflected light of a full moon makes their outlines so clear I can even distinguish individual branches. Other nights are pitch-black, as if nothing at all exists beyond the window glass. I don't pull a blind to cover this window at night. There's no one out there. And whether I can see them or not, my friendly trees are always standing guard.

One very dark night I was just drifting off when my eyelids fluttered open and I saw a flash of light in the room. It couldn't be—all the light switches were off, and no moon was in sight. But there it was again! I awakened my husband, who promptly but gently assured me that I was seeing imaginary things and that there was medication available to solve that problem. A jab in the ribs from my elbow brought him fully awake with open eyes. There it was again! We both exclaimed together, "It's a firefly!"

"And it's inside," I mused. "Must have slipped in when you fetched the cat for the night."

We both lay awake for some time, commenting on the little bug's pluckiness. The poor thing was searching for a mate it wouldn't find in the confines of our house. Around and around the room it flew, always surprising us with its glow in an unexpected spot. It felt rather comforting to have the little creature with its lamp.

Jesus tells us that He is the light of the world. Without Him is darkness. He warns us to walk while we have light because we can't tell where we're going when it's dark.

Sometimes my life goes through a time of blackness, as if a heavy blind has been pulled across the sun to blot out its rays. At such times I cling to the promise that Jesus will light my path. It may be only a flicker from a tiny firefly or reflected light from a full moon, but it's always enough to guide my steps so long as I keep my eyes fixed on Jesus, the author of light.

DAWNA BEAUSOLEIL

Playtime

Is anyone among you suffering? Let him pray. Is anyone cheerful? Let him sing psalms. James 5:13, NKJV.

THE SUMMER TEMPERATURES in northern Minnesota had been extremely sweltering. Week after week of hot, humid weather with temperatures in the nineties had kept me from doing my gardening chores. Knowing I needed to remove the volunteer grasses, weeds, and little trees that had decided to take up residence in my flowerbed, I went out before sunrise to work. Day was just beginning to break when I welcomed Princess for company as I began my chore.

As I pulled, Princess reached out with her paws to bat the moving greenery. I reached over to scratch her and play with her. Keeping her claws shielded, she gently reached out to touch my hand and play with me. Becoming more brave in her play, she opened her mouth and gently took my finger in her mouth. Part of the time was spent working with one hand and playing with Princess with the other. For more than an hour the young kitten was my companion. I couldn't keep the smiles from my face as I enjoyed our playtime. She made me relax and savor the moments we shared.

I praised God for the wonder of His creation and for the playfulness He instilled in the kitten. Princess did much to add to the cheerful beginning of my new day. The days come and go, and I often become busy and burdened with the cares that come my way. I forget to allow the smiles to come to my face. My heart doesn't sing the praises that should be springing forth. The joy of life isn't as radiant as I would like it to be. When this happens, I know it's time to take a mini vacation and play. A few moments spent relaxing and thinking happy thoughts will once again bring praise and joy to my heart.

Dear God, as I begin each new day, instill songs of praise in my heart and mind. Remind me to express the joy and love that are gifts from You. May I often take a few moments to play and reap the benefits that come from these pleasant intervals in my life. Thank You for early-morning hours in the garden and for little kittens.

EVELYN GLASS

The Sea

Even the winds and the waves obey him. Matt. 8:27, NIV.

THERE'S SOMETHING ABOUT the sea that attracts people of all ages. Is it its calming beauty when we see the sun shimmering and skimming over the calm and tranquil waters? Or is it the sense of adventure a sailor feels when out in his boat? Or is it the excitement we have all felt when watching a child splashing through the waves, running and playing?

During the past few years our family has experienced the many moods of the sea: adversity and joy. On returning from a vacation in Spain, we got caught for 30 hours in a storm with gale-force winds. We felt extremely vulnerable and frightened.

In a totally opposite type of event, our two daughters decided to get baptized in the sea of Aberdaron, north Wales, giving their hearts to the Lord and creating a witness to others looking on. Our 10-year-old son loves to play in the sea on his body board, riding the waves and swimming in the ocean.

Many a sailor has lost his life in the sea; families have lost their loved ones. And yet many creatures live in and depend on the waters of the deep for their very survival. However we view the magnificence of this part of creation, there's only one who controls it—God. It was He who once told the waves of the sea, "Peace, be still!" and they obeyed. It is to Him that we owe homage and eternal gratitude.

Being a Christian can be likened to the sea. It's an experience that isn't to be taken lightly. We can have periods of storm, periods of calm, and periods of fun and beauty. It can be full and rewarding if we let God control our lives and let Him be the captain. And it can be frightening when He isn't in command. Let's welcome the One who has control over the seas of the world and allow Him to control our daily life and encapsulate us in His everlasting love.

God, our Father, ruler of the sea, rule over our lives. Clean us each day in the waters of Your love and forgiveness. Thank You for being the captain of our ship as we sail the daily waters of life.　　　　ANNETTE KOWARIN

Kissin' Cousins

Praise the Lord. How good it is to sing praises to our God, how pleasant and fitting to praise him! Ps. 147:1, NIV.

THE BEST SOUVENIR FROM my trip to the Middle Eastern Kingdom of Jordan was a reignited excitement for the Old Testament. Those Bible stories we learned as kids aren't just sweet fairy tales. The struggles were real, and the people were real.

Take the children of Israel, for example. God shoots off a fireworks display of miracles to get His people out of very tough circumstances. He even personally escorts them, but they grumble over minor matters. Think about it: if God can displace millions of gallons of water so one can walk on the sea bottom, how hard can it be for Him to put a little spring of brackish water through an aqua filter? I hate to admit it, but many times I must be kissin' cousins with those Israelites.

Then because they were too chicken to dream big dreams with God, mumbling about their inabilities instead of focusing on God's infinite abilities, the Children of Israel wandered 40 years in the wilderness. *H'mmm . . . The Big 4-0 is a number I've become familiar with. Lord, have I gone in circles?*

What's so great about God is that He never gave up on them. While they were wandering all those years He never failed to overnight manna for a.m. delivery. He provided a huge, cloudy umbrella for shade from the desert sun, and a toasty fire for warmth at night.

God wanted to take them on the direct express through Edom and Moab, but as usual they dillydallied, missed the train, and had to walk the long way around. At least this route was many degrees cooler than what they'd been traveling through. But were they grateful? No. Grumble, grumble, grumble. "I wish I had." "I don't like what I have." "Why can't I have?" "Why have you?" Snakes were so fascinated with the questions that they came out to investigate.

Lord, so often I'm not grateful either. I grumble when I could—and should—be praising. You deserve praise. Forgive me. Help me to keep my eyes on You, the one who volunteered to hang naked as a snake on a pole to take away my guilt and shame.

All because You never stop loving me.

HEIDE FORD

Days of Clouds and Darkness

As a shepherd looks after his scattered flock when he is with them, so will I look after my sheep. I will rescue them from all the places where they were scattered on a day of clouds and darkness. Eze. 34:12, NIV.

WHEN I WAS YOUNGER I loved a really good storm. When the clouds were black and boiling, when the wind blew fiercely, and especially when lightning split the sky, I would laugh and say, "This is a good one!" But that was when I was inside, watching from a safe window. I didn't have to walk (or drive) through that storm.

Since then I've walked and driven through many of life's storms, and I think I've weathered them pretty well—some better than others. But recently a horrible storm has blown my way, and I don't know that I've completely come through it. The clouds have been menacing, dark, and angry. They seethe and boil and rain down pain upon my heart. Lightning often races across the threatening sky, piercing the gloomy darkness with flashes of thundering brilliance. The wind angrily whips about me, clutching at my hair, my face, and my clothing. At every thunderclap, I cringe in fear. I run and I hide in places I have never been before. I close my eyes and wish with all my heart that the rain, the pain, and the gloom will all just go away. I don't know if my face is wet more from tears or from raindrops. I feel as if I'm completely alone.

Then the raging storm subsides, and, thinking it's over, I look up toward the sky. But the sad, dark clouds remain. I find myself thinking that I'll never again see the light of the sun. I think I'll never find home again. I cry out, "Where are You, God?" And even as I speak those words, I know He is near. As if in answer to my cry, a single sunbeam pierces through the clouds. I can almost see the hand of God reaching down to me in the place where I have become lost.

Even when I can't see Him, even when I can't feel Him, God is here to rescue me from the places where I've run in fear.

Dear Father, I thank You that no matter how the storm may rage, You are here. I reach back to You today.   Lynda Mae Richardson

God's Water

As the deer pants for streams of water, so my soul pants for you, O God. My soul thirsts for God, for the living God. Ps. 42:1, 2, NIV.

IMAGINE A PARCHED COUNTRY with dry bush grass that's taller than you are. The green leaves of the mango trees on the roadside are no longer green but covered with red dust. Ash flakes from the bush fires fall softly from the sky where the grass has been burned down. It's been hot and dry for many, many months. Not a drop of rain. Although you drink enough water, you feel parched inside. Although you have enough water in your bucket shower to get clean, you long for a really good, long, cool shower with the water pounding on your head and shoulders. And then the wind starts blowing and the first clouds gather. *Oh, how I wish it would rain soon!* is your first thought. And you watch and wait for the first raindrops. And then they start falling, a few solitary drops at first, but soon it's like a massive waterfall. The children run outside and enjoy the water pouring from the sky. Even you would like to step into the rain for a shower. Maybe you do, holding your face into the spray. How you have longed for this experience!

This was my experience during the years we spent in central Africa. In the local language Sango there is no word for "rain," but it is called *"ngou ti Nzapa"*—God's water. Rain is indeed God's refreshing water. It washes the red dust from the trees, and suddenly the leaves are green again. Not long after the first rain, the burned ground is covered by soft green grass.

I used to live in England, and rain was always to be expected. But rain in Britain is vastly different from tropical rainstorms. England's rain is a light drizzle, something that surrounds you gently. I loved to walk in the rain, my feet in Wellingtons (rubber boots) and my head covered by an umbrella. But the ever-present rain was often taken for granted and grumbled about.

Do you long for God's refreshing water of life as you would for a good, long shower? Do you want to expose every part of your body to the delicious downpour? Are you letting God's water massage away the stiffness in your muscles and your heart? Are you letting God refresh your life every day? Are you letting Him surround you like a steady drizzle? Let's think of God every time He sends His water onto the earth and thank Him for His presence in our lives.

HANNELE OTTSCHOFSKI

God Can

Those who hope in the Lord will renew their strength. They will soar on wings like eagles; they will run and not grow weary, they will walk and not be faint. Isa. 40:31, NIV.

IT WAS AUGUST, and my eldest son, who had been dating for seven years, arrived home with the young woman he had chosen to be his wife and announced his wedding date for December 15.

I was happy, and now the family plans converged for the big day they had chosen. But 15 days after they had announced the wedding plans, I had some medical examinations done and received a devastating report. I had breast cancer and should immediately prepare myself for radical surgery that would be followed by chemotherapy. The news shook me deeply, as it did my children, relatives, and friends.

My son asked me, "And now, what about my wedding?"

I answered him with the calm strength and serenity that only God can grant at a moment like this. "Son, your wedding was already in God's plans; my cancer is an invader, an intrusion that will be removed. Your wedding should not suffer any change. God can do all things."

By September 25 I'd already had surgery, which was followed by chemotherapy treatments. On December 15 my husband and I, as well as our dear relatives and friends, gathered for the wedding blessing. And it was a beautiful wedding.

The festivities passed, but my struggle continued. Problems multiplied. Dear friend, the Bible tells us that in this world we will have afflictions, but it also furnishes us the necessary support to overcome obstacles. I felt the arms of Jesus holding me, just as He was holding my two sons and today, two daughters-in-law.

We feel a tug at our heart, but we perceive the precious promises of God in the details of our necessities. Good angels visit us, care for us, and give us support. Through the breaks in these struggles God's opportunities open up to us. Jesus Christ uses our lives, our hands, as we learn to live to serve Him.

Each day I hear, "Daughter, My grace is sufficient." It is He who strengthens us.

CASSANDRA MARTINS

Pass It On!

God is love. Whoever lives in love lives in God, and God in him. 1 John 4:16, NIV.

A FEW YEARS AGO I lived in an apartment complex with a lot of children. It was a very lively house. Once I approached the heavy entrance door as a boy of about 4 struggled with all his might to open the door. You could see it wasn't easy. I commented, "The door is heavy and hard to open, isn't it?"

"No, not for me!" he declared.

I held back my smile and said that sometimes it was hard for me. And then this little child said, "Well, if I'm around, you can call me. I'd be glad to help you."

What adorable beings children are! He was so small, yet he cared about my needs.

Another day I rode a bus to town. It wasn't very full, so everybody could have a seat. A young woman was sitting next to me. On the seats in front of us were her two daughters, who wanted to sit by themselves. An older woman got onto the bus. She looked unkindly at the two little girls and sat down next to them without a word. The girls squeezed together and looked at their mother with anxious eyes. I wondered how I would have reacted had I been the woman. I decided I would have at least have smiled and asked for permission. Maybe I would have shared something funny, and we would have had something to laugh about. I imagined that this ride could have been a good time.

It's our responsibility as adults and Christians to show children how to be friendly and kind. How can they learn if we do not give them a good example? Even if they're not our own children, our actions have an influence on how children learn to react to people.

Everybody wants to be loved, accepted, and valued. Yet we find it difficult to pass on the love we all need. Maybe we could learn from children in this respect. We can't always wait for somebody to begin. I can begin myself!

Little things are important. The little boy who showed he cared made my day. I left the house joyfully and was able to pass on a smile. God has shown us in many ways how much He loves us. Isn't it wonderful to pass on this love? It will certainly come back to us more than once.

CHRISTEL SCHNEIDER

A Challenging Situation

A gentle answer turns away anger. Prov. 15:1, Clear Word.

I PRAY OFTEN THAT God will help me to be kind, encouraging, or just a good listener. But sometimes He answers my prayer, and I'm not aware of it until the experience is over and I hear the end of the story.

I was a registered nurse, working in a new hospital in a large city. I'd heard that one of our specialists in the hospital had a bad temper. Four of us nurses were having a meeting at the desk when this doctor came in and asked for help to do a spinal tap on a small child. When he noticed we were in a meeting he commented, "Some other time will be OK." I was in charge of the afternoon shift and was accustomed to accommodating the doctors, so I said, "Oh, no, you won't need to wait. Two of us will help you now."

Another nurse and I got the material and the child ready for the procedure. The other nurse held the child in what she thought was the proper position. I got the sterile tray ready. I wasn't wearing my glasses and started to open the tray upside down. I quickly noticed my error and immediately turned it over. Quick as a wink the doctor lost his cool and barked, "What are you doing?" I didn't say a word (which was a miracle), and nothing more was said.

The doctor was very unhappy with how the other nurse was holding the child. Since I'd done the procedure before, I offered to take over for her. By now the doctor needed a new pair of gloves, so I started to get them for him. Somehow he reached for the gloves too quickly and cut his finger on the paper covering. Then he really yelled at me. I was amazed at my calmness as I looked him in the eyes and quietly said, "I'm sorry." Which again was amazing.

I then held the child, and we soon got through the procedure. It was an intense time, and all four of us nurses felt our day was ruined.

Some days later, when we were all in the supervisor's office, she told us the rest of the story. The doctor had gone to her office and reported, "We had a problem in pediatrics today, but the nurses handled it perfectly."

Thank You, God, for helping us in our times of stress. FRIEDA TANNER

Just Beyond the Wall

If ye be willing and obedient, ye shall eat the good of the land. Isa. 1:19.

FOR MANY YEARS MY mom planted and tended flowers and Dad looked on with pride at a job well done. In recent times, however, by beholding he has become changed and now is actively involved in the process of acquiring new varieties for the ever-expanding garden and greenhouse.

On one of their frequent trips into the city his eyes caught a glimpse of a fern-covered wall. He began to imagine his own wall in like splendor. Mom shared his excitement, and soon he was convinced to stop and "acquire" a small bit. "This could not possibly make a difference to this densely covered wall," he reasoned. His conscience, however, chipped in and reminded him of the need to receive permission.

Upon opening the gate, they were both invited into an unforgettable experience. They stood surrounded by some of the most beautiful and exotic plants they'd ever seen. The owner had a 30-year collection of orchids and was the recipient of several international horticultural awards. Anthurium, a wide collection of ferns, and orchids of all colors, shapes, and origins, even hybrid orchids that the owner had developed, competed for their attention.

The feast to their eyes was second to none of any they had ever experienced. In addition, they received cuttings, suckers, plant-care manuals, and tons of good advice. To think that they could have missed all this—just beyond the wall.

Many times we've traded life-changing experiences for instant gratification and self-righteous rationalization. The Lord understands, we muse. We're aware of the right way to go, but rationalize our consciences into submission. The angels of heaven many times stand disappointed as they hover over us, bearing gifts we fail to receive. The reminder comes to us: "Seek ye first the kingdom of God, and his righteousness; and all these things shall be added unto you" (Matt. 6:33).

Today as you make each decision, keep in mind the blessings specially designed for you just beyond the wall of obedience.

PATRICE E. WILLIAMS-GORDON

The Best Part of Relationships

Pleasant words are a honeycomb, sweet to the soul and healing to the bones.
Prov. 16:24, NIV.

HONEY IS A SWEET substance with a pleasant taste and peculiar flavor. It's formed of the juice from flowers and fruits collected by bees. Honey is a highly nutritive food, a product of the bee and of all the bee collects. I too am the totality of all that I live.

Sweetness is not easily obtained. It requires processes, mixtures, and much work. Sweetness is our capacity to influence and bring about good fruit. It's not something that is static and still; it's dynamic and is composed of small nothings, such as kindness, tenderness, disinterested service, a smile, a friendly word, a phone call, a visit, a flower given with care. Each kind act is "sweet to the soul and healing to the bones."

The queen receives royal jelly, a special honey, while the other bees receive regular honey. My life reflects the nourishment that I receive. In my spiritual life I can feel the same effect, depending on the type and quantity of daily prayer, moments of reflection, and communion with God.

There are various types of bees. Parasite bees steal nectar from other bees. Social bees live together in large colonies in nests called combs. But not all bees live in colonies. The majority of them are solitary bees that do not produce honey, either because of their species or their disorganization.

What type of bee am I—parasite, solitary, without courage? Am I helpful or depressing to those around me? Or am I productive, sociable, committed, dynamic, and diligent?

To produce six grams of honey a bee has to visit from 60,000 to 90,000 flowers. In my spiritual family or my professional journey, have I done enough to fill those whom I love and with whom I come in contact daily with the nectar of joy and happiness?

Lord, help me to be like a bee—organized, dedicated, and busy—and may the fruit of my life be like the effects produced by honey: calming, regenerating, sweetening, giving courage, and creating new strength.

IVONE FELDKIRCHER PAIVA

Our Day Out Back in Time

Thou makest him master over all thy creatures; thou hast put everything under his feet. Ps. 8:6, NEB.

THE STEAM TRAINS OF the West Somerset Railway travel more than 20 miles of unspoiled countryside beside the Quantock Hills and the Bristol Channel. As a small group of Taunton church members, we were ready for a great day out. We stopped at all 10 restored stations, each with its "olde world" charm.

We moved slowly, winding our way through the scenic route and admiring the beauty around us. The Lord was blessing us with delightful views and glorious sunshine. We finally arrived at the last station, feeling very relaxed. All the tension of town and city life was behind us. We crossed the road and sat beside the beach to have our packed lunches in the old Victorian seaside town. A fresh sea breeze completed the peace we were experiencing.

It was great to get away from the pressures of modern life and enjoy our surroundings. It's in times like these that we're able to praise the Lord for the peace and harmony He has given us. We can also look ahead to the time Jesus has promised us far more beauty than we can imagine. If we follow Him in our lives now we can be saved in His everlasting kingdom where we'll see even more than we can imagine. Not for just a day, but forever.

The sounds of the children playing on the beach and the trees behind us rustling in the wind reminded me of Psalm 118:24: "This is the day which the Lord hath made."

Before returning to our train in the afternoon, we took a slow and leisurely stroll around the bay. Our journey home was just as picturesque. We passed the famous Dunster Castle and decided to stop at Stogumber station and visit the Bee World and Animal Centre. The children were fascinated with the ponies, rabbits, and bee life. They even saw the birth of a lamb. We wandered around the stalls of highland cows and rare breeds of sheep and goats.

The children were delighted with the animals and birds. Everyone enjoyed the outing and appreciated the natural beauty of the hills and sea. Our heavenly Father has made us rulers over all these precious gifts. Let's remember that we are stewards too.

Thank You, Lord.   PHILIPPA MARSHALL

Spider in Church

Resist the devil, and he will flee from you. James 4:7, NIV.

MANY YEARS AGO, when my children were still very small (7, 4, 2, and 3 months), my husband was pastoring his first district in Mississippi. We had already attended two churches that Sabbath day and arrived at our third church at 3:00 in the afternoon. It was a hot summer day, and my children and I were all tired. We had stopped to eat a picnic lunch on the way from the second church.

The little white church, situated on the outskirts of a small town, had only 30 members. The building was made of bricks and contained a sanctuary, a multipurpose room with a kitchen at one end, and two bathrooms. Instead of pews, rows of folding chairs lined the sanctuary on a carpeted floor. Along the left side of the sanctuary were four stained-glass windows.

I always sat with my children on the left side, near the back. That way I could take them out if they got too loud or needed diapering. We had just sung the opening song and knelt down to pray when one of my boys noticed a black spider on the windowsill. He started blowing at it but kept a safe distance. I whispered to him to leave it alone and to close his eyes as we were going to pray to Jesus. My husband was praying, and everyone was quiet.

All of a sudden my son screamed "Spider!" at the top of his lungs. It was a scream of fear followed by uncontrolled crying. My eyes flew open, and I grabbed him. Pulling him to me, I tried to soothe him and quiet him down. As it turned out, he had continued to blow at the spider and had moved closer to it to try to get it to move. As he moved closer for the final blow, the spider jumped at him—but missed. Through the years of childhood, adolescence, and teens my son hated spiders and tried as hard as he could to avoid being around them.

This story reminds me of how we sometimes play with the devil. He seems so harmless and still, but as we get closer to him he tries to attack us.

Today I have choices—to play with spiders, or to repeat the prayer You taught us: "Lead us not into temptation." Help me to make the right choices, Lord.
CELIA MEJIA CRUZ

Heading Home

Yea, the stork in the heaven knoweth her appointed times; and the turtle and the crane and the swallow observe the time of their coming; but my people know not the judgment of the Lord. Jer. 8:7.

IT WAS THE END of August and the last few days of a long and very hot summer. Our bedroom window was wide open. Waking early to yet another bright, cloudless sky, I was immediately aware of an unusual sound filling the predawn silence. Hurrying to the window, I looked out on a never-to-be-forgotten sight. Hundreds of small birds were gathering on the electric cables overhead in preparation for their annual migratory flight to the warmer climes of central Africa. The house martins, cousins of the better-known swallows, were twittering and chirping in a frenzy of excitement, moving around on the wires and jostling each other like a group of unruly children gathering for a school excursion. Some of them had made this journey before; for others this would be their first experience of long-distance travel. Not all would reach their ultimate destination safely. They seemed, however, totally unconcerned by the daunting prospects ahead of them. Suddenly, at some invisible signal, the twittering stopped. As one bird they lifted off and, turning, wheeled into the predawn skies in perfect formation.

We, too, are preparing for a long, long journey. When Jesus comes, He will take us home with Him to heaven. Perhaps, as we wait for that great day, we could learn a few lessons from these cheerful little birds. First, the birds were fearless. In fact, they were bubbling over with excitement. They had a joyful, positive attitude that should surely fill every Christian heart as we wait for our Savior's promised return.

They also knew where they were going. What a wonderful sense of certainty! They recognized their impending time of departure and were ready for it. Nor were they disobedient to the promoting of their internal clocks. And finally, they didn't travel alone but in a group so that they could encourage and help each other when the way was hard.

Thank You, Lord, for simple lessons from Your creation. May our own lives be enriched as we learn from these happy little birds.

REVEL PAPAIOANNOU

Beware the Boxthorn

Thorns and snares are in the way. Prov. 22:5.

IT WAS FUN GROWING up in the country. My sisters, a younger brother, and I made huts in the hay barn and played for hours in a little shed at the end of the garden. We were doctors, we were nurses, we were dentists. Then there was a hedge to hide in, and toward the back of our farm was a small area of native bush with supplejack to swing on. The dampness of the bush soil there made it very slippery, so we took turns pulling each other down a slope while sitting on a punga frond.

Of course, there were chores to be done—hens to be fed, washing to be brought in from the clothesline, ironing the easy things—but looking back, it was a wonderfully carefree childhood.

Around the neighbor's paddocks, however, were hedges of boxthorn. So whenever I went over to see my school friend, Judy, I always wore something on my feet—shoes, sandals, or gum boots, depending on what I could find.

One afternoon after school there was no time to play; we were needed to help Mom. We had relatives coming to stay, and many more jobs than usual had to be done. I soon tired of the polishing I was assigned to do and sneaked away to play with Judy. I didn't want to be seen, so I didn't stop long enough to find footwear. As I ran down the neighbor's drive, the inevitable happened. I stepped on a thorn—a nasty, large, poisonous boxthorn—and it became embedded in the heel of my foot.

After I came home it wasn't long before my mother saw me limping and guessed what had happened. It really was a case of "be sure your sin will find you out" (Num. 32:23). Because the thorn was so deeply embedded, I had to soak it out, which meant many hours sitting with my foot in a bucket of very hot water and disinfectant.

How disappointed I was not to be able to run down the paddocks to the hay barn to make huts in the hay with my siblings and my cousins. It was punishment indeed to sit at home with my foot in a bucket when I could have been enjoying myself. My mother never said one word in discipline, for she knew my sin had found me out. I had learned a valuable lesson in obedience.

LEONIE DONALD

Ballet From the Sky

For ye shall go out with joy, and be led forth with peace: the mountains and the hills shall break forth before you into singing, and all the trees of the field shall clap their hands. Isa. 55:12.

A S I WAS TAKING in the beauty of an early snow on my walk one brisk September morning, I heard a musical sonnet. There, amid the mist, flew a dozen lovely Canada geese. They floated down into a large field. Soon there were groups of 8, 14, and 25, gliding through the air, descending. They emerged from east, north, and west—all horizons except the south.

They arrived at 5- to 15-minute intervals. What a lovely sight as they bent their wings earthward like umbrellas to sit on top of the snow and chat among themselves. Once in a while a large single bird would fly over as if he were the king of Canada geese—and maybe he was!

For two hours I watched as hundreds found open spots and covered the white earth. Others found shelter from the wind near some small trees. All of a sudden there came a "knack, knack," and about a hundred of them flew up and away, turning south.

I went home and got my car and came back to the field. I snuggled into my sleeping bag and sat with the motor off and the window down. The third hour approached, and my tummy told me that I'd forgotten lunch, yet I didn't want to leave. Then suddenly, they all flew up and away—quietly, without a honk. I scanned the horizon with my binoculars. None to be seen. Yet I lingered, hoping more would come.

As I drove home I was sad to see them all leave but glad to have witnessed such a sight of living beauty. I have a heavy heart when I realize I've missed much the past 50 years.

When you find beauty and wholesome pleasures, treasure the moments. Make them last as long as possible. Go out of your way to find them, or they'll pass away before you know it. Go out to see the aurora borealis (northern lights); sleep under the open sky. Think of occasions to experience, and your day will be very rewarding. If you don't, your years and your life will be almost over, and you'll wonder where all the joy in your life went.

VIDELLA MCCLELLAN

Untold Blessings Promised

For I will pour water on the thirsty land, and streams on the dry ground; I will pour my spirit upon your descendants, and my blessing on your offspring. Isa. 44:3, NRSV.

HAVE YOU EVER PONDERED at times how foolish your wishes were when you were younger? Well, I'm no exception. Recently I was talking with someone who had been my best girlfriend when we were in college. We worked in the English Department then, as readers. Somehow, both of us ended up with boyfriends who were taking theology. During our free time we would dream of marrying them and becoming foreign missionaries. However, since we both came from poor families, we promised each other that we'd work first as English teachers in Hong Kong. Our dream and aim was to work hard, save lots of money, and then purchase pump organs, typewriters, projectors, and other important gadgets that would be helpful in the meetings our husbands-to-be would be conducting. We were very certain that our boyfriends would be called to work in the Philippines after their graduation.

As my friend and I were reminiscing about the wistful musings and cheap talk, we both said, "Wasn't that just foolish on our part?"

Then she added, "I can't believe how small our faith was in our big God, who had so much in store for us. He was more than willing to pour floods of blessings upon us."

She and I didn't end up teaching English in Hong Kong after our graduation; however, we did marry our boyfriends and were sent to foreign lands as missionaries. They went to Zimbabwe and Lebanon, and my husband and I went to Laos and Thailand. We thank and praise our big God, who saw fit to let us serve in those countries.

Today we still aren't rich, but we live comfortably. Our children and their respective families are very blessed. In so many ways God has shown His guiding hand in all His dealings with us and with our children. How true it is when our God proclaims in His Word, "For I will pour water on the thirsty land, and streams on the dry ground; I will pour my spirit upon your descendants, and my blessing on your offspring." Truly God is good and remarkable and worthy to be praised.

OFELIA A. PANGAN

Recycling

A new command I give you: Love one another. As I have loved you, so you must love one another. John 13:34, NIV.

I RETURNED TO MY country after more than three years to find a new way of disposing of refuse. I learned about it at my mother's house. She showed me several boxes lined up by the garbage can outside. She pointed to each box, saying, "You wash the containers, remove the labels, and put the tins in this box, the glass in this one, the plastic here."

I said, "What? You have to do all this?"

"Yes," she said. "We want to be good citizens. Our seniors' club even makes crocheted place mats from used bread wrappers, and we sent one to the president!"

I saw one of the unusual place mats. I had to laugh, but I obediently recycled all the while I was there, and I have ever since. I learned that those used containers are reprocessed into useful objects to be sold on the market. The landfills are then less full of debris and less hazardous to the environment.

One day I was looking at a picture of a waterfall and thought about recycling. *The water in the falls the day that photo was taken is long gone to the sea by now,* I thought. We have water because the rain forms streams and rivers that flow to the sea, rise in vapor as clouds, and return as rain to water the earth and give us food and beautiful landscapes. Recycled.

There are other examples of recycling in God's creation. Some caterpillars turn into moths and butterflies that lay eggs that turn into larvae and begin the cycle over again. Birds eat seeds that are digested and dropped to sprout into new plants that produce more seeds. Recycled.

God's love is recycled, too, through me. As today's verse says, God's love flows through me if I let it flow out to others. Like the "living water" Jesus talked about to the woman at the well, living water of His love. I want to be part of God's love-recycling plan.

Dear Lord, I need Your living water to flow through me like a river of love to others all around me that they will never thirst again for Your living water.

BESSIE SIEMENS LOBSIEN

Without Spot or Wrinkle

That He might sanctify and cleanse it with the washing of water by the word, that He might present it to Himself a glorious church, not having spot or wrinkle or any such thing, but that it should be holy and without blemish. Eph. 5:26, 27, NKJV.

I WAS GOING THROUGH one of the most difficult trials ever and felt totally abandoned by God. In desperation I cried out to God, "Please tell me why. Haven't I had enough trials the past couple years?" I felt I couldn't bear this unless God gave me some answers.

The next morning I picked a blouse to wear that I thought might pick up my spirits. It was very wrinkled, which is why I hadn't worn it. I hate ironing, so I usually buy only wash-and-wear. However, I started ironing. The more I ironed the blouse, the prettier it became. *Wouldn't it be nice if Jesus could just iron out my life and make me like new again?* I thought.

The Holy Spirit spoke to me. "I can and I will, Joyce. In fact, I am doing that right now."

My life is like that blouse, wrinkled and often stained with sin. God needs to clean me up. He fills His washing machine with water. Slosh, jerk, pull. It certainly doesn't feel good, but I'm here with my friends, family, and church members. Surely I'll be able to bear it. He pours in the washing powders and the bleach. *Lord, don't be too hard on me. I've got just a little stain.* He shows me another stain, and I say, *Oh, that's little, too. No one will ever notice it. Go easy on me, Lord.* He points out another. *OK, Lord,* I admit, *I'm a sinner.*

Finally the machine stops. *God is so good to allow rest periods between my diverse trials and heartaches,* I think. Now I can blow in the outdoor gentle breeze to dry, I figure. But again I hear His voice: "I really need to use you right away, so into the dryer you go." The constant spinning makes me very sick, and oh, the heat! After some time He takes me out, shakes me off, and says, "Joyce, you have several bad wrinkles. I'd better iron you so you'll look as good as new for when I need to use you." I complained about the dryer, but I hadn't felt the iron yet!

Lord, please help the material of my life to be so durable that I can stand all You need to do to make me a fit garment for Your service. I realize You care what I'm going through, but there's a purpose for it. I will praise You continually because I want to be without spot or wrinkle. JOYCE MAPLES

Where I Want to Be

But I trust in you, O Lord; I say, "You are my God." My times are in your hands. Ps. 31:14, 15, NIV.

FROM ELEMENTARY SCHOOL days on through high school, I've known the sting of being picked last to play on a team. But not being chosen at all was devastating.

We'd known for some time our department was going to be shut down as part of the restructuring going on. They told us they'd try to find places for as many of us as possible, but there wouldn't be room for everyone. So we waited through week after anxious week.

I found out I was among those being laid off when my dad, who's also the vice president of my former department, stopped by our house after work to deliver the news. It was a very difficult thing for him to have to tell me, and he didn't have to be the one to do it, but I love and respect him all the more because he did.

The next morning I went up to the personnel office and discovered that when the week ended, so would my employment. There were lots of hugs and tearful goodbyes those final three days, and I expected to burst into tears when I walked out the door for the last time. But instead of being overwhelmed by sadness that final day, I felt a growing sense of exhilaration and freedom, which really caught me by surprise. It was as if God was telling me He and I would still be having a new but different adventure.

It's been a little more than a month now since I joined the ranks of the downsized, since I lost my sense of purpose and belonging. I still believe there's a reason I'm no longer employed, but there are days when I'm terribly frustrated by my inability to discover what it is. People have been asking me since the day I left if I knew what I was going to do next. I didn't know then, and I still don't have an answer for them. Or for me.

But I've been thinking. Even though I haven't found a new job, maybe I'm still doing what God wants me to do by simply living one day at a time and trusting that whatever He's called me to do will eventually become clear to me. In the meantime, I'll remind myself that God still wants me on His team, even when it seems nobody else does. Now, if I can just figure out which position I'm supposed to play this season . . .

TOYA MARIE KOCH

New Every Morning

But this I call to mind, and therefore I have hope: The steadfast love of the Lord never ceases, his mercies never come to an end; they are new every morning; great is thy faithfulness. Lam. 3:21-23, RSV.

WHEN MY SON STARTED second grade his new teacher had a system of classroom discipline that involved green, yellow, red, blue, and black light. The children began with a green light. A yellow light was a warning about a behavior. The red light involved the loss of five minutes of recess. Blue and black lights were more serious disciplines involving parents and the principal.

After reading over the teacher's information, I thought the system made sense and made sure my son understood what was expected of him. I noticed, however, that after a few days of school my son didn't want to go to school. This was very unusual; normally he loved school. It didn't take long to discover that the problem was a holdover red light. This meant that he had committed an infraction of classroom rules after the last recess, so his loss of recess time was held over to the first recess of the next day.

My husband and I spoke to our son's teacher several times about finding ways to let him serve his time for misbehavior at the end of the school day, or in some other way, so there wouldn't be a holdover to the next day. We were concerned about the fact that he was no longer eager to get up and go to school. We didn't want to see his love for school evaporate over a discipline system. Nothing could be agreed upon. My son, however, learned to be especially careful about his behavior after the last recess of the day so that he wouldn't have to begin the next day with the dreaded red light.

This whole event reminded me of the love of God. I love the verses in Lamentations 3: "This I call to mind, and therefore I have hope: The steadfast love of the Lord never ceases, his mercies never come to an end; they are new every morning; great is thy faithfulness." Each new day we can begin with the assurance of God's love and mercy to us. We can accept His forgiveness and are given the opportunity to start afresh each morning in Him. Praise God, there are no holdovers!   SANDRA SIMANTON

The Wrong Door

The meek will he guide in judgment: and the meek will he teach his way. Ps. 25:9.

I CHECKED INTO THE hotel and scrutinized the room that was to be home for the next five days. The little room was quaint with matching floral drapes and bedspread. I was hot, tired, and thirsty after the long three-hour drive. Before unpacking, I headed to the ice machine some two floors down. After filling the small bucket with ice, I made my way back to the room.

I put the small key into the keyhole and turned the key, but the door didn't open as I expected it to. I took out the key, examined it, and tried again. After several attempts I convinced myself that something had happened to the lock or the key.

Reaching for the hall phone, I dialed the front desk to ask for some assistance. Before I could hang up the receiver it seemed, an attendant came to my rescue. "I'm sorry, madam, you have the wrong room. Your room is 201; this is 102." The words stung my ears.

I'd been so sure that I was putting the key in the correct door. How could I have made such a mistake? How could he be right? I inspected the tag on the key ring and looked again at the bold white number on the door; 102 peered at me mockingly. My face burned with embarrassment as I told him thanks and walked away.

Sometimes we think—we believe—that we're sure about something, but we can be dead wrong. How do we perceive a decision or comment that another person has made? Often we have to pause and ask ourselves some pointed questions. What did the statement mean? Did we misunderstand a motive? What sometimes seems right to us is really not right at all.

We are apt to make mistakes, but God, our merciful, sympathetic Father, makes no error. He is capable and willing to guide you through today. Go ahead and trust Him; He doesn't know how to make a mistake.

Dear Father, thank You for the reassurance that I can trust You with my thoughts and my actions today. I surrender all my plans for Your approval. Help me to remember that as long as we walk together I have nothing to fear. Thank You for Your unfailing love.

GLORIA GREGORY

An Awesome God

Hearken unto this, O Job: stand still, and consider the wondrous works of God. Job 37:14.

FROM EARLIEST CHILDHOOD I've always loved camping. Going into nature and sleeping in cabins with my friends was so much fun. Besides that, there were no parents around. I looked forward each year to Pathfinder camp and, as I grew older, to youth camp.

On my island of Trinidad and Tobago, camp occurred once a year at carnival time. This was the time to take the children and youth away from the carnival crowds, music, and possible temptations. My favorite campsite was Camp Balandra, a picturesque site deep in the countryside, perched at the top of a cliff by a beautiful but dangerous seashore. My special spot was a flat rock near to the edge of the cliff overlooking the sea. I loved to watch the waves roll in and crash on the huge rocks below. As I came back to that spot in later years I would always look to see if the rocks had grown any smaller or smoother from the constant crashing of the waves and would sit there thinking how mighty and powerful is the God we serve.

In later years my joy in returning to that site again and again was to enjoy that spot by the sea. Unknown to anyone else, I had claimed it as my spot. As I sat there one morning I thought of the words of a favorite hymn that says "O love of God, how strong and true! Eternal, and yet ever new; uncomprehended and unbought, beyond all knowledge and all thought."

Now when I make mistakes and become discouraged in my Christian walk and wonder if I am growing spiritually, I think of my favorite spot by the sea and remember my God and His awesome love. He is strong and true.

I see myself in those rocks. Many times I'm stubborn and resistant to the will of God, yet, like those waves, God's love keeps washing over me, slowly but surely smoothing the rough edges and cleansing me from sin. That scene constantly reminds me that there's nothing that God can't forgive, and He will never forsake, but will always keep seeking me out to save me from myself.

O love of God, keep me strong and true is my prayer today.

HEATHER-DAWN SMALL

God of the Refrigerator

But God has surely listened and heard my voice in prayer. Praise be to God, who has not rejected my prayer or withheld his love from me! Ps. 66:19, 20, NIV.

RELAXING AFTER DINNER, I went to the refrigerator for dessert. As I got the box of orange sherbet out of the freezer, I noted that the box was soft. *My mother would like this,* I mused as I thought about how she liked her ice cream soft.

My son Nathan interrupted my thoughts. "Mom, I think the milk is spoiled. I got a bowl of cereal this morning, and when I poured on the milk, it came out in clumps and it tasted sour."

I looked in the refrigerator. Yes, the setting was on the highest level, but it felt only cool, not cold.

The next day my knowledgeable husband commented about the refrigerator. "See? The rubber cushion is hot; the motor's going out. The appliance man said we'd probably have to get a new refrigerator." *Oh no, not another unexpected expense!* Finances had been tight, especially since we'd decided to send our second oldest son to Pine Forge Academy, a Christian boarding school 600 miles away. We definitely could not afford a new refrigerator!

In my quiet time I prayed desperately to the Lord. *Lord, please fix the refrigerator! You know we can't afford a new one now or even in the near future. You're going to have to fix it, Lord. Amen.*

Two days later my husband commented, almost complainingly, that his juice was too cold. "It's almost frozen!" Quickly I got the sherbet out of the freezer, and my serving spoon almost broke on the truly frozen dessert.

"Well, I prayed that the Lord would fix the refrigerator," I told my husband.

Praise the Lord! Praise the Lord that in a world full of turmoil and disturbing events, God still looked down on one of His children and answered a desperate prayer. He'll answer your prayers, too, when you honestly come to Him.

CHARLOTTE VERRETT

On a Mission

Therefore be ye also ready: for in such an hour as ye think not the Son of man cometh. Matt. 24:44.

AFTER MORNING WORSHIP I pondered my priorities. First I voted in the primary, then dropped my neighbor at the Department of Motor Vehicles. Finally I went to visit my friend, as I had promised.

She was emotional as she opened the door. "A plane just hit one of the twin towers!" she said as she tearfully pointed to the television. "They think it was an accident," she continued.

Clouds of smoke and flying debris sent camera operators, reporters, police, EMT workers, firefighters, and everyone running for their lives as we witnessed a second plane plow into the side of the remaining tower. It literally became a burning inferno before our eyes as we stood watching in horror. This was no longer thought to be an accident. We were being attacked by terrorists!

"My friend works down there," my friend exclaimed, her voice cracking.

"My niece, my niece," I stammered. "This is the second time . . ." My voice faded as we watched the buildings crumble to the ground. We joined hands and knelt to pray. We prayed for everyone, including the terrorists.

We learned later that the Pentagon had been hit, and while a plane in Pennsylvania didn't hit its target, everyone on board was killed in the attempt. Terrorists were truly on a mission, a mission for the foe, to kill and to destroy.

We tried to make calls to find out about our loved ones, but my friend's phone line went dead and my cellular phone malfunctioned. Eventually we did find out they were safe. I, too, would have become a victim of this catastrophe had I not arrived in New York City's Port Authority Building September 10 instead of September 11, 2001, as planned.

Christ is on a mission for His children (1 Thess. 4:16, 17). He is coming as a "thief in the night" (1 Thess. 5:2). Television pictures won't be necessary. There will not be time for phone calls. "Every eye shall see him" (Rev. 1:7). We may not know the day or the hour, but we know for sure that Christ Jesus will be back. My desire is for us to be ready to meet Him in the air when He comes to claim His own.   CORA A. WALKER

What Matters Most

And we know that all things work together for good to those who love God, to those who are the called according to His purpose. Rom. 8:28, NKJV.

WHO CAN FORGET September 11, 2001, that infamous day when thousands died from terrorist attacks on the World Trade Center in New York City, the Pentagon in Washington, D.C., and the plane crash in rural Pennsylvania? We were all affected. Whether or not you were directly connected to any of the victims, your sense of security was shattered and your perspective on what is really important in life was changed.

As I looked at the magnitude of the attack, soaked up every bit of the news, and listened to the stories, I was devastated. *How can human beings be so vile?* As the days wore on and I looked at the news coverage and read the newspaper, I must admit that even though I saw evil in its rarest form, I also saw God's love and mercy.

Our text for today states that all things work together for good to those who love God. What was intended to not only kill innocent civilians but also the spirit of America galvanized Americans to unity and patriotism. The outpouring of love, sacrifice, and donations was phenomenal. Never in the nation's history have we witnessed such care and togetherness, so many people calling upon the name of the Lord, people unapologetically thanking God and quoting Scriptures. Not in the nation's history have we seen so many of our leaders seeking spiritual guidance or heroes redefining who a hero really is. No, the terrorist acts were not completely successful. Yes, lives were forever changed, but people's perspective on what is really important was changed, too.

Lord, I don't know what today may bring, but I do know that You can work it out for good. Help us to realize, Lord, that it isn't what we attain in this life that's important, it's what we maintain that's really important and of eternal value. Help us to maintain good relationships with our family, friends, and fellow human beings. Help us to realize that a good relationship with You should be of paramount importance.

ANDREA BUSSUE

Shoestring Weddings

Jesus knew that the lack of drink would soon embarrass the bride and groom, so He turned to the waiters and said, "Fill these water jars to the rim." And they did. . . . When they poured out what they thought was water, it looked like wine. John 2:7, 8, Clear Word.

MY SISTER HAD BEEN a single mother for several years. When she decided to get married, she knew she wanted to start her new relationship in the house of God. A church wedding, however, didn't fit into her tight budget. So we decided together that it would be a simple wedding. We would do the flowers and reception ourselves, she would borrow a wedding dress, and the attendants would wear something they already had in their closets. Her daughter was her only bridesmaid, and my two daughters were the candlelighters.

Several weeks before the April wedding, my daughters received a package from their aunt-to-be on their dad's side. (They were going to be flower girls at her wedding in June.) The girls danced around with glee in their new dresses that Auntie Connie had purchased in California. "Mommy, couldn't we pleeeeeeease wear these at Auntie Val's wedding too?"

I was a little hesitant because I didn't want my sister's daughter to feel as if she was the only one without a matching dress. She was planning to wear a dress my mother had made her the year before with fabric purchased at a discount store in Oklahoma. But after getting my sister's and her daughter's approval, I finally conceded that they could wear the dresses.

We were able to arrive several days early to help with all the last-minute preparations. My girls rushed up to their cousin's bedroom to show her their pink floral dresses. We soon heard squeals of sheer delight coming from the bedroom, and it wasn't long before three very excited little girls, all wearing dresses made of perfectly matching fabric, stood before us. Mom, Val, and I stood there with our mouths dropped open, unable to even speak.

It didn't take long to conclude that this surprise went far beyond the stroke of luck. We had a Friend who takes special delight in helping with the smallest details of our lives, especially, it seems, at weddings. After all, wasn't He the one who graciously provided at another wedding long ago where the shoestring budget hadn't quite allowed for enough punch?

CINDY WALIKONIS

Lighting My Way

In him was life, and that life was the light of men. John 1:4, NIV.

WHEN I WAS ABOUT 12 I went camping with a group of girls. It was a well-kept camp with groups of tents and a large public rest room. I was extremely nearsighted, having clear vision of only a few inches without glasses or contacts. When we settled down for the night, my friend put my glasses in her purse on the far side of the tent so no one would roll over on them by accident.

I woke up in the middle of the night, needing to use the rest room. I tried to wake up a couple of the other girls, but they went right on sleeping. I couldn't find either my glasses or a flashlight and ended up leaving for the rest room by myself without a light. Finding my way down to the rest room wasn't too hard. I couldn't see the ground, so I shuffled my feet as I walked. I kept my eyes on my objective—the lights glowing from the rest room. It shone like a lighthouse in the darkness.

Getting back to the tent, however, was another story entirely. I knew that I could get there by following the path, but there was nothing but darkness at the end of the trail. For a moment I considered spending the night in the rest room. It would be cold and uncomfortable with no sleeping bag, but I wouldn't freeze or anything. I finally decided that it wasn't that far back to the camp and I could make it if I was careful.

With no light to point my way, and being unable to see the ground, my shuffling method didn't work very well. I kept stumbling and straying off the path. After falling several times, I dropped down to my hands and knees and crawled back to our tent.

I sometimes look back at things I did when I was young and think how stupid I was. I've done a lot of dumb things on my spiritual path, too. One of my worst mistakes is when I take my eyes off Jesus. When I don't follow His teachings, I find myself stumbling around in the darkness. Reading His messages in the Bible, meditating on His words, and communicating with Him through prayer all help me to find my way. Jesus is the light along my journey.

GINA LEE

Sensitivity

A merry heart doeth good like a medicine: but a broken spirit drieth the bones. Prov. 17:22.

I WAS 3 OR 4, recovering from a serious illness, when the circus came to Omaha. Mama took my sister, Mary, and me, and we sat in the front-row seats, directly behind the balustrade that separated the floor of the circus from the audience. At one point in the program the famed clown, Emmett Kelly, walked around in front of the balustrade, watching the faces of the crowd as they became aware he was there and switched their attention from the center ring to him.

He stopped when he came right in front of me. He stared at me a long time from his painted, woebegone face, his hands behind his back. Then he elaborately reached into a pocket and took out a peanut. He placed the peanut on the balustrade right in front of me and stood there staring at it. After a while he looked up at me, staring at me a while before he took his other hand from behind his back. In it was a maul with a monstrous head. He looked at me, then at the peanut. Then he made an exaggerated swing with the maul at the peanut.

The crowd was going wild with laughter, but I just stared, waiting for what he would do next. He removed the maul, and there was the bare peanut, the crushed shell lying all around it. He looked at the peanut and the crushed shell, then at me. He picked up the peanut, looked at Mama for an OK, then gave the peanut to me, bowed low, and walked to a nearby exit, to the roars of laughter and applause of the audience. The whole while I stared at the peanut in my hand—the peanut the great Emmett Kelly had shelled just for me.

A great man saw a sick little girl and gave a wonderful, moving performance in a big auditorium, a performance just to bring a smile to her peaked face.

Beloved heavenly Father, thank You for the Emmett Kellys of this world who are willing to single out the sick, the sorrowful, the lonely, and work to bring a smile to their faces. Lord, may I be blessed by being one of these people. Amen.

DARLENEJOAN M. RHINE

Majestic Mountains

In his hand are the depths of the earth, and the mountain peaks belong to him. Ps. 95:4, NIV.

MY HUSBAND AND I were doing medical relief mission service in Nepal. It had been a stressful time for the country and for us. Two days after we arrived, the royal family was massacred. There were riots in the capital (Kathmandu), Maoist uprisings, and a minor earthquake. We needed a getaway break, so we went to Nagarkot, 7,000 feet (2,134 meters) above sea level, and booked into the almost deserted hotel for one night. This was the rainy season, and we arrived in a dense cloud and a driving rain. Where were the wonderful views we'd hoped to see? On a clear day one can see the snowcapped Himalayas, of which Everest is the highest on earth.

Our wake-up call came at 5:30 the next morning—we wanted to see the mountains at sunrise. I stepped out on the balcony. The rain had stopped, and the clouds had cleared somewhat. What I saw almost took my breath away. Below me the steep hillside rice fields dropped in step fashion into the nearest valley, where a wisp of cloud still lingered. Beyond, another range of mountains rose up before giving way to another cloud-filled valley. I counted four mountain ranges stretched out before me, and then, in the very far distance and almost totally obscured by clouds, I could see the tips of two snowcapped mountains. I watched as the clouds rolled back over them, and then I wrote in my prayer diary out there on that balcony, "How majestic are the works of Your hand, Lord."

Overwhelmed by awe at the scene before me, I was grateful that I'd been given the opportunity to see it. We dressed and went out to the lookout point a mile or two away, where the view was just as spectacular. The clouds then rolled right back in, and again there was nothing to see. How glad I was that we'd gotten up early enough to see that view!

This experience helped me to put the troubles of this world into perspective and to realize again that our God is greater than all those troubles.

Thank You, God, for allowing me to see the wonders of Your creation in those majestic mountains. Thank You for reminding me of Your great power. Help me to trust You more.
RUTH LENNOX

Hurricane!

Watch therefore, for ye know neither the day nor the hour wherein the Son of man cometh. Matt. 25:13.

EXCITEMENT WAS IN THE air—the National Hurricane Advisory Committee had issued a hurricane watch. That meant a hurricane was in the area, and it was possible that our island would be hit. As a member of the Community Health team, I was called in to assist my coworkers in securing our clinic. We were to report to our respective hurricane shelters the following day with enough supplies to last for three to five days. I was reminded instantly of the session on hurricane preparedness that I'd attended several weeks earlier. We'd been instructed to keep a constant supply of nonperishable food items and to prepare our homes in such a way that we'd be able to leave them on short notice.

I began a mental scan of my kitchen cupboards—a few cans of beans and not much else. How was I going to survive three to five days in the shelter with just that? Furthermore, what was my husband going to eat if indeed this hurricane came near us? I suddenly felt like one of the characters in Jesus' parable about the 10 virgins in Matthew 25. I was unprepared!

The storm veered to another course and came no closer to us, and I didn't have to go to the shelter. I breathed a sigh of relief and determined that I'd go that week to buy the necessary items to be prepared for the next storm. My husband began to question the wisdom of that decision. His rationale was that we likely wouldn't have another hurricane come into our area this season, and anyway, we already had enough things to fill our home. Why add more that we'd never use? My motivation to prepare was instantly diminished.

There will be those who are cynical about Christ's return, too, and who will scoff at our attempts to be prepared. How easy it is to listen to these persons and have our motivation affected. We don't need an advisory committee to tell us that Christ is coming, however. We have the steadfast Word of God to let us know beyond a shadow of a doubt that He will return. Any day, any hour. Let's be ready!   ABIGAIL BLAKE PARCHMENT

Before I Asked

Your Father knows what you need before you ask him. Matt. 6:8, NIV.

MY PROPOSAL WAS FINISHED, and I'd finally received approval from the University of Alabama in Birmingham to proceed with my research investigation. As I gathered the necessary material to place into envelopes, I was in an attitude of prayer, asking the Lord to impress the nurses who would receive the surveys for my doctorate dissertation to quickly fill them out and return them to me. I was working late, trying to get all of the stapled surveys, along with the introductory letter, into the envelopes so they could be distributed to the hospital nurses the following evening. As I was putting the next survey into the envelope, I noticed that the last page wasn't attached. As I looked at the page my heart sank. It was printed improperly. I checked the previous and following surveys and found several other surveys with spoiled pages. After replacing the damaged pages with new ones, I sat back to think about what had happened.

Chills ran up and down my spine as I thought back to when I'd printed the surveys. It was shortly after the infamous September 11 tragedy. Only one survey out of 130 was improperly stapled—one of those with the spoiled pages that needed to be replaced. I was awed and in wonder as I comprehended the full significance of this "casual" occurrence.

The Lord took time to remember me and knew the importance this event had had on my life and my pursuit of higher education, even while He was so busy with world events. It was a rather insignificant occurrence in the scheme of all that was going on in this world at that time, but it was very important to me. All the surveys with incomplete information would have been ruined and would have had to be thrown away. They might have been the very surveys that were needed to complete the allotted numbers necessary to finish my dissertation. I realized that He had answered a prayer that I hadn't even known I needed to pray. As I bowed my head to thank Him, I realized what an awesome God I serve.

MARYANN ROBERTS

The Intervening Years

Train children in the right way, and when old, they will not stray. Prov. 22:6, NRSV.

I WAS ALWAYS PUZZLED by this passage of Scripture. As a young person I'd often seen children of Christian parents "depart" from the lessons and principles taught by their parents. I'm even more puzzled now that I'm a mother of young adults.

There's no question that parenting isn't an easy job. It's the one profession for which there are no preparatory courses from which you graduate. I've often asked God, "Where did I go wrong?" My husband and I tried our best to provide a loving, nurturing Christian home environment for our children. At great financial sacrifice we sent them to church-related schools. We did our best to impart to them the principles of a Christlike life both by work and example. In spite of our best efforts, they've not truly embraced these principles the way we'd like to see them manifested.

My early-morning walks have given me a wonderful opportunity to talk with God. It's during these times that I feel most assured that God, who is the Promise Keeper, will keep the promise made in Proverbs 22:6. Solomon, the wise man, speaks of a beginning—childhood—and an end— old age. He makes no mention of a "middle"—the intervening years. Could it be that Solomon, too, experienced the straying of children during these intervening years?

I'm convinced that the intercessory prayers of parents on behalf of their children touch the very heart of God. Our Father knew firsthand the terrible pain of separation from His only Son, Jesus Christ. Sometimes when I sit in the pew at church and listen to parents testifying about the strong Christian young people they've raised, I can only lift my thoughts to heaven and pray like the thief on the cross, "Lord, have mercy on me!"

Dear Lord, You always keep Your promises to us, sinful though we be. You know how deeply we love our children and how we want them in Your kingdom. Please take away any hint of discouragement. Help us to continue to love them, pray for them, and encourage them so that by Your mercy and grace and through the Holy Spirit they will choose to walk with You all the way.

AVIS MAE RODNEY

Confidence

I consider that our present sufferings are not worth comparing with the glory that will be revealed in us. Rom. 8:18, NIV.

AT THE MOMENT I am in the midst of a personal crisis and keep asking "Why?" This crisis was triggered by September 11, 2001. Nothing seems to be as it was. Even in my private life the ground on which I stood suddenly pulled away. *I feel helpless and insecure. What's wrong? What's happening to me? Where are You, God? You seem to be so far away. There's no room for hope. Everything is so senseless; where are You, God? Have You forsaken me? Can't You see how I'm suffering? Can't You hear me? I cry over all the pain and suffering on this earth. I cry because of my own trouble. I am so devastated. It's enough. I can't take any more.*

And then Bible verses come to my mind, promises that Jesus will come again to make everything new—will wipe away all tears. Two thousand years ago Paul wrote to the church in Rome that suffering began with the Fall in Paradise. Ever since that time it has influenced our planet and its inhabitants. Suffering increases; we have only to turn on the TV or look at the newspaper to be convinced. We could just give up, yet God didn't want us to suffer; it's not His fault. We humans are responsible for our suffering—or rather Satan, God's enemy, is. There is a conflict between God and Satan, influencing all facets of life.

The Bible, God's Word, has good news for us. Paul suffered, but he didn't lose his confidence. He knew that suffering, and even death, is not the end. In the midst of suffering Paul stayed confident. He considered our present sufferings not worth comparing with the glory that's waiting for us. This is one of the most precious promises in the Bible.

Our heavenly Father has prepared something better for us than this life. He loves us and wants us to be close to Him.

Thank You, Lord, for my personal crisis! It has brought me closer to You; at first, You seemed so far away. Sometimes I have to endure things to be brought where You want me. But You are always at my side, even though I don't always perceive it. With Your help we can endure suffering, and our prize is waiting for us—everlasting life with You. Thank You, Lord.

HEIDI MACHO

Until She Finds It

What woman having ten silver coins, if she loses one of them, does not light a lamp, sweep the house, and search carefully until she finds it? Luke 15:8, NRSV.

I HOSTED A DINNER party as a parting gift to some friends who were leaving the country. It was a wonderful occasion, made more special by the fact that they all insisted on clearing the table and washing the dishes after the meal. I was only too happy to oblige them.

As I was putting away the cutlery, however, I noticed that one of my forks was missing. As soon as my friends left, I searched the silver chest, the china cabinet—everywhere. No fork. I went to bed sad that night, asking the Lord to help me find that fork, trying to rejoice in the fact that I had other forks. But it was difficult.

Tossing in bed, I began to understand the persistence of the women in the Gospels. The woman in today's text and the importunate widow (Luke 18:2-8) shared something in common with most of us. They were persistent. They knew that what they were seeking was valuable. Their search was worthy of steadfast effort. The same could apply to me.

I woke at break of day the next morning, suddenly sure that the fork had been accidentally thrown out with the garbage. As I went out to the bin and pulled out the bag, I was repulsed at the sight of the remains of yesterday's dinner—day-old tomatoes and soggy lettuce, mashed potatoes, corn casserole, peanut-butter cheesecake, and a mass of other gooey stuff. I didn't hesitate for more than a moment, though. I sank my hands into the slimy contents of that bag, feeling around in the squishy mess for what seemed like ages. Then I felt something solid and cold. It was my fork!

Rushing to the faucet, I washed my hands and the fork, praising God. I thanked Him for showing me that He is in control. He had shown me where to look. I thanked Him for my tactile sense—I could feel, even if I didn't want to look at the repulsive gunk. I thanked Him for the graphic reminder that He had to search through more than mere potatoes and corn when He came to rescue me from a world besmirched with sin. I thanked Him that He didn't hesitate.

Lord, thank You for modern-day parables that remind us of Your gospel. Most of all, I thank You for delving into this sin-filled world that is so unlike Your infinite purity—just to save me. GLENDA-MAE GREENE

273

612 Decisions

Then choose for yourselves this day whom you will serve. . . . But as for me and my household, we will serve the Lord. Joshua 24:15, NIV.

I READ SOMEWHERE THAT the average woman makes 612 decisions a day. I have no idea how they came up with such a figure but decided to see how many decisions I have to make in a day. I discovered that the decisions started before I even got out of bed: Should I get up, or try to snooze a few more minutes? Should I hit the snooze button, or risk waking up again on my own? Or maybe I should just face the day and get up. Should I read in the bathroom, or hurry on to the tasks of the day? And then there came getting dressed—oh dear, what to wear!

My husband fixes breakfast, so I don't have to decide what to fix, but I do have to decide which of the things to eat—wheat and bran, with or without honey; toast, with or without margarine—more and more decisions. And that doesn't even include how much to eat of each.

All morning there are decisions about money, budgets, programs, letters to answer, e-mails to care for, now or later. Do I tackle those big projects now, or put them off again?

Lunchtime. Again, what and how much to eat. But now I have to decide with whom to eat and even where to eat. Eat in the cafeteria, or go back to my desk to get some reading done? Decisions, decisions!

At home the decisions get a little easier, if not fewer. I know immediately that I'll put on my jeans—but which sweatshirt? Shall I open the junk mail? (Maybe there's a dollar in one of them—I heard of that once.) Next comes eating again. Is it supper or dinner? More decisions.

Finally, after more decisions through the evening, I head for bed and time once again with God. I'm sure the best decision of the day was to begin the day with God. I had decided to give Him control. Did I always remember to let Him do what He knew was best? Sometimes I feel as if I can make the decisions myself. That usually turns out to be a mistake. Other times I know I'm in over my head and remember to pray for guidance.

"Choose for yourselves this day." It doesn't really make much difference how many decisions you make as long as you make the most important one first.

ARDIS DICK STENBAKKEN

Fluffy-Puppy Love

For God sent not his Son into the world to condemn the world; but that the world through him might be saved. John 3:17.

MY GRANDDAUGHTER, RILEY, was thrilled with the gift of a puppy. She immediately named her Fluffy-Puppy. The first hour, holding Fluffy-Puppy was wonderful. Then Fluffy-Puppy was put down on the carpet. Immediately she squatted and did what dogs are usually trained to do outside. We assured Riley the puppy would learn.

But no amount of training helped Fluffy-Puppy. No amount of praise, treats, smacks with a rolled-up newspaper, trips outside after eating, convinced Fluffy-Puppy of her duty to potty outside. The family questioned Fluffy-Puppy's intelligence. However, in a very short time we taught her to sit, lie down, and dance on her hind legs for a treat. We sought help from a professional dog trainer, who advised that we feed her and immediately put her outside, lavishly praise her success, and then give her reinforce-the-behavior treats. Sure enough, she now eats, goes outside, potties, receives praise and treats—then returns inside to potty again on the carpet! We keep working with her, but Fluffy-Puppy's behavior keeps her from becoming an integral part of the family. In fact, Fluffy-Puppy's destiny is hanging in the balance.

Unfortunately, Fluffy-Puppy isn't capable of understanding people thoughts and therefore is unmoved by the tears of the little girl who begs to keep her, even though she "has a problem." She doesn't know that her behavior is a barrier to the very love she craves.

In a sense, we humans are just like Fluffy-Puppy. We keep repeating the same sinful behaviors that keep us from becoming an integral part of the family of God. Just as we keep working with Fluffy-Puppy, God keeps working with us. Just as Riley cries to keep her precious pet, Jesus cries to keep us, even though we, too, "have a problem."

But unlike Fluffy-Puppy, we are capable of understanding God's love for us. We are capable of understanding the great sacrifice God made in giving up His Son to die for us. What a price to pay for the precious humans He created! "For God sent not his Son into the world to condemn the world; but that the world through him might be saved." How can we ignore such great love?

ELLIE GREEN

Failure Is the Beginning of Success

Man's goings are of the Lord; how can a man then understand his own way?
Prov. 20:24.

THE PICTURE OF IPOTI, bathed in the beauty of bright moonlight, is
indelibly engraved in my brain. I fell in love with that town that night. I
was 8 years old and visiting my hometown for the first time. My grandmother had died, and I went home with my father for the burial.

This bright picture of peace affected all that happened during those few
weeks I spent in Ipoti. It was the end of the year, when examinations were
conducted for pupils to determine promotion to the next class. Since I
wouldn't be able to take my promotion examination where we lived, my
father had me join the class in the mission school in Ipoti a few days before
they started the promotion examination. I can't remember what questions
were asked or how the examination really went, but I do remember the day
the results were to be given.

In those days results were announced publicly. The first, second, and
third positions were praised; those who had failed were also exposed. I
caught the excitement of my fellow pupils and prayed that morning during
devotions that the Lord would help me to pass my examination.

Alas! I failed woefully. It probably wouldn't have hurt so much if my
siblings hadn't laughed at me after my prayer for success that morning.
They said I should have prayed for help during the examinations, not after
they were graded and ready to be announced.

I still remember that singular experience in my life and always use it to
counsel my children that we should cast our all on God at all times—not
only when we're tested or when we're getting the results. I always let them
know that I had faced being jeered at. But praise the Lord, I've also experienced victory in every sphere of life through my Lord Jesus Christ.

Since the Lord is the one directing our steps, why should you or I question why things happen the way they do? Do I need to know everything that
happens along the way? It's enough that He is leading and I am following.

BECKY DADA

Tornado

To thee they cried, and were saved; in thee they trusted, and were not disappointed. Ps. 22:5, RSV.

IF YOU HAVEN'T EXPERIENCED the devastation, it will be hard for you to understand the fear that goes with a tornado. My husband and I will never forget our first encounter with one.

At the office we were told to delay going home because of a tornado warning. After waiting for 30 minutes, we decided to drive the four miles home. As we neared home, the road was jammed with cars; we could barely move. We were horrified to see huge trees uprooted, cars overturned, electric lines blocking the roads, roofs and walls blown down, and loose objects such as patio chairs, tables, and umbrellas all over the place. Our area had been hit by the tornado.

Two hours later we finally entered our street and got home. The two-hour wait was torture. My husband was so concerned and worried about the damage that might have been done to our house. I told him to trust everything to the Lord, that He would take care of us. Deep in my heart, for some reason, I felt that our place was safe. I knew for sure that our children, parents, brothers, sisters, and friends were always praying for us, and that God answers prayers.

As we entered our street we saw that our neighbors' houses had been badly damaged. We went around our house and examined the damages. Remember when Moses told the Israelites to put blood on the doorposts of their houses? We had the blood, in the form of prayers of loved ones and friends, on our doorpost. This is the reason our house was spared. Yes, a few shingles of our roof were missing and two huge trees had been uprooted, but that was nothing compared to the damage surrounding us. We prayed a thanksgiving prayer right at that moment.

When we cry to the Lord and trust Him, we will never be disappointed; He will save us.

Lord, as we start our day, we call upon You to hold our hands that we may walk with You and be safe from all harm and danger. We pray also, Lord, for all our loved ones and friends; our prayers may be just what they need for today, so please take care of them. Thank You, Father. JEMIMA D. ORILLOSA

Nothing Is Too Small for God

If you believe, you will receive whatever you ask for in prayer. Matt. 21:22, NIV.

BECAUSE IT WAS A holiday, I decided to utilize my time profitably and wash all the comforters and blankets that hadn't been used for a long time. So I went to the basement closet and got out all the things I wanted to launder, loaded them in the car, and went to the nearest Laundromat. It took me two hours to wash and dry all of them, but I felt good about getting this big job done.

That same evening my son and I wanted to go to wish his aunt Bernice a happy birthday. As I got ready, I looked for my watch on my dresser and couldn't find it. It was nowhere to be found. I knew I'd worn it before going to the Laundromat. I was feeling anxious and worried about losing my favorite Citizen watch.

Since the black leather strap had been wearing out, I had a feeling it may have dropped somewhere. The only place I'd gone that day was the Laundromat. So at 8:30 that evening we went to the Laundromat to look for it in the parking lot and to ask the attendant if he'd found a watch. The attendant told me I should check with the woman who was on duty during the day shift and gave me her home phone number. However, when I called, it was a wrong number. I decided to go to the Laundromat the next day to ask if the woman found my watch. Before going to bed that night, I asked God to please help me find my watch if He felt I should have it.

Early the next morning I went to the basement closet to get my work clothes. As soon as I walked into the closet, right there in front of me on the floor was my watch! I was so thrilled that I prayed aloud to God. I was very grateful to Him for making sure the watch fell in my house and not in the Laundromat, where it would have been almost impossible to find.

Our God is a great God, and yet He cares for us even in small matters. I love this beautiful promise in the Bible: "Are not two sparrows sold for a farthing? and one of them shall not fall on the ground without your Father. But the very hairs of your head are all numbered. Fear ye not therefore, ye are of more value than many sparrows" (Matt. 10:29-31).   STELLA THOMAS

Remove the Frogs!

Blessed are all they that put their trust in him. Ps. 2:12.

AFTER THREE YEARS OF marriage my husband, Steven, and I were blessed with a little girl. As the years pass and I watch our child grow, I'm amazed to see the parallels in her development to my Christian walk. She's been able to show me where my faith is not as strong as it should be. One night in particular was extremely poignant.

I had an entire day to spend with my 2-year-old daughter. Declaring the day a holiday, I decided to have as much fun as possible with Lillian. After a quick breakfast I told Lillian, "Honey, Mommy is home today. We can spend the day playing." She was so happy she laughed and jumped up and down. After breakfast we played house, played with all of her dolls, changed their clothes, combed their hair, and put them down for a nap. After lunch and a short nap Lillian and I spent the remainder of the day playing at the marina. All too quickly the day was over, and it was time for Lillian to go to bed. After a short story and her prayers Lillian finally fell asleep.

I'm not sure how long I slept before I heard Lillian calling out pitifully in her sleep. "Mommy! Mommy!"

When I reached her bedside I said, "Sweetheart, what's the matter?"

She cried out, "Mommy, make them go away! Take the frogs off me!"

I assured her there were no frogs on her and that she was just dreaming. Her eyes fluttered open, and she smiled and said "OK, Mommy" before she rolled over and promptly went back to sleep.

After thinking about what had just happened, I realized I had learned quite a lesson from my daughter. She had cried out in her despair for the one she knew could make everything better. She had cried out to the one she knew would respond to her call and comfort her.

How often do I try to remove my own frogs? I know I need to go to the One who can make things right, yet I don't call out to the Lord as often as I should. Lillian was smart. She didn't try to remove her "frogs" herself.

Lord, help me to have the faith and trust of a small child. Today I lay all my cares on You and ask for the faith of a mustard seed. I know You will sustain.

TAMARAZ MARQUEZ DE SMITH

The Power of Assembling

Let us not give up meeting together, . . . but let us encourage one another.
Heb. 10:25, NIV.

WE SAT TOGETHER, WATCHING candlelight flicker at the end of each pew. Wondrous melodies swirled around us from the majestic organ pipes.

"Thank you for bringing me," the woman beside me whispered.

It began in the checkout line at a grocery store. The talk had been about the latest terrorist incident and the relative sense of security that had evaporated into thin air. "Funny, but somehow I feel the urge to attend church," the woman had said, "but I haven't stepped inside one for years!" Fortunately, I knew of an upcoming memorial service and invited her to go with me.

The choir asked us to sing "O Beautiful for Spacious Skies." Our voices harmonized as one ensemble. Tears welled up from my heart and spilled down my cheeks. The synergism was powerful! We heard the Gospel according to Matthew: "Surely I am with you always" (Matt. 28:20, NIV). The pastor invited us to repeat the Lord's Prayer. There were tears on her cheeks, too.

Why is it, I asked myself, *that in times of disaster people often return to churches, temples, cathedrals, or mosques and seek solace in ritual, prayer, and singing? Why the sense of urgency to connect with one's Higher Power often in the congregation of others?*

Perhaps it's because we humans are spiritual and relational. Perhaps it's because that little clump of cells in the right temporal lobe of the brain, believed by researchers to enable us to find meaning in spiritual experiences, pushes us to connect with a Being outside ourselves.

We abhor disasters, especially when they're deliberate and fueled by hate. Nevertheless, such incidents offer us another opportunity to reassess and strengthen our personal and spiritual relationship with God and to unite with others in a deeper and more meaningful way. These experiences strengthen our immune system, lower blood pressure, and reduce the release of harmful stress hormones.

"I feel so calm," my new friend said as we made our way outdoors. "I think I'd like to come back again next week." Her voice was tentative.

"Easy to arrange," I responded, smiling. There really is a silver lining to every cloud.

ARLENE TAYLOR

God Does Not Change

The heavens declare the glory of God; and the firmament shows His handiwork. Ps. 19:1, NKJV.

Behold, God is great, and we do not know Him. . . . For He draws up drops of water, which distill as rain from the mist, which the clouds drop down and pour abundantly on man. Indeed, can anyone understand the spreading of clouds, the thunder from His canopy? Job 36:26-29, NKJV.

FOR SOME TIME I'VE had the habit of looking at the beautiful skies from my bathroom window every morning between 2:00 and 4:30. It's an awesome sight to behold God's magnificent handiwork at the dawning of a new day. The different scenes never cease to amaze me. Once I observed a huge round moon illuminating the sky with its beautiful and dazzling light. A myriad of twinkling stars added to the splendor of the view. Another morning as I gazed at the sky a sea of fluffy white clouds of all shapes and sizes cascaded across it. The intricate formation of the clouds reminded me of a gorgeous painting depicting the second coming of Jesus. The scene was breathtaking.

Later in the week the scene changed to clear skies. Not a single cloud was visible from my window. Many bright stars, large and small, lined the sky, providing a panoramic view. A few days later the once beautiful and picturesque sky filled with thick black clouds that emptied torrential rains on rooftops. The thunder crackled, the lightning flashed, and the tall trees tossed to and fro. It was a frightening scene.

Yes, the same skies, but each day the scene changed. These varied scenes remind me of my own life's experiences that change from day to day. One day is full of sunshine and laughter, and the next sometimes brings scattered showers of pain and heartache. Another day may bring tumultuous storms with torrential rain and winds that threaten to wash away my peace of mind and blow me to bits. As I reflect on these changing scenes, I'm thankful that no matter the situation, my heavenly Father is always the same yesterday, today, and forever. He is constant; He does not change. He is always there, a present help in time of trouble, always waiting with loving and outstretched arms, beckoning me to come to Him.

Thank You, Jesus, for being my unchanging friend.

SHIRLEY C. IHEANACHO

A Flower in Need

My God will meet all your needs according to his glorious riches in Christ Jesus. Phil. 4:19, NIV.

THE PLANT LOOKED VERY healthy at first. Its full pink flowers cascaded over the sides of its pot and onto the shelf above the sink. For a few days, whenever I visited the women's rest room at work, its blossoms cheered my heart—a touch of beauty and nature in an urban world.

But after a few days I noticed that the plant wasn't doing so well. Once or twice I topped up the pot with water when it felt dry, but still the plant looked tired and sad.

Then one day I realized what was happening. The plant was in a room with a timed light switch that gave us enough light for a few minutes. What the plant needed was some real light! The cubicle itself had a window, so I moved the plant onto the windowsill, hoping that the sunlight would revive the plant again.

The next day, though, someone had moved the plant back to the windowless sink area. I returned it to the windowsill, realizing that this was its only hope. Once again, someone moved it back to the dark sink. The plant, being juggled between the two spots, finally came to rest on the cubicle windowsill, and it's been there ever since.

Sometimes we treat people as we treated the plant. We treat them in certain ways because of what our needs are rather than in ways that meet their needs. We needed a prettier rest room, but the plant had a more basic need: to be where it could experience the warmth and light of the sun. But the beautiful flower nearly died before we discovered this.

Jesus was aware of people's needs. He met their real needs even when they themselves weren't aware what their own needs were. He forgave people who thought they needed healing, gave them grace when they thought they needed punishment, and gave them new perspectives when they thought they needed only pat answers.

Father, help me today to be more aware of the needs of those around me and the ways I can show them Your warmth and light in a cold, dark world.

KAREN HOLFORD

My Husband

For thy Maker is thine husband; the Lord of hosts is his name; and thy Redeemer the Holy One of Israel; The God of the whole earth shall he be called. Isa. 54:5.

A father of the fatherless, and a judge of the widows, is God in his holy habitation. Ps. 68:5.

ONE CHILLY OCTOBER evening we stumbled into our cold mobile home. Exhausted, I sent the children directly to bed and collapsed there myself. As I shivered between the sheets, I knew I had a lot for which to be thankful. I'd found myself alone to raise my two boys, 4 and 8 years old, and I had only a high school diploma. I had no idea how I could provide the three things I was convicted the children needed for a good Christian upbringing—a country home, their own mother's daily care, and a Christian education.

All three needs were provided for when I secured a position at a Christian boarding high school in the country. For this I was thankful. However, the job was a very demanding one, often 12- to 15-hour days, after which I still had all the household responsibilities to meet. The house we were living in was heated with wood and retained no warmth once the fire was out, but I was simply too exhausted to kindle and build a fire from scratch. As I lay in bed, dreading to face the cold, cold morning, I mentally cried on the Lord's shoulder, praying, "Lord, I know You are a husband to the widows and a Father to the fatherless. You've provided so well for us, and yet I have to do all the work. If I had a husband right now, he'd build a fire for us because I'm just too exhausted. Even if there were just a little fire in there, and all I had to do was add the logs, I could handle that, but to have to kindle and build it from scratch is just too much."

As I lay there, grieving, I suddenly heard a *tick, tick, tick,* like the sound a woodstove makes as it heats up. *What on earth?* I wondered, knowing the fire had long since died out. But when I got up and opened the door of the stove, there was a flame rising up out of the cold ashes in the back of the stove! All I had to do was pile in the logs, and we awoke to a warm home the next morning.

Praise the Lord! You are indeed a Father to the fatherless and a husband to the widows. What a comfort this promise was and continues to be. How You care for us—even about the little things.   BARBARA L. SAVAGE

Punish or Discipline?

God's temple is sacred, and you are that temple. 1 Cor. 3:16, NIV.

I HELPED MYSELF TO A generous serving of luscious strawberries. My mouth watered as I watched them sprawl out over homemade shortcake. "I love berry season," I murmured, and passed the cut-glass bowl.

"No, thank you," Melissa said, "none for me. I'm punishing myself today."

My fork hung in midair. "Punishing yourself?" I gasped. "For what?"

"I didn't finish my assignment at school today," she explained. "So no supper for me."

My mouth fell open so far my chin hit the plate. I did a quick reality check. Yes, it was the twenty-first century, although her comment sounded straight from the Dark Ages. "How did you come up with that?" I asked, endeavoring to keep my voice neutral and steady.

It turned out that a classmate at school had been waxing eloquent about the concept of penance. In that girl's home, actions were quickly labeled as good or bad, positive or negative. Punishment for bad/negative actions, of course, was swift. "Her folks said that the goal was to learn to punish yourself before anyone else had to," Melissa explained.

I shook my head. "What will this self-punishment achieve?" I asked. "Will it guarantee that you'll finish your assignment next time?"

Melissa, her face rueful, finally admitted, "Not necessarily, I guess."

"Unfortunately," I mused between juicy, satisfying bites, "some individuals confuse discipline (to train or develop by instruction) with punishment (suffering, pain, or loss inflicted as retribution)." One helps us to mature and become the person we were designed to be. The latter drains our energy and can move us toward addictive behaviors and diminished health. We talked about setting realistic goals and expectations for schoolwork and of the need to avoid self-flagellation of our body temple.

As we conversed, an emerging gleam in Melissa's eye signaled that she was beginning to view her classmate's admonition in a new light. I'd almost polished off the last morsel of my strawberry shortcake when Melissa said, "Please pass the berries." What a relief!

Do you punish or discipline yourself?

ARLENE TAYLOR

Diligent as a Squirrel

*He becometh poor that dealeth with a slack hand: but the hand of the
diligent maketh rich. Prov. 10:4.*

KING SOLOMON ADVISES US to go to the ant and "consider her ways,
and be wise" (Proverbs 6:6). We Canadians would suggest one study the
habits of the beaver, our national symbol. One probably could find any
number of resident animals to observe for object lessons in diligence.

From my condo window I've admired the perseverance of the squirrels.
Tall spruce trees surround our building on three sides. The squirrels scurry
up the trees, scamper around on the ground, and dash away on business.
One of our neighbors throws peanuts on the patio to tempt the squirrels.
They snatch them and stash them away.

I followed a squirrel from one side of the building to the other to see
where it was hoarding the peanuts. In the next lot was a pile of debris left
by the renovators. Somewhere under the heap the squirrel found a "secure"
place for the peanuts. Every now and then it would stop, sit up, listen, and
look around with quick jerks of its head. It was as though it was scouting
for danger or thieves. When finished, it ran back for more peanuts and repeated the same scenario.

A few days later, a front-end loader came and hauled the debris away.
Gone were the peanuts. I wasn't lucky enough to see the look of bewilder-
ment on the squirrel's face when it made the discovery, but I do know it
didn't give up. It found another place for its provisions.

This time it put them inside a four-inch underground drainpipe. We
condo owners were concerned that the squirrel's cache would plug the
drain and cause problems, but a heavy rain gushed down the drain and sent
all the squirrel's provisions out with a whoosh. You'd think the squirrel
would give up. But no. It continued to work before the winter storms blew.

I've often wondered if my efforts are worthwhile. Then I think of the
squirrel. God can make something good out of every setback, if we trust Him.
"In all labour there is profit" (Prov. 14:23). The profit may not be money or
what I expected, but if I'm patient I may find the purpose of failures. So let's
go about our business today with the tenacity of my squirrel neighbors.

EDITH FITCH

Righteousness and Filthy Rags

*We are all as an unclean thing, and all our righteousnesses are as filthy rags.
Isa. 64:6.*

FOR NEARLY TWO DECADES we lived next to a hoarder. Fences and trees helped hide the sight of empty cans, bottles, plastics, yellowed newspapers, broken furniture, and other accumulated junk. The old woman kept to herself, quietly puttering about among her dogs and the rabbits she kept in broken crates.

Only a handful of people ever spoke to old Belle. Even hawkers blanched and turned away when they saw the yard and the piles of cartons and rolls of rotting carpet on the porch.

Gradually she became a miser as well as a hoarder. The hot-water system broke down. Instead of having it repaired, she gave up bathing and washing clothes, and her surroundings stank.

As the years passed, the grass grew taller and the vines and bushes more tangled. My husband mowed the strip of grassy verge outside her front fence. Once in a while I visited over the gate that kept the dogs at bay and took her a home-cooked meal or hot soup on a bitingly cold day, but the offerings were spurned. Belle had a fierce pride.

Then Belle suddenly collapsed, and the ambulance came and took her to the hospital. I shuddered when I saw her unwashed body and ragged, dirty dress lying on the snowy sheet. I pitied the nurses who would have to bathe her.

I thought of Isaiah 64:6. In God's eyes I appear like Belle—unclean, filthy, full of rottenness, wretched, and ragged. "All our righteousnesses are as filthy rags."

Really? I'm a commandment-keeping Christian; do I look like that? The Bible says I do. It's a humbling reality. But God loves me. He offers me a clean robe of Jesus' righteousness to cover my filthy rags; perfume for the stink, a new house and garden, and, best of all, an eternity to spend with Him and the saints of all ages.

Dear Lord, help me to always look on others as souls for whom Christ died, and use me to tell them the good news of salvation. Amen.

GOLDIE DOWN

On Growing Old

Godliness with contentment is great gain. 1 Tim. 6:6.

IT IS A TRUISM that we're all growing older, even the babies in their cribs. Growing old, though, has a different connotation to them. To each of us it has a meaning that's dependent on the years we've lived and what we've done with them. What the years have done to us depends on the way we've responded to the hurts that have come through the years.

One of John Maxwell's books reminds me that what's important is our response to events rather than the events themselves. The same author also calls our attention to the fact that when we have problems they should teach us a lesson rather than cause depression.

How old is old? Some say they're not old till they feel old. Others look in the mirror and let it tell them when old age has arrived. As we get older, our memories sometimes play tricks on us. We remember things that never happened; we need to be willing to stand corrected by those whom we trust. We worry about our properties and moneys lest someone attempt to take our things from us. By keeping close to Jesus in prayer, we can know that He will care for us. He says, "Let not your heart be troubled."

Through Jesus comes the peace that only He can offer me, and the contentment that comforts and takes the fear of the future from old age.

God is the Ancient of Days. He never grows old. We are His created beings and were not intended to grow old, but we do. We may live long and be healthy and happy. If we do live longer, we have the obligation to look back and count our blessings every day. First, we can be thankful for the fact that we're able to count them. We give thanks for our families and friends, who care for us. We're thankful for the degree of health we enjoy, for the comforts of life that are provided for us, for the ability to bring comfort to others unable to do for themselves, and for the things of nature that remind us always of God's love.

It's not great to grow old, but if we stay flexible it can be made tolerable, even enjoyable and profitable.

I'm thankful, Lord, for the privilege of growing old.   GRACE STREIFLING

Embarrassing

I am sure that God, who began this good work in you, will carry it on until it is finished on the Day of Christ Jesus. Phil.1:6, TEV.

WE HAD MOVED FROM Vermont to Maryland, and one day an old friend from Vermont came to visit us. His head was slightly balding on top, and our little dog, Mickey, a fox terrier-cocker spaniel mix, decided it looked good to lick. Before I knew it, Mickey had leaped to the top of the couch and was licking the top of his head. How embarrassing! I quickly leaped to my feet and took her off the couch.

"Oh, I am so sorry," I apologized. "I have no idea why Mickey did that. Please forgive us!"

"It's all right," he responded. "I'll continue to be your friend." And he did remain a friend for many years.

Dogs can be good pets, especially for elderly people, but they have their embarrassing moments, as I had discovered many years ago. I wonder, however, do we embarrass Christ and God at times? We're told that we each have two guardian angels. I am sure they must cringe at times when we do or say things that are hurtful to others. It's so easy to pop out with the wrong words at the wrong time, even though we would never say those same words if we took the time to think before we spoke. Hopefully, as we grow older, we have more control over our words.

Some of us grew up in loving families, and self-control is easier for us; others of us never knew a loving mother or father, and it takes years longer to learn that same control. We are a product of our background. I'm so glad that the Lord "takes note of where we come from."

Only a year or so ago, I found myself saying hurtful words to someone. I was horrified afterward. "Where did that come from, Lord?" I asked. I later called the person and apologized to her.

It's so easy to speak and then think, rather than to think and then speak. My prayer today is for guidance over the things I do and say that I will be a Christian example for the Lord, and not an embarrassment.

LORAINE F. SWEETLAND

First Pray, and Then Do It

You will keep in perfect peace all who trust in you, whose thoughts are fixed on you! Isa. 26:3, NLT.

SEVERAL YEARS AGO I received a small card from a nutrition center, that was said to be a "stress thermometer." If I held my thumb on the black square in the center and it stayed black, I was stressed. It turned red when I was tense, green when I was normal, and blue if I was calm. Medical people say there's a scientific reason for this that has to do with the pressure at which you hold it, the body temperature, as well as the circulation in the fingertips.

For years I'd been working at a highly stressful job, putting in 18-hour days. I knew I shouldn't be burning the candle at both ends, but somehow I seemed trapped in a situation and didn't see a way out.

One day I took out the stress card and placed my thumb on the black square. It stayed black every time I tried. I then decided to try it on our granddaughter. Immediately, it turned bright blue. We tried it on a number of other people, and no one got an all-black reading, as I did. This was just another reminder that my lifestyle needed change.

Our granddaughter got a big kick out of my getting the black, but then she looked at me so seriously and said, "Grandma, first pray, and then do it." Such wisdom from a small child!

Sadly, I was reminded that I hadn't taken enough time for prayer and study of the Word. Our granddaughter thought that if I prayed, God would take away my stress right then. She had complete faith that He would.

That afternoon in the park Andrea and I did pray, and I explained to her that even with the prayer I would first need to make some changes to have my stress level improve.

It's years later now, and I still have the card. Sometimes I can get it to show green or blue, but, more important, I remember the words of Andrea on every occasion: "First pray, and then do it." That's what Jesus would have us do with everything in our lives.

I thank God for the blessings of little ones and for their simple faith. I do need time with the One who keeps us in perfect peace.

DARLENE YTREDAL BURGESON

Hornets

Be self-controlled and alert. Your enemy the devil prowls around like a roaring lion looking for someone to devour. 1 Peter 5:8, NIV.

I WAS ONLY 6 when I first went with my parents to visit my aunt and uncle in the small town of Higganum, Connecticut. Their charming cottage was like a storybook house, nestled in a forest far away from noisy distractions.

I was fascinated by the quaint furnishings and details of interest in every room. With my hands behind me, as mother had instructed, I explored it all, scrutinizing Aunt Hattie's lovely needlework and breathing the fragrant wood aroma from the fireplace. But I loved her delightful kitchen best.

On this particular fall day, Aunt Hattie needed to have the woodbox replenished, so she asked my 16-year-old cousin, Needham, to go and chop enough wood to fill it. I loved my cousin and wanted to be with him every chance I could, and of course the woodpile was no exception. Staying a safe distance from where he split the logs, I watched every move he made.

"Just one more log, and we'll be finished," Needham told me, and down went the ax again. In that instant hundreds of angry hornets rose from the woodpile. He had chopped right through a hornet's nest that had been concealed in the pile.

Needham shouted at me to follow him as he headed for the house, and my legs lost no time in responding. But the hornets had targeted us and followed in hot pursuit. By the time we had stomped into the kitchen, the hornets had triumphed. Needham sustained more stings than we could count. I didn't have as many, but the few I had are still a painful memory.

Our adversary seems to work somewhat like the hornets in Higganum. He stays securely and artfully hidden until we come close enough to temptation for him to track and attack us. Then too late, we realize how powerless we are in our own strength.

What a blessing it is to know that, if we allow, our precious Friend stands ready to stop the enemy in his course, and rescue us. Then He gently applies His antidote of grace and connects us to His sweet, transforming power. All we have to do is give Him full control.

LORRAINE HUDGINS-HIRSCH

Angel Assist

The angel of the Lord encamps around those who fear him, and he delivers them. Ps. 34:7, NIV.

I HAVE TO FIND a rest room," I told my husband. We were driving home from a weekend with family in a nearby state.

"Fine," he answered, "but can you wait until we get through this town we're coming up to? I'd like to get past that highway construction before the true rush hour starts."

"No, I really can't wait; I need one now," I said, not wanting to be a pest but having a sudden urgent need.

"All right, we'll pull off and find a place at the next exit," he patiently replied.

We soon approached the next exit and found what I needed. In a few minutes we were back on the highway again. We passed the construction area my husband had mentioned and resumed normal traffic flow. But a few miles later we found ourselves in a quickly forming line of traffic. There was no indication what was causing the traffic jam, and we inched slowly along.

Emergency vehicles passed us as we approached an overpass. When we cleared the other side, it quickly became clear that an 18-wheeler had turned a little too fast onto an entrance ramp. When it overturned, the enormous spool of cabling it carried came loose and rolled down the hill onto the highway, hitting another 18-wheeler broadside, sending him across the median and into oncoming traffic. Fortunately, it didn't appear that anything had been approaching from the opposite direction. The truck had ended up across both lanes of traffic, blocking the road. No one appeared to be hurt, as the large truck had been able to stay upright.

I looked at my husband, and he looked at me. The implication was evident to us. The accident had obviously happened minutes before—just when we would have been passing had we not stopped earlier. Our sport utility vehicle, while larger than most passenger cars, was definitely smaller than the truck and could have been crushed by the rolling spool.

We thanked God for His protection and for the angels who had been assisting us.

FAUNA RANKIN DEAN

Seeds That Give Life

Still other seed fell on good soil. It came up and yielded a crop, a hundred times more than was sown. Luke 8:8, NIV.

AT THE CLOSE OF a seminar the participants presented a little gift to me—a tiny little plant. The young man mentioned that this little "tree" would grow and one day produce many, many seeds. If those seeds fell on good soil, they would produce new life.

I placed the plant in a light, sunny spot in my study. I watched and tended it carefully, but it didn't thrive—it looked sad and miserable. After about a year I decided to put it in a larger pot with fresh soil. I got good soil and a big pot and carefully planted my wee tree. The little plant looked so tiny in the big pot. But to my amazement, after only a few weeks the plant started producing new leaves and growing rapidly. What a difference the fresh soil made!

This experience reminds me of the parable Jesus told in Luke 8 of the farmer who went out to sow seed. The seed is the Word of God, seed that produces life. But this seed will only grow properly if it falls on good soil. When people hear God's Word and keep it in their hearts, these seeds will bring forth new life. I've learned that it's not enough to simply read a portion of the Bible now and then. We have to take care that the soil in our hearts is well tended. If we wonder why we aren't growing and reaping fruit, maybe we should look for more fresh soil so that we have enough to grow in. Take the time to dig a little deeper in God's Word. Turn the soil so it's light and the roots can grow. Keep at it, and you'll be surprised what happens!

The apostle John tells us that Jesus is this living Word that will transform us and give us new life. He tells us that he looked at and touched this Word of life (1 John 1:1-3). He had a personal relationship with Jesus, his very special friend.

My tiny little plant has grown and become a tree. It has produced a lot of seeds that have grown into new little plants. I've been able to give away four little plants. Every time I enter my study this plant reminds me of the parable of the seeds. It's a wonderful thing to be able to proclaim and pass on seeds of life. The crop is produced by persevering. A speaker at a seminar once said, "Open God's Word to the people, and it will have its effects."

INGRID NAUMANN

He Is Awesome

Let all the inhabitants of the world stand in awe of him. Ps. 33:8.
But my heart standeth in awe of thy word. Ps. 119:161.

THE MEDIA HAD BEEN releasing news of a weather change over the weekend. "Wednesday is fine; Thursday will be OK; but take note: on Friday there will be a drastic change of temperature. There will be a hard freeze."

The meteorologist invited the county agriculturist to talk to the gardeners about how to protect the new flowers and vegetable seedlings. He recommended that they be put back in the pots and be brought in. He also said to cover the trees with natural fiber coverings.

To get the full benefit of sunshine before the cold weather happened I waited until the last minute, just before the temperature dropped, then I followed the instructions. I doubted that my procedure would be effective. I thought that the covers were "too flimsy" and not of any good; nevertheless, I did what I could and left the rest in God's hands.

I covered the plants just a few minutes before prayer meeting started. When the prayer requests were called for, I told the prayer leaders, "My prayer requests are childlike: I want someone to pray for my plants, that they'll be protected from harm." That night I also prayed by my trees for God to guard all my plants.

The following morning the sun shone warm again, so I quickly unveiled the plants. I found them all perky and unharmed. The drooping buds were looking up and doing fine.

The Lord is awesome! He has made His infinite power available to us. Where two or three are gathered, there He is also. His creation is full of promises, and so is His Word. God fulfills them according to His will, fashioned according to our needs, especially when it's humanly impossible to do anything about the problem.

If God takes care of His plant creation, how much more will He care for someone whom He created according to His image. My faith in Him was made stronger with the evidence of love He had shown me. Psalm 121:2 says our help comes from the Lord, who "made heaven and earth." He will also take care of us today and every day, "and even for evermore."

ESPERANZA AQUINO MOPERA

Thank God for Simple Remedies!

And his servants came near and spoke to him, and said, "My father, if the prophet had told you to do something great, would you not have done it? How much more then, when he says to you, 'Wash, and be clean'?" 2 Kings 5:13, NKJV.

NAAMAN WANTED TO BE cleansed from his leprosy—but he wanted to do it his own way. Disappointed that Elisha didn't come in person to heal him, Naaman balked at following the simple instructions of Elisha's servant to "go and wash in the Jordan seven times, and your flesh shall be restored to you, and you shall be clean" (2 Kings 5:10, NKJV). Fortunately, Naaman yielded to the pleading of his servants and received the help he so desperately needed.

Are we sometimes like Naaman, so caught up in our own ideas about how things should be done that we pay no heed to plain advice, especially in matters of health? I know I've been, at times. All my life I've heard advice from health sermons, health classes, and doctors: "To stay healthy, you need to drink at least six to eight glasses of water a day."

But I didn't like water. I preferred milk, juice, Postum, or soft drinks. Being a very busy person, I thought I did well to get down a couple of glasses a day. After passing painful kidney stones twice, I had the second stone analyzed. "How can I avoid having more such spells in the future?" I asked. "Take medicine? Change my diet?"

"No need for that," my doctor replied. "Simply drink at least six to eight glasses of water daily, in addition to all your other liquids. That will keep those uric-acid crystals in solution."

How inexpensive! How reasonable! How easy! I began following Dr. Keim's advice. I've had no more problems with kidney stones.

Maybe it's time to check out how most of us (myself included) fare when it comes to our spiritual health. Are we daily drinking deeply enough from the water of life that our Savior can come into our lives and change our "stony" hearts? Or are we, perhaps, among those who feel that the plan of salvation is too simple, that we can't rely fully on Christ, that we must try to somehow work our way to heaven?

Thank God that a childlike faith in Christ and His grace can fill all our needs, whether they are physical, mental, or spiritual!   BONNIE MOYERS

The Crossing Guard

A merry heart maketh a cheerful countenance: but by sorrow of the heart the spirit is broken. Prov. 15:13.

EACH WORKDAY STARTS out with a whirlwind of activity. Breakfast needs to be served, lunches need to be packed, children need to be dressed, and the list goes on and on. It's very easy for me to get caught up in the turbulence of the morning. Driving to work helps me put things in perspective.

As I make the trek to work I ponder my to-do list. Usually, I'm so engrossed in my thoughts that I don't pay attention to my surroundings. But something changes when I come to the church school zone in a neighborhood on my route. I look forward to seeing the crossing guard who monitors the area. Not only does she direct traffic; she's always smiling. It amazes me how she can smile, regardless of the weather, being in the middle of the road, heavy traffic, and inconsiderate drivers.

The first time I saw her she made an immediate impact on me. I could feel her joy and felt warm inside. After that, I looked forward to seeing her each morning. I'd watch her as I waited my turn. There were days when I actually needed her smile. It seemed to eliminate the beginning of a bad day. Eventually I noticed how other drivers responded to her, as well. The other motorists seemed to be doing the same thing I was. Her smile was contagious. Sometimes they'd even leave their cars to give her a gift.

It's been a blessing to see this woman, and I've learned a great deal from this situation. Not only is she a crossing guard; she's a guard of the cross of Christ.

We can exhibit a positive or negative countenance and how the results affect people. When I am engrossed in my thoughts, I've found that I don't look very friendly. It's not intentional, but as the saying goes, "a picture is worth a thousand words." I wonder what my countenance has looked like to others.

My prayer today, Lord, is to have a merry heart, one that spreads joy to others and that people look forward to seeing. I thank You for the people You put in our lives when our hearts are empty.   MARY WAGONER ANGELIN

Spaghetti Sauce

Keep yourselves in God's love as you wait for the mercy of our Lord Jesus Christ to bring you to eternal life. Jude 21, NIV.

HAVE YOU EVER noticed that if you're doing anything with any type of tomato sauce that it's sure to get on your clothes (especially if you are wearing a white blouse)? Now, I'm quite certain that there's nothing sinister about spaghetti sauce, but I certainly notice its presence more than any other food.

It's always seemed to me that if I wore something new, it was certain to get a tear or rip or snag the first time I wore it. It seemed my children would fall and rip the knee of new pants every time. If one got past that first time, the item would last for years. The same principle seems to work with panty hose—if they don't get a run the first time, they have a good chance of lasting quite a while. Of course, this isn't totally true, but it certainly seems like it. Probably once the item is old, I don't care that much anymore and pay little attention.

What we're thinking about and paying attention to comes to our notice the most. There's a woman in the building where I work who has a suit exactly like one I have. I always notice when she wears it but pay little attention when she wears anything else, even though she dresses very nicely.

A few years ago we bought a new car. I'd never paid much attention to that make of car before, but after we got ours, I saw them everywhere. The same is true of expressions, names of books—all sorts of things. Once I become aware of something, it seems to pop up all over the place.

Which all leads me to believe that what I think is important, or that to which I give attention is noticed, remembered, and valued more than other things. So I have to ask myself, Where does Jesus Christ fit into the picture of my life? Do I concentrate on His life, His values, His wishes? Do I think of His desires when I'm making a decision or making a value judgment?

I want to keep myself centered on Jesus until He is the most important thing in my life and my thoughts. Then spattered spaghetti sauce won't even matter.

ARDIS DICK STENBAKKEN

God's Light

Let your light so shine before men, that they may see your good works, and glorify your Father which is in heaven. Matt. 5:16.

M Y FAMILY WAS IN the West Indies, and I was in England studying to become a registered nurse. I missed my family and found pleasure in singing hymns. It helped fill the void.

The patients assigned to us were severely ill, but I enjoyed helping people. After finishing the night shift, my classmates, colleagues, and I would go to the dining room to have breakfast. I observed one of my classmates staring at me. I tried not to let it disturb me, but it annoyed me. I couldn't imagine why she stood and stared at me. I felt very uneasy and found it difficult to eat.

I proceeded to eat slowly as I engaged in conversation with those sitting at my table. The classmate who had been staring eventually came over and sat beside me and blurted out angrily, "I hate you! I hate you! I hate you!" The room was filled with silence. I got a cold chill. I couldn't believe what I was actually hearing. I was respected by everyone I came in contact with, and had never experienced any bad encounters with any of my classmates, teachers, or coworkers. I was in total shock and honestly had no idea why she was shouting that she hated me.

I finally mustered up enough courage to ask, "Why do you hate me?"

She replied, "You're always happy! You're always singing. You never go to dances, movies, or parties. You don't wear makeup or lipstick. You always follow the rules and never get in trouble. I do all these things and am never happy!" She shouted, "You're so different. You're always happy, and I hate you for this! I hate you!"

I froze, praying silently that she wouldn't strike me. Lost for words, I quickly excused myself from the table, went to my room, and knelt in prayer. She said I was "different." I thanked God for helping me to uphold the standards of a Christian.

Gradually she warmed up to me. She said she stopped doing some of the things she hated me for not doing. We became true friends afterward. She seemed to be much happier.

At an early age I learned the importance of letting the light of Christ shine so that others might see His good works in me and glorify my heavenly Father.

GERTRUDE E. BURKE

God's Plans

"For my thoughts are not your thoughts, neither are your ways my ways,"
declares the Lord. Isa. 55:8, NIV.

TIME FLIES. JUST THE other day we were beginning the year, full of expectations, and now we see the second half of the year going by at an
accelerated pace.

The months went by so quickly that at times we tended to believe that
together with them our unaccomplished plans also vanished. Perhaps you
have regrets because your dreams were unfulfilled, and now you feel half
lost or frustrated. But as you pray, don't question the Lord. Continue praying that God's plans, which are always better than ours, may be carried out
in your life. "For my thoughts are not your thoughts, neither are your ways
my ways, saith the Lord. For as the heavens are higher than the earth, so are
my ways higher than your ways, and my thoughts than your thoughts" (Isa.
55:8, 9). "For I know the thoughts that I think toward you, saith the Lord,
thoughts of peace, and not of evil, to give you an expected end" (Jer. 29:11).

What a blessing to know that the Lord wants to give us the end that we
desire. At times, though, our mind is obscured by lack of faith, and we're
not able to see beyond our problems. We want, like Abraham, "to help" the
Lord. Our finite mind attempts to comprehend His plans, and it's clear
many times that we're not able to understand. At these times we need to
open our eyes of faith to believe that "all things work together for good to
them that love God" (Rom. 8:28). We need to believe that our loving
Father works in our favor. He loves us and is concerned for us, and best of
all, He has the power to do everything that is the best for us.

As you begin this new day be encouraged with the surprises that our heavenly Father is preparing for you. Certainly your heart will praise the Lord!

My thoughts are inadequate to even address You or know what I should
ask for. Bless me this day, I pray, in accordance with Your love and Your will.

REGINA MARY SILVEIRA NUNES

Inner Beauty

The king's daughter is all glorious within. Ps. 45:13.

OUR ELDEST SON RECENTLY married. Prior to the wedding I decided to pass on to my new daughter-in-law a family heirloom that originated in my generation—a 24-karat, gold-plated, rose-filigreed, beveled-glass jewelry box. I had received it on the day of my wedding. I got it out to dust it off and wrap it for her. But its appearance shocked me. I'd been remembering how it had looked 34 years before. Its present condition was appalling. It looked like an ugly old antique.

I hadn't remembered that years of mission field diesel fumes, mingled with African humidity and dust, had ascended from the jungle road below our house, coating the palm branches an ugly brown, as it also coated the crafted rose petals on my jewelry box.

The local jeweler wouldn't touch the box for fear of damaging it but told me how I might try to restore it. So one morning I gently and meticulously scrubbed the nooks and crannies of the sculpted roses and leaves on the outside of the box. Eventually years of grime clumped up until I could wipe it away. But when I stood back to admire the fruit of my labor, it still looked tawdry.

Why? I wondered. Then, through the hundreds of airy openings in the filigreed rose vines, I started seeing deeper coats of grime on the backs of the sculpted leaves and flowers down in the box. I opened the lid and went to work on the inside of the box. At long last I finished my project and closed the lid.

The gasp of pleasure, the sparkle in my daughter-in-law's eyes when she first saw the restored jewelry box, and the spontaneous bear hug she gave me all testified to the fact I'd done a pretty good job.

Cleaning and restoring that jewelry case reminded me that we, too, are God's jewelry boxes, often tarnished with unforgiveness, unacknowledged pride, dark thoughts, and pet sins. But when we let Christ through the "lid" to work on our inner beauty, we can stop worrying about external appearances.

When *true, lasting* beauty radiates from our hearts, others will always find us attractive—on behalf of the One who is living within.

CAROLYN SUTTON

The Phone Call

And it shall come to pass, that before they call, I will answer; and while they are yet speaking, I will hear. Isa. 65:24.

SEVERAL YEARS AGO MY husband suddenly became ill and was hospitalized. I needed to contact one of his brothers, who lived in the United States, to inform him of the situation. Unfortunately, he had recently moved and, in my frustration, I was unable to find his current address. Feeling helpless and anxious, I decided to pray about it.

Going to my bedroom, I knelt by the bed. *Dear Lord, You know how urgent it is for me to get in contact with my brother-in-law. I don't have his new address and phone number. I need Your assistance and divine intervention. Please help me!*

While still on my knees, I heard the sound of the telephone. I immediately rose from my praying position to answer it. How overjoyed I was to hear the familiar voice of my brother-in-law. I excitedly exclaimed, "I was just asking the Lord to help me locate you, and He heard and answered immediately!"

I thanked God for His prompt response and was reassured of the scripture found in Isaiah 65:24: "It shall come to pass, that before they call, I will answer; and while they are yet speaking, I will hear." Surely, if we trust Him, He will hear and answer our earnest petitions.

Two biblical accounts flashed into my mind after that incident. One is found in Daniel 9:21, 22. There the story is recorded of Daniel's experience nearly 3,000 years ago when the angel Gabriel was sent from heaven to answer his request while he was yet praying. Then there is the deliverance of Peter from prison (Acts 12). While the church members fervently prayed for his release, he was standing and knocking at the door of the house where they were praying. I realized that God had done the very same for me.

What a wonderful, caring, omnipresent heavenly Father we serve, who knows our needs and desires even before we ask.

Father, may we always put our faith in Your promises.

MARJORIE BOYCE

The Tale of Two Cakes

Now therefore stand and see this great thing, which the Lord will do before your eyes. 1 Sam. 12:16.

S O MUCH FOR GOOD intentions. I honestly thought I was being help- ful, but my actions to this day are misinterpreted, and there remains a standoff at my house. You see, it began quite innocently—I remember it as though it were yesterday.

It was my birthday, and my husband's schedule had seemed hectic for the past month. Not wanting to put added pressure on him, I had remained silent about any birthday wishes and hoped-for plans for celebrating the day. Then I got what I thought was a brilliant idea. Since the kids love par- ties almost as much as their mother does, I let them plan my birthday. I put the oldest, 5-year-old Brandon, in charge. "Would you like to plan a party?" I asked in a hushed tone.

"*My* birthday?" he said matching my whisper. When I informed him it was my birthday, he asked quite matter-of-factly, "When is it?"

I informed him it was that very day. "Well," he said, "we've got to get a cake and ice cream and a clown."

I was quite impressed with his list and tickled by his contagious enthu- siasm, though I did have to nix the clown idea. So after school, off we went.

When we got home, however, guess who was already there, cutting his day short with his own party surprises—and an even nicer cake. Oops!

"You couldn't wait, could you?" he began. "How could you think that I'd forget? And to top it off, how could you buy your own birthday cake?"

"Well," I began weakly, " I thought—"

His disappointment still echoes.

Unfortunately, there are many times the Lord has had to say the same thing when I've "helped" Him. My human good intentions have gotten me into situations that I then had to pray for a way through or for deliverance from. No wonder the psalmist emphasized it thus: "Wait, I say, on the Lord."

Lord, help me not to help You, but instead to wait on Your guidance, for You have promised, and You are faithful. MAXINE WILLIAMS ALLEN

Someone's Kiss

They will see his face, and his name will be on their foreheads. Rev. 22:4, NIV.

WHILE FLIPPING THROUGH channels with my remote, I recently discovered a cable TV channel called "Animal Planet." Their program, *Emergency Vets,* is a favorite of mine. On this show cameras follow the doctors and patients around in an animal hospital.

An elderly dog in a recent show made a big impression on me. His hind legs could no longer support him, so his human "mommy" took him for walks by holding up his rear with a special harness. The duo were quite a pair as they came into the clinic, the woman carefully made up and the happy dog walking by her side. When the vet decided to keep the dog overnight for tests, the woman told the dog goodbye and planted a big kiss on his forehead, leaving a big lipstick mark. Everywhere the dog went people smiled to see the lipstick kiss on his head. It was clear evidence that the animal was much loved, and some hospital employees gave him more kisses.

The old dog died, and the woman brought out a photograph album to share pictures of his life. In every picture, from puppyhood on, the dog's forehead featured a lipstick kiss.

I was thinking how marvelous it would be to wear someone's kiss on your forehead. No matter where you were, everyone would know you were loved. The mark would be right there, out in the open, for everyone to see.

The Bible talks about the faithful wearing the Lord's name on their foreheads. When we become Christians, we're using Christ's name to identify ourselves. But we write His name in our hearts, not on our foreheads.

Most Christians don't wear a particular type of clothing to identify themselves. There's no special hairstyle or handshake that lets people know we're Christians. Not showing physical signs to our identity, it's all the more important that we show who we are by our actions.

I want people to recognize me as a Christian by the love that I show them. I belong to Jesus, and I want everyone to know it. I pray that I can live my life as though people could see Someone's kiss on my forehead.

GINA LEE

The Fog Will Lift

For God, who commanded the light to shine out of darkness, hath shined in our hearts, to give the light of the knowledge of the glory of God in the face of Jesus Christ. 2 Cor. 4:6.

I TURNED OFF THE RADIO alarm and lay in bed, listening to the beautiful music. Finally deciding I should get up, I walked over to the window to see what God's daybreak had brought. Surprised, I saw a dense fog. In fact, it was such a thick fog that I decided to call it the Fog of 2000. I couldn't see whether the cars were red, blue, or black. I only knew they were passing by because I was able to see the headlights and hear the sounds as they carried people to work at a very slow pace. The weather report called for school bus delays, air-flight delays, and even rail travel delays.

God always has a purpose, and I thought, *Well, on this October morning of the year 2000 He wants everyone, including me, to slow down and listen to His still, small voice through nature.* As I watched the thickness of the fog, I couldn't help saying, "How majestic are Your works, Lord God Almighty!" I began my chores for the day, and in less than a couple hours the fog began to lift, and soon the light of God's glorious sunshine shone brightly.

The morning fog of the year 2000 is something like life's experience. Sometimes our lives may become foggy with car problems, physical problems, financial problems, and school problems (to name a few). But good news came to mind as I watched the October's fog. Regardless of the density of life's fog, the One who sent October's fog and then lifted it can lift the fog in our lives as well, no matter how thick it may seem.

I pray to the Fog Sender that the fog in my life, and in others' lives, will lift. But I want His will to be done. He alone knows how, when, or whether He'll lift our fog. Our part is to have faith and to wait and accept His answers.

ANNIE B. BEST

Imaginary Fears

Yea, though I walk through the valley of the shadow of death, I will fear no evil: for thou art with me; thy rod and thy staff they comfort me. Ps. 23:4

MY LITTLE BOY WAS afraid of sleeping in the dark. He wouldn't sleep in the room he shared with his brother because his brother wouldn't allow him to turn on the light. So he slept in our room. My husband doesn't like to leave the light on at night, either. It was therefore a war of words between father and son, each trying to convince the other why the light should be on or off.

My little boy devised a means of getting attention. As soon as the light was off, he'd leave his bed and climb in beside me, saying there were ghosts in the room that wouldn't allow him to sleep. At first, I allowed him to sleep beside me, but when I found that he needed to learn to overcome the fear of the dark, I started staying up, reading to him from *Uncle Arthur's Bedtime Stories* until he fell asleep. Little by little he overcame his fears and started sleeping in his own bed. After a few months he felt he was big enough to go to his room. No more night ghosts.

When I think back on my son's experience, I feel I'm like that, too. I have my imaginary fears—fears of the unknown, fears about the future. Shortly after my father died, I found that I depended heavily on my older sister. There were four of us, and I was the baby of the family. The first sister was in an overseas country, so I couldn't lean on her. My second sister accepted the family responsibilities and helped me immensely. Because of this I feared I might lose her, just as I'd lost my father. Anytime she traveled, I'd find my eyes glued to the highway, waiting and watching for her. My imagination was so fertile that I'd think of all kinds of things that could happen to her. Praise God, she always came home and allayed my fears. However, I carried this fear into my adult life. When I got married, I was always watching for my husband whenever he traveled and was headed home.

Today I've learned to take John 14:1 sincerely: "Let not your heart be troubled." I believe every word of that verse. When God says do not be troubled, He sincerely means it.

BECKY DADA

Angels Took Charge

There shall no evil befall thee. . . . He shall give his angels charge over thee. Ps. 91:10, 11.

IT WAS FRIDAY NOON on the Lowry campus. A huge tamarind tree was being cut down, but the branches were loaded with half-ripe fruit. As I passed that way returning from my friend's house, I was tempted to get some tamarind for making pickles. I found Alwyn, my son, playing with his friends. I asked him to get some fruit from the tree, since he knew how to climb it.

As I watched Alwyn climb the tree, I felt uneasy and guilty about asking him to do this. He started picking, slowly advancing toward the end of the branch where there was a lot of fruit. I could see the joint of the branch cracking and shaking, and I sensed the danger. I got scared. Suddenly I could see and hear the branches breaking and falling. I could see my son slowly falling down along with the branch. I closed my eyes for a second, and my heart stopped. When I dared to open my eyes, I saw my son gracefully land on a lower branch. He dropped lightly to the ground and smiled. I heaved a sigh of relief and breathed, "God, You are great." I didn't even bother to collect the tamarind, but walked with my son toward our house.

I was so ashamed of my cravings for tamarind and unhappy with myself. If something had happened to my son, I could have never forgiven myself. At vespers that night, with a grateful heart we rededicated Alwyn and thanked God for sparing his life, because Alwyn's angels again took care of him.

The devil knows our weaknesses and waits for a chance to trap us. The devil knew my weakness for tamarind pickle and took advantage of that. He knows each of us and also knows our desire for money, position, and the things money can buy. This is how we fall prey to the traps the devil sets for us.

Dear Lord, take away the desire for worldly gratification and fill our lives and hearts with heavenly things.   WINIFRED DEVARAJ

Giving Up on Getting Even

Be kind and compassionate to one another, forgiving each other, just as in Christ God forgave you. Eph. 4:32, NIV.

SINCE I'VE SPENT ALMOST 30 years in working to strengthen families, I was fascinated by the story of a man who spent the last decades (yes, decades!) of his marriage sleeping down the hall from his wife. It seems that some 30 years previously his wife felt that he didn't show enough empathy when their 5-year-old daughter became ill. To teach him a lesson, she moved out of their bedroom to a spare bedroom. Every night for 30 years he's waited for her to come to him and say, "I'm sorry." Every night for 30 years she's waited for him to come to her and say, "I'm sorry." Each waits for the other, and no one makes the first move.

We might say, How ridiculous! It would have been so easy for one to go to the other and say I'm sorry and have it over with. But sometimes we can think of a hundred reasons why we shouldn't forgive someone who has wronged us. We say, "It's not up to me to make the first move," or "I'll forgive her when she says she's sorry," or "If I forgive her, she might act this way again!"

But it is forgiveness, and forgiveness only, that can stop the cycle of blame and pain. The Greek word for forgiveness literally means to release, to hurl away, or to free oneself. The state of an unforgiving heart leads to resentment. Resentment clings to the past, reliving each moment of the hurt, turning it over and reviving it again and again.

Forgiving a wrong offers a solution to the problem. When you initiate the "I'm sorry," it begins to thaw the heart of the guilty one. It may not determine who is right and who is wrong. The question of who is right and who is wrong will not be settled. Saying "I'm sorry" allows a relationship to begin anew. Forgiveness allows us to reconnect with someone from whom we have been alienated. As long as we don't forgive the person we remain bound to them.

Author Phillip Yancey states, "The only thing harder than forgiveness is the alternative." Is there anyone in your life whom you need to forgive? If the answer is even a half yes, there's no better time than now to initiate the "I'm sorry." You'll break the chains of what binds you to that person. Forgiveness offers true freedom.

Why not claim that freedom today? NANCY L. VAN PELT

The Retread

Trust in the Lord with all your heart and don't depend on your own understanding. Put the Lord first in everything you do and He will direct your life. Prov. 3:5, 6, Clear Word.

RETREAD. I DIDN'T LIKE the word then, and I don't like it now. Many years ago, after being a stay-at-home-mother for 20 years, circumstances propelled me back into the world of nursing. My first job was scary, but the seasoned nurses were kind and very helpful. However, I was less than enchanted with their title for me—"the Retread"—like getting more miles out of worn-out tires.

After a few years as a retread, the Lord led me to the rewarding world of academia. Twenty years on the nursing faculty was a great experience, but I did look forward to retirement. I began to ask God daily, "What do You want me to do in my retirement?" I had some ideas. I could continue my routine shift at the hospital (I worked a shift a week during my teaching years to keep up my nursing skills) and do more church work, or perhaps some community service, such as working with the homeless or serving in the community soup kitchen.

Astonished, I heard God say "retread." As it turned out, my years of teaching experience were to be utilized in coordinating a learning assistance program for nursing students to assist them in "putting it all together." Amazingly, my community service ambition had the word "retread" written all over it, also. There were numerous nursing graduates from the various schools in the area who had not been successful in passing state board examinations. They felt alone and abandoned. I'm not sure how it all came about except for God's leading. I started study groups for these graduates. One by one these graduates were able to pass their state boards and now contribute their special talents to the nursing profession.

The lesson I want to share is don't depend on your own understanding. God proved to me that His ways are higher than my ways and His thoughts higher than my thoughts. The reward? My retirement activities have been stress-free, fun, and the most rewarding of my nursing career. I still don't like thinking of myself as "the Retread," but God led me in that direction, so I accept the title.

BONNIE HUNT

Safe Shelter

The Lord is God, and he has made his light shine upon us. Ps. 118:27, NIV.

LIKE A MOVIE, the events of the past few days passed through my mind. They had been difficult days; I felt tired and discouraged. Then I remembered an old song that says, "If a ray of sun said, 'Today I am not going to shine,'" and the song goes on to describe the consequences, what would take place if all the rays of the sun decided not to shine. Of course, there would be unsupportable coldness, dense darkness would form, and the entire ecological cycle would suffer.

Was I perhaps being a ray of sunshine that had decided not to shine? Was the routine of many activities, deadlines, daily work, and periodic feelings of failure and inability leaving me exhausted? Was my light hidden behind a screen, under a basket?

I once read that there's nothing wrong in feeling tired, but it's totally wrong to abandon ship in the middle of the battle. When punished by bad weather or taken over by a storm, we need to find shelter and refuge. But to whom could I tell my problems? Where could I find encouragement? David, when he felt cornered and wounded by his adversary, wrote, "O my Strength, I watch for you; you, O God, are my fortress" (Ps. 59:9, NIV). Like David, I have found refuge and shelter in the promises of God. Jesus is the Sun of justice, and His warmth, His light, and His power produce inexhaustible life and joy in us.

I once read in *God's Devotional for Women:* "Look around and you become tired; look within yourself and you become depressed; look to Jesus and you become rested."

Don't allow yourself to be suffocated by unfavorable circumstances. For each situation, no matter what you're facing, God has already prepared the necessary provision of strength, wisdom, and patience. There's no affliction, weariness, or tribulation that is greater than the grace of God. Partake of this grace and be a ray of sun that has decided to shine!

Truly, You are my strength, and Your light shines upon us. I pray for the necessary strength to meet the challenges of this day in Your grace and power.

MARIA BALDÃO QUADRADO

Teeth

He has covered me with the robe of righteousness. Isa. 61:10, NKJV.

IF THERE'S ANYTHING I hate, it's going to the dentist. That's no reflection on the dentists I've had over the years; they've always been very nice people. Maybe it's the dentist chair that bothers me.

As soon as I sit down in the chair my body stiffens, and I grab on to the arms and hang on for dear life. I've heard of "painless" dentists but never seem to get one of those. Mine plays music, which is supposed to relax the patient, but I'm still gripping the arms of the chair.

Now, the grip varies. When the drilling starts, I grip the arms harder. The sound of the motorized dental equipment really sets off my panic alarms. By the time the dental appointment is over, whether it's a routine checkup or really digging in to some problem, I'm sure I've reduced the size of the arms of the chair. Maybe this is good exercise for arm muscles. If so, twice a year I get a workout.

I brush my teeth three to four times a day, using whitening toothpaste. By now my teeth should be whiter than snow. But not so! They still seem to have a brownish tinge. My dentist says it's old age. I can remember when they introduced fluoride to our water systems. One of the results, we were told, was that it would make our teeth brown. Well, they were right! So now we have all these products to whiten and brighten our teeth.

Well, I'll keep brushing my teeth and going to the dentist. I've lived through it this many years; I guess a few more won't harm me. Besides, where can I get a workout of arm muscles on the side? At least I still have teeth to brush!

We have the stains of sin in our lives that discolor our souls. Soon we'll stand before the King of the universe and see Him in person. We will be clothed in the white raiment of Christ's righteousness. All the stains of sin are gone with this celestial raiment.

Will you accept the Master's gift of this glorious righteousness made especially for you? It's much more important than anything else in our lives.

PEGGY CURTICE HARRIS

The Rest Room Experience

Do not lay up for yourselves treasures on earth, . . . where thieves break in and steal. Matt. 6:19, RSV.

WHILE WAITING FOR A flight, I used the airport rest room. Never would I expect what happened next. I went in the stall, locked the door, and placed my carry-on bag on the floor by my feet. I placed my purse in the plexiglass receptacle mounted on the wall of the stall. When I was ready to leave, I picked up my bag, but there was no purse.

I yelled, "My purse is gone. Someone has taken my purse!" As I quickly washed and dried my hands, a young woman came out of nowhere, looked at me, and pushed my purse into my hands. She said, "Here is your purse."

Shocked, I said, "Thank you, but how did it get over there?"

She said nothing, but walked off. I couldn't believe it. With many women in the rest room, she had come directly to me.

My husband was waiting for me, so after checking my purse, I went out to tell him. I keep our black passport case in my handbag with our tickets and a little emergency money. The money was gone! I knew immediately that the young woman had taken it. I could identify her. Retracing our steps, I saw the woman standing outside the entrance to the rest room. I said to her, "You returned my purse to me." Sort of smiling, she said yes, and I continued, "You took my money." Of course, she denied the allegation. She and I walked to Customer Services, reported the theft, and waited for the police. Because it was almost time for our next flight, I was anxious.

The police came. After recounting the incident to them, they questioned both of us. I was not surprised when nothing but a written report was made. Even though I was angry and upset, I apologized to the woman for any inconvenience she may have experienced.

In spite of the loss, we were blessed. We had our tickets, all our credit cards, and money I had in another place. I decided that whoever took the money needed it more than we did. I reasoned that though they may enjoy it now, eventually they would lose much more. You will reap what you sow.

I learned some valuable lessons: always keep my eyes and hands on my belongings, be aware of my surroundings, pray daily for protection, don't get too attached to material things, pray for those who do evil against me, and finally, give thanks to God in all situations.   MARIE H. SEARD

Jericho, 2000

He shall deliver thee in six troubles: yea, in seven. Job 5:19.

THE RAISED THUMB OF the superintendent elicited a joyous, calm but explosive "Thank You, Lord, thank You!" This was indeed a time for celebration and rejoicing in what had been a time of anxiety, despondency, and fear.

It had been almost 12 months to the day since the groundwork for the church construction had begun—discussions, plans, permits, building size, cost, community concerns, etc. Now it was three days before the publicized opening of the church. Extensive preparations had been made, but all was not well. Anxiety filled the atmosphere. Most taxing of all was the antici-pated visit of the fire marshal. No one was ready for him. He'd given distinct directions for certain types of equipment and materials for specific areas in the building. Not being readily available, these things were not in place, although genuine effort had been made to secure them. The frustrated contractor informed the pastor the materials wouldn't be delivered until some weeks after the scheduled opening.

The pastor informed the membership about the situation, and everyone began to pray. A group of women, who called themselves the "Prayer Warriors," made a daring move. They took the initiative to talk with the contractor. Exactly what was said is not known; however, the contractor agreed to join them as they presented their case to the Fire Marshal above all fire marshals.

When the local fire marshal arrived and started to make his rounds with the contractor, the "Prayer Warriors" started marching around the building, talking with the Lord. Later, as the contractor exited the building, the superintendent quietly gave them a jubilant thumbs-up!

Another Jericho? Well, the walls of rejection did fall down, as the triumphant praises went up from the "Prayer Warriors" and those around them.

Everyone lifted joyful hearts in thanksgiving and reconsecration as they welcomed the more than 300 individuals who joined in the celebration on October 29 in acknowledgment to God, whose answer to prayer broke down the walls.

QUILVIE G. MILLS

The Bumblebee and Me

Hasten to me, O God! You are my help and my deliverer. Ps. 70:5, NASB.

I OPENED MY CAR door and stepped out into the parking lot on an absolutely perfect autumn day. Balmy. Sunny. *Great day to enjoy the outdoors,* I thought. Suddenly, out of nowhere, a bumblebee made a wild dive for my head. I was scared to death of bees and made a mad, screaming dash for the front seat of my car.

The bee, undeterred, flew right into the car with me. I screamed and jumped from the car, flinging my arms every which way to scare the bee off. In hot pursuit, the insect circled my head, flying toward my face again and again. Panicked, I slammed the car door and quickly tried to gather my belongings, which were now strewn on the pavement near my car. Breathing hard from the almost attack, I walked as fast as I could toward the building. The bee hovered nearby, flying offensively at me every chance it got. After I'd gone about eight feet, it disappeared.

Not convinced that it was actually gone, I continued to wave my hands to ward off any sneak attacks. I wanted to be ready. My heart continued to race as I moved quickly. There was no time to lose; I had to make it to the safety of the building. I made a quick backward glance now and then, but there was no bee anywhere. Phew! The little pest was gone, probably to annoy someone else.

I entered the building at last and made by way toward the elevator. I was safe! Another employee, who was walking toward the elevator, caught my eye and commented, "Wow, you were really having a fierce battle out there in the parking lot!" Embarrassed, I laughed. I'm sure it must have looked pretty comical to anyone else who wasn't close enough to see the little bumblebee. Eager to explain my crazy-looking actions, I relayed what had happened. She agreed, the bee—determined to win the battle—was surely after me!

I know another pest who shows up on the balmy, sunny days of our lives when things seem just perfect. Creating havoc. Attacking from all sides. Following closely and coming at us again and again, despite our best efforts to get rid of him. Making us run scared. And thank God, we can run to Him for safety when we feel scared, threatened, or distressed.

Thank You, Lord, for Your daily help, protection, and deliverance in times of distress. May I always stay close to You and be safe from the enemy's vicious attacks.

IRIS L. STOVALL

Secret Prayer

But thou, when thou prayest, enter into thy closet, and when thou hast shut thy door, pray to thy Father which is in secret; and thy Father which seeth in secret shall reward thee openly. . . . For your Father knoweth what things ye have need of, before ye ask him. Matt. 6:6-8.

OUR NECESSITIES ARE GREAT; we're always in need of something, even besides the satisfaction of a complete spiritual life. But God says that He has enough power to supply these necessities.

"I'll be upstairs," I told my family. "I'll be busy with some things, so I don't want to be bothered by anyone."

I prepared myself with the Bible, pen, and paper. I surrounded myself with the necessary accessories to begin my secret prayer. I was going through a difficult time in my life. There were some debts to be paid, and the money to do this hadn't appeared. The amount I was to receive wasn't enough to take care of the debts. What was I to do? Everything in my life seemed so dark; a feeling of emptiness wanted to take control of my being.

I needed to tell this to God. I prayed, then read today's text. A sensation of well-being, of acceptance before God, began to fill my heart. When I read "your Father knoweth what things ye have need of, before ye ask him," I knew a feeling of confidence. Although the world and its traps were attempting to destroy my faith, God would strengthen me to continue the struggle in the direction of heaven.

Yes, I will continue praying in secret, and my Father, who sees me in secret, will reward me. I won't be a hypocrite; I'll tell Him all the things that I am in need of. He knows that you and I are really needy, and He will grant us blessings from the heavenly regions. *My loving Father, I will always pray to You in secret.*

Set aside a moment of your life to pray alone with God, only you and Him, Father and daughter. God will certainly give us what is best.

Dear Lord, come each new day to take our needs, both material and spiritual, into Your powerful hands and renew our life. We ask in the name of Jesus. Amen.

ROSA CARNEIRO

Innocence of Faith

I tell you the truth, unless you change and become like little children, you will never enter the kingdom of heaven. Therefore, whoever humbles himself like this child is the greatest in the kingdom of heaven. Matt. 18:3, 4, NIV.

LANDON WAS 5, a delightful age. A typical little boy, he was half-adorable cherub and half-mischievous imp and the center of the attention in the family, always commanding the limelight. His innocent observations and comic antics were a never-ending delight.

Then it was time to start school. The first few days he was filled with the excitement of being a big schoolboy, and he'd come home with reports of the neat things they were doing. But to sit still and be quiet just seemed to be an impossible task. His teacher patiently explained that when they weren't quiet or if they disobeyed, a magnet with their name on it would be placed on the blackboard. If five magnets were put up in one day, a visit to the principal's office was required.

Each day Landon would solemnly report, "Mom, I got two magnets up today, but I really tried to be quiet." As hard as he tried, he'd forget, get out of his seat, or start talking. Weeks went by, and even promises of a special prize didn't help. Then it happened—five magnets with his name on them. Landon was fearful. His mother was called and told of the disciplinary action.

The whole family expected to see a frightened, dejected little boy that afternoon. But to their surprise, he bounced in with his usual smiles and hugs. "Mom, guess what? I had to go to the principal's office." His mother had to ask what had happened. "Oh, he had me sit beside him and talked to me about how I have to learn to sit quietly and listen in class."

"Well, Landon, is that all he did?" she asked.

"Oh, no, Mom, he prayed for me and told me to pray to Jesus to help me. And Mom, do you know what? It worked, just like that! Jesus just did it, and I was still all afternoon!"

In a simple way, an innocent 5-year-old learned the greatest lesson: when you have a problem or a need, tell Jesus. And his family also learned a valuable lesson. When we turn to Jesus with our problems, exercise the trusting faith of a little child, He takes care of the need.

BARBARA SMITH MORRIS

Seeking the Lost

Father, I want those you have given me to be with me where I am. John 17:24, NIV.

IT'S NATURAL FOR ONE to want to be near someone he or she loves. As my husband and I grow older, we grow closer to each other. It's not un-usual, when we are apart a little while even in our home, for him to come looking for me to be sure I'm all right. This is love. It reminds me that God loves us and wants us with Him. In the beginning God came to walk with Adam and Eve in the garden (Gen. 3:8).

Later, when Moses wanted assurance that God would be with the chil-dren of Israel as they broke camp at Sinai and were planning to move on, the Lord said to Moses, "I won't leave you. I'll go with you and help you." Moses said, "But suppose we leave here and then along the way you decide not to go on with us, then it would be better for us to have stayed here. . . ." The Lord said, "I will go with you and stay with you. . . . I . . . know you love me" (Ex. 33:14-17, Clear Word).

In the beautiful story of Ruth and Naomi, Ruth said, "Don't ask me to leave you. I want to go wherever you go and live where you live. Your peo-ple will be my people and your God, my God" (Ruth 1:16, Clear Word).

And then Jesus, when He came, told His Father that He wants His chil-dren to be with Him where He is (John 17:24).

After my friend lost her husband, she got a beautiful little white dog named Nikky, who rarely lets her mistress out of her sight. If Nikky is left alone at home for even a short time, there's a joyous reunion with lots of yapping and "talking" upon my friend's return.

Jesus' promises of His return are precious to all Christians. One of the favorites is John 14:1-3: "Don't let your hearts be troubled. You believe in God, so trust me. In my Father's house there's plenty of room for everyone. If that weren't so, I would have told you. I'm going home to prepare a place for you. And if I go to prepare a place for you, you can be sure that I'll come back to take you home with me, so you can be with me forever" (Clear Word).

My daily prayer is that my loved ones, friends, and I so love the Lord that we may enjoy fellowship with Jesus in that home. That will truly be love.

RUBYE SUE

What Do You Think?

If anything is excellent or praiseworthy—think about such things.
Phil. 4:8, NIV.

IT'S GOING TO BE a complete, unmitigated disaster!" Melissa exclaimed emphatically.

"If that's what you believe, then that's what it'll be," I replied, trying to keep my face straight. As she grew, so did the length of the words she pulled from her dramatic vocabulary.

"Once upon a time there lived a very old woman who was known for her wisdom," I began. Melissa sat down. "It so happened that a mischievous little boy also lived in the small village," I continued the fable. "One day he decided it would be great fun to trick the wise old woman, so he caught a tiny sparrow. Cupping it in his hands so only the tail feathers could be seen, the boy took the captive bird to the wise old woman.

"I'll ask her if it's dead or alive, he said to himself. No matter what her answer, however, the boy planned that it would be wrong. If she said it was alive, he'd give a quick squeeze and show that the bird was dead. If he answered that it was dead, he'd open his hands and allow the bird to fly away.

" 'Is this sparrow alive or dead?' the boy demanded.

"Looking directly into the boy's eyes and not at his hands, the wise old woman answered, 'It's whatever you want it to be.' "

I watched Melissa's face. "I can see how the boy's thoughts could control the fate of the bird, but I can't control the whole play!"she protested.

"Of course not," I countered. "But you can control what you think."

"And how will that help?" she persisted.

"Thoughts precede actions or, as Emerson put it, 'the ancestor of every action is a thought.' If you think the play will be a success, your actions will help to move it in that direction. Or vice versa," I added.

"Can do!" Melissa said (just like that!) and moved toward the telephone.

A problem I was dealing with niggled into conscious awareness. With it came the swift realization: *I need to change my thoughts about it.* "Can do!" I said decisively.

What do you think?

ARLENE TAYLOR

Listen to What He Has to Say

And thine ears shall hear a word behind thee, saying, This is the way, walk ye in it, when ye turn to the right hand, and when ye turn to the left. Isa. 30:21.

ONE MORNING WHILE I was presenting my daily radio program, I received a telephone call that touched my life. A woman, Generosa, wanted to talk to me off the air. While some songs played, she explained what bothered her.

Her friend, a young mother, had cancer in an advanced stage. The previous day Generosa had visited her friend, who cried because when she passed away she'd leave her 6-year-old daughter an orphan. What most saddened Generosa was that the friend's minister, who was also present during the visit, affirmed that the young mother's illness was a divine punishment for sins, perhaps not confessed or not abandoned.

That night Generosa was not able to sleep. She had prayed, wept, and struggled with God for her friend. "Lord," Generosa said, "do not punish my friend. She's one of Your daughters, also. You know that she's a good person. She's helped the needy so much. Why, Lord? Why have You punished her with a terrible illness? Why can't You forgive her?"

After saying this, Generosa asked me if God could still forgive and cure her friend. Was this a punishment? I had the opportunity to give her beautiful and comforting Bible promises of the certainty of God's unconditional forgiveness and how He never treats us as we deserve.

Generosa asked me to quote the verses so that she could copy them and repeat these comforting promises of God to her sick friend.

Before hanging up the telephone, she stated, "Now I know why as I struggled with God this past night, it was as though I heard a suggestion to turn on the radio."

Have you ever felt you were being God's answer to someone? I felt I was on that day. Since then I've become more dependent on the Holy Spirit, allowing Him to direct me in each interview when I counsel with someone. Only God knows each individual's needs.

Help me, Lord, to hear Your voice so that I can be Your answer for those who come in contact with me today.

SÔNIA RIGOLI SANTOS

Cast Your Bread

Cast your bread upon the waters, for you will find it after many days. Eccl. 11:1, NKJV.

WRITE A CHECK AND give it to her."

The voice was loud and clear as I lay in bed, unable to go back to sleep.

"I don't think I have enough money to cover it, Lord. I'm low on funds and have so many needs."

"Write a check. You'll be helping her. She needs it even more than you do. Remember, she's been sick for months."

"OK, Lord. I'll do it tomorrow. Or what about next payday?"

"I want you to write it in the morning and give it to her. Don't wait for your next payday. Trust Me. If only you would trust Me."

This entire conversation took place at 2:00 Saturday morning. After agreeing to write the check, I fell asleep. When I awoke at 7:30, the conversation was still fresh in my mind. Had I been dreaming? No, it was real. However, I then heard a voice telling me to wait. I recognized that it was the voice of Satan. He wanted me to disobey by procrastinating.

"Get behind me, Satan. As a matter of fact, if you keep whispering in my ears not to, I will increase the amount. How about that?"

When I got to church, I wrote the check and placed it inside a card, sealed the envelope, and gave it to her. I felt peaceful inside, peaceful even though I had sacrificed the money I'd allocated for my transportation and lunch. Four days later I received a letter from my sister, Guenlyn, who was living in the Caribbean. When I opened the envelope I was shocked to find the exact amount of money I'd given away four days earlier. Was this a coincidence? This gift was totally unexpected. I was then reminded of the verse for today. It didn't take many days for my "bread" to return. I thank God I had chosen to obey His voice.

Today is a new day, Lord. Please help me to stay in tune with You. Help me to develop the habit of listening to Your voice and give me the strength to obey and follow Your leading. And Lord, please help me to be able to distinguish Your leading from Satan's temptations.

ANDREA BUSSUE

Threads of Friendship

For the Lord does not see as mortals see; they look on the outward appearance, but the Lord looks on the heart. 1 Sam. 16:7, NRSV.

THE START OF THE excavation season in Israel was rapidly approaching, and I was duplicating reports for dig supervisors when the copy machine quit. Sy, the dig director, tried in vain to fix it. The repairman was unavailable, and there were no copy centers in Jerusalem.

"We must be finished by tomorrow," said Sy, looking at me with concern. "Talk to the secretary at the ecole." Although the directors of the Ecole Biblique were interested in archaeology, Sy knew that the secretary, who met each visitor, was a formidable obstacle.

I remembered my first encounter with her. Armed with a letter of introduction, I had expected a welcome to the institution. Instead, she frowned at me. I received similar frowns as I entered the ecole during the fall and winter to do research. In fact, I jokingly talked to my husband about "the dragon lady" guarding the front desk.

But I also remembered a different sort of encounter in the spring. I was smiling after a profitable day of research. The secretary, in the intervals between checking researchers' credentials, was cross-stitching. I asked about the design she was creating.

"This," she said, "is one the women in my hometown have used for many years. But," she added, with a sparkle in her eyes, "I'm changing it just a little bit."

Emboldened by her enthusiasm, I mentioned that I'd been on a quest to find local embroidery patterns. An Arab shop owner had lent me a book of them; a woman had even urged me to borrow several of her cushions so I could copy the patterns for myself.

From that day on the secretary (no longer "the dragon lady") and I talked. We shared ideas about handiwork; we admired each other's embroidery; she copied a family pattern and gave it to me. We had even begun chatting about our families.

"I'll be happy to go to the ecole," I said to Sy, collecting the stack of papers and noticing the look of surprise—and relief—that spread over his face.

As I walked up to her desk, the secretary—my friend—dropped her embroidery and said, "What are you doing?" And with a smile she added, "How can I help?"

DENISE DICK HERR

Getting Ready to Serve

It is more blessed to give than to receive. Acts. 20:35, NIV.

ANOTHER YEAR HAD PASSED, and it was time for the annual collection of money to support the church's development and relief agency. Church members go to various businesses to ask for donations. This isn't easy. You become aware of your dependence on other people and on God. Humans don't like to be dependent. Each time it takes a lot of willpower for me to get started. Each year it's a special time of praying and asking for support from my colleagues at work.

When the big day came, there were no more excuses. The beginning was bad. One shop owner wasn't present; another one decided not to support the agency any longer. I prayed that God would influence the heart of the person I was going to meet next. A young man received me in a friendly way in his office. Without hesitating, he gave me some money. "You're always welcome," he added. "Come back next year."

Things were getting better. I then met a woman who I realized was discouraged, so I asked the Lord for His guidance. She opened her heart and told me that she had recently lost her mother and five other close people. She didn't know about her future or if she could keep her shop. Spontaneously, I hugged her. Before leaving, I was even able to tell her of the hope that we have in Jesus Christ, that He offers us a new life on the new earth. Despite her financial and emotional hardship, even she contributed something to the collection.

The last person I met was also very nice. I presented my request, and he got up from his chair to look for some money. When he realized that he didn't have any change, he decided to give me the banknote that he had. It was a generous amount of money. I could hardly believe it and thanked him profusely.

When I returned to my working place, I shared this news with my colleagues, who'd prayed for me, and we all praised God. I know that it will be difficult to start again next year; however, it wasn't the first time that I'd experienced God in such an extraordinary way. It's more blessed to give than to receive. Are you ready to serve God?

HEIKE EULITZ

Free at Last!

Weeping may endure for a night, but joy cometh in the morning. Ps. 30:5.

YOU MIGHT NOT TAKE me for a former jailbird, but when I was about 4 years old my grandfather was elected to a term as sheriff of our county. Our family lived in an apartment in the same building as the jail. Our town was fairly small back then, and much of the county was rural, so most of the prisoners were not the hardened criminals that could be found in big cities. I quickly became a favorite with them. I delighted in passing toast, hot rolls, or other goodies through the bars to them, thanks to the help of the cook.

Some prisoners were considered trustworthy enough to be allowed to work around the jail during the day, and that's how I got to know Frank. He'd carry me around on his shoulders, as he might have done if I'd been his child.

The day came when Frank completed his sentence and was released, but he didn't know that in his absence things had changed. Another family had moved in with his wife, and they didn't want him to come home. Finding the door locked, he attempted to break it down and was met by a shotgun blast that killed him instantly. As he was my special friend, Mother took me to the funeral and then to the poorly kept country cemetery where he was laid to rest. As an excuse for my tears, I said the briers were scratching my legs.

Perhaps it was this experience that has made me dislike attending funerals, even to this day. In fact, we used to say that I went to the weddings, and my husband went to the funerals. Now we go together to both—and I cry at both of them!

Someday soon Jesus will come as a bridegroom to claim His own. That will be the happy occasion—and it will be the end of the sad ones. After that there will be no gunshots, no funerals, no tears, no scratchy briers, no good-byes. The "goodies" won't have to be passed through jail bars, for all will be free and everyone will have access to all that heaven has to offer. What a day of rejoicing that will be! Free at last! Let's make our calling and election sure, that our tears may be dried when "joy cometh in the morning."

MARY JANE GRAVES

Teach Us to Number

Now the man Moses was very meek, above all the men which were upon the face of the earth. Num. 12:3.

THE OTHER DAY AT a Bible class my husband made a mistake in counting how many years had elapsed since 1982. He missed by 10 years, and I gave the correct answer to the class. He then said, "Even the math teacher makes mistakes!" One of the members of the class laughed out loud. (He was my husband's former student when he was in high school.)

As we grow older I discover not just the mistakes of my husband but my own mistakes, as well. I find it hard to recall names and appropriate words to use. We then have to rely on each other for help. Quite often my husband will ask, "What is his name?" Then I'll say, "First of all, who is he?" It probably sounds amusing. We have a great time as long as we exercise patience with each other.

Not long ago we both reached the "threescore and ten" milestone. We don't feel as if we've passed it, but when our memory fails, we realize we have. In Psalm 90:10 Moses wrote about this milestone. He said that one may reach fourscore by reason of strength. Probably because he was 80 and was called to deliver a nation of captives from their bondage.

Can you imagine what a challenge it must have been to face the angry Pharaoh? To get the release of the captives? To execute judgment? To brace against the murmuring multitudes in the harsh desert? To exercise faith to perform miracles, to urge them to enter Canaan by faith?

Weary and exhausted at the age of sixscore, his patience ran out. We can't blame him. Doing all that hard work at that age, one man against an obstinate and ungrateful multitude, and without any pay at that. With that one sin, Moses missed out on Canaan. But God had a better plan for him. Satan was there, too, to condemn him, but the Lord was there to rebuke Satan (Jude 9). Psalm 90:12 says, "So teach us to number our days, that we may apply our hearts unto wisdom." And Jesus has said, "Blessed are the meek: for they shall inherit the earth" (Matt. 5:5).

O that we pray daily, *Lord, teach us to be patient and meek and prepare us to enter the heavenly Canaan.*   BIRDIE PODDAR

Lesson From the Cruise

Wait for the Lord, and keep to his way, and he will exalt you to inherit the land. Ps. 37:34, NRSV.

LAST DECEMBER MY HUSBAND and I fulfilled our dream of cruising through the Panama Canal. The closer we came to Panama, the more excited we passengers became. We were ecstatic when the ship's captain announced that we would begin the nine-hour trip through the Panama Canal at 9:00 the next morning.

We, along with scores of other passengers, arrived on the ship's upper front deck before 6:00 the next morning with our water bottles and snacks in hand. All the deck chairs were already occupied, but we were able to improvise the deck's plastic tables into front-row "seats." By the time our ship passed under the Bridge of the Americas and the canal came into view, passengers were sitting and standing in rows four to six deep. Everyone was enjoying the friendly closeness, moving so that others could see and snap pictures, and watching the harbor tugboats.

Suddenly a latecomer ran up behind the crowd. "Move over and let me in," she loudly demanded. "I've paid for this cruise, and I deserve to be on the front row as much as any of you!"

Instantly the dynamics of the friendly crowd changed. A low murmur of disapproval arose. Many, like me, ignored her. When she realized that verbal abuse wasn't going to win the coveted front-row seat, she resorted to physical abuse. She began pushing past a man, his wife, and adult children, stepping on toes and elbowing backs and sides. This was too much—the man commanded his family to stand up and block the woman's entire view. At that, unrepeatable words were exchanged, ending when the woman stomped away in great anger.

My husband and I looked at each other, and each had the same thought: *This is how it will be when Jesus comes.* There will be those who have prepared and waited expectantly and those who failed to prepare, believing they had plenty of time before the event and, if not, confident they could join the waiting crowd at the last minute.

Speaking of Jesus' coming, the Bible warns us in Matthew 8:12 that "there shall be weeping and gnashing of teeth." May this not be you or me. May His coming find us eagerly waiting in a front-row seat!   ELLIE GREEN

Empty Petrol Tank

But my God shall supply all your need according to his riches in glory by Christ Jesus. Phil. 4:19.

THE FIRST POLITICAL COUP in Fiji occurred while my husband and I were in Suva, doing business for Fulton College, where he was the principal and I was a lecturer. We knew that Fiji would never be the same again, although life on our campus continued much the same as before, with students from 13 countries living, studying, and worshiping together.

When a special Bible conference convened, we were invited to participate, so we happily packed the car and set out in time to reach the venue located up the beautiful Sigatoka Valley. What a blessed experience it was to meet with God's people and share their enthusiasm and dedication to our Lord. The singing was fervent, and the messages from the Word stirring.

On Saturday evening, when someone turned on the radio, our peace was shattered with news of a second coup and that there was to be no commerce on Sunday.

As Allan and I talked and prayed about the situation, we felt impressed to leave early on Sunday morning to return to Fulton College and give some leadership to the faculty and students. But we had a real problem. Our trip to the Bible conference had used up nearly all of our fuel. Under normal circumstances this wouldn't have been a problem, as there was a trade store not far away where we could purchase petrol for our return trip.

As we prayed and set off, Allan decided to go to the back of the little bush trade store to see if he could buy some fuel. The man came furtively to speak with him and sold him about a gallon of petrol in bottles. It was so little; we had so far to go. But we set off, praying all the way, and didn't stop at any point on the road. No one stopped us. Military police seemed to be off the main road the whole way, and the fuel kept our motor going and going and going until we drove into our garage at Fulton College.

Everyone was so surprised and glad to have us back. We wondered again at God's gracious provision for us by making that small amount of petrol last, like the oil and flour in the story of Elijah and the widow and her son.

Our God was the God of miracles that day, and we humbly knelt to praise His name.

URSULA M. HEDGES

Without Fear

Fear thou not; for I am with thee: be not dismayed; for I am thy God: I will strengthen thee; yea, I will help thee; yea, I will uphold thee with the right hand of my righteousness. Isa. 41:10.

AFTER TWO MINOR SURGICAL procedures, two cesareans, and surgery on an ovary, I'd promised myself that I'd never have another surgery. But now I sat with the results of an ultrasound examination in my hand and the doctor telling me that I had a cyst eight centimeters in diameter that needed to be removed. I confess that I surprised myself as I agreed to surgery. I was sad but resigned.

After the necessary preparations, I entered the hospital, filling my mind with thoughts of gratitude. God gave me a good hospital, a good room, a doctor who was a friend, and my mother to stay with my children. Above all, God had been with me through the other surgeries, and I knew He would be with me in this one also. That night in the hospital all was calm. Early in the morning I consecrated myself to God, and it wasn't long before they took me to the operating room.

I don't know why, but at one time everyone left the operating room, one by one, and I was left alone. It wasn't cold, but my body trembled. I couldn't stop. I even felt pain trying to make my body relax. It was useless. I was more tense than I'd ever been before. I prayed in the solitude. Then I remembered numerous promises of comfort and put myself in His hands—not only myself, but also the doctors. I asked Him to be the Great Physician.

The anesthesia was local, but I was also given a sedative. When I woke up, the doctor was by my side. He told me that at the end of the surgery I'd had a hemorrhage that had greatly concerned him. Now, however, everything was under control. I was immensely grateful to God!

As I remember this episode, I think about how many times in our lives Christ is just waiting for our call so He can give us peace and take fear from us and sustain us.

Many times we remain alone, attempting by ourselves to make our bodies stop trembling, seeking peace on our own. Then I remember the great peace and assurance He gave me on that day, and I'm grateful to Him for such great love, for such a great gift. REGINA MARY SILVEIRA NUNES

God's Promises

For you shall not go out with haste, Nor go by flight; For the Lord will go before you, And the God of Israel will be your rear guard. Isa. 52:12, NKJV.

ONE THING THAT I learned when I accepted God as my Savior was to claim His promises through His Holy Word. Whenever I need guidance, or when I am in distress and need to be comforted, I sincerely pray and ask God to lead me into His Word of inspiration. Always, He answers my prayers.

For the nine years of my stay in South Africa I feared one thing—the nonrenewal of my work permit. Every year it was mandatory that I apply for the extension of my work permit, and every year I'd go through the tension of waiting for its approval. During the past two years the procedure had gotten so tough that there was a real possibility of its nonrenewal. I was so afraid I'd be told to pack my bags and leave the country in a week's time or so. This had been done to other foreigners. I felt so insecure.

Then a friend came to visit me. "Minerva," she said, "I know you're feeling really nervous and apprehensive. I have just the text for you!" And then she shared Isaiah 52:12 with me. In fact, she read it aloud: "'For you shall not go out with haste, nor go by flight; for the Lord will go before you, and the God of Israel will be your rear guard.'" That was exactly what I wanted to hear, an assurance that God would not let me "go out with haste, nor go by flight." I would have time, even if I didn't get an extension.

God was true to His promise. He gave me ample time to prepare for my departure. Though my work was terminated on March 1, 2001, I had three months to do some volunteer work at the college as I prepared for my trip home. I didn't leave South Africa in haste, but in peace and quiet.

As the plane took off, I saw my friends watching and waving goodbye. The flight home wasn't only safe but also peaceful, because God was before me and He was my rear guard. He had kept His promise.

MINERVA M. ALINAYA

The Vase of Flowers

I will be like the dew to Israel; he will blossom like a lily. Like a cedar of Lebanon he will send down his roots. Hosea 14:5, NIV.

THE STORY IS TOLD of a porcelain vase that always complained because it lived alone, empty, and without vitality. The vase said that it would like to be useful, that it would like for someone to plant a flower inside of it so that it could show all the beauty that flowers have.

One day, surprisingly, the opportunity came. Someone approached the vase and attempted to plant a rosebush. The stem had a beautiful rose on it. In spite of the good proposal, the vase protested vehemently, "I'll not allow them to put dirt inside of me." In an argumentative manner it continued, "If they want to make me useful, they should use water instead of dirt."

"With only water, my existence will be much shorter," objected the beautiful flower. "If you allow them to put dirt inside you, I'll have a long life. You'll be noticed and will no longer live alone. Everyone will see that we're united, that we can live for each other."

"But I can continue living alone, without the necessity of swallowing dirt," retorted the vase. And then it added, "In fact, I've even grown accustomed to living alone."

"Well, since you don't want me to live with you, there's nothing I can do. Perhaps I can find support from another. However, I advise you to be more careful, because one day you could turn into something that just gathers dust or holds dead things."

"You know, you are almost convincing me!" exclaimed the vase.

"Great! It's only this way that my existence will be extended!" exclaimed the dear rose, giving off an excellent perfume.

So the next day, in the indoor garden of a beautiful home, there was the lovely couple—the former single porcelain vase and the beautiful flower. And everyone who looked at them was amazed so see such beauty together. Finally, the vase understood that to be happy it's necessary to make others happy.

We, too, can be vases of blessings in the lives of many people when we allow God to use us. Together we can help others to develop their faith by bringing Jesus into their lives. RAQUEL COSTA ARRAIS

Handicapped, but Not in Spirit

I have great confidence in you; I take great pride in you. I am greatly encouraged; in all our troubles my joy knows no bounds. 2 Cor.7:4, NIV.

IT WAS OUR FIRST camping experience. When we arrived at the park where we had planned to pitch our tents, all campsites were taken, and we weren't allowed inside the gates. Some friends nearby kindly allowed us to camp on their lawn. These friends were four senior citizens, two brothers and two sisters. They had raised their own families, had lost their spouses, and had now returned to the family homestead to live together again, as when they were children.

One sister, Mary Lou, was so tortured by arthritis that she was helpless and couldn't get out of bed. Her siblings kindly cared for her needs. We felt sorry for her, completely confined to her room day after day, and thought we should visit her and cheer her up. So before we left, we visited her room, expecting to see a decrepit old woman, looking very much in pain and filled with sadness and gloom.

What was our surprise when she greeted us with great cheer and enthusiasm and appreciation for our visit. She had no words of complaint or discouragement. She explained that her church was going to build a new structure, and she was raising money for the project. Would we be interested in buying some pencils from her to help raise money? Of course we would! And we gave her much more than the pencils were worth. We were the ones who were encouraged and uplifted by the visit. True, she was disadvantaged in body, but not in spirit.

There are many stories of people who have accomplished great things, not letting a disability prevent them from reaching high goals. One example is the artists with paraplegia who paint by holding a paintbrush in their mouths.

Jenny didn't allow old age to dampen her positive spirit. When she became so helpless that she had to move into a nursing home, she looked around the lobby at the worn-out people, and said, "Well, another new adventure!" She began teaching them the gospel, and soon several people accepted the love of God, which gives us joy that knows no bounds.

Even if we have personal disabilities or troubles, our joy—our spirit—may also know no bounds.

RUTH WATSON

Happy Hobby

Do not withhold good from those who deserve it, when it is in your power to act. Prov. 3:27, NIV.

L ET ME TELL YOU about my hobby. It's not knitting, scrapbooking, or quilting (though I enjoy some of these). Mine is a hobby without any tangible objects to arrange or make. Better yet, it costs no money. This hobby is done anytime, anyplace, anywhere—well, anywhere people are present and qualify.

Qualify? Yes, I search for people who qualify, because my hobby is handing out compliments. Not quick, frivolous ones, but genuine, heartfelt, kind words. That's not a hobby, you say? Why not? Isn't a hobby something you enjoy doing, something that gives you a satisfied feeling? Isn't it fun to involve other people in your hobby? I think so!

Once as I pushed my grocery cart past a woman I said in a loud whisper, "Your outfit is very nice."

She turned around and said, "Really?" Then she proceeded to tell me how she had retrieved it from the back of her closet and almost didn't wear it because she felt it was too worn. When I assured her it still looked quite nice to me, she beamed. Both our spirits were lifted—she was affirmed, and my feelings soared because I had encouraged her.

My hobby reversed itself one day in a care center. On my way down the hall a woman in a wheelchair said to me, "Don't you look cute today!" She must have been partially blind, but I enjoyed her comment and told her so. I thought, *It does something wonderful to my soul to get a compliment. Others must like it, too.*

It takes so little to add a positive spark to the lives of others. If people deserve a good comment, it's our duty to tell them. Doing so serves a dual purpose: it invokes an uplifting moment for both giver and receiver. Even a pat on the head or a smile at a baby or small child with "What a sweet baby you are!" buoys a young mother's day.

Now I'm trying to come up with another hobby that's as much fun and as economical as passing out compliments. But I'll still keep this one. I plan to do it for life!

MARYBETH GESSELE

Vital and Green in My Old Age

But the godly will flourish like palm trees and grow strong like the cedars of Lebanon. Even in old age they will still produce fruit; they will remain vital and green. Ps. 92:12-14, NLT.

I COULDN'T BELIEVE HOW that tomato plant grew and grew and grew. I'd planted it, thinking it would occupy a small corner of my herb garden. However, just after the tomatoes began to grow, we left for a month. A couple weeks later my sister-in-law announced that she was enjoying the tiny tomatoes but that the plant had outgrown its wire cage. When we got back I could see what she meant! I constructed a stronger cage, but the tomato plant soon outgrew that support, too.

As the vine extended, I devised ways to keep it from smothering the herbs and invading the lawn. Finally, in late September, there was a lull in its growth. The bowlfuls of tomatoes dwindled to mere handfuls. Obviously, the tomato plant's bearing days were coming to an end. I began to think of ways to use that spot of garden.

And then a new surge of green leaves and tiny yellow flowers made my tomato vine look fresh and promising. *Maybe I should give it a few more weeks,* I thought.

As days grew shorter and nights colder, I realized that those flowers wouldn't make tomatoes this year. One bright November day I got out the shovel and started my demolition. I felt sorry for the plant, but the vine was past its prime, so I dug it up. It was still producing, only not as much as before. It was doing what it could with the best of its strength, yet I uprooted it.

After a year of retirement, I compared myself to that vine. Useful? Yes. Productive? Not too much. Destined for the shovel? *Oh, no!*

Evidently David had similar feelings. In Psalm 71:9 he pleaded, "In my old age, don't set me aside" (NLT). After contemplating God's power and goodness in the next few verses, he made a request: "Let me proclaim your power to this new generation, your mighty miracles to all who come after me" (verse 18, NLT). Now, that's something useful for me to do! After years of experience, certainly I have something to say about God's loving care and guidance in my life.

Thank You, Lord, for not treating me as I did the tomato vine! Thank You for giving me something fruitful to do in my senior years!

NANCY JEAN VYHMEISTER

Be Strong

Be strong and courageous. Do not be terrified; do not be discouraged, for the Lord your God will be with you wherever you go. Joshua 1:9, NIV.

THIS IS ONE OF my favorite Bible texts. It came alive for me through an experience I had on my way home. Something had happened that had hurt me deeply, but I wasn't able to express my pain. Not even to my best friend. And so I prayed, "Dear God, You know how I'm hurting. I feel so alone; I'm not able to talk to anybody. Please help me! Show me that You are here. Please let there be a letter in my mailbox so I can feel that You are with me!"

When I got home, the mailbox contained only one large brown envelope—no letter. I was desperate. Hadn't God understood that I needed it this moment? Maybe He had let go of me and didn't want to bother with me anymore. Many vicious thoughts flashed through my mind. In my apartment I threw the envelope on a chair and wallowed in my grief.

When I finally opened the envelope, I discovered it was mail from a good friend who leads a women's Bible breakfast group and regularly sends me material she uses. Among other things in the envelope was a beautiful table card with the text from Joshua 1:9.

Can you imagine how this text helped me in that moment? The situation was still the same, but the Bible verse had become a special message for me. I became calm, fell on my knees, and thanked my heavenly Father. He had seen to it that this letter was sent at the right time, with the right Bible text in it, because He knew that I needed it right then.

Joshua was in a difficult situation himself. Moses had died, and God had chosen Joshua to lead the Israelites to Canaan. No easy job! He must have been afraid, too. Maybe he didn't trust in his abilities. The people were difficult to lead. Again and again they chose their own paths, although they should have known that God would lead them if they'd let Him. Joshua knew that God expects us to do a good job, but He also will help solve our problems. God keeps offering possibilities and shows us what we can do, just as He spoke to Joshua.

I thank God for His words: "Do not be afraid; I am with you in everything you will do." Won't you trust in Him today? It's worth it!

CHRISTEL SCHNEIDER

Disaster Plan

So do not fear, for I am with you; do not be dismayed, for I am your God. I will strengthen you and help you; I will uphold you with my righteous right hand. Isa. 41:10, NIV.

BECAUSE OF THE TERRORIST attacks in the United States, many people there have become paranoid with fear. In the area where I live we've recently been given elaborate disaster plans for any sort of disaster. And they are being taken very seriously!

These plans call for carefully planning an escape for a family, detailing evacuation steps to take, supply kits to have ready at all times, lists of what to take along, travel routes to go on, how to arrange for the disabled and pets, first-aid directions, emergency rescue shelters, and community centers. I'm sure every area of the country has some variation of this plan.

I thought of the first item I would put on my supply kit list for a disaster plan of escape: my Bible, God's Holy Word. It is full of good promises for survival in almost any situation. I've marked many verses that offer comforting words for times of fear and frustration. That's my disaster plan—not to be afraid. Besides taking all the commonsense precautions and supplies, I will cling to God's promises of assurance that He will be with me in whatever happens.

Isaiah 43, the Psalms, and many other scriptures are comforting promises in times like these. I take with me each day the promise in Philippians 4:6, 7: "Do not be anxious about anything, but in everything, by prayer and petition, with thanksgiving, present your requests to God. And the peace of God, which transcends all understanding, will guard your hearts and minds in Christ Jesus" (NIV).

Ellen White promises, "God's people are not to fear. Satan cannot go beyond his limit. The Lord will be the defense of His people. He regards the injury done to His servants for the truth's sake as done to Himself. When the last decision has been made, when all have taken sides, . . . God will arise in His power and. . . . Every opposing power will receive its punishment" (*Maranatha*, p. 191).

Dear Lord, it is with thanksgiving for the power in Your promises that I come before You today to claim Your promises of deliverance from fear of disasters by trusting in Your care.

BESSIE SIEMENS LOBSIEN

Ask and Ye Shall Receive

Give, and it shall be given unto you; good measure, pressed down, and shaken together, and running over. Luke 6:38.

ONE MORNING I JOINED my friends at our regular women's prayer group. The ladies were requesting prayer for special needs. The Holy Spirit impressed me to request prayer for a video player that I needed badly. I said I'd like a four-headed model, if possible. A good used one would do.

A sweet 80-year-old friend objected. "No, ask for a new one!"

So as we knelt for prayer the ladies prayed for a new four-headed VCR for me.

When the prayer session was over, we sat around talking. One of the ladies mentioned that she'd like to go to a graduation but her car was being repaired, and her husband wouldn't be able to get his check cashed to pay for the repairs until after the weekend. I felt impressed to lend her the money so she could go.

Then my elderly friend asked for a ride home. Once there, she asked me to come in and told me to sit down. She disappeared into the other room and returned with a box in her hand. "Here's something you may be able to make use of, if you want it," she said, handing me a new VCR.

When I had recovered from a moment of shock, I thanked her for the wonderful present. She held up her hand. "Don't thank me; thank the good Lord."

The VCR had been given to her some time before, and she had asked the Lord what she should do with it, as she already had one. The Lord impressed her to hang on to it, as there would come an opportunity to give it where it could be best used.

When we give ourselves, unreserved, we receive in return showers of blessings, pressed down and running over. You may say, "Oh, that was just a coincidence that the right person was in the group who just happened to have a VCR." But I know that my Lord impressed her long before that I'd be needing one. The Lord is still in control. He is waiting to help in all aspects of our lives, if we will only ask—even for material things.

VIDELLA McCLELLAN

Feed the Hungry

I was hungry and you gave me something to eat. Matt. 25:35, NIV.

IT WAS IN THE early 1970s. I was sweeping the front yard when a man entered through the gate and walked up to me. "Good morning, Mama."

"Good morning," I replied, not even looking at him.

"Could you give me a piece of bread?"

Still continuing with my sweeping, I replied, "I have none." The man left, and I still continued sweeping. I didn't know it, but my father had overheard the conversation. He stepped out on the veranda and asked what the man had wanted. "Bread," I replied.

My father asked me in a soft tone, "What would you have done if the man had dropped dead just outside the gate because of hunger?"

My conscience pricked me; guilt and fear took hold of my soul as I asked myself what I really would have done. I dropped the broom and rushed to the gate to call him back, but he was gone. I stood for a moment, hoping I could see him walk out in the neighborhood, but all was in vain. I lived with my haunting guilt, praying so hard that the Lord would bring some hungry person, but as time went by I only hurt the more.

One day as I was sweeping the veranda another man walked in through the gate. "Good morning, Mama. I have not eaten for the past two days." Without hesitating, I dropped the broom, went into the kitchen, cut some bread, filled a large glass with milk, and gave them to him.

As I watched him eating I became afraid that he might choke, he was so hungry. "Thank you, Mama; you have saved me," he said, and left. I ran to the gate to see which direction he took, but he was nowhere to be seen.

There are many souls in the world who are hungering and thirsting for God's Word, as well as bread for the stomach, and we have sometimes turned them back when they were at our doorstep.

Thank You, Jesus, for teaching me this never-to-be-forgotten lesson.

ETHEL DORIS MSUSENI

In the Hands of Jesus

Let him have all your worries and cares, for he is always thinking about you and watching everything that concerns you. 1 Peter 5:7, TLB.

IT WAS ONE OF THOSE mornings. You know the kind. You wake up in the morning and start your day, thinking all is going well. Then, bam! Out of nowhere the devil starts trouble, and you fall right into the mix before you have time to think. You have one of those disagreements with your beloved, the man the Lord gave you to love and honor and cherish. It doesn't take much fuel to keep a small fire burning, and hurtful words are spoken hastily and without much thought. We parted with an unresolved disagreement looming over our day.

I felt utter and complete defeat. I melted into tears and sat down on the couch. As I considered the long day I would have until my husband returned home, Emily, our 5-year-old daughter, crawled up on the couch to sit beside me. "Mommy, why are you crying?"

At that moment I realized how painful this unresolved issue was. I desired so much to have the time needed to resolve what was such a silly disagreement and move on to the activities of the day.

I paused a moment to see how I could put into words what had just occurred between her father and me. "Honey, your daddy and I had a small disagreement, and we didn't have time to work it out before he had to leave for work. I just don't know what to do."

Without missing a beat, she said to me, in that sweet little-girl voice, "Mommy, the only thing to do when we don't know what to do is to put it in the hands of Jesus."

I was amazed at the calm and confident manner of this small child. We bowed our heads as my little Emily prayed that Jesus would help her mommy and daddy work out their troubles. When she finished praying, the same calm, sweet spirit I'd seen in her filled me, and I too felt calm and confident in the Jesus she so lovingly believed in.   CATHY L. SANCHEZ

A Ray of Sunshine

A happy heart makes the face cheerful. Proverbs 15:13, NIV.

OUR LUNCHTIME FLIGHT was canceled, and we were rescheduled for early evening. It had been a long day, and when it was announced that there would be a further delay our hearts sank. All the passengers looked tired, dispirited, and miserable, and few were talking. When a young mother walked into the airport lounge, pushing her child in a stroller, her extremely short skirt and low-cut blouse caused something of a diversion. As she struggled to fold the stroller after taking her daughter out of it, we all sat in silence and watched, too immersed in our own misery to think of helping.

The child, about a year old, had obviously just learned to walk. For a while she played with a rag doll, but when she tired of it her mother gave her a ball. At first the baby walked around with it, but then she started rolling it along the floor, where it came to rest at the feet of a tall, distinguished gentleman who was reading his paper. The little girl toddled after it, looked at the ball, and then at the man. A delighted grin spread across her face, and she gave a little giggle. Looking down, the man allowed a faint smile to cross his face before returning to his reading.

Next, she rolled the ball to the feet of a girl, giving an infectious giggle as she lurched after it. The girl smiled tentatively, and so did the lady next to her. The next target was a young man. He grinned as he gently kicked the ball back to the tiny feet. Before long we were all watching to see where she would go next, and it wasn't too long before a game of "football" had developed. Those who weren't kicking the ball looked on indulgently at those who were, and as the child's smiles and little squeals of delight filled the room, the passengers began to talk to her and about her.

It seemed no time at all until the flight was called, and our broad smiles as we boarded the plane owed more to a child than to the anticipation of the flight. Her mother didn't lack helpers this time! Smiles are infectious. Make some happy hearts and cheerful faces by giving some of yours away today.

AUDREY BALDERSTONE

The Other Side of Through

The Lord watches over the righteous, and He listens to their cries. Ps. 34:15, Clear Word.

IT WAS THANKSGIVING morning, and as I opened my eyes to greet the day the tears began to run uncontrollably down my ebony cheeks. I continued weeping as if my heart were breaking. As I tossed and turned in my bed, the phone rang. I quickly dried my tears, held my breath to gain composure, and in a naturally optimistic voice said, "Happy Thanksgiving!" The caller didn't detect my depression, but there I lay under sheets that felt like iron bars, holding me down. I was a prisoner of my emotions, and I felt utterly alone.

More calls came in, and finally someone sensed something different in my voice, and with that validation my tears were released more freely. The caller prayed with me and encouraged me not to cancel dinner plans with family and friends in Huntsville. She said I didn't need to be alone.

It was almost noon when I finally gained enough strength and courage to remove those heavy sheets. The face that looked back at me from the mirror had bloodshot and swollen eyes, quivering lips, and furrowed brows, all testifying to my deep sadness. Then I stepped into the shower, and something within me began to sing again, and as the warm water cleansed my body, the music inside of me cleansed my soul. I opened the blinds, and the sun shone brightly through my windows. I looked out into the fall sky and asked God to be with me and to show me in a dramatic way that I wasn't alone and that He would get me through this emotional storm.

Almost forgetting my request, I grabbed my bags and began the dreaded drive to Huntsville. Because my radio/cassette player wasn't working, it was going to be a much too long and too quiet trip. As I started the car, with almost absentminded faith I turned the radio on. Immediately, music filled the car! I was startled but overjoyed, because in that moment my car was filled with God's presence. Then the music ended as quickly as it had begun.

As I drove, it was now with tears of joy. It's been four months since that morning, and my radio hasn't worked since, but the memory of God's intervention rings loud and clear. God will get you through any storm. I know, because now there's a smile on my face, peace in my heart, and a stronger faith on the other side of "through."

TERRIE RUFF

337

Love Notes

His banner over me was love. S. of Sol. 2:4.

MY 5-YEAR-OLD granddaughter came for Thanksgiving dinner two years ago. As the rest of us got busy with the preparation for the meal, she retired to my study. Dinner was wonderful. My daughter-in-law's dishes were delicious.

It was only after little Briana left with her family that evening that I noticed something heartwarmingly special. She had printed a three-word line on several pages of a Post-It Notes pad and pasted them on walls all over the house. Her words "I love you" declared her affection for me everywhere. I saw it on my desk. I noticed it on the refrigerator. I glimpsed it in her scribble by the telephones.

Her words reminded me that God's love is written everywhere in our world. We see it in the beauty of creation—from the pristine beauty of the golden sunrise to the awesome glory of a coral sunset. We feel it in the delicate breezes. I sense it in the tangy aroma of the orange blossoms. We taste it in the crispy crunch of a just-pulled carrot. I hear it in the gentle cooing of the doves each morning.

Briana's notes also reminded me of the tiny box of Scripture message cards that my secret pal had once given me. Those words continually assure me of God's love and His promises to care. He will protect and guide us, if we will let Him.

My favorite writer tells us, "Everything speaks and acts the will of the Creator. Cloud and sunshine, dew and rain, wind and storm, all are under the supervision of God, and yield implicit obedience to His command.... And can it be that [woman], made in the image of God, endowed with reason and speech, shall alone be unappreciative of His gifts and disobedient to His will?" (*Christ's Object Lessons,* pp. 81, 82).

I can't help appreciating His blessings! But I know we have to keep our eyes and minds open for His love notes. We mustn't let them go unread and unheeded. I plan to share some of God's Post-It-Notes—messages of His love to us—with at least one person I meet today. That might be His only note that she reads. Won't you join me?

CAROL JOY GREENE

Always Grateful

In every thing give thanks: for this is the will of God in Christ Jesus concerning you. 1 Thess. 5:18.

EVERY TUESDAY BEFORE going to the radio station to present my nightly program, I passed Terezinha's house. She was a middle-aged woman with quadriplegia who had lain in bed for almost 40 years; she looked like a porcelain doll. Recently she also had been diagnosed with breast cancer.

On one of my visits she told me she wasn't well. The skin all over her body was irritated, and she had an allergic rash. I sought out a dermatologist who visited and prescribed medication. On my following visit, her despair was visible. How could she find relief for the itching if she couldn't move? I felt unable to help her because her skin was thin, delicate, and sensitive from being in bed for so many years. Her skin could not be rubbed. The only thing to be done was to pray for her, asking God to speed up her cure, and that the medication would soon be effective.

As I was leaving, she made a request. Would it be possible on the following Saturday to hold a worship of thanksgiving in her home? She noticed my surprise. "Sônia, I want to thank God for my rash, for my pain. In reality, I want to thank God because He has given me life these 39 years. I want to invite my relatives who don't know Jesus to come to this worship so that they can also get to know Him and can learn to love Him."

The worship was held. As she had wished, almost all of the relatives and friends she had invited attended. A short time later she passed away, and I again saw all of those people at her funeral.

I had never held a worship of thanksgiving to God! I had never thanked Him when I was sick. How could she do this?

How could Paul, the author of today's verse, thank God, even after being cruelly whipped and handcuffed in an uncomfortable position in a cold, dark prison in the city of Philippi (Acts 16)? Like the apostle Paul, Terezinha walked so intimately with Jesus that she never felt alone. Even in the pain and suffering that life reserved for her, she could see Him, feel Him, and touch Him.

Help me today, Lord, to walk as closely with You as did Paul and Terezinha, so that my life can always be a hymn of gratitude and praise!

SÔNIA RIGOLI SANTOS

A Frozen Garden

Therefore I take pleasure in infirmities, in reproaches, in needs, in persecutions, in distresses, for Christ's sake. For when I am weak, then I am strong. 2 Cor. 12:10, NKJV.

I LOOK OUT MY WINDOW into the backyard and see the remnants of a garden that recently boasted masses of beautiful flowers. The autumn frosts have accomplished their task and killed the tender plants. Yet even after temperatures in the teens and 20s, the roses cling to some of their leaves; the chives maintain their green, and the grass continues to grow. The calendulas seem to send out new growth in defiance of the cold during these last nights of November.

I wonder how some plants have found the ability to stay bright and green through the nights of falling temperatures, while all around the landscape is displaying the ravages of cold fall weather. A few diehards exhibit unusual stamina and respond to the warmth of daytime sunshine.

These hardy plants give me courage. I may experience cold and frosty greetings from those I have thought of as friends. Others may falsely accuse me of various things of which I have no knowledge. Some may even tell me they are able to correctly interpret the recesses of my mind by reading my "body language," thereby ascribing to me thoughts the like of which I haven't even imagined. I know that the blanket of God's love will protect me from these assaults and keep me strong and growing through the difficult times.

Even though the outward atmosphere isn't always comfortable, I can grow in the warmth and love I feel in my innermost soul. This is that which comes from the One who loves me supremely, the One who was willing to die for me, a sinner. He carries me through the times when there's an absence of earthly friends to encircle me and help me on my journey.

When the sun shines on my soul and all seems well, He is there too. He sends friends and family to bring the brightness back into my life. Then, like my garden, I can flourish and grow strong and reflect His love to all.

Father, I ask You to help me be more trusting in Your goodness and less dependent upon the affirmation of fellow humans. They may fail me, but I have the assurance You are always there to make me strong and help me over the humps that impede my pathway.

EVELYN GLASS

Help at the Right Time

For he shall give his angels charge over thee, to keep thee in all thy ways.
Ps. 91:11.

THAT MORNING I DIDN'T want to go to work, and my body did not want to get out of bed. My daughter cried because she didn't want to go to day care. Something wasn't right.

It had been two months since I had decided to sell natural medications to supplement the family income. A dear friend had asked me to go out with her for a time to see if I could sell the products. I agreed. Three of us women traveled to nearby towns, and it seemed that I had a certain talent for that type of work. The only problem was that I didn't like to ride in a car. One day the car slid and almost threw us down an embankment. We felt the hand of the Lord protecting us from a fatal fall. Then, once again we were on the highway.

But this particular morning was different. I really didn't want to go to work. After talking to the Lord about my day, though, I went. We sold products in one town, delivered products in another, and decided to work one more town that day. We were already tired as Marinalva got behind the steering wheel, and we were off once again.

As we chugged up a small dirt hill, we could see the town at the end of the dirt road. Suddenly the car zigzagged on a small slope, and the tires skidded in the sand. I don't know how Marinalva lost control of the car, but suddenly we, and the trunkful of boxes of medications, were bouncing down a ravine. Only seconds elapsed, but it seemed like hours.

We finally got the door open and saw a car stop near us. Three men jumped from their car and offered to help us. They pulled the car from the ravine and calmed us down. Then they fixed our car so that we could be on our way again. When we checked, not one bottle of medicine had broken, thanks to the unfailing care of our Creator.

When the men said goodbye and left, the other woman with us commented, "It is possible that those men were angels."

If those men were angels or not, we don't know. But at that moment it is as though they were. Once again the Lord God had kept His promise; He deserves our praise each day.   AURÍSIA SILVA BRITO RODRIGUES

East to West

Great is our Lord, and abundant in power; his understanding is beyond measure. Ps. 147:5, RSV.

IT WAS GOING TO be one of our long drives from the East Coast to the West Coast. We were excited; it was to be a family trip, just the four of us. We needed this time together because my husband and I had been too busy lately in our work, and the girls needed help with their schoolwork.

All the preparations were completed, and the car was neatly packed with our stuff. We had planned to drive at least 12 hours each day, so with prayers, we started our journey on a beautiful day. As we traveled Route 80, we enjoyed the lush green trees and hills all dressed with beautiful wildflowers. The music played, and the girls giggled and sang at the top of their voices.

Suddenly my husband frantically called out, "There's no power! I'm stepping on the gas, but it doesn't work! What shall we do?"

I could hear the urgency and fear in his voice. "Take the next exit," I suggested. "We have to have this car checked."

"Oh, this will cost us a lot of money," my husband kept saying, worrying about our finances and all the time we were going to lose.

"There's the exit—you just missed it!" I called out. "You were worrying so much that you missed the exit. I hope we don't get stranded on this highway," I fussed.

By this time the car was going slower and slower. "Pray, everybody, pray," I said. Everyone was silent for a moment. While my husband kept driving, the three of us closed our eyes and prayed. Our prayers were interrupted by my husband's excited voice: "It's working again; it's working! Your prayers were answered."

Instantly the Lord had answered our prayers. We still don't know what happened to the car, but we never had any further problem throughout our journey.

When we pray, we get recharged. We get power from the Lord to face whatever comes our way. As we go through the challenges of the day, let's start it with the power capsule—prayer. With God at our side, we'll always be on the winning team.

JEMIMA D. ORILLOSA

Transforming Power

Therefore, if anyone is in Christ, he is a new creation; old things have passed away; behold, all things have become new. 2 Cor. 5:17, NKJV.

IT WAS LATE NOVEMBER, and my family and I were driving from New Hampshire to Kentucky. The bare landscape looked stark under an overcast sky, reminding me of my own life. I had made a commitment to follow Christ about four years before, and even though I was so determined to honor the promise I had made, I still felt far away from my goal. I was tempted to believe that it was beyond my reach. I had tried so hard, longing for Christ's beauty to cover me, for His love to fill me, so I would be transformed.

We stopped in Erie, Pennsylvania, to spend the night. The snow that had started falling sometime that afternoon was starting to stick. I was rest-less, so while my husband and son slept, I looked out the window. The snow was falling faster now; big flakes of white merged to cover the bare earth with a blanket of white. The transformation was amazing. Instead of brown stubble and stones, the countryside snuggled under a fluffy white comforter, providing not a hint of what had previously been. It was beautiful!

As I sat there, I felt the Holy Spirit speaking to my heart. I realized that what I lacked was patience. I'd been expecting to change instantly. Indeed, what I'd been trying so hard to do was beyond my ability to accomplish. I had to allow a power greater than myself to take control and do the work. Slowly, I began to understand that just as the winter whiteness starts with one tiny snowflake and builds to a crescendo, so the Holy Spirit comes in at our invitation. At first we may not notice a difference, just as one tiny snowflake by itself seems so insignificant; but with the passage of time we realize that there is indeed a change. Little by little we see less of ourselves and more of Him until one glorious day we no longer see ourselves at all. Others, beholding us, see the change, too.

I had a better understanding of what David was asking God to do when he said, "Wash me, and I shall be whiter than snow" (Ps. 51:7, NKJV). I'm in awe of what the transforming power of snow can do to a sin-scarred landscape.

RACHEL ATWOOD

The Battle Is for Real

For we wrestle not against flesh and blood, but against principalities, against powers, against the rulers of the darkness of this world. Eph. 6:12.

IT WAS FRIDAY AFTERNOON. I was very excited because I had just completed training to become an Online Bible Course instructor. I'd already entered four of the 27 responses into my computer, and now I'd set aside a block of time to enter the other 23 required responses. My newly upgraded word processor was in top form, and I could hardly wait to get started.

Then disaster struck. After entering the fifth response, I clicked on "save," and my computer went blank—nothing was there. I restarted the computer, but of course nothing had been saved. I was devastated, but that was only the beginning. I repeated this process four times, and every time either the computer quit or a message came up indicating I needed to restart before continuing, and nothing had been saved.

Something very strange was going on here; I hadn't had any problems of this type before. I knew this was something that really needed to be done, and I would be helping people to learn more about God and His great love. The devil wouldn't like that! I felt that I was in the middle of a real battle between good and evil, so I bowed my head and earnestly petitioned the Lord to intervene on behalf of the work I knew He wanted me to do, to rebuke the devil and allow me to finish what I wanted to do for Him. I opened my eyes, turned the computer back on, and confidently typed in the fifth response once again. I clicked on "save"—and there it was, waiting for me to give it a title! I entered the remaining 23 responses that afternoon and never had even the hint of a problem again.

It was kind of scary when I thought about the implications of what had just happened, yet I was elated that God truly was there with me and showed me He would be with me through all my battles with the evil one.

ANNA MAY RADKE WATERS

A Prayer for Schaquan

Be careful for nothing; but in every thing by prayer and supplication with thanksgiving let your requests be made known unto God. Phil. 4:6.

I WAS VERY CONCERNED about my nephew, Schaquan, who had experienced one of the worst seizures ever in 16 years. He was in the hospital and had been placed on life support. As I entered the critical-care unit with his mother, I noticed the medical team making their rounds. Two people were on ventilators. One was a woman, who was fully alert. The other was Schaquan, who was unresponsive. Having worked with critical-care patients for 15 years, I knew things did not look promising. My heart ached for his mother.

When the doctors had completed their rounds, we were approached by a doctor and nurse from the team. "I'm sorry," the nurse said. "We've done everything we can for Schaquan." The doctor nodded in agreement. I wondered if Schaquan's mother had actually heard and understood. If not, I wondered if it was my place to try to get through to her. I knew she truly loved her son. I also knew that God loved all of us and was waiting to hear from us.

I began to talk to Schaquan. I knew he could hear me, so I spoke loudly and clearly. He didn't move. I began to pray. The Holy Spirit took full control as I prayed and prayed. I noticed his eyelids moving, as though he was trying to force them open. They continued to twitch until one opened, then the other. He appeared dazed. We talked to him and rubbed his arms, head, hands, and legs until he acknowledged our presence.

We asked the doctor and nurse to come see the sudden change in his condition. They came running, unable to believe their eyes. "What did you do?" they asked in amazement.

"We prayed," I responded, thanking God from deep within my heart.

A woman visiting the lady on the other respirator came over and began talking to me about the power of prayer. We prayed for all the sick, as well as Schaquan.

It's a wonderful feeling to know we can be saved from sin the same way God saved Schaquan from death. All we have to do is ask. Whatever burdens you may be carrying, won't you try Jesus?

CORA A. WALKER

The Donated Wood

Prove Me now in this . . . if I will not open for you the windows of heaven and pour out for you such blessing that there will not be room enough to receive it. Mal. 3:10, NKJV.

THERE ARE STILL SOME people in this world of gas and electric heaters who actually heat their houses with woodstoves. My parents always had a woodstove, and when I married, David and I decided to heat with woodstoves. The only problem with woodstoves is that you get warm twice—when you cut the wood, then when you burn it. Believe me, cutting the wood is three fourths of the battle.

Finding time to cut wood has always been part of our battle, as my husband works full time and I work part-time. I'm also a mother, which we all know is a 24/7 job. During the summer David and our children did a lot of odd jobs to earn the extra money needed for private school tuition. Mowing lawns, building fences, nothing seemed too small to do—and God provided many of these jobs. Along the way, we seemed to find extra wood.

The Nuhns called and needed an electric fence put up in their backyard. While we were there, they offered us a large tree, already cut up into stove-length sizes. "Maybe you know of someone who can use this, but if you'd just help us by getting this old oak out of our yard, we would appreciate it," Irene had said. Indeed, we *did* know someone!

Then, while cleaning house for a local, we found a pretty good amount of wood piled in the yard. More wood for the Robinson woodpile! Another day, while driving along the highway, I noticed that the highway department was cutting wood back to the fence lines. I stopped and asked what they were going to do with the wood. The crew boss said, "Give it to you." So my children and I returned with the pickup, gathering wood from the side of the road.

By October we had a large woodpile, more than four stacks. It seemed that God knew something we didn't. My husband suggested that, like Joseph of old, God was giving us goods before the famine—or the cold, as the winter of 2000-2001 was in Arkansas. We had enough wood to last all winter and never had to turn on our backup central heat. God opened the windows of heaven that winter.

CHARLOTTE ROBINSON

A Missionary at Home

How happy is the one whom God reproves; therefore do not despise the discipline of the Almighty. Job 5:17, NRSV.

I'VE OFTEN ADMIRED PEOPLE who were missionaries in other lands. But for 23 years Satan had control of my life. I left the Lord for the ways of the world, while others went to teach people a better way of life. Then during an altar call, God took hold of me, and my life changed, and I began walking hand in hand with Jesus.

Going back to church made a big difference. I took part in a fund-raiser for a soup kitchen in New York and heard experiences from some who went to Mexico to build an orphanage. I was plagued with thoughts that I wasn't doing anything for my Lord. Isn't this what the Christian message is about, bringing to others the knowledge of the Savior?

I decided to make it a matter of prayer, and let the Holy Spirit speak to me. It wasn't long before my mind turned again to thoughts of sharing my faith. I had married a "nonbeliever" during my years of wilderness wandering. I couldn't see why he didn't believe what was so plain in the Bible. Then there are my three adult children, who had attended Christian schools but now had different opinions. When I started going to church they said, "Mom, we're happy for you, but don't come preaching to us." How could I tell them about my experiences with the Lord?

With the words "This gospel of the kingdom will be preached in all the world . . . , and then the end will come" (Matt. 24:14, NKJV), ringing in my ears, almost as if there had been a radio or tape turned on, I heard a voice say, "Why are you so concerned with the mission field? Have I not called you from your worldly life that you may witness where you are? Your mission field is right here within your own four walls."

Now I was filled with guilt, knowing I hadn't been the kind of witness to my family that Jesus would have me be. I'd been quick to wrath, sharp-tongued, impatient, loudmouthed, hypocritical, and intemperate.

O Jesus, forgive me for wanting to be somewhere else, and teach me how to witness to my family and those with whom I come in contact. Amen.

VIDELLA MCCLELLAN

Sounds in the Night

You will not fear the terror of night. Ps. 91:5, NIV.

WHY SHOULD SOUNDS IN the night cause more anxiety than the thousand sounds of the day? Of course, there are comforting sounds in the night, such as crickets, the breathing of a sleeping child or spouse, the familiar sound of the family car turning into the driveway, and laughing voices of our loved ones as they enter the house. These sounds dispel worries and fears.

Nighttime can be terrifying when we're alone or in a strange environment. Dogs barking, cats fighting, steps in front of the house, a bump against the door—strange noises can dispel sleep for hours.

I remember some of the night sounds of our six years in Africa that kept me on the alert: ripe mangoes falling on the corrugated iron roof, twigs snapping, electrical storms, disoriented bats flying around the mosquito net of our bed, the night watchman snoring like a roaring lion because he had no roof in his mouth, a frog that we'd caught in a cardboard box on our bookshelf trying to jump out, a special kind of cricket that sounded like a circular saw, early-morning visitors to our orange and grapefruit grove, goats scampering around the house.

As long as I wasn't alone in the tropical night I didn't worry, but when my husband was away on bush trips, leaving me in charge of our home and the children, the night sounds took on a more threatening aspect. After all, I was there, all alone, with my small children. My friendly daytime world would change into a hostile environment as soon as the tropical night fell. We didn't have electric lights, so I would leave an oil lamp burning all night. But these little lamps only make the shadows even darker. I would send the girls to bed shortly after nightfall, then sit bravely on the terrace in front of our house, enjoying the cooler evening air, reading or listening to the radio, trying to ignore the lurking shadows. But soon I would long for the comparative security of closed doors and withdraw into the house.

Of course, I knew that most of my anxiety was unnecessary. God had promised to protect us. But we often forget we aren't alone—not even when we seem to be so. God is always there and will take care of us. Even in the midst of the sounds of our lonely nights. HANNELE OTTSCHOFSKI

I Believe in Miracles

I will sing to the Lord, for he has been good to me. Ps. 13.6, NIV.

I WAS GETTING READY to leave for the airport when I received a call from a friend who gave me the telephone number of a friend about whom I had inquired earlier. I decided to call her before leaving. That call began a succession of events culminating in the answer to our prayers.

My husband was living temporarily in another city, where he was receiving medical treatment. The one-bedroom apartment where he was staying was $800 a month. We prayed and searched but couldn't find a cheaper apartment within walking distance of the hospital. The second month's rent was due that afternoon.

When I called, my friend was surprised to hear my voice and came immediately to see us. "Why don't you come and stay at my place? I have an extra bedroom with a private entrance no one is using," she said. She lived about five miles away. But my husband didn't want to rent a car. To our amazement, she said, "My son's car is sitting in the parking lot. You can use it."

Everything was happening so fast. I told my friend we'd been praying that God would provide a cheaper place. Although we were impressed that He would answer our prayer, our faith became weak as only a few hours remained before the rent was due. My husband seemed still in shock when I left for the airport. By the time I reached home, our friend had helped him move, and he was settled in his new place. That night we rejoiced and praised God for providing a place rent-free. Our friend refused to take any rent because she was deeply impressed with the way God had answered our prayers and didn't feel comfortable taking the money.

She told us that tears come to her eyes every time she thinks of how God miraculously provided a place for us. When I had called, she was hurrying to take care of last-minute details before traveling overseas. She was outside her apartment when the phone rang and didn't want to answer it, but God impressed her to do so. It's amazing how He works on our behalf!

When you're tempted to doubt, trust in God and have faith to believe that He is able to work everything out for your good. We serve a loving God who specializes in answering prayers, and nothing is too hard for Him to accomplish.

SHIRLEY C. IHEANACHO

Freedom Isn't Free

For this reason Christ . . . has died as a ransom to set them free from the sins committed under the first covenant. Heb. 9:15, NIV.

FOR FOUR YEARS WE lived on the ridge of the Aliamanu volcanic crater that rises just off Pearl Harbor, Hawaii. We could walk up the slope behind our house, or up the street to the end of the block, and look down over the quiet waters of the harbor. I made it a point each December 7 to walk up to a vantage point and contemplate what had happened there that quiet Sunday morning in 1941. One could look off to the north to the Kolekole Pass, through which the Zeros appeared, bringing their death and destruction to Hickam Air Force Base and the ships resting in the harbor. Several times I'd watched battleships coming in past Fords Island and saluting the *Arizona* as they passed. I'd visited the USS Arizona National Memorial several times, once with a group of my English language students, most of them from Japan. An interesting experience!

One year while we lived there, a naval exercise called RIMPAC (Rim of the Pacific) took place. Ships from all our allies around the Pacific Rim were lying at anchor below. The local news reported that Soviet submarines also lay just offshore, observing, waiting. Waiting for what, no one knew. Because this was before *perestroika*, it made everyone nervous.

On December 7, 2001, I was glued to the History channel, watching the sixtieth anniversary of the attack. The survivors were getting old and introspective and were well worth listening to. One in particular grabbed my attention. He said, "I have a grandson named for me, and two granddaughters. And I want them to know that freedom isn't free."

Because my husband spent nearly 24 years in the Army, including one year in Vietnam, I know many individuals who willingly went off to war, and at least one whose name is engraved on the Vietnam Veterans Memorial wall. But most important, I have a Friend who died that I might be free, not just here and now, but forever. He has invited me into a relationship with Him, but He always leaves me free to choose or reject His offer. That is real freedom. But it didn't come without cost. Jesus paid it, paid in full, paid with His own life, the supreme price. Freedom isn't free, but thanks to Jesus Christ, I am free. And so are you.

ARDIS DICK STENBAKKEN

The Necklace

Weeping may endure for a night, but joy cometh in the morning. Ps. 30:5.

MY SISTER AND I spent a delightful day shopping in a local mall. Linda and her family live several hundred miles away, so an afternoon together was a real treat. We were in the dressing room of the last store of the day, tired and eager to finish and head home.

"Look at this!" exclaimed Linda, holding up an exquisite gold necklace with a large center pearl, surrounded by baguette diamonds. She had picked it up off the floor. "We need to turn it in."

We quickly gathered our belongings, went to the Lost and Found desk upstairs, and showed the necklace to the clerk. We told her where we found it, and she asked me for my name, address, and phone number.

After we unloaded our packages at home, the phone rang. My husband answered and handed the phone to me. A breathless woman explained she'd been shopping in Bakersfield with her mother, and while driving back to Los Angeles she realized her necklace was gone. "I feel terrible," she said, her voice shaking. "It was a gift from my father." I asked her to describe the necklace, which she did in perfect detail.

I turned to Linda with a big grin. "She's on her way," I said.

Soon there was a loud knock at the door. A young woman with reddened eyes entered. I quietly handed her the precious necklace. Throwing her arms around me, she hugged me, and between sobs told me her father had died a short time before, and the necklace had been a gift from him. As she turned to leave, I felt a piece of paper pressed into my hand—a check! With a big smile I tore it into pieces and handed it back. "We don't want this. It's been a thrill to return it to you." She hugged us all again and left.

"Wasn't that wonderful!" said Linda, smiling broadly as we hugged each other.

A few days later I got a lovely card. "Thank you so much for returning my necklace," it read. "We came to Bakersfield to shop and never expected to find a couple of angels there."

How exciting it was to return a lost valuable to the rejoicing owner! Imagine how our Father in heaven rejoices whenever one of His lost children returns to Him. There will be tears of joy and hugs all around when we meet together with Him in the clouds of heaven. I can hardly wait!

CHERYL HURT

351

Transformed

Do not conform yourselves to the standards of this world, but let God transform you inwardly by a complete change of your mind. Then you will be able to know the will of God—what is good and is pleasing to him and is perfect. Rom. 12:2, TEV.

A S I WAS WATCHING a weekly nationally televised church service, the camera focused on a woman who was singing in the choir. She had to be the homeliest woman in the choir. Interestingly enough, the next time I watched the choir on this program, the camera panned the singing group and focused on the same woman. But how different she looked now! Somehow a new hairdo and some makeup had transformed her looks. She was no longer the ugly duckling, but had been transformed into a beautiful woman. As I would notice her from time to time after that transformation I checked to see if she still held the same beauty. It has lasted!

Sin has stained those of us on this planet, and we so desperately need a transformation. All our own efforts at improving our "looks" are to no avail. We need the heavenly hand of God to bring about the transformation in our lives. This transformation will reflect a heavenly glow to beholders as we put ourselves into the hands of the Master Artist. Our very being is changed into something worth looking at.

The woman singing in the choir must have had a lovely voice or she wouldn't have been there. We too have something special that God sees in us. If we'll allow Him to touch our life, it will cause our countenance to be changed for the better.

When God changes us, we become attractive magnets who will share this special beauty that comes only from God; we share with others so that they might in turn be transformed.

What about you, friend? Have you felt God making changes in your life? Is His Spirit working in your life to bring this dramatic transformation to light in you? He wants to give you a heavenly makeover. Will you come today to allow Him to work in you?

Don't put it off. You too are a beautiful transformation just waiting to happen.

PEGGY CURTICE HARRIS

The Spirit of Forgiveness

Be merciful, just as your Father is merciful. Luke 6:36, NIV.

WITH A LITTLE REFLECTION, you can remember someone who hurt you with words or who has had a disagreeable attitude toward you or someone you know. This is reality. How many wounded, sad, and offended hearts go about on the avenues and streets of a city? These hurts corrode the soul and bring serious consequences to the physical and emotional being. Why? Because we aren't able to forgive. We prefer to caress hurts and carry all the negative and injurious symptoms for the rest of our lives.

From the human point of view, it's impossible for us to naturally have a spirit of forgiveness. But when we pray for strength from our Creator, we obtain courage and power to forgive.

A doctor once treated a member of my family in an incorrect manner. He used a procedure that greatly injured the health of this individual. I confess I developed a great dislike for this professional. I even doubted the individual's competence as a doctor. I thought that this professional should lose his credentials. A very negative feeling in relation to him grew within me. I began to pray, asking God to remove all these negative feelings. I had to fast and pray a great deal to be able to overcome the evil that had settled in my heart. By God's grace and with His powerful assistance, the battle was won, and I could forgive this doctor.

God is merciful to the ungrateful and cold of heart, and He hopes that His children will reflect this same spirit in their daily lives. We receive in the measure that we give—this is the great law of life. When we have to appear before the Judge of the earth, we will count on divine mercy and forgiveness. How important it is that we use mercy and forgiveness toward each other! If we keep bitterness in our heart, we can't be open individuals in a relationship, we won't feel the presence of Jesus, and our prayers won't reach the altar of God.

It's worth asking our friend and companion, Jesus, to grant us a spirit of forgiveness—that He will take us in His arms of love, free from resentment and open for a better relationship with Christ and those around us. Today, may you find God's power to forgive and to live authentic Christianity, showing the world that it is worthwhile to be a Christian.

MEIBEL MELLO GUEDES

The Lord Bless Thee

The Lord bless thee, and keep thee. Num. 6:24.

I 'VE SPENT MOST OF my money, but there's something I really want to buy for you." Tommy, who was about 7, had been very generous with his Christmas shopping money. He had found appropriate gifts for his parents, siblings, and grandparents, and he had only a few dollars left. "Come here, Grandma; I want you to see how pretty it is!"

I went over to where he was looking at some key chains. "I think you would really like it," he said, pointing to one that had a shiny heart attached. The heart was inscribed with the words, "The Lord Bless Thee."

It was beautiful and brought tears to my eyes to think that he was thinking of what would please me. He knew I liked most things that are heart-shaped, and the message was so precious. "Yes, Tommy, I think it's lovely," I said as I regained my voice, "but you've already bought me a gift."

"Grandma, I really want you to have this," he insisted.

"All right," I agreed. "I'll give you some money so that you'll have enough to buy it." He was very pleased that he was able to give me such a beautiful gift. I don't remember much about the rest of the gifts I received that long-ago Christmas, but I will always treasure the heart with the touching message and the handsome young man who wanted to buy it for me. I have a very special key on the chain.

I love to pick up the phone and hear his cheery "Hi, Grandma!" He never ends a conversation without assuring me, "I love you, Grandma."

God is a faithful and generous giver, a great example to each of us, constantly assuring us of His love and protection. He wants us to live with Him forever in that glorious place He has prepared just for us. He wants us to enjoy His bountiful love and countless gifts, day after day and year after year, without end.

LILLIAN MUSGRAVE

No, Never Alone

I will never leave you nor forsake you. Joshua 1:5, NIV.

I DON'T REMEMBER HOW many times I've said, "I'd rather be sick than lonely." As one who has experienced both of these options many times, I still adhere to my opinion. Being sick and surrounded by sympathetic loved ones is preferable to having good health and being lonely.

Loneliness and being alone aren't the same thing. A person can be desperately lonely in the most crowded place on earth.

My husband's work often separates us by half a world. It wasn't so bad when we had children at home. I missed him, but I still had company. I wasn't lonely or alone. Now the children are grown and gone. Health reasons prevent my going with him, so I have to find ways to combat my loneliness.

My foremost comfort is the Lord. He says to me, as He did to Joshua, "I will never leave you nor forsake you." These words assure me that I'm never really alone. So I talk to my Best Friend or read about Him.

The weekend is the loneliest time of the week for me, so I don't sit at home waiting for someone to invite me to Sabbath lunch. If I'm well enough, I prepare food and invite others to join me. Or I invite other ladies to bring a dish and all eat at my house. If the church is having a potluck, I take my contribution and eat with the crowd.

I know other women who are alone, and on Friday nights I telephone them in turn. I begin with a cheery message or a harmless little joke, and from then on all I have to do is change the receiver from ear to ear. Most of them are so eager for someone to talk to that I have only to listen. I throw in a comment every little while so that they know I'm still there, and we have a delightful visit.

Being alone is owing to circumstances; being lonely is homemade. Don't let it happen to you. Talk to your heavenly Father, your Big Brother, your Faithful Guide, however you choose to look upon our Lord. He is the best companion of all.

GOLDIE DOWN

Time Enough for God

There is a time for everything, and a season for every activity under heaven. Eccl. 3:1, NIV.

MY FRIEND ROSA complained to me about how tired she was. "You're seven months pregnant; you're supposed to be tired," I told her.

"But I wasn't this tired with my first baby!" she protested.

So I asked her what she'd done the day before. After working eight hours as a secretary, she had picked up her son from school and bought groceries on the way home. Before dinner she threw in a load of laundry. She cooked dinner, paid bills, helped with homework, and got her son to bed. She cleaned the kitchen and changed her dirty shelf paper. She still had an hour left before bed, so she did some ironing.

Before she finished her tale I was howling with laughter. I think it was the picture of this insane pregnant lady climbing up on her counters to put down fresh shelf paper that pushed me over the edge. She felt a little better when I explained that such a schedule would make any person tired, pregnant or not. And I warned her never to open my kitchen cabinets to check out the state of my dirty shelf paper!

No matter who you are, rich or poor, married or single, you still have only 24 hours a day. That's it. You make choices about how you will spend that time. You choose to hold down a job rather than live in poverty. You choose to clean your house. You choose to take care of your children or aging parents. You make decisions every day—should I go waterskiing or take my child to the park? What we call "demands" on our time is the price we pay for being responsible rather than selfish.

Students in a writing class I teach are always complaining that they don't have time to write, and I tell them they'll just have to take the time away from something else—maybe watching TV, chatting on the phone, or washing the windows. I freely admit that my house only gets cleaned just before I'm expecting company. That's where I get my writing time.

More important than my writing time is my "God time." It's a matter of priorities. I decided that I needed to spend daily time communing with God. Considering that most of my waking time is spent taking care of my needs and wants, I still don't spend nearly enough time with Him. But I'm working on it.

GINA LEE

Comforted Through Pain

I will not leave you comfortless: I will come to you. John 14:18.

SHE WAS BACK. It was getting close to Christmas, and I hadn't seen my sister in months. Now, as I gazed at her sleeping on the hospital bed, I promised I would visit her every day. Two days later we were arguing. "Do you know why I am still alive?" she asked me.

Sullenly I said, "No."

With tears in her eyes she said, "Because I'm afraid you'd kill yourself if I die."

I walked out of the room, but she was right. She was what I was living for, too.

I went to stay with my cousins. It was great—no church, no Sabbath, just fun. I realized that my sister wasn't getting better and that I hated God for her illness. I wanted nothing to do with the kind of God who would make His children suffer so. She loved Him, and she was dying.

I was baby-sitting my cousins. Soon we got tired with the video games and decided to play hide-and-seek. Then I came up with the idea of hiding in the master bedroom, which was filled with boxes of Christmas decorations, waiting to be stored.

I don't remember falling. I tried to get up. Pain such as I'd never felt before tore through my left knee. My screams brought the girls. I managed to stop crying as I closed my eyes against my surroundings. Both girls were holding my left hand when I closed my eyes. I felt pressure on my right hand, so I opened my eyes to see who it was, but no one was there. I could still feel Someone holding my hand and started to cry softly again. But these were tears of joy. The hurt didn't stop, but somehow knowing that He was there with me made it bearable.

At the hospital they bandaged my leg. Many times that night, while my mother was with me, I started to tell her I wanted my sister to know that Jesus had found me, but somehow it never came out. I never saw my sister alive again.

At her funeral I told my mother, "I wish I could have told her. I wish she could have known I'm saved."

My mother smiled at me. Softly she said, "I told her."

Even when I hated Him, God never left my side, or my sister's side. He gave us comfort when we needed it to face our most difficult test. Thank God, He never changes.

ASENATH BLAKE

Breakfast Invitation

Jesus said to them, "Come and have breakfast." John 21:12, NIV.

FOR THE PAST 10 years it's been my privilege and joy to travel to many churches, sharing the message of building a close relationship with God through prayer. But now and then my enthusiasm hits a snag.

My favorite way to speak is to be invited for an entire weekend so that I can get to know the people—and they can get to know me. That way I can build up messages over the weekend, showing a clear outline of developing an intimate relationship with God. But when I'm asked to speak for only one service, I find it hard to figure out what I can possibly say in only 20 or 30 minutes of sermon time that will make a difference to anyone.

So here I was, preparing to preach a Sabbath sermon in a big city church with a dwindling congregation—30 minutes at the most to speak. *Lord, what can I say?* I pleaded. My mind was blank. Time was closing in on me. One morning in my prayertime I read in John 21 the story of Jesus and the miraculous catch of fish. In my mind's eye I saw the discouraged disciples coming in from their fruitless night of fishing. I heard the Stranger on the shore call out, "Friends, have you caught any fish?" I heard His suggestion that they throw the net out again, this time on the right side of the boat. I saw the commotion as the net immediately filled up with fish. I heard John call to Peter, "It is the Lord!" I saw Peter leap out of the boat and set out for shore. As the rest of the disciples brought the boat in and tugged the heavy net onto the beach, I heard Jesus call, "Come have breakfast with Me!"

God had given me the topic for my sermon! I would challenge the congregation to begin each day by answering the call "Come have breakfast with Me!"

"Here I am!" Jesus calls to you and me. "I stand at the door and knock. If anyone hears my voice and opens the door, I will come in and eat with him, and he with me" (Rev. 3:20, NIV). Another day Jesus told a disgruntled crowd who craved free food, "My flesh is real food and my blood is real drink" (John 6:55, NIV).

Every day God spreads a table before us, calling, "Come have breakfast with Me!"

CARROL JOHNSON SHEWMAKE

In Their Hands

For he will command his angels concerning you to guard you in all your ways; they will lift you up in their hands, so that you will not strike your foot against a stone. Ps. 91:11, 12, NIV.

WE'D BEEN CHRISTMAS shopping at the Fairfield Mall all day. It was late afternoon, and a gentle rain had begun to fall as my 5-year-old son, James, and I were heading home. The splatter of rain on the car lulled James to sleep. His tired little form was curled up in the back seat as he dozed on and off. As we climbed the winding road that leads to Pacific Union College, the rain came down harder. I began to anticipate home, imagining myself lying down, closing my eyes, and putting up my tired feet!

Then, as we rounded a long curve near Linda Falls Terrace, I suddenly realized my tires had lost traction and the car was no longer following the curve of the road. It was making a slow but sharp curve of its own. The car began to spin, and in what seemed like a split second we were spinning out of control. The car crossed the centerline, and I could see the side of Howell Mountain looming up on James' side of the car. James had awakened and was staring out the window, his eyes, wide as saucers, filled with fright. I struggled not to panic. We were traveling at more than 50 miles per hour, and I feared we were going to slam up against the rocks and James would be killed.

No longer in control of the car, I took my feet off the pedals and let go of the steering wheel. I took James's little hand and whispered, "O dear God, please save us!"

And just like that, we sat as still as could be. Everything was quiet. We sat there for a minute, looking at each other. We hadn't even felt a jolt from the car stopping. I looked out James' window and saw that we were only a foot or two from the rocks that jutted out from the side of the mountain. We bowed our heads and thanked Jesus for sending His angels to stop the car from smashing against the rocks.

Slowly I turned the car around and headed up the road to Angwin once again. We knew that our guardian angels were riding with us.

SHIRLEY JOHNSTON

Little Things

The generous prosper and are satisfied; those who refresh others will themselves be refreshed. Prov. 11:25, NLT.

A T MY HUSBAND'S REQUEST, I was busy baking cookies. "Don't worry," I told him. "There will be plenty of cookies for you."

There would be plenty to share with friends, too. Our friendly mechanic, who always seemed to do something extra without charge, was on the list of those with whom we wanted to share. Then I was prompted to think of our neighbors. They didn't have much and would probably enjoy some cookies, especially since the wife suffered from Alzheimer's and her husband had to do all the cooking.

Since we live in a rural area and our mailboxes are about a quarter mile from our house, the neighbors usually pick up our mail along with theirs. That afternoon when Louise dropped off our mail, I brought out a container of cookies and said, "Here, let's trade."

"For me? Oh, thank you!" She was so happy and surprised. It was such a little thing, but in making her happy, it made me happy.

I had ordered extra women's devotional books as gifts and still had one left. While thinking to whom I should give it, I thought of my friend who had lost her little daughter a few weeks earlier. She must be suffering, and it would be a hard Christmas for her family, so right away I wrapped the book and mailed it to her. Later I found that she'd been wanting the book, but hadn't found the time or energy to get it. She felt as though it was a hug from God to get just what she wanted during a very difficult time.

It's almost Christmas again. There are so many around us for whom the most simple of gestures can mean so much. It's one thing to pray that God will use us; it's another to do something. And yes, there will be plenty of blessings left to refresh you and me, too.

Thank You, Father, for Your prompting to be Your instrument. Help me not to forget the little things that are so important. BETTY J. ADAMS

The Free Gift

Whoever wishes may have the water of life as a free gift. Rev. 22:17, NCV.

DURING ONE OF OUR visits to the mall I made the mistake of filling in one of those forms one can pick up in any shop. "Free Gift," it boldly announced. "Enter your name to win a beautifully embroidered cushion."

Several days later a note came through the mail requesting me to stop by and pick up the cushion I had won. I was so excited I begged my husband to take me to town immediately. In my imagination I knew what the cushion would look like: it would be large and beautifully embroidered, with wildflowers or a quaint English cottage set in a tranquil garden. As soon as we reached the mall, I raced into the shop, leaving my husband to park the car. I looked around at the embroidered tablecloths, cushions, and wall hangings, wondering which one would be mine.

"Oh, yes!" said the lady when I handed over my slip. She dived under the counter and came up moments later with a cushion, a very small cushion, a pincushion, in fact, about the size of a postage stamp. My face must have mirrored my disappointment as I mumbled "Thanks" and fled. "If I ever see you filling out a form for a free gift," my husband muttered on the way home, "I'll—" He didn't need to finish the sentence.

Somehow, though, I can't resist the lure of a free gift and continue to naively fill in forms with more or less the same disappointing results. There is, of course, a free gift that is going to take all eternity to enjoy, to plumb its depths, to really understand and appreciate. This free gift is what the woman at the well was seeking. Jesus addressed her need when He said, "If you knew the gift of God and who it is that asks you for a drink, you would have asked him and he would have given you living water" (John 4:10, NIV).

Like her, we are offered a free gift that sounds too good to be true: "Whoever is thirsty, let him come; and whoever wishes, let him take of the free gift of the water of life" (Rev. 22:17, NIV).

Thanks be to God for His unspeakable Gift! EDNA MAY OLSEN

Divine Appointment

You will keep in perfect peace all who trust in you, whose thoughts are fixed on you! Isa. 26:3, NLT.

IT WAS ABOUT 4:00 in the morning when I heard a forceful voice say, "Get up and call 911." I didn't know why the voice said that, so I knelt down to ask God. The voice once again said, "Get up and call 911." I was concerned about alarming my 86-year-old mother, so I went into the living room. I could feel my heart beating fast. Once again the voice said, "Go call 911."

This time I didn't hesitate. As I began to call, I realized that my breath was short and I was having difficulty breathing. I explained my breathing problem to the operator who answered, then I decided to wake my sister, who came upstairs and waited with me.

Before long the fire department rescue unit arrived and proceeded to take my blood pressure. It was 220/114, going into stroke level. The paramedics came and took my blood pressure again, confirming what the firefighters had gotten.

They got me into the ambulance, then stabilized me before transporting me to the hospital. When I arrived at the hospital, the night crew went into action to lower my blood pressure and to reduce the fluid buildup. They took blood at least three times, did an EKG, and put a heart monitor on me. The doctor finally came in and told me that I'd almost gone into congestive heart failure.

When you are a child of the King, you get royal treatment. When I arrived at my private room, a nurse named Ali greeted me. She said that she'd been waiting for me for a long time and that before I left that hospital, I would be spoiled.

That night, as she was making her rounds, she came into my room and talked for a while, then asked me if I would pray for her. The next day I wrote a song of praise and let her read it. She asked me to write her a poem. I believe that she was my divine appointment.

I do believe that You, Lord, are in control. Even in the midst of our 911 moments, may we, in perfect peace, put our trust in You.			OLIVE LEWIS

Back in the Day

[God] will wipe every tear from their eyes. There will be no more death or mourning or crying or pain, for the old order of things has passed away. Rev. 21:4, NIV.

BACK IN THE DAY, as our son would say, Christmas Eve was set in stone. About 7:00 p.m. we put on our coats and stepped out into the Texas night to walk next door to my aunt and uncle's home. We were quite a crowd—about 12 of us packed around the tree, Aunt Lona in her rocker and Uncle Bob in his reclining chair. There was a comfortable sameness to the evening—finger sandwiches, homemade cookies, gifts exchanged. Robbie, my cousin, set a beautiful table, though, way back in the day, and we wondered why it took so long to get everything together.

I remember the year our firstborn toddled among us. "Mama would be so thrilled with this baby," we said. But Mama (our grandmother) had died five years before. More years passed. Now we bundled up three little girls for the short walk next door on Christmas Eve. Aunt Jimmie, widowed, joined us, too. It was the more the merrier, back in the day.

Holidays came and went and came again. Rainy . . . balmy . . . icy. (Texas weather is fickle, as is life.) Now it's been 20 years since we spent Christmas in Texas. Over the years we added a son but lost five precious people. These days my sister and I host a much smaller party, and wonder why we're not ready before 9:00 p.m.

I'm looking forward to "Christmas" in heaven. No, not exchanging gifts, but our family crowded together—dusting off the old jokes and laughing at them all over again. I'm eager to finally meet Grandpa Jim and my dad's mother, Annie, who died when he was 4. I'll tell Mama that I've been to Bukovina, Romania, her birthplace, and that her great-grandchildren lived her dream of mission work. I can't wait for my mother to see our grownup daughters and meet the son she had predicted but didn't live to know. I'm going to hug her for a hundred years.

Christmas way, way back in the day. The longings of eternity wrapped with the Babe in swaddling clothes. The balm for the loneliness gifts cannot heal. The promise of tomorrow in today's dying light.

PENNY ESTES WHEELER

Anita's Christmas Gift

But we had to celebrate and be glad, because this brother of yours was dead and is alive again; he was lost and is found. Luke 15:32, NIV.

MY SON, SCOTT, LOVES Christmas. He especially enjoys Christmas shopping and wrapping the gifts he purchases. His wife, Anita, also loves Christmas but can't stand the suspense. Scott foils her snooping by hiding her gifts at our home until Christmas Eve.

Last Christmas Eve, soon after Scott picked up Anita's gifts for wrapping, I received a frantic phone call. Anita's primary—and most expensive—gift was missing. Scott was devastated. The entire family began searching. For several hours we looked high and low. I called my husband, who was in his car, and we agreed to pray. No sooner had he said amen than his eye caught the corner of the bag under some files in the back seat of his car. With great joy the news spread throughout the family. The gift had been found!

This incident refocused our Christmas when someone pointed out that God searches for us just as we had searched for Anita's gift. God loves us so much He searches for us! I've never heard Luke 15 used as part of the Christmas story, but it should be because it tells of the great lengths to which God will go to search for lost sinners. In the first story a shepherd loses one sheep out of 100, yet he goes out and scours the countryside. The second story tells of a woman who loses one coin out of 10. She searches high and low until she finds it. In the third story the loss is a worthless son. You and I may have written off the wicked prodigal as hopeless, but not God! Jesus' stories show that God places tremendous value on every person.

The intense search for Anita's lost gift gave our family a deeper understanding of the true meaning of Christmas. It caused us to rethink the unfathomable love of God. We realized that Christmas is not just about Christ's birth but also about each individual's rebirth.

When one sinner is saved, all heaven is ecstatic, just as they were at Christ's birth. If "there is joy in the presence of the angels of God over one sinner who repents"(Luke 15:10, NKJV), we should be searching for those who are lost with the same diligence and fervor we used to search for an earthly, perishable gift. This Christmas let's think not of our gifts, but of those precious souls we can win and present as gifts to God.   ELLIE GREEN

Lost

And ye shall seek me, and find me, when ye shall search for me with all your heart. Jer. 29:13.

THE DEPARTMENT STORE WAS crowded with Christmas shoppers. My 7-year-old son and I had gone for last-minute items before the store closed. I had made my purchase and was delayed at the counter for the item to be brought from the stockroom. "It'll be about a 10-minute wait," the clerk explained, so I directed my son to a small play area within sight as I waited and watched him walk toward it.

A full 10 minutes later, with my item in hand, I went to retrieve my son. But he wasn't there! In near panic, I searched the area. Every minute seemed like hours. He wasn't inclined to wander, and I always felt I could rely on his obedience. Perhaps I had trusted him too much!

I made my way to security, and they joined me in the search. Throughout the store we went, and even out to the busy mall. Fear gripped my throat as I realized the possibility of an abduction. Wherever he was, I wondered what he must be thinking now. I couldn't bear the anguish of his loss.

It was nearly closing time. *O God, please help me find him.* My silent prayer ascended almost audibly now, in my terror of losing him. "Please, God, don't let the store close!" I couldn't—I wouldn't—leave without my boy.

After what seemed an eternity, my precious little son was finally found. He had misunderstood my directions when I sent him to the play area and had walked beyond it to a small restricted area. He'd been there all the time, patiently awaiting my return, and I had overlooked him.

I've thought about my heavenly Father, who patiently waits for me to come to Him. He has given His word that He will never leave or forsake me. But how often, in my busyness, I forget He is there! Because He has endowed me with the power to choose, He doesn't impose Himself on me, and too often He is overlooked. Finally, when I come to realize that my own strength is far from adequate, I begin searching for Him.

Oh, what a precious Savior we have, waiting for us with His arms outstretched, but we must seek Him with our whole heart.

LORRAINE HUDGINS-HIRSCH

God's Special Gifts for Women

Everything good in life is a gift from heaven, and it comes from the Father of lights. Unlike shadows which shift with the turning earth, God never changes. James 1:17, Clear Word.

SOMETHING WENT WRONG after my third chemotherapy injection. Instead of bouncing back in a few days, as I'd done before, I got a respiratory infection and spent five days in bed. Wimpy, nauseated, and hairless, my self-esteem and stamina had about slipped away.

Finding me half asleep in bed, my husband whispered, "Ulla sent this for you." In his hand was a small black travel case. I smiled as I remembered my friend in Germany. She loved black and white, and her home was elegant with these simple tones. Inside the case was a card not just telling me to get well soon, but a note in her delicate handwriting reminding me that God's hand was over me.

The travel case contained several small packages, the kind women love to give and receive—perfume, candles, lotion. There was even a collection of tiny white rosebuds, seemingly waiting to burst into bloom. Each piece was wrapped lovingly and carefully with ribbons and more flowers. I knew Ulla, a busy gynecologist, had taken a lot of time and care to prepare the contents of the little travel case to make me feel special and so it would be able to withstand the pressures of the baggage compartment of the big Lufthansa jet traveling from Germany to Nepal. She had made this exquisite gift just for me.

I sat up in bed and looked out the window as I thought of another gift. Two thousand years ago God wrapped a gift. Tenderly, carefully, He wrapped His gift for every human on earth, even though it would be 2,000 years before some of us would receive it. He chose black and white, too—a starry winter night in Palestine. No jet taxied down the runway—God sent His gift among thousands of singing angels. Flowers, lotion, candles? No, God's gift was the gift of His Son. God sent us the priceless gift of eternal life wrapped in rags in a Bethlehem manger. I looked out the window again. A woman was threshing rice in a nearby field. Today God uses you and me to deliver His gift. Had I taken His gift to my sister in the rice paddy? Would I soon?

SHERRY SHRESTHA

Unto Us a Child Is Born

For today in the city of David there has been born for you a Savior, who is Christ the Lord. Luke 2:11, NASB.

THE BABY WAS SLEEPING, but I just wanted to hug him and look at his wide-open blue eyes some more. But I know little newborns need their sleep. We were so excited about Thomas Alexandre's arrival. We'd flown all the way to Switzerland from Maine for his birth and had waited day after day, and now he was here. We were all so happy for the safe birth. And could there be a more handsome little boy? We all agreed—his parents, the grandparents, my husband and me—he was the one.

As I gloried in Thomas's birth, I thought of another baby named Jesus. No one had room in the little town of Bethlehem for a mother who was ready to give birth. Finally, the parents found a manger, with the farm animals as guests to greet that Baby. Today every need of mother and baby is attended to. Mary and Joseph had no relatives or friends there to share the joy of Jesus' birth, but shepherds came to see the Baby and told Mary of the angels' singing to them in announcing His birth. Mary's heart must have been full of joy as she knew again the certainty that He was really the long-promised Christ child who would save His people.

Then I think of King Herod's law to kill all babies 2 years old and under. I look at my little grandson and think, *How could the king do that?* These sweet little children are so precious to each family. And Jesus said in Matthew 19:14, "Let the little children come to me, and do not stop them; for it is to such as these that the kingdom of heaven belongs" (NRSV).

Baby Jesus grew up to be our Savior. He died and was resurrected that we might have eternal life. Little baby Thomas is God's gift to us. And may he grow up to love this other baby, Jesus, the baby who was born so long ago in the manger. May we as parents and grandparents love our children and train them for that eternal life Jesus has made available to all of us.

DESSA WEISZ HARDIN

Unwanted Gifts

Let us thank God for his priceless gift! 2 Cor. 9:15, TEV.

HAVE YOU EVER RECEIVED an unwanted gift? I have. Have you ever given a gift to a loved one that cost you some sacrifice, and then it was unwanted? I've had that experience too, and certainly didn't feel good about it. I loved to crochet baby shawls and give them as gifts to pregnant mothers. Some showed appreciation; others didn't.

I once had to go to the hospital for an operation. I met a patient there who talked so much she told me her life story. When we were discharged, she phoned me every day. One day she announced that she was pregnant with her second child, so I decided to crochet a baby shawl for her. I bought the three-ply yarn and selected a very special pattern. When I completed the shawl, I contacted her. She said she didn't want it—without even seeing it! I felt so bad. I was really hurt. I'd made this gift with all the love in my heart, and now it was refused, an unwanted gift.

I decided to sell the shawl, and someone bought it for a friend. After a few weeks passed, the woman whom I originally made the shawl for phoned me and asked if I still had the shawl. Her husband had told her she was foolish not to accept the gift I made—but it was too late.

Jesus' mother didn't have the privilege of delivery in an air-conditioned maternity ward. There was no room in the inn. This Baby didn't have a beautiful nursery decorated in pastel blue. He was born in a manger where animals were fed. No relatives and kind friends brought Him soft, cuddly baby-grows to wear. He was wrapped in swaddling clothes—strips of cloth to clothe His naked body. Even King Herod wanted to destroy this Babe. But Joseph was warned in a dream to take the young child and His mother and flee by night.

This Baby was Jesus, the King of kings! Born in such humble conditions—an unwanted gift—"He came unto his own, and his own received him not" (John 1:11).

Today you have the opportunity to accept Him and love Him with all your heart—no longer as an unwanted gift, but as a priceless gift. Tomorrow may be too late.

PRISCILLA ADONIS

Singing in Jail

About midnight Paul and Silas were praying and singing hymns to God, and the other prisoners were listening to them. Suddenly there was such a violent earthquake that the foundations of the prison were shaken. . . . The jailer called for lights, rushed in and fell trembling before Paul and Silas. . . . He then . . . asked, "Sirs, what must I do to be saved?" Acts 16:25-30, NIV.

TON PIRON* FACED DANGER, as did Paul and Silas. When a foreign political group took over her country, she joined the army, accepted their atheistic doctrine, and became a lieutenant. Later her son became seriously ill. God answered the prayers of a Christian and healed her son, so she became a Christian herself and began preaching to others about the true God. She was arrested. In prison she prayed and was released with a harsh warning not to preach again. That didn't stop her, so she was arrested again and again. Instead of complaining and becoming discouraged, she sang behind the bars and composed original gospel songs.

In court she was charged with having taught a foreign religion. She replied, "If you are going to get rid of all foreign beliefs, you must expel Buddhism and Islam. Our country has no original religion of its own." The officers couldn't answer her, so they threatened to kill her. She said, "If you kill me, you will not rid the country of Christianity. Many more will come up in my place. It will only grow the more." They threw her back into prison, and she sang again. Two weeks later she was released with a court warning. She still preaches and sings.

This brave woman hikes back into the mountains on trails so steep and rough that no other pastors will go. When she has converts ready to baptize, she brings them down the trails to the river where a pastor will meet them for the baptism. She has preached the gospel to thousands. In one village alone she has 270 members. She walks the mountain trails, teaching and singing the gospel with the 1,500 believers she has in her parish.

We may not be faced with the same challenges as brave Ton Piron, but we can use the same solution to our problems that Paul and Silas did: "Sing and make music in your heart to the Lord, always giving thanks to God the Father for everything, in the name of our Lord Jesus Christ" (Eph. 5:19, 20, NIV).

RUTH WATSON

---

* Not her real name.

Praise God

Praise the Lord. How good it is to sing praises to our God, how pleasant and fitting to praise him! Ps. 147:1, NIV.

CONFLICTS AND STRUGGLES always produce results. The newspapers are filled with heated rhetoric on right and wrong. People are always fighting somewhere over something they deem worth dying for. Friends refuse to talk to friends, and family members decide they're better off apart from each other. It seems as if everyone is talking of enemies and war and hatred. So many are bitter. Everyone, it seems, except Betty.

Betty and her husband of 46 years live in a little house in a poor section of Orlando. Twelve years ago, having spent their lives struggling physically and financially through bitterly cold winters in upstate New York, this newly retired couple managed to move their meager belongings to Florida. Leaving family and lifelong friends was hard, but the hope of a peaceful retirement seemed too good to pass up. Within months of the move Betty's husband suffered a stroke. Weeks of intensive therapy and exhausting exercises followed. Betty was always right there with him, cooking meals at home and carrying them into the rehab unit so he could eat "what he likes."

Over the course of the next 12 years Betty's husband struggled through three more strokes, each one stealing another fragment of his independence. He is now confined to a wheelchair and dependent on her for everything, from feeding to bathing. Betty has ample reasons to feel bitter, or at least shortchanged in her bid for happiness. But Betty is doing an incredible thing. She is saving her money until she has enough to pay for one night in a hotel. A caring neighbor has agreed to watch over her husband so that Betty can go to that hotel room and spend 24 hours, without interruption, praising God!

Betty says God has always been there when she needed Him—sometimes before she even knew she needed Him. He's listened to her countless requests, and she just can't find enough time at home to "properly praise Him."

Without struggles it's impossible to grow. Don't let your struggles overcome you—instead, praise your awesome Father and radiate God's grace.

SUSAN WOOLEY

Downsizing

Surely I am with you always, to the very end of the age. Matt. 28:20, NIV.

A T FIRST I COULDN'T believe they'd do it. How could they cut a service from two people down to one and expect it to continue to function, when it really needed six to do the work adequately? Why would the Lord allow such a thing to happen? Even though there was no cure for it, I'd recently recovered from a rare disease that was self-limiting.

My assistant was married, with a little boy who'd been born with a handicap. The administration was planning on letting him go and retaining me. I felt the stress of the job loss would be too much for him, and I felt my health was too important to try to do the work myself. So I chose to leave and let my assistant stay. He was well trained, an excellent worker, and young enough to cope with the lack of help.

I knew the Lord would be with me and would open doors so that I could pay the mortgage and other bills. My husband was retired on Social Security. It would be up to me to earn the extra income. Before my job ended at the library, I had another job working from home as a self-employed person, working for a correspondence school grading and teaching seventh-grade language and eighth-grade English. I had about 200 students from all over the world. I also taught and graded teacher education courses for the same school.

In addition to doing the correspondence courses, I tutored students in my home, working with a first grader and a ninth grader. It was a challenge going from first grade to ninth grade, but interesting. One part of the day I'd be teaching reading and phonics. Later that same day I'd teach algebra.

The next year I lost my first grader—she had learned to read! But the Lord opened up a job for me to do medical journal indexing. That lasted for a summer, and I had my algebra student back again. When he finished his last test, the very same day I received a call to do medical journal indexing for another company.

That's the way the Lord blessed me when I stepped out in faith and left a job to someone else. My prayer today is that all who read this and are facing something similar will remember how the Lord can bless and lead in their lives, regardless of the circumstances. LORAINE F. SWEETLAND

Above the Clouds

For the Lord God is a sun and shield. Ps. 84:11, NRSV.

DECEMBER 29 FINALLY CAME. I rushed home from work to start packing for a long-awaited trip to California for the New Year's holiday. Did I ever need this vacation! It had been an exceptionally difficult year and a busy month with work and the holiday activities. I was ready to fly away!

Tennessee weather in late December calls for wool suits and light jackets. I realized this would be inappropriate dress for sunny southern California, so I pulled out summer slacks and a light sweater. However, I felt quite underdressed at the airport, as it was a dark, chilly day. *Never mind,* I thought as I shivered in my sweater; *I'll be just right when I arrive.*

Our flight to Minneapolis took us through gray cloud cover. Swirling white snow with blizzard-like winds greeted us in Minnesota. The runways were buzzing with activity as snowplows and deicing machines attempted to clear the runways. We disembarked for a three-hour layover. Now I really felt underdressed. Crowded all around me were people in heavy, long coats, boots, and gloves. It was obvious to all that I wasn't a local.

As we took off I saw nothing but darkness out my window. Just then our pilot announced that we were going to climb to a high altitude to rise above the storm clouds. Seconds later, a flash of brightness beamed through my window. As we broke through the clouds, it was like a miracle. The sky was a brilliant blue with not a cloud in sight. The sun awaited us in all its glory.

Do we do that in life? Do we stay muddled in the darkness of sin and despair? Are we always out of place in the situations in which we find ourselves? Do we fail to soar above those earthly cares that bind us? We must remember that above the clouds the sun is always shining with the warmth and brightness of God's love and mercy.

I landed in Los Angeles to 86-degree temperatures and again realized that I was inappropriately dressed. I quickly peeled off my sweater and rolled up the sleeves of my long-sleeved shirt. *What a world our Father has created!* I thought. Nature itself proclaims the cold and darkness of life's experiences but also reveals the brightness and warmth of the Son—if we will just reach above the clouds in faith to receive Him.

BARBARA SMITH MORRIS

Scarred for Life

He himself bore our sins in his body on the tree, so that we might die to sins and live for righteousness; by his wounds you have been healed.
1 Peter 2:24, NIV.

EVERY MORNING I WAKE up and examine my most recent injury to see how it is healing. In the past three weeks I've watched it go from an open, bleeding wound to pinkish raised skin—almost normal again. When I look back I realize how unnecessary it was for me to have gotten hurt in the first place. I fed a leftover sandwich to a Bernese mountain dog that I really didn't know well. His jaws clamped down on my thumb knuckle just as I pulled away. I let out a yelp. His top teeth scraped across my finger, tearing a flap of skin.

As far back as I can remember, I was always getting hurt. As a preschooler, I did something very naive. I jumped out of a boat by stepping on the upright point of an anchor. I can still feel the half-inch long scar on the bottom of my foot. At 5 I was roller-skating on a sidewalk and tripped on a crack, splitting my chin open. As if that wasn't enough, before it was even healed I was running around the outside of our house, trying to jump the sandbox. I caught one foot on the front side and my chin on the other.

Every scar on my body has a story behind it. I've got scars from getting cut with glass, poked with sticks, grazed by cinders, burned on exhaust pipes of a motorcycle, and from removing the scabs of chicken pox. As an adult, the scars have been of a more serious nature, from biopsies and surgeries, the two longest from the removal of both breasts. Then there are the invisible scars from the wrongs committed against me through life. Most of these scars are known only by the Lord Himself.

I don't know about you, but I'm looking forward to the resurrection and a new body, inside and out. The only scars in heaven will be on Jesus, and we'll know the story behind them. It's a story that we will think about, discuss, and never fully comprehend for eternal ages. In the meantime, we can tell His story—which puts all of our scars into proper perspective. How great is God's love for us!

DONNA MEYER VOTH

Restored and Renewed

Anyone who belongs to Christ is a new person. The past is forgotten, and everything is new. 2 Cor. 5:17, CEV.

THE FIRST TIME I attended a Celebration of Recovery weekend retreat, I went to learn some skills that would enable me to help others (especially some people close to me) overcome their shortcomings, weaknesses, and addictions, such as overeating, workaholism, drugs, legalism, perfectionism, alcoholism—things no one likes to admit to. After all, who would honestly want to admit they weren't a perfect Christian? Before long I realized that I had addictions that I'd never owned up to. I was flabbergasted! I could just picture how my family or friends would react:

"So that's what's wrong with you?"

"Well, it's about time you saw yourself for who you really are."

"We knew you had problems. Anyone could have told you that."

I was feeling quite perplexed and very uneasy. What was I to do to get rid of my old self, my addictions? How could I become new? I didn't have to wonder long.

The attitude of the other "addicts" there—many who had attended recovery weekends for numerous years—and their love, encouragement, and spiritual support were just what I needed. Their deep love for Jesus Christ was thrilling. I finally understood how powerless I really was and how completely Jesus Christ could restore and renew me. Through group sharing experiences, break-out sessions, workshops, praise, and prayer, my road to recovery was being paved. I was ready to give up old thoughts, habits, and behaviors. I accepted my shortcomings and invited recovery. I was fixable! Further, I found myself more empathetic to others and their addictions. Together we addressed concerns and needs, knowing that only through God's power would we fully recover. To culminate the weekend, there was a ceremony to count down our minutes/hours/days of recovery and to celebrate those accomplishments. My past was forgotten—I was healthy and whole, a new person, by the power of the Holy Spirit. I felt great!

Lord Jesus, I give You myself. Make my thoughts Your thoughts; my ways Your ways. Help me do my best to know You and to serve You. Make me new again. Amen.

IRIS L. STOVALL

BIOGRAPHICAL SKETCHES

Betty J. Adams is a retired schoolteacher, wife, mother of three, and grandmother of five. She has written for *Guide* magazine and for her church newsletter. She's involved with community services in her church and enjoys her grandchildren, quilting, and traveling, especially on mission trips. **Apr. 20, July 27, Dec. 17.**

Priscilla Adonis is active in women's ministries. She is a DGL (discussion group leader) for a Bible class at church. She loves writing and has pen pals in many places. She misses her children, who are living overseas. **Mar. 2, May 1, June 2, July 20, Dec. 25.**

Sally J. Aken-Linke resides in Norfolk, Nebraska, with her husband, John. Her experiences as a single mother, raising two children, and a strong Christian faith provide a basis for her poetry and short stories. Sally and her husband are active in air medical transport and are near completion of an airplane. She enjoys reading, music, and working with young people. **June 23.**

Minerva M. Alinaya is a former senior lecturer at Bethel College in South Africa. Her hobbies are reading, playing the piano and the recorder, and doing cross-stitch. Her dream is to be a dedicated missionary and to be with Jesus in heaven. **Mar. 1, Nov. 13.**

Maxine Williams Allen resides in Orlando, Florida, with her husband and two small sons, where she has her own computer and business consulting company. She loves to travel, meet people, and experience different cultures. Her hobbies include writing, reading, and computers, and she has a special interest in family, children's, and women's ministries. **Apr. 9, Aug. 10, Oct. 19.**

Mary Wagoner Angelin lives in Tennessee and is communication director and newsletter editor at her church. She is a social worker at an inpatient psychiatric facility. Mary and her husband, Randy, have two girls, Barbara, 4, and Rachel, 2. Hobbies include therapeutic humor, exercising, hiking, writing, vegan cooking, volunteering, and being a mom. **Mar. 7, Oct. 13.**

Raquel Costa Arrais is a minister's wife who has developed her ministry as an educator for 20 years. Currently she works as associate director of her church's women's ministries for South America. The mother of two teenagers, she enjoys being with people, singing, playing the piano, and traveling. **Feb. 11, July 31, Nov. 14.**

Rachel Atwood is a stay-at-home mother of three boys and is married to a construction superintendent. They have lived in eight different states at last count, but plan to retire to Kentucky soon. At the time of this devotional, she was writing from New Hampshire. She enjoys nature, music, and helping out at church. **Apr. 28, Nov. 30.**

Rosemary Baker of Iowa is the author of a children's book, *What Am I?* and has had contributions in *Shining Star, Kids' Stuff,* and other magazines. She's a member of the Iowa Poetry Association and the Quint City Poetry Guild. Active in church and volunteer work, she also enjoys working with children and pursuing her interests in arts, crafts, poetry, writing, music, and painting. **June 10.**

Audrey Balderstone helps her husband run their garden landscaping company in England, where they are both involved in church and community activities. Audrey raises thousands of dollars for charity through flower festivals and is chair of the editorial board of *The Flower Arranger* magazine. **Feb. 12, Nov. 23.**

Jennifer M. Baldwin writes from Australia, where she is clinical risk management coordinator at Sydney Adventist Hospital. She enjoys church involvement, travel, and writing, and has contributed to a number of church publications. **Apr. 14.**

Dawna Beausoleil lives with her spouse in rural northern Ontario. Her active lifestyle has been curbed sharply by chronic fatigue syndrome, but she still loves to sing and write and play with her cat and dog. The long winters are great for jigsaw puzzles, and the glorious summers perfect for flower gardening. **Jan. 26, Aug. 18.**

Annie B. Best, a retired public school teacher and mother of two grown children, enjoys being with her three grandchildren, reading, and listening to music. She's worked as leader in the cradle roll and kindergarten departments of her church, which she enjoys and finds rewarding. Her husband of 53 years passed away in November 2001. **Jan. 2, Oct. 21.**

Dinorah Blackman lives in Panama with her husband and baby, Imani. **Mar. 3.**

Asenath Blake was a student at Newbold College in southern England and in her second year of behavioral science when she wrote her devotional. Her home church is in the Cayman Islands. She enjoys cross-stitch, sewing, and reading and writing short stories and poems. **Dec. 14.**

Fulori Bola is the women's dean and a lecturer in the primary education department at Fulton College, Fiji. She is a single parent of two children and enjoys working in women's ministries, running seminars on prayer in local churches, and studying God's Word. Her hobby is developing skits and readings based on Scripture. **Apr. 13, July 25.**

Marjorie Boyce writes from Regina, Saskatchewan, Canada. She is the widowed mother of five adult children and has eight grandchildren. She's active in her church and was, until recently, head deaconess. **May 11, Oct. 18.**

Darlene Ytredal Burgeson is a retired sales manager. Her hobbies include sending notes and seasonal cards to shut-ins and people living alone. She also enjoys writing, gardening, and photography. **May 24, June 16, Oct. 7.**

Gertrude E. Burke, a first-time contributor, is a retired registered nurse. She's married and lives in Queens, New York. An active member of her local church, she enjoys gardening, cooking, and sewing. Her greatest joy is making others happy. **Feb. 17, June 17, Oct. 15.**

Andrea Bussue, born on the Caribbean island of Nevis, holds a master's degree in education. She's an administrator and consultant in issues regarding special education in Washington, D.C. She started the children's choir in her local church and served as Bible school superintendent. She enjoys public speaking, traveling, sewing, and meeting people. **Feb. 24, Apr. 11, May 19, July 10, Sept. 12, Nov. 5.**

Rosa Carneiro writes from São Luís in Brazil and is a first-time contributor. She is married and has two children—Laercio, 17, and Leanderson, 12. She likes to travel with her family on vacation. **Oct. 31.**

Virginia Casey is a retired municipal collections clerk, and resides with her husband in Conception Bay South, Newfoundland, Canada. She enjoys immensely her involvement in church-related duties, and is a volunteer with the Discover Bible School. Her hobbies include cross-country skiing, walking, reading, writing, and spending time with friends. **June 18.**

Frances Charles is a retired school principal. She is a bereavement counselor for the "Compassionate Friends" and a caregiver at a hospice. She is the author of *My Tears, My Rainbow.* Her hobbies include reading, writing, and making pretty things. **May 10.**

Ginger Church, a mother and grandmother, writes from Williamsport, Maryland. She serves the Review and Herald Publishing Association as director of periodical sales and of the Women's Ministries Resource Center. **Mar. 9.**

Marsha Claus taught elementary school for two years. After having a child seven years ago, she chose to be a stay-at-home mom. Her husband is the manager of the Illinois and Wisconsin Adventist Book Centers. They enjoy traveling around the state on the bookmobile. Her hobbies include traveling, writing, and crafts. **Mar. 19.**

Clareen Colclesser, a retired L.P.N. and widow since 1994, has two children, six grandchildren, and five great-grandchildren. She enjoys her family, homemaking, and quiet times with a good book. Clareen stays active in her church. Hobbies include short stories and her collection of interior decorating magazines and writing letters. **Jan. 15, Mar. 29.**

Celia Mejia Cruz is a pastor's wife, mother of five adult children, and grandmother of five. A church elder and women's ministries leader, Celia works as the operations administrative assistant for the Albany Youth Opportunities Movement in Georgia. She enjoys entertaining, reading, playing with her dog, and collecting Siamese cats. **Apr. 26, July 9, Aug 30.**

Becky Dada is principal of a secondary school in Nigeria. She and her pastor-husband have four children. She's been active in women and development programs, in publishing Bible games and youth magazines, and is now writing the history of Adventist women in west Nigeria. Her hobbies are conducting Revelation seminars, giving talks, reading, and writing. **Feb. 18, Apr. 21, Aug. 9, Sept. 24, Oct. 22.**

Fauna Rankin Dean, a published freelance writer/photographer, lives in northeast Kansas with her husband. They have one adult son and two teenagers who light up their lives. In her spare time she enjoys reading, gardening, and sewing. **Feb. 21, May 25, Oct. 9.**

Winifred Devaraj was a teacher for more than 25 years. Now she is a women's ministries director in India and a pastor's wife. They have one son, who is a medical director at the Adventist hospital, Ottapalam, in Kerala, India. **Oct. 23.**

Leonie Donald has lived in Brisbane since 1987 and enjoys the warm climate. Her hobbies are reading, exercise, and spending hours in her garden, which tells her of God's love. She has held many church positions over the years, but really enjoys being with and teaching the little ones. **Jan. 16, Mar. 28, May 3, June 5, July 18, Sept. 1.**

Goldie Down is a retired minister's wife, writer, teacher, and mother of six children and was a missionary in India for 20 years. She has 25 nonfiction books to her credit, as well as numerous stories and articles in magazines and newspapers. She helps her husband, David, produce two archaeological magazines that uphold the Bible. **Feb. 3, July 11, Oct. 4, Dec. 12.**

Louise Driver lives in Beltsville, Maryland, with her pastor-husband, Don. They have three grown sons and four grandchildren. At church she is involved with music and women's ministries. She works in the Potomac Adventist Book Center as children's coordinator. Her hobbies are singing and music, skiing, reading, crafts, gardening, and traveling to historical places. **May 15.**

Joy Dustow is a retired teacher who enjoys taking an active part in the social and spiritual activities of the retirement village in Australia, where she resides with her husband. **Feb. 8.**

Karen Edris is employed as an assistant property administrator in Takoma Park, Maryland. One of her duties as a member of her church is being the coordinator of the fellowship meals. Music (especially piano), animals, flowers, intercessory prayer, and giving out hugs bring special joy to her life. **Mar. 31, May 27.**

Heike Eulitz comes originally from Germany. She left her home country when she was 19 to became a secretary in Bern, Switzerland. She is an active member in the prayer ministry of her local church. Her hobbies include all kinds of crafts, baking, nature, and swimming. **June 29, Nov. 7.**

Edith Fitch is retired after 41 years of teaching, most of them at Canadian University College. She volunteers at the school's archives and devotes many hours in research for church and school histories. Her hobbies include needlecraft, cryptograms, and traveling. **Jan. 21, Apr. 3, July 14, Oct. 3.**

Heide Ford, the associate editor of *Women of Spirit,* lives with her husband, Zell. She holds a master's degree in counseling and loves reading, flowers, and whale watching. **Feb. 4, Aug. 21.**

Edna Maye Gallington is part of the communication team in the Southeastern California Conference of Seventh-day Adventists and is a graduate of La Sierra University. She's a member of Toastmasters International and the Loma Linda Writing Guild. She enjoys freelance writing, music, gourmet cooking, entertaining, hiking, and racquet ball. **Mar. 22.**

Marybeth Gessele lives with her husband in Oregon. She enjoys country living, making miniature quilts, and being with her two granddaughters. She has a home economics degree and is currently working with people with special needs. Marybeth is the author of *No More Cinnamon Bear Cookies,* a book explaining death to children. **Jan. 31, Nov. 16.**

Evelyn Glass enjoys her family and loves having her grandchildren live next door. She and her husband, Darrell, live in northern Minnesota on the farm where Darrell was born. Evelyn is active in her local church and community. She writes a weekly column for her local paper and serves as women's and family ministries director for the Mid-America Union Conference of Seventh-day Adventists. **May 12, June 14, Aug. 19, Nov. 27.**

Mary Jane Graves retired in North Carolina after working at many jobs, from society editor of her hometown newspaper to years spent as a school librarian and registrar. She and her husband have two adult sons and two granddaughters. Gardening takes up much of her time during the spring and summer months. **Mar. 20, June 19, Nov. 8.**

Shirley Kimbrough Grear writes from New Jersey, where she lives with her husband, Carl. She is a speaker and seminar/workshop leader throughout the United States, and a master quilter. Her articles and quilts have been widely published and exhibited. **July 23.**

Ellie Green, a retired registered nurse, and her husband, Lloyd, live in North Carolina near their adult children. Ellie preaches in public evangelistic campaigns in the United States, as well as overseas, and is a presenter at women's conferences and retreats. She modestly admits that her two grandchildren are the smartest, brightest, most adorable, sweetest, and cutest in the entire world. **Apr. 23, Sept. 23, Nov. 10, Dec. 21.**

Carol Joy Greene writes from Florida, where she has retired. She is the mother of three adult children, and the grandmother of four. She is active in women's ministries in her church. **July 5, Nov. 25.**

Glenda-mae Greene was formerly the assistant vice president of student services at Andrews University in Berrien Springs, Michigan. She finds pleasure in writing, teaching, and preaching for various church groups, and enjoys most the company of her God, her three nieces, and her nephew. She is now retired and living in Florida. **Mar. 21, Sept. 21.**

Leila Fay Greene writes from Florida, where she and her husband have retired. She is the mother of five adult children and the grandmother of six. She is the Bible school superintendent in her church. **June 13.**

Gloria Gregory is a minister's wife, mother of two girls, and associate director of admissions and records at Northern Caribbean University, Mandeville, Jamaica. With a master's in education, her hobbies include handcrafts, playing word games, sewing, and gardening. **Jan. 25, Apr. 25, July 3, Sept. 8.**

Meibel Mello Guedes is the wife of Pastor Arlindo Guedes, mother of three daughters, and grandmother of Maressa. She is a women's ministries and Shepherdess director for South Brazil and is completing her master's degree in education. Her hobbies are reading, studying, and talking about Jesus. **May 9, Dec. 10.**

Heather Hanna lives near Newbold College in England. When not parenting two boys under 5 and leading cradle roll Bible school, Heather is studying for a degree and working part-time as a neonatal intensive-care nurse. She has previously written and directed sketches for drama and mime. **Mar. 13, Aug. 16.**

Dessa Weisz Hardin has three adult children scattered around the world—which increases her love of travel. She likes to read and write and still works with children on a reading appreciation program. She enjoys walking in her bit of the Atlantic Ocean. **Mar. 18, May 21, July 4, Dec. 24.**

Peggy Curtice Harris serves as an elder in her church and coordinates two Net Care ministries—hospitality and regeneration. Peggy and husband, Melvin, have two children, Melanie and Mark, and two granddaughters, Kristina and Kimberly. **Oct. 27, Dec. 9.**

Ursula M. Hedges, a retired secondary school teacher/administrator and women's ministries director in Australia, was born of missionary parents in India. She and her husband have served for 10 years as missionaries. Ursula, an elder at her church, has published books, stories, and articles. She's an interior designer who enjoys reading, producing dramas, sewing, and cooking. **Apr. 16, June 28, Nov. 11.**

Denise Dick Herr teaches English at Canadian University College in Alberta, Canada. She participates in archaeological excavations in Jordan and is interested in connections between biblical narratives and the contemporary world. She is the author of *Men Are From Judah, Woman Are From Bethlehem: How a Modern Bestseller Illuminates the Book of Ruth.* **May 22, Aug. 3, Nov. 6.**

Joyce Hill is a retired church school teacher who has found a new interest in writing for a hobby. Several of her pieces have been aired on Adventist World Radio, England. She is a new author to the devotional book series. **July 15.**

Karen Holford works with her husband in family ministries in the south of England. She loves finding new ways to be a channel of God's love in a hurting world. She has three school-age children and a neglected garden. She enjoys writing, quilting, and creative worship. **Jan. 6, Mar. 23, May 8, July 29, Aug. 1, Sept. 30.**

Lorraine Hudgins-Hirsch is retired in Loma Linda, California. She has worked at Faith for Today, the Voice of Prophecy, and the General Conference of Seventh-day Adventists. Her articles and poems appear frequently in various publications. She has also written two books of poems. **Jan. 9, Mar. 6, May 26, July 24, Oct. 8, Dec. 22.**

Viola Poey Hughes, originally from Malaysia, lives with her husband, Chris, and two boys in Silver Spring, Maryland. She works in the United Nations Liaison Office of her church world headquarters in Washington, D.C. When she's not working on her graduate degree, Viola leads out in family ministries for her local church and teaches the junior-age children with her husband. **May 4.**

Bonnie Hunt is a retired nursing professor from Southern Adventist University in Collegedale, Tennessee. In her retirement she coordinates a "learning assistance" program for nursing at the university. The fact that her three grown children and five grandchildren live nearby is, she feels, one of God's greatest blessings to her. **Oct. 25.**

Cheryl Hurt is a retired registered nurse, a Bible worker, and the communications secretary of her church. She enjoys swimming, baking, and collecting antique phonographs. She and her husband, Brett, live in Bakersfield, California. **Dec. 8.**

Christine Hwang, a family physician who worked in Toronto, Ontario, Canada, moved to London, England, to study at the School of Hygiene and Tropical Medicine from October 2001 to September 2002. Her hobby is food—from eating to cooking and baking. **July 12.**

Shirley C. Iheanacho resides in Huntsville, Alabama, with Morris, her husband of 32 years. She has three adult daughters and two grandsons. Shirley taught for four years in Nigeria before moving to Huntsville. An elder in her church, she loves singing in the choir, playing handbells, sharing God's love, meeting people, and reading. **Jan. 22, May 7, June 12, Sept. 29, Dec. 6.**

Aleah Iqbal is a freelance writer who lives with her family in Willimantic, Connecticut. She home-schooled her children for 10 years. Her publishing credits include a book of poetry, original recipes for community cookbooks, and health store newsletters. In the past she has hosted her own local cable television show. She's currently writing a children's book. **Mar. 4, Aug. 15.**

Lois E. Johannes is retired from overseas service in Southern Asia and the Far East and lives near a daughter in Portland, Oregon. She enjoys knitting, community service work, patio gardening, and her four grandchildren and two great-grandchildren. **Jan. 11, June 11.**

Elaine J. Johnson lives with Peter, her husband of 35 years, and her Nanday Conure bird, Samantha. At church she is Bible school superintendent and a greeter. She is a teacher in daycare/preschools and has an associate in mental health technology and a certificate in community social work. Her hobbies are reading, writing, drawing, and meeting people. **Jan. 27, July 17.**

Pauletta Cox Johnson and husband, Mike, live in a small town in southwest Michigan, where she grew up. She is an interior designer, a freelance writer (mostly children's books), and does gardening, sewing, and crafts. Active in her home church, she's the proud mother of three grown sons, two daughters-in-law, and two young grandsons. **Apr. 10.**

Shirley Johnston is a wife and mother of four children and one stepdaughter. She works as the business manager for an elementary school, enjoys reading, writing, scrapbooking, and teaching her children about God through the Bible and nature. Her son James is now 14, and his guardian angels are always busy keeping up with him! **Dec. 16.**

Marilyn King is a retired registered nurse who lives in Oregon with her husband, Marvin. She holds a master's degree in business and is active in her church and community. Her interests are her family, church, and reading, walking, and enjoying country life. **Jan. 7, Mar. 10, June 6.**

Toya Marie Koch is a freelance writer and designer living in Hagerstown, Maryland. She leads out in praise and worship at the Highland View Academy church, as well as volunteering at the academy. She's married, has no children, but has two cats and two dogs. She's an amateur musician and photographer. **Jan. 3, Sept. 6.**

Annette Kowarin, a first-time contributor from England, is married to Terry (for more than 21 years) and is the mother of three teenagers. As a nurse, she cares for ventorlatory dependent children in their homes, working with their families. She is joint youth leader in her local church. Each year she helps organize and run a family holiday program in Aberdaron, North Wales. **June 15, Aug. 20.**

Mabel Kwei is the wife of a Gambia Mission president, director of Gambia women's ministries for her church, lecturer at Gambia College and the University of Gambia College. She helps in the pastoral work with her husband and loves reading. **Jan. 17, June 7.**

Gina Lee is the author of more than 650 published stories, articles, and poems. In addition to writing, she works at a library. She shares her home with four cats. **Jan. 18, Mar. 14, June 30, Sept. 14, Oct. 20, Dec. 13.**

Ruth Lennox is women's ministries director for the British Columbia Conference of Seventh-day Adventists in Canada. She writes and produces monologues of first-person stories of Bible women. A retired family physician, she and her husband have three married children and four granddaughters. **Apr. 27, Sept. 16.**

Olive Lewis is a caregiver and medical technologist. She attends church in Atlanta, Georgia, where she is a youth teacher and a former youth director. She's written a book, poems, plays, and is working on two more books. As an advocate for youth, she writes with them in mind. **Dec. 19.**

Bessie Siemens Lobsien is a retired librarian who worked in foreign mission service and the United States. Her published works include articles and poems. She enjoys sewing, reading, gardening, and visiting her two grandchildren. **Jan. 13, Feb. 29, May 30, July 19, Sept. 4, Nov. 19.**

Hattie R. Logan works at Ford Motor Company. She has published a daily devotional book, *Peace, Prosperity and Spirituality,* and a handbook, *Living Within Your Means—Writing a Budget and Sticking to It.* She has a religious CD entitled *In Times Like These.* Hattie has two sons, David and Darnell. **Aug. 13.**

Heidi Macho was born in Offenbach, Germany. She has two small children. Trained as a wholesale merchant, Heidi paints watercolor paintings and loves to sing. **Sept. 20.**

Pearl Manderson is retired along with her husband and resides in Florida. She is the mother of two sons and has four grandsons. She's a devoted church worker who plans and organizes church programs. She is a lover of flowers, enjoys doing embroidery, crocheting, writing letters, reading, and walking. **June 24.**

Joyce Maples is a mother and grandmother who is very involved with her grandchildren. She lives in Morganton, North Carolina, and is active with church and women's ministries. She is currently a part-time literature evangelist. **Mar. 27, Sept. 5.**

Salome Marks is a student in southern England. She has two brothers and two sisters. She says, "I love teaching Sabbath school in the church I grew up in. I love animals and wish I were able to have a pet, but it's forbidden in my flat. I like writing short stories, having Bible study, and reading poetry by the fire." **June 20.**

Alicia Marquez was born in Montevideo, Uruguay, and has lived in New York for more than 30 years. She is a senior accountant and worked previously with the Spanish television program, *Ayer, Hoy Y Manana.* She collaborates with the family and women's ministries presenting seminars and preaching. **July 22.**

Clarissa Marshall has worked in radio and television and has been considering what to do next. Formerly a missionary on the island of Guam, she is extremely grateful for the opportunity to reach the world in these last days with the gospel of Christ. **May 2.**

Philippa Marshall enjoys writing as a ministry and meeting other writers. She's active in her church and loves being with her family and friends. **May 14, Aug. 29.**

Cassandra Martins is an educator, journalist, and marketing operator in the publishing house Hoje Maringá. She is a member of a church in Paraná, Brazil, and the mother of three children. **Apr. 8, Aug. 24.**

Deborah Matshaya is a teacher at Marian High in Elsies river in Cape Town, South Africa. Previously, she taught at Bethel College. She has had several devotionals published and enjoys gym and loves gospel music. **Mar. 11.**

Vidella McClellan (aka Vie Mucha) is a homemaker and repertory care worker in British Columbia, Canada. A grandmother of seven, her hobbies are gardening, crafts, writing, redecorating, travel, camping, and cats. She's had a few articles published in local newspapers and has written 28 stories for casual family reading. **Feb. 13, Mar. 25, July 2, Sept. 2, Nov. 20, Dec. 4.**

Patsy Murdoch Meeker, of Virginia, twice-widowed, is a mother, stepmom, stepgrandma, and stepgreat-grandma. She's been a frequent contributor to the devotional books. **May 13.**

Christel Mey is an author of several volumes of poems and has written articles for various periodicals. She is a vocal soloist and painter, is married, and has two adult children. **Apr. 24, July 30.**

Quilvie G. Mills is a retired community college professor who's now actively engaged with her husband, Pastor H. A. Mills, in the operation of their church. She loves people, makes friends easily, and does all she can to assist young people in achieving their educational aspirations. Her hobbies include music, reading, traveling, and gardening. **Oct. 29.**

Marcia Mollenkopf, a retired schoolteacher, lives in Klamath Falls, Oregon. She is involved in local church activities and serves as a school board member. Marcia enjoys reading, bird-watching, hiking, and crafts. **July 13.**

Esperanza Aquino Mopera is the mother of four adult children, grandmother of five, a registered nurse at Virginia Beach City Public Schools, and director of women's ministries at her church. She likes gardening and watching birds and fish in the backyard lake. **Apr. 7, Oct. 11.**

Barbara Smith Morris is executive director of a nonprofit retirement center and presents a devotional over the speaker system daily. She served seven years as a Tennessee delegate, representing housing and service needs of low-income elderly. Barbara is a presenter of seminars on elder life issues, mother of four grown children, and grandmother of six. **June 4, July 16, Nov. 1, Dec. 29.**

Bonnie Moyers lives with her husband and four cats in Staunton, Virginia. The mother of two adult children and grandmother to a 3-year-old, she works as a laundry assistant at a local bed-and-breakfast, is a musician for a Methodist church, and does freelance writing whenever she can fit it in. She's been published in a number of magazines and books. **Feb. 6, July 8, Oct. 12.**

Ethel Doris Msuseni is a retired professional nurse and teacher living in Umtata, Eastern Cape, South Africa. She likes cooking, listening to music, and sewing. **Nov. 21.**

Lillian Musgrave and her family have enjoyed the uniqueness of northern California for more than 40 years. She enjoys having time for family and church responsibilities. Her interests include but are not limited to music and writing (including poetry). She's been active in the HIV spiritual support group in her area and has established a parents support group. **Feb. 5, Dec. 11.**

Ingrid Naumann has been director of the women's ministries department for her church for all of southern Germany since 1993. She's the single parent of a son who is studying theology to become a pastor. **Apr. 30, Oct. 10.**

Judy Neal is a former registered nurse and is currently pursuing a Master of Divinity degree at Andrews University in Berrien Springs, Michigan. She is a mother and grandmother, enjoys reading, music, sewing, and camping (when there is time from all the reading and paper writing that college demands). Currently living in the Chicago, Illinois, and Berrien Springs, Michigan, area, she calls herself a gypsy. **June 1.**

Joan Minchin Neall, a registered nurse, was born in Australia, lived in England, and now makes her home in Tennessee. She and her retired pastor-husband have four adult children and nine grandchildren. She is the women's ministries leader for her church and enjoys journaling, young women's Bible study groups, and spending time with her family. **Jan. 1.**

Anne Elaine Nelson, a retired elementary teacher, is still tutoring. She has written a book, *Puzzled Parents.* Her husband passed away in 2001. She has four children who have blessed her with 11 grandchildren. She lives in Michigan, where she is active in church work and women's ministries, and enjoys sewing, music, photography, and creating memories with her grandchildren. **Feb. 25.**

Regina Mary Silveira Nunes is the wife of a district pastor, a dentist, and mother of two teenagers. She lives in Maringa, Parana, Brazil, and likes to read, write, cook, and work in counseling. **Oct. 16, Nov. 12.**

Edna May Olsen is retired and living in Simi Valley, California, with her husband, Roger. Her hobbies include swimming, hiking, and writing. She has three daughters and three granddaughters. **Dec. 18.**

Jemima D. Orillosa works as an administrative office assistant at her church world headquarters in Silver Spring, Maryland. She loves visiting elderly people and talking to them about Christ. She is active in her local church and lives with her husband and two teenage daughters. She enjoys gardening and making friends. **Jan. 4, Mar. 24, June 25, Sept. 25, Nov. 29.**

Hannele Ottschofski lives in Germany with her family. She is editor of the local Shepherdess newsletter and loves to read and write. From time to time she presents seminars and workshops at women's ministries retreats. She is a piano teacher and directs a choir in her local church. She did the translation work for the German edition of this devotional book series. **Feb. 2, Aug. 23, Dec. 5.**

Ivone Feldkircher Paiva is a minister's wife, mother of two children, and grandmother of two granddaughters. After working 23 years as director of schools, she now works in education administration for her church in North Parana, Brazil, and has a daily radio program. She likes to read, embroider, write, travel, and present seminars on education and family. **Aug. 28.**

Ofelia A. Pangan is a retired teacher who still serves God and people with her minister-husband. She loves her three children and their spouses and her grandchildren. Ofelia enjoys reading, traveling, walking, gardening, and playing Scrabble. **Jan. 8, Mar. 30, May 28, Sept. 3.**

Revel Papaioannou was a pastor's wife for 40 years in various parts of Greece and is an English teacher. She especially enjoys her eight grandchildren; climbing mountains; reading; and collecting stamps, coins, and phone cards. **Aug. 31.**

Abigail Blake Parchment is a family nurse practitioner. She and her husband, Sean, reside in the Cayman Islands. She is the women's ministries and family ministries director for her local church. She's had an article published in *Women of Spirit* magazine. **Sept. 17.**

Gwen Pascoe is a wife, mother, granny, and published author of children's books, and recently completed a master's degree in history at the University of Melbourne, Australia. **Apr. 19.**

Birdie Poddar lives in northeastern India. She and her husband enjoy retirement but keep busy. She enjoys gardening, cooking, baking, sewing, reading, writing, and handcrafts. They have a daughter, a son, and four grandsons. **Feb. 7, Apr. 29, Nov. 9.**

Lanny Lydia Pongilatan, from Jakarta, Indonesia, works as a professional secretary. She's been an English instructor and enjoys playing the piano, listening to Christian gospel songs, reading religious books, playing tennis, and swimming. **Jan. 29, Mar. 15, May 31, Aug. 17.**

Maria Baldão Quadrado is a minister's wife and mother of two children. She taught in two high schools for 23 years. Currently she's women's ministries and

Shepherdess director in Brazil, and has a program on the local radio station. She lives in Maringá, Paraná, Brazil, and enjoys preaching, working with women, and traveling with her family. **Oct. 26.**

Darlenejoan M. Rhine, born in Omaha, Nebraska, raised in California, and schooled in Madison, Tennessee, is a widow with one adult son. She holds a B.A. in journalism and has for many years been public relations secretary for her church, Los Angeles Central City, in California. **Sept. 15.**

Lynda Mae Richardson is an administrative assistant for an architectural and engineering firm in Southfield, Michigan. She's had two short stories published, and her hobbies include writing, singing, baking, hiking, and bicycling. **Aug. 22.**

MaryAnn Roberts is a baccalaureate program coordinator in the School of Nursing at Southern Adventist University in Tennessee, where she teaches. A deaconess in her church, she enjoys camping (if her creature comforts are tended to), traveling, and always has a book or two that she is currently reading. Her two children are her pride and joy. **Sept. 18.**

Charlotte Robinson is a wife, and mother of three. She's had stories published in numerous magazines. Between taking her junior- and earliteen-age children to school and cleaning two post offices, she likes to mow lawns, write letters, and do almost anything but clean house. **Mar. 17, Aug. 5, Dec. 3.**

Avis Mae Rodney is a justice of the peace for the province of Ontario, Canada. As women's ministries leader for her church, she gives motivational talks, particularly to youth and women. She enjoys long walks, gardening, and crocheting. Avis is a wife, mother of two adult children, and grandmother of five grandchildren. **Feb. 9, May 17, Sept. 19.**

Aurísia Silva Brito Rodrigues is the women's ministries director of the Vila Nova Nanuque Church in Minas Gerais, Brazil. She is 23, married, and has a 5-year-old daughter. She likes to read, listen to music, go places, talk, and raise animals. **Nov. 28.**

Terrie Ruff is a team social worker and supervisor with Alexian Brothers Community Services PACE Program in Chattanooga, Tennessee. She is also an adjunct professor at Southern Adventist University in the Social Work Department. Terrie enjoys public speaking, writing, singing, and traveling. Her life motto is "I'm too blessed to be stressed or depressed." **Jan. 10, Apr. 5, Aug. 4, Nov. 24.**

Cathy L. Sanchez and her husband live in southern Illinois with their daughter, Emily. She leads an active life as a full-time homemaker, home-school parent, women's ministries director, and leader of several "Bible Studies for Busy Women" groups. Her special interests include writing, gardening, small group studies, and, most of all, her family. **June 9, Nov. 22.**

Deborah Sanders has shared from her journal, *Dimensions of Love,* since the beginning of this devotional book series. Deborah (pen name "Sonny's Mommy") lives in Canada with Ron, her husband of 35 years. They've been blessed with Andrea and son-in-law Bill, and Sonny, who is severely mentally challenged with autism. Deborah serves her church as a deaconess. **Jan. 30, Apr. 2, June 8, Aug. 11.**

May Sandy was an active women's ministries leader in her local conference in South Australia and worked in her local church until she passed away in June 2002. She was a library manager in a school community library in Tailem Bend, and enjoyed gardening and breeding colored sheep. **Apr. 6.**

Sônia Rigoli Santos has a degree in theology and was the first Brazilian woman to obtain a master's degree in this area. A minister's wife and mother, she worked for almost 20 years as a teacher. Currently she's a leader of women's ministries in Ijuí, Rio Grande do Sul, Brazil. She likes to produce and present radio programs and enjoys writing. **Apr. 15, Nov. 4, Nov. 26.**

Barbara L. Savage's life took a dramatic turn for the better after meeting Christ at the age of 23. After raising her two sons, she worked as a sculptor and commercial artist. Now a massage and hydrotherapist at the Black Hills Wellness Center in South Dakota, she helps people maximize their health by using God's eight natural remedies. She is a first-time contributor. **Oct. 1.**

Sabine Schlicke has worked as a Bible instructor in a church-planting project in southern Germany. She is in training for geriatric nursing. She loves to sing and compose songs. **June 27.**

Christel Schneider is a women's ministries leader in South Bavaria and lives in Bad Aibiling. She is the single parent of a grown son. A trained nurse, she works in the office of a nursing home. **Feb. 20, Aug. 25, Nov. 18.**

Marie H. Seard, a native of Alabama, has been retired for nine years. Among other activities, she is the chaplain of the Washington Inter-Alumni Chapter of the United College Fund. She enjoys listening to religious CDs and working with the Say It Now With Flowers committee that pays tribute to church members whose faithfulness and good deeds are unnoticed. **Feb. 19, Oct. 28.**

Donna Lee Sharp's hobbies are reading, bird watching, and entertaining college-age grandchildren. Her church duties include music responsibilities, working as a parish leader, and occasionally as Bible school teacher. Community outreach includes being the pianist for the Christian Women's Club and teaching English to Mexican farmworkers. **Apr. 18.**

Carrol Johnson Shewmake is an author and speaker. Her passion is for a relationship with Jesus through prayer. She and her retired pastor-husband lead out in prayer ministry in their home church. Their hobby is building their retirement house. They are the parents of four, grandparents of eight. **Dec. 15.**

Judy Musgrave Shewmake and her husband, Tom, live in northern California. They have a married daughter, a son studying for the ministry, and a son and daughter still at home. Judy has always home-schooled her children and is editor of *The Adventist Home Educator*. Her favorite hobby is writing, but she also enjoys reading, genealogy, and making memory scrapbooks. **Apr. 12.**

Sherry Shrestha and her husband, Prakash, are family practice physicians at Scheer Memorial Hospital in Banepa, Nepal. They have three teenage daughters. Sherry is doing well following chemotherapy for breast cancer. **Dec. 23.**

Sandra Simanton is a family therapist in Grand Forks, North Dakota. She lives with her husband and two children, Grant and Alana, in nearby Buxton. She is involved with children's Bible school and is women's ministries leader for her church, as well as being involved in a thousand projects at her children's school. She enjoys sewing, rubber-stamping, and reading. **Feb. 27, Sept. 7.**

Heather-Dawn Small is the associate director for women's ministries at her church's world headquarters in Silver Spring, Maryland. A native of Trinidad and Tobago, she is the mother of a college-age daughter and an elementary school son. She says she loves travel, reading, embroidery, and stamp collecting. And "joy" is her favorite word. **Jan. 24, Sept. 9.**

Dolores E. Smith is a retired registered nurse and certified midwife. She worked as a nurse practitioner for many years in a large metropolitan hospital. She holds a master's degree in education, and she received the Woman of the Year Award from women's ministries in 1996 for outstanding and dedicated service. She enjoys traveling. **Feb. 28, Aug. 8, Aug. 12.**

Tamara Marquez de Smith writes from Long Island, New York, where she lives with her husband, Steven, and their daughter, Lillian. Tamara has held numerous offices in her local church, including head deaconess, assistant youth leader, and choir leader. **Mar. 5, Sept. 27.**

Ginger Snarr graduated from Walla Walla College School of Nursing in 1960. She and her husband, Dudley, recently moved to Surprise, Arizona, where they are retired and thoroughly enjoying the sunshine. They continue to be involved in mission projects. **Feb. 16.**

Candace Sprauve is a reading teacher and the parent of three adult sons and a daughter. She has two grandchildren and serves her church as an elder and the general Bible school superintendent. She is a Literacy Link of America volunteer, and her hobbies are reading, gardening, and sewing. **June 22.**

Ardis Dick Stenbakken edits the submissions to this book as she travels the world, leading out in women's ministries worldwide for her church. She and her husband, Dick, a retired Army chaplain, have two married children. She especially enjoys helping women discover their full potential in the Lord. **Feb. 1, Mar. 12, May 23, July 1, Sept. 22, Oct. 14, Dec. 7.**

Risa Storlie is a busy college student who loves coming home to see her cats and dog. In her spare time she enjoys reading, crocheting, writing, cooking, and hiking in nature. **July 6.**

Iris L. Stovall, a certified CLASS (Christian Leaders Authors and Speakers Services) communicator, is lay pastor and head elder at her church. Administrative secretary and assistant editor of *Mosiac*, a women's ministries newsletter, she is married, has two sons, one daughter, and two granddaughters. Singing, videotaping, and watching beautiful sunsets bring smiles. **Jan. 12, Apr. 1, June 26, Aug. 6, Oct. 30, Dec. 31.**

Grace Streifling is the proud mother of four adult children and is a retired nurse. She taught school for four years and has had children's stories published. Her hobby is quilting, and she enjoys Bible study, visiting neighbors, and watching someone else mow her lawn. **Oct. 5.**

Rubye Sue is a retired secretary working at a small self-supporting school, where she enjoys interaction with the students. Rubye (80 years old) and her husband (87) still travel and look forward to visits with their children, grandchildren, and great-grandchildren. **May 5, Nov. 2.**

Carolyn Sutton, freelance writer and speaker, lives in Grants Pass, Oregon, with her husband, Jim. They enjoy camping, gardening, and sharing Jesus in practical ways. **Feb. 22, July 28, Oct. 17.**

Loraine F. Sweetland is a retired librarian and teacher who resides in Tennessee with her husband, 98-year-old mother-in-law, and three little dogs. She keeps busy as school board chair, church clerk, communications leader, gym-building chair, and treasurer of her local food co-op. She writes a weekly article for her local newspaper about church doings. **Jan. 23, Apr. 4, May 18, Aug. 2, Oct. 6, Dec. 28.**

Frieda Tanner, a retired registered nurse, keeps busy by sending Bible school materials all over the world. She now lives in Eugene, Oregon, to be near her two grandchildren. **Aug. 26.**

Arlene Taylor is director of Infection Control and risk manager at St. Helena Hospital in California. As founder and president of her own corporation, she promotes brain-function research. She is a professional member of the National Speaker's Association and received American Biographical Institute's American Medal of Honor for Brain-Function Education in 2002. **Jan. 14, Mar. 16, May 29, July 21, Sept. 28, Oct. 2, Nov. 3.**

Tammy Barnes Taylor runs her own daycare. Married 17 years, she has three sons and one daughter. She enjoys Creative Memories scrapbooking and loves to read and write stories. She is a first-time contributor. **Aug. 7.**

Stella Thomas works as a secretary in her church's global mission office. She is grateful to God for giving her the opportunity to work for Him and to see the work of the Holy Spirit in spreading the gospel in many unentered areas of the world. **Sept. 26.**

Nancy L. Van Pelt is a certified family life educator, best-selling author, internationally known speaker, author of more than 20 books, and has traversed the globe, teaching families how to really love each other. Her hobbies are getting organized, entertaining, having fun, and quilting. Nancy and her husband live in California and are the parents of three adult children. **Feb. 10, Apr. 22, June 21, Oct. 24.**

Nancy Cachero Vasquez is volunteers' coordinator for her church in North America. She and her husband are the parents of three adult daughters. She is coauthor of *God's 800-Number: P-R-A-Y-E-R*, and a former missionary who enjoys reading, writing, shopping, and spending time with her husband. **May 16.**

Julia Vernon has been a hospice chaplain for 15 years, is married, and has three children. She lives on a farm in Utah and attends church in Salt Lake City. Her hobbies are crocheting and writing. She is a first-time contributor. **Jan. 28.**

Charlotte Verrett is a family practice physician in rural North Carolina. Married to Leon Verrett III, she has three wonderful sons and says her most precious degree is "M.O.M." Children are truly her calling. She is chair of her church's elementary school, and enjoys writing, a wide variety of sports, and spending valuable time with her family. **Sept. 10.**

Donna Meyer Voth is a substitute teacher and volunteer for the American Cancer Society. She enjoys giving Bible studies, watercolor painting, traveling, and camping. She and her husband live in Vicksburg, Michigan, and have a daughter in college. **May 6, Dec. 30.**

Nancy Jean Vyhmeister is a semiretired seminary professor who now enjoys church activities, gardening, homemaking, writing, and three long-distance grandsons. **Aug. 14, Nov. 17.**

Cindy Walikonis is a mother, pastor's wife, and registered dietitian. She lives in Walla Walla, Washington. Her hobbies include hiking, creative writing, creative vegetarian cooking, teaching health and nutrition classes in the community, and working with the women's ministries committee at her church. **Sept. 13.**

Cora A. Walker lives in Queens, New York. She is a retired nurse and an active member in her local church. She enjoys reading, writing, sewing, classical music, singing, and traveling. She has one son. **Mar. 8, May 20, July 7, Sept. 11, Dec. 2.**

Anna May Radke Waters and her husband, Herb, have celebrated their fiftieth wedding anniversary. A retired administrative secretary, she has five children and seven grandchildren, is a church elder, and a greeter. Her top hobbies are helping others know Jesus better through Internet Bible Studies, being a prayer warrior, and her family. **Jan. 5, Mar. 26, July 26, Dec. 1.**

Ruth Watson served in Thailand with her physician-husband for 13 years. Though now retired, she has served briefly in Dominican Republic, Fiji, Thailand, Laos, and Cambodia. She loves helping her grandchildren and her primary children in Bible school, and is a deaconess at her church. **Feb. 14, Nov. 15, Dec. 26.**

Dorothy Eaton Watts is an administrator for her church headquarters in India. Dorothy is also a freelance writer, editor, and speaker. She was a missionary in India for 23 years, founded an orphanage, taught elementary school, and has written more than 20 books. Her hobbies include gardening, hiking, and birding (with more than 1,400 in her world total). **June 3.**

Betty Welch is an emergency room nurse in Loveland, Colorado. She loves to cross-stitch and spend time with her four grown children and spectacular daughters-in-law. **Feb. 15.**

Penny Estes Wheeler, mother and grandmother, cherishes her Texas childhood and still feels most at home in wide-open, barren places. She enjoys reading and rubber-stamping, and recently established a book reading club in her community. The editor of *Women of Spirit*, Penny is a freelance author and speaker at retreats and other events. **Dec. 20.**

Mildred C. Williams lives in southern California and works 13 hours a week as an almost-retired physical therapist. The rest of the time she enjoys studying and teaching the Bible, writing, gardening, public speaking, sewing, and baby-sitting her granddaughter. **Jan. 19.**

Patrice E. Williams-Gordon lectures in the Natural Science Department at Northern Caribbean University in Mandeville, Jamaica. An active minister's wife, she enjoys team ministry with her husband, Danhugh. She delights in her two daughters, Ashli and Rhoni, while trying to keep up her hobbies of reading, speaking engagements, and planning special events. **Aug. 27.**

Ingrid Ribeiro Wolff de Oliveira is married, is the daughter of missionaries, and spent three years of her childhood in Angola. She's an educator and an elementary school teacher who loves children. She makes handicrafts and likes to write children's poetry and programs. She dreams of one day writing a children's book. **Jan. 20.**

Susan Wooley lives with her husband, Steve, and two boys in Oviedo, Florida, where she works as a home health nurse and edits a monthly newsletter for her church in Winter Springs. **Feb. 23, Dec. 27.**

Velna Wright is a stay-at-home mom of two boys. Married, she is a deaconess, a bulletin editor, and is active in her church's cradle roll department, Vacation Bible School, and women's ministries. She enjoys home-schooling her older son, floral arranging, crafts, sewing, and cooking. **Feb. 26.**

Gundula Zahalka is a pastor's wife and mother of two adult sons. She lives near Schorndorf, in southern Germany, and works as a receptionist and assistant in a medical practice. She has a diploma in health education. **Apr. 17.**

PRAYER REQUESTS

_____

_____

_____

_____

_____

_____

_____

_____

_____

_____

While I live will I praise the Lord:
I will sing praises . . . while I have any being.
—Psalm 146:2.

PRAYER REQUESTS

_____

_____

_____

_____

_____

_____

_____

_____

_____

Thou hast said it. I take Thee at Thy word.
—Ellen G. White, Signs of the Times, *Dec. 25, 1893.*

PRAYER REQUESTS

_____

_____

_____

_____

_____

_____

_____

_____

_____

The Lord is nigh unto all them that call upon him.
—Psalm 145:18.

PRAYER REQUESTS

_____

_____

_____

_____

_____

_____

_____

_____

_____

Let the words and example of my Redeemer
be the light and strength of my heart.
—*Ellen G. White,* Review and Herald, *Aug. 10, 1886.*

PRAYER REQUESTS

_____

_____

_____

_____

_____

_____

_____

_____

_____

He shall give thee the desires of thine heart.
—Psalm 37:4.

PRAYER REQUESTS

_____

_____

_____

_____

_____

_____

_____

_____

_____

_____

Here am I, Lord, and all that I am is Thine.
—Ellen G. White, Review and Herald, *Jan. 4, 1887.*

PRAYER REQUESTS

_____

_____

_____

_____

_____

_____

_____

_____

_____

_____

Evening, and morning, and at noon, will I pray.
—Psalm 55:17.

PRAYER REQUESTS

_____

_____

_____

_____

_____

_____

_____

_____

_____

_____

Take me, O Lord, as wholly Thine. . . .
Use me today in Thy service.
—Ellen G. White, Steps to Christ, p. 70.

PRAYER REQUESTS

_____

_____

_____

_____

_____

_____

_____

_____

_____

_____

_____

Trust in him at all times; . . .
pour out your heart before him.
—Psalm 62:8.